Equatorial Guinea

the Bradt Travel Guide

Oscar Scafidi

edition

1

www.bradtguides.com

Bradt Travel Guides Ltd, UK
The Globe Pequot Press Inc, USA

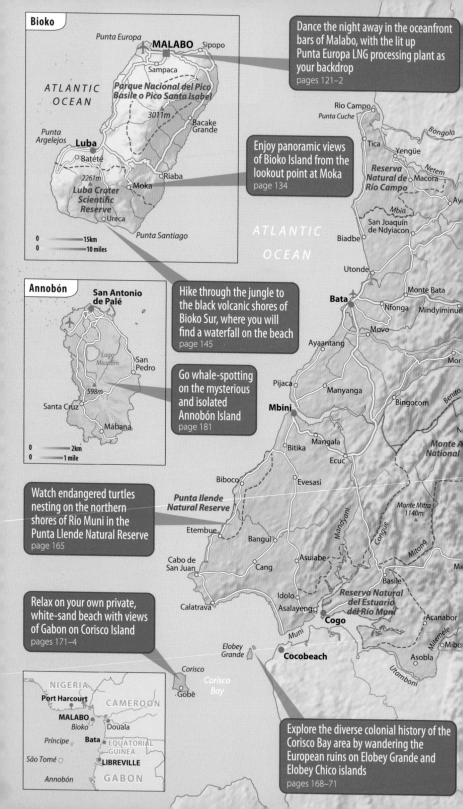

Bioko

Punta Europa
MALABO   Sipopo

ATLANTIC
OCEAN   Sampaca

Parque Nacional del Pico
Basile o Pico Santa Isabel
3011m
Bacake
Grande

Punta
Argelejos   **Luba**
Batété   Riaba

2261m   Moka
Luba Crater
Scientific
Reserve
Ureca   Punta Santiago

0 —————— 15km
0 —————— 10 miles

Dance the night away in the oceanfront
bars of Malabo, with the lit up
Punta Europa LNG processing plant as
your backdrop
pages 121–2

Enjoy panoramic views
of Bioko Island from the
lookout point at Moka
page 134

Annobón

San Antonio
de Palé

Lago
Mazafim   San
Pedro

598m

Santa Cruz
Mábana

0 ——— 2km
0 ——— 1 mile

Rio Campo
Punta Cuche

Tica   Yengüe   Bongola

Reserva
Natural de   Netem
Río Campo   Macora

Mbia

San Joaquín
de Ndyiacon   Ay

Biadbe

Utonde

Monte Bata

Bata
Nfonga   Mindyiminue

Mavo

Ayaantang

Pijaca   Manyanga   Bingocom   Benito

Mbini

Mangala   Monte A
Bitika   Ecuc   National

Biboco   Evesasi

Punta Ilende
Natural Reserve   Monte Mitra
1140m
Etembue   Banguí
Mandyani   Congüe   Mitong
Cabo de
San Juan   Cang   Asuiabe
Basile
Idolo   M
Calatrava   Asalayeng   Reserva Natural
del Estuario
del Río Muni   Acanabor
Muni   **Cogo**
Mikemele   Mibo
Elobey   Asobla
Grande   **Cocobeach**   Utamboni
Corisco
Corisco
Gobe   Bay

ATLANTIC

OCEAN

Hike through the jungle to
the black volcanic shores of
Bioko Sur, where you will
find a waterfall on the beach
page 145

Go whale-spotting
on the mysterious
and isolated
Annobón Island
page 181

Watch endangered turtles
nesting on the northern
shores of Río Muni in the
Punta Llende Natural Reserve
page 165

Relax on your own private,
white-sand beach with views
of Gabon on Corisco Island
pages 171–4

NIGERIA
Port Harcourt   CAMEROON
MALABO   Douala
Príncipe   Bioko
Bata   EQUATORIAL
GUINEA
São Tomé   **LIBREVILLE**
Annobón   GABON

Explore the diverse colonial history of the
Corisco Bay area by wandering the
European ruins on Elobey Grande and
Elobey Chico islands
pages 168–71

KEY

Capital city	■
Main town	●
Other town	○
Airport	✈
Border crossing	⤫
Main road	
Other road	
National park/reserve	---

CAMEROON

Marvel at the scale of Oyala: the new capital city rising out of the jungle
pages 202–5

Ngoa

Micomeseng

Acom

Esong

Ebebiyin

Mimbamengui

Andoc

Moyo

Ncue

Ebongo

Nsang

Tool

Reserva Natural del Monte Temelón

Dumandui
~~aman~~

San
Carlos

Temelón

Abia

Oboronco

Ngong

Ngosoc

Niefang

Mfaman

Niefang

Añisok

*Piedra Bere
Natural
Monument*

Nonkieng

Mbam

Efualn

Amwang

Elonesang

Ndúmensoc

Ncumekie

Bisun

Mengomeyén

Nyong

Mongomo

Bicurga

Oyala

Ncomo

Nkumekie

Yen

Manseng

Nsung

Uoro Mbini

Asoc

~~Laña~~

Eñang

Monte Chime ▲

Mecoga

*Piedra Nzas
Natural
Monument*

Misergue

Evinayong

Abia

Ntoro

Mindong

Oveng

Acoga

Abenelang

Cucumancoc

Aconibe

Ngon

Ebomicu

Be

*Los Altos de Nsork
National Park*

Ngüelensoc

Nsoc

Nchengayong

Esong

Medouneu

Macula

Efon

Acurenam

Alum

Track wildlife along the abandoned trails of Monte Alen National Park
pages 187–9

Edum

N

Bradt

Follow the forest elephants' trail of destruction around the forests of Altos de Nsork National Park
page 201

GABON

| 0 | | 30km |
| 0 | | 20 miles |

Equatorial Guinea
Don't miss...

Bioko
The 250m-tall Iladyi Cascades, located only a short trek from Moka in central Bioko

(CM/A) page 143

Nesting turtles
The beaches of Equatorial Guinea, both on Bioko and mainland Río Muni, are important nesting sites for rare sea turtles such as this leatherback (*Dermochelys coriacea*)
(SS) page 162

Malabo

Malabo's waterfront skyline includes the Santa Isabel Cathedral, the Sofitel hotel, the presidential palace and the infamous Black Beach prison

(I/A) pages 105–36

Annobón

Locals await the return of fishermen with their daily catch in San Antonio de Palé, Annobón

(OS) pages 175–93

Corisco

The last vestiges of Spanish colonialism, here in the form of a Claretian mission house, are being slowly reclaimed by the jungle on Corisco island

(OS) pages 171–4

Equatorial Guinea in colour

top   The Catholic missionary Iglesia Parochial Maria Reina still serves as a spiritual and educational focal point for the community of Niefang (OS) page 187

above left   La Basílica de la Inmaculada Concepción in Mongomo is one of the largest and most highly decorated cathedrals in all of Africa (OS) page 198

above   The Iglesia Parroquial Corazón de Maria was renovated in 2010, marking a new wave of investment on the isolated island of Annobón (OS) page 181

below left   Overlooking Corisco Bay and neighbouring Gabon, this church and mission house is one of the few places to stay in Cogo (OS) page 168

below   The Torre de la Libertad dominates Bata's coastal skyline, and features a great Italian restaurant with panoramic views (OS) page 161

above left   Pico Quioveo, the extinct
             volcanic peak at the centre
             of Annobón (OS) page 181

above right Frogs are common on Bioko,
             such as this modest forest tree
             frog (*Leptopelis modestus*)
             (PM/BBPP) page 11

right   The unspoilt Arena Blanca
             beach, less than an hour south
             of Malabo (OS) page 134

below   Bioko's lush rainforests are
             teeming with wildlife and are
             easily accessible from Malabo
             (SS) page 137–45

above Football is the national sport of Equatorial Guinea, with informal games taking place wherever space will permit (WS/F) page 125

left Most Equatoguineans are subsistence farmers, growing tropical crops such as this papaya (GD/F) pages 50–1

below left The shores of the sacred Lago Mazafim on Annobón are used for subsistence agriculture (OS) page 180

below Riaba, once a global centre for cocoa exports, still processes a small harvest every year in the traditional manner (OS) page 50

AUTHOR

Oscar Scafidi was raised in Italy, then the UK, and has spent six years living and working in Africa as a teacher. When not in the classroom, Oscar is a travel journalist focusing on difficult destinations such as Somalia, Afghanistan, Liberia and East Timor. Some of his work can be found on Sean Rorison's website about conflict and post-conflict zones, Polo's Bastards (*www.polosbastards.com*). His Twitter feed is @OscarScafidi.

AUTHOR'S STORY

Equatorial Guinea has fascinated me for years. Like many Europeans, I first read about it in detail following the highly publicised 2004 attempted coup d'état. Prior to this point, I knew of the country only vaguely, in the wider context of Portuguese and Spanish colonialism in Central Africa, as well as through the documented horrors of the Macías regime in the early independence years.

In 2013, I was refused a tourist visa to enter Equatorial Guinea during an overland trip from Angola to Cameroon. That same year I read a United Nations' report that ranked Equatorial Guinea as one of the ten nations least visited by tourists in the world. Having seen the wonders of neighbouring Cameroon and Gabon, I was intrigued: what was this tiny Spanish-speaking country like, and why was it so difficult to get in? After nearly two years and a lot of hard work, I finally have the answers. My aim in writing this guidebook is to equip visitors with the tools required to enter the country and then get around safely and successfully, whether they are a business visitor, a 4x4 overlander, a backpacker on a tight budget, an ecotourist or anything in-between!

Equatorial Guinea is by no means an easy destination, but it is certainly worthwhile. Some of its problems, such as the endemic corruption, are not unique to this country, although they do manifest themselves in some pretty interesting ways given Equatorial Guinea's tiny size and vast oil wealth. But don't write it off too quickly or you will be missing out on a remarkable place: the only hispanophone nation on the continent, with a dizzying variety of landscapes and peoples, linked together by some of the best road networks in Africa. Whether you are visiting for the first time or are an expatriate resident of Malabo or Bata, I hope this guide encourages you to head out and explore some of the sights that very few other tourists have had the privilege of seeing.

PUBLISHER'S FOREWORD   *Adrian Phillips, Managing Director*

When Oscar Scafidi told us that Equatorial Guinea sees fewer tourists than almost any other country on the planet, we of course knew we had to publish a Bradt guide! It's perhaps less of a commercially bonkers decision than it might seem – there are many expats working in the oil industry who will find this guide invaluable. But it's also clear that Equatorial Guinea has the natural resources to attract adventurous tourists, with tropical wildlife, empty beaches, volcanic islands and dense rainforest. Oscar's guide – the first and only one available – provides all the practical advice they'll need to make the trip.

First edition published November 2015

Bradt Travel Guides Ltd
IDC House, The Vale, Chalfont St Peter, Bucks SL9 9RZ, England
www.bradtguides.com
Print edition published in the USA by The Globe Pequot Press Inc,
PO Box 480, Guilford, Connecticut 06437–0480

ISBN: 978 1 84162 925 4 (print)
e-ISBN: 978 1 78477 136 2 (e-pub)
e-ISBN: 978 1 78477 236 9 (mobi)

British Library Cataloguing in Publication Data
A catalogue record for this book is available from the British Library

Front cover Red-eared guenon monkey (TL/G)
Back cover A child in Malabo (WS/F); Mongamo Cathedral (OS)
Title page Fisherman on Annobón (OS); Red colobus monkey (AO/BBPP); the highlands of Evinayong (OS)

Photographs
Alamy: Carlos Mora (CM/A), incamerastock (I/A); Bioko Biodiversity Protection Programme: Araks Ohanyan (AC/BBPP), Patrick McLaughlin (PM/BBPP); Fractures Photo: Guillame Darribou (GD/F), William Sands (WS/F); Getty Images: Tim Laman (TL/G); Oscar Scafidi (OS); SuperStock (SS)

Maps David McCutcheon FBCart.S; colour map base by Nick Rowland FRGS

Typeset by BBR and Wakewing
Production managed by Jellyfish Print Solutions; printed in India
Digital conversion by www.dataworks.co.in

Acknowledgements

Writing a guidebook to a country with no previous guidebooks and very few tourists has presented a wealth of serious challenges. I would not have been successful in this undertaking without the help of a wide variety of people. Firstly, I wish to thank Rafael for his selfless generosity while I was in Río Muni. My exploration of the continental region, and especially Bata, would have been much harder without him. Also, thanks to Jesus (of Colombia, not Nazareth) for looking after me while I was in Bata and helping out with my language translations and his friend Andres for all the assistance around Cogo and Corisco. Lastly, thanks to Annibale for the guided tour of Utonde, and all the Italians for their warm hospitality.

On Bioko, I owe a debt of gratitude to Autumn and Scott Elliott Florida of The Ladybug Project. Your hosting in Malabo was great, and who knows how I would have obtained a visa without you! Thanks also to their housemate Serra Brandes for accompanying me on a number of road trips around the island. Alastair proved himself invaluable throughout my time on Bioko, helping out in a variety of areas, and was always willing to provide detailed information to assist in my travels. Thanks to Barry Maguire for lending me his vehicle (and introducing me to the joys of China Pub!). I am also very grateful to all the staff of the Bioko Biodiversity Protection Program, especially Drew Cronin and Bryan Featherstone for their assistance in-country, as well as Angel Vañó at Ruta47 for his tireless efforts to make this book a success. Thanks also to Jim O'Brien of Native Eye who read early proofs of the book.

Regarding the language appendices, I had help from a group of scholars spread across the globe. My thanks go out to Daniel Duke, Dr Justo Bolekia Boleká, Kofi Yakpo, Pedro Mba and Dr John Lipski. In my wider research I was assisted by a huge number of contributors, who are listed in the appendices, but particular thanks to Yolanda Marta Aixela Cabre, Dr Igor Cusack, Fred Swengel, Luke Powell, Jacob Cooper, Martin Bohnstedt and many of the staff at BirdLife International for their detailed contributions.

Finally, I wish to thank my friends and family for their support throughout this process, especially Steph who took a big leap moving back from Angola with me. I hope you all think it has been worthwhile!

Contents

LIST OF MAPS

MAPS

Keys and symbols Maps include alphabetical keys covering the locations of those places to stay, eat or drink that are featured in the book. Note that regional maps may not show all hotels and restaurants in the area: other establishments may be located in towns shown on the map.

Grids and grid references Several maps use gridlines to allow easy location of sites. Map grid references are listed in square brackets after the name of the place or sight of interest in the text, with page number followed by grid number, eg: [110 C3].

FEEDBACK REQUEST AND UPDATES WEBSITE

The influx of oil wealth means Equatorial Guinea is developing at a rapid pace. Inevitably, things will change between when this book is published and when you read it. If you wish to stay up to date with developments in the country, follow our dedicated Twitter account (@BradtEGguide) or look for updates on the Bradt website www.bradtupdates.com/equinea, which will supplement the printed guidebook. Also, if you have any information about changes in the country, or feedback regarding the book, please direct them to this site so that future editions can be as current as possible. Alternatively, contact us on 01753 893444 or info@bradtguides.com, or you can add a review of the book to www.bradtguides.com or Amazon.

FOLLOW BRADT

For the latest news, special offers and competitions, subscribe to the Bradt newsletter via the website www.bradtguides.com and follow Bradt on:

- www.facebook.com/BradtTravelGuides
- @BradtGuides
- @bradtguides
- www.pinterest.com/bradtguides

Introduction

Equatorial Guinea is not a very well known country. Random straw polls of my secondary students elicited mainly blank stares or they confused it with one of the world's three other nations containing 'Guinea' in the title. There was the occasional mention of the 2004 attempted coup d'état or perhaps news articles relating to the president's eldest son's extravagant spending habits. My enquiries with adults fared little better. Those around in the 1970s sometimes recalled reading about former president Macías's rule of terror, and how Equatorial Guinea used to be a Spanish colony. They might perhaps tell me it is an oil-rich country. Beyond that, the place is a mystery. Hardly anyone goes there, and if they do, it is for work purposes, and they are often hidden away in hermetically sealed expatriate compounds. So what should tourists expect upon arrival?

The first thing is a unique blend of diversity. Yes, it is a Spanish-speaking nation but there are also remnants of British and Portuguese influence to be found in the languages of Malabo and Annobón respectively. By the continental border regions, you may also hear French from neighbouring francophone countries, Gabon and Cameroon. Setting aside these European influences though, there are dozens of African languages, some found only in Equatorial Guinea and some regional, which highlight the ridiculous nature of the straight-line artificial colonial boundaries. But we cannot discuss the place simply with reference to European and African influences. Here you will find representatives from the Americas, the Caribbean, the Middle East and Asia, all playing a part in the rapid oil-fuelled development of the country.

Visiting Equatorial Guinea you will find not one capital but two, with the second under construction deep in the jungle. The regions are connected by an advanced network of highways, ports and airports, far removed from the stereotype of slow, pot-holed African roads. Outside the population centres are vast, empty stretches of pristine beach, volcanic black or crystal white. Expect jungles and mountains and waterfalls and volcanic islands, all teeming with wildlife if you know where to look. Best of all, you will likely have most of these landscapes all to yourself. This is one of the last true African frontiers, and even high-end ecotourism has not taken off here yet. In the cities you will find an eclectic mix of cuisines, cultural events and nightlife, a testament to the diverse populations that call this place home.

Equatorial Guinea is not an easy place to get into or to travel around independently. However, the tourism sector is a focus of the government's Horizon2020 development plan, so hopefully things will improve. In the meantime, jump through the hoops, get yourself a visa and head over to Central Africa's best-kept secret, before everyone else does.

Part One

GENERAL INFORMATION

Location West Central Africa. The main island, Bioko, is approximately 40km off the coast of Cameroon. The island of Corisco is 30km southwest of the Río Muni estuary, which divides Equatorial Guinea and Gabon. The island of Annobón is 180km southwest of São Tomé. The mainland continental territory, Río Muni, is bordered by Gabon to the east and south and Cameroon to the north.

Size 28,051km² (Río Muni 26,003km², Bioko island 2,017km², Annobón island 17.5km², Corisco island 14km² plus several uninhabited islets)

Status Independent republic

Government Multi-party democracy; presidential system

Population 722,254 (international estimate July 2014): Bubi, Pygmy, Bantu, Spanish, Portuguese, Angolan, Creole descent, mixed-race

Life expectancy 54 (estimated 2012)

Capital Malabo on Bioko island (new capital Oyala under construction in Río Muni)

Economy Oil, gas, subsistence farming

Religion Roman Catholic (83%), Protestant (6%), indigenous religious beliefs (5%), Muslim (<1%)

Currency Central African CFA franc (CFA or XAF). Also the euro (€), which is widely used, and the US dollar (US$)

International telephone code +240

Time WAT (West Africa Time), UTC/GMT +1 hour

Electricity supply 220V round, European two-pin sockets

Flag A coat of arms in grey with a silk cotton tree and above, six yellow stars on three horizontal bands of green, white and red with a blue isosceles triangle on the hoist. Under the coat of arms is the motto: Unidad, Paz, Justicia (Unity, Peace, Justice).

Public holidays 1 January, Good Friday, 1 May, Corpus Christi Feast, 5 June, 3 August, 15 August, 12 October, 8 December, 25 December

GUIDEBOOK UPDATES

You can read the latest updates and make suggestions of your own by following @BradtEGguide on Twitter or by posting a comment on the Bradt website @www.bradtupdates.com/eguinea.

1

Background Information

GEOGRAPHY

Equatorial Guinea is located on the west coast of Central Africa. The nation is divided between the mainland and numerous islands. The small coastal piece of territory on the mainland, known as Río Muni, is sandwiched between Gabon and Cameroon. It has a 265km-long Atlantic coastline, stretching from the estuary of the Río Campo river in the north to the estuary of the Río Muni river on the southern border. The landscape here features a narrow coastal plain backed by a range of coastal hills and mountains, the highest of which is Mount Mitra (also known as Biyemeyem), standing at 1,200m. The interior is mainly covered by a 500m-high plateau that stretches across the border into Gabon, where it forms the Monts de Cristal. The highest point of this plateau within Equatorial Guinea is Mount Fijelvingue, standing at 1,500m. This plateau is dissected by three main rivers: the Temboni in the south, the Campo in the north and the Mbini in the centre.

Equatorial Guinea also features a number of islands, some of which are volcanic, stretching along the Cameroon Line. Five of these islands are inhabited. The largest volcanic island, Bioko, is around 40km off the coast of Cameroon, and has the capital Malabo at the northern end. Formerly called Fernando Pó under Spanish rule, it is around 67km long and 40km wide, with a 270km coastline. The highest point of the island is Pico De Basilé at 3,011m, which is a volcanic cone. The island is covered in tropical rainforest.

At the mouth of the Río Muni estuary lie four smaller islands, also heavily forested: Corisco, Elobey Grande, Elobey Chico and Belobi. Further south are three small disputed islets in Corisco Bay: Conga, Cocotiers and Mbañe. Only Mbañe is inhabited, by a few Gabonese fishermen. Gabon has been occupying and administering these islands since the 1970s, however, both parties are looking to the International Court of Justice to settle the territorial dispute. Given the potentially lucrative oil deposits around these islands, they have been a source of tension between the two nations for decades.

Almost 600km southwest of Bioko island, past São Tomé and Príncipe, lies Annobón, the southernmost volcanic island of Equatorial Guinea. This tiny island is just under 18km², with a number of volcanic cones. The highest point on the island is Pico Quioveo at 598m.

At just over 28,000km², Equatorial Guinea is one of the smallest nations in Africa. While reliable statistics on the country are difficult to obtain, the population was estimated by the World Bank at 722,254 in 2014. Almost half of Equatoguineans live in the two principal cities of Malabo on Bioko island and Bata on the mainland.

CLIMATE

As the name suggests, much of the country enjoys an equatorial climate: warm, rainy and humid all year round. Malabo is consistently warm, with an average temperature that sits around 26°C. Between January and May it is slightly warmer, and between July and October slightly colder, but the temperature difference is rarely more than 4°C. The city is often overcast, with the most cloud cover between May and November.

Rainfall over **Bioko island** is variable due to the relief. In Malabo, rainfall is highest between June and October, with drier months between November and February. The south of the island is much wetter, with Ureca receiving a staggering 10,450mm of rainfall per year, making it the wettest place in Africa and one of the wettest in the world.

Río Muni is also equatorial, however the average temperatures in Bata are slightly lower than in Malabo. There is also a noticeable drop in temperature between June and August, during which time precipitation also reduces significantly, before recovering over the course of the year (almost the opposite of Bioko). Along the coast of the mainland rainfall levels increase the further south you travel, with the Río Muni estuary being particularly wet with over 4,500mm of rainfall annually. This rainfall declines the further inland you head, with the higher points of the plateau being relatively cooler than the coast. Humidity is always high.

Annobón's average temperature is just over 26°C, with little annual variation. Relative humidity is always above 75% and the island is frequently cloudy. The northern end of the island is drier than the south, but average rainfall is still high at around 1,200mm annually. There is a dry season from June to October and a wet season from November to May.

NATURAL HISTORY

Although a relatively small country, Equatorial Guinea contains an incredible wealth of biodiversity. Situated in the globally significant Gulf of Guinea, the country encompasses Congo Basin forests, extensive coastal and marine areas, and a number of islands harbouring high diversity and endemism. It has the fourth-highest primate species richness in all of Africa, including chimpanzees, the critically endangered western lowland gorilla, and drills, among many others. Bioko island, with an area of just 2,017km², is a true 'hotspot within a hotspot', and is considered among the most important sites in the world for the conservation of primate diversity and forest bird species. The island is home to 11 types of primate, of which seven are found only on Bioko, and one of these, Pennant's red colobus, is often considered among the most endangered primates in the world. It is also a critical nesting site for four species of marine turtles (leatherback, green, olive ridley and hawksbill), and contains numerous unique birds, at least 40 endemic plants and a host of other rare wildlife.

FLORA Equatorial Guinea is one of the most biologically significant locations in all of Africa. Bioko island, separated from the rest of Africa after the last Ice Age, is home to a diverse collection of endemic subspecies that have evolved separately from their mainland counterparts over the last 12,000 years. It has been recognised by the International Union for Conservation of Nature (IUCN) and the World Wide Fund for Nature (WWF) as a Centre of Plant Diversity. The nation is home to 3,250 plant species with around 66 endemic and 23 threatened plant species. On Bioko alone there are 1,105 plant species of which 12% are endemic. There are a further 20 endemic species on Annobón. Visitors hiking up Bioko's Pico Basilé might spot the small flowers of *Solanecio lainzii*, which occur nowhere else in the world. Likewise, those visiting Monte Alen National Park on the mainland get a chance to see the small yellow flowers of *Begonia aequatoguineensis*, which occur nowhere else. Even today, Equatorial Guinea's flora is not well documented, and new species are being discovered all the time. Sharing the space with these endemics are alien species such as cocoa and coffee which were introduced on plantations during European colonisation.

Forests cover around 79% of inland Río Muni and its offshore islands. This is a mixture of Atlantic equatorial coastal forests, Cross Sanaga Bioko coastal forests,

ENDEMIC PLANTS   *Fred Swengel*

Equatorial Guinea is home to around 66 endemic plant species, and possibly many more, given the lack of exploration and research throughout the territory. Endemic plants include types of orchids, shrubs, flowering plants, riverweed, ferns, quillworts, relatives of ginger, ferns and mistletoe. Some of these species are not just endemic to Equatorial Guinea, but limited to an extremely small geographic range within the country. Some key species to look out for are:

- *Acalypha annobónae* Low tropical flowering shrub found only on Annobón
- *Afroligusticum townsendii* Found on the IUCN Red List of Threatened Species
- *Asplenium annobónense* A fern found only on Annobón
- *Asplenium carvalhoanum* A large West African fern
- *Begonia aequatoguineensis* A small, yellow-flowering species of begonia found in Monte Alen National Park
- *Bertiera annobónensis* A tropical flowering plant found only on Annobón
- *Chonopetalum stenodictyum* A vascular plant
- *Crossandrella cristalensis* Found in the Equatoguinean portion of the Crystal Mountains, mainland Río Muni
- *Cyathula fernandopoensis* Found on the IUCN Red List of Threatened Species, this plant occurs in only four locations on Bioko island
- *Discoclaoxylon pubescens* Member of the spurge family, found only in the south of Annobón Island
- *Ficus annobónensis* A shrub found only in the north of Annobón
- *Genyorchis saccata* A type of orchid
- *Isoetes spinulospora* A quillwort found in Equatorial Guinea's freshwater and marsh areas
- *Macropodiella uoroensis* A type of riverweed, which grows on hard surfaces such as rocks in fast-flowing river water (such as rapids and waterfalls)
- *Polystachya engongensis* A type of orchid
- *Polystachya reticulata* A type of orchid
- *Polystachya riomuniensis* A type of orchid
- *Renealmia mannii* A type of ginger found on Bioko island
- *Schoenoplectus heptangularis* A type of sedge (resembling grass) that grows only on the shores of Lake Biaó, Bioko
- *Solanecio iainzii* A member of the sunflower family found on the slopes of Pico Basilé, Bioko island
- *Viscum grandicaule* A mistletoe found only on Annobón

and Mount Cameroon and Bioko montane forests. Central African mangrove ecoregions can also be found in the numerous estuaries.

Between 80% and 90% of the country's population rely directly on the forest for food, fuel, building materials and medicines. This widespread reliance, along with the incredible biodiversity found in Equatorial Guinea's forests, has attracted many conservation groups to the country, as the lowland forests of West Africa are home to more than a quarter of Africa's mammal species. This interest from conservationists is welcome news as the UN estimates that between 1990 and 2010 Equatorial Guinea lost 12.6% of its forest cover, around 243,000ha, due to deforestation.

The Ministry of Agriculture and Forestry in Equatorial Guinea, through collaboration with groups such as the World Resources Institute, has recently taken steps to improve its forest management. In 1997, the government introduced the 'Ley De Uso Y Manejo De Los Bosques [Law on the Use and Management of the Forests]', followed up in 2000 by more legislation on 'Areas Protegidas'. The level of protected areas has been increased, while forest concession areas decreased. There has also been a policy shift away from timber-only extraction to a more sustainable approach. While these are welcome legislative steps, deforestation is still an issue today.

The Bioko Diversity Protection Program was set up in 1998, as an academic partnership between Drexel University in Philadelphia, USA, and the Universidad Nacional de Guinea Ecuatorial (UNGE) in Malabo. Originally with a focus on protecting Bioko's primate species, it has since expanded its efforts into other conservation areas.

FAUNA Equatorial Guinea is home to 194 known species of mammal (including whales, dolphins and manatees), 418 birds and 91 reptiles, although these numbers are subject to frequent change given the lack of research into this biodiverse country.

Primates

There are 21 species of primate spread across Equatorial Guinea, and Bioko island is home to Africa's greatest concentration of endangered primates. Within the Luba Crater Scientific Reserve alone you can find seven primate species and this is the best and most accessible location in the cuntry to view them.

Two full primate species are endemic to Bioko: the Bioko squirrel galago (*Sciurocheirus alleni alleni*) and the Bioko red colobus (*Procolobus pennantii pennantii*). The island is also home to numerous endemic subspecies of drill (*Mandrillus leucophaeus poensis*), Preuss's guenon (*Cercopithecus preussi insularis*), red-eared guenon (*Cercopithecus erythrotis spp. erythrotis*), putty-nosed guenon (*Cercopithecus nictitans spp. martini*) and crowned guenon (*Cercopithecus pogonias spp. pogonias*). Four species have been identified as endangered by the IUCN. Primate densities in this region are among the highest recorded anywhere on the continent.

The forests of Río Muni are home to a small population of critically endangered western lowland gorillas (*Gorilla gorilla gorilla*). The most famous member of this population was Copito de Nieve ('Snow Flake'), an albino gorilla who was removed from the forest in 1966 and taken to Barcelona Zoo, where he was kept on display until his death in 2003. The forests around the Río Muni estuary are also home to the Calabar angwantibo (*Arctocebus calabarensis*) and potto (*Perodicticus potto*). These big-eyed nocturnal creatures are relatives of the slow loris, which became a YouTube sensation a few years ago thanks to its supposedly cute appearance and affable nature. You might also see the southern needle-clawed bushbaby (*Euoticus elegantulus*), Bioko Allen's bushbaby (*Sciurocheirus alleni*) and collared mangabey (*Cercocebus torquatus*).

Aquatic mammals Humpback whales (*Megaptera novaeangliae*) migrate past Annobón island in autumn each year and the Río Muni Estuary Natural Reserve is home to a sizeable population of African manatee (*Trichechus senegalensis*).

Atlantic humpback dolphins (*Sousa teuszii*) are present in the waters off Equatorial Guinea and this is the species of dolphin you are most likely to see. The nation's waters are also home to Clymene dolphins (*Stenella clymene*) and Fraser's dolphin (*Lagenodelphis hosei*), although these prefer deep water so you are unlikely to see them unless out on a boat. The very uncommon pygmy killer whale (*Feresa attenuata*) also has Equatorial Guinea within its range.

Other mammals Mbini area is home to significant populations of forest antelopes and rare rodents. Buffalo can also be found there, but are threatened. Ten different species of fruit bat can be found on the mainland, as well as manatee (*Trichechus senegalensis*) in the Río Muni estuary and hippopotamuses in the Río Ntem estuary. Forest elephants can also be found in the southeastern forests, by the Gabonese border.

There are also at least four small mammals endemic to the country. Eisentraut's mouse shrew (*Myosorex eisentrauti*) is a critically endangered species endemic to Bioko, and the island is also home to the Bioko forest shrew (*Sylvisorex isabellae*), Father Basilio's striped mouse (*Hybomys basilii*) and endemic subspecies of blue and Ogilby's duikers.

Birds with Jacob C Cooper and Luke L Powell, Equatorial Guinea Bird Initiative
Home to five Important Bird Areas, Equatorial Guinea harbours more than 400 species of birds: Annobón (pages 175–81), Pico Basilé (page 133), the Luba Crater Scientific Reserve (page 143), Monte Alen National Park (pages 187–9) and Altos De Nsork National Park (page 201). Several species occurring in this part of the world were originally described from Bioko, and any species with the scientific name 'poensis' was named after Bioko's former name, Fernando Pó. The vast lowlands of Río Muni host a wide range of Central African rainforest species, whereas the isolated island peaks contain some of the world's rarest birds, including three species found nowhere else on earth: the Bioko batis (*Batis poensis*), the Bioko speirops (*Zosterops brunneus*), and the Annobón white-eye (*Zosterops griseovirescens*).

The birds of Equatorial Guinea generally fall into three categories: Afromontane, Gulf of Guinean and Lower Guinean. Most birdwatchers travel to the region for the Afromontane birds. These Afromontane species occur only in Central African mountain ranges, and in Equatorial Guinea are restricted to the highlands of Bioko and Monte Alen National Park. Such global rarities as Cameroon pigeon (*Columba sjostedti*), mountain sawwing (*Psalidoprocne pristoptera*), black-capped woodland warbler (*Phylloscopus herberti*), and Shelley's oliveback (*Nesocharis shelleyi*) occur in the highlands, and these species are relatively easy to find when hiking the trails and roadways. The second category, the Gulf of Guinea endemics, are restricted to the island of Annobón and share more in common with São Tomé and Príncipe than the rest of Equatorial Guinea. Scouring Annobón won't yield very many species, but if you're lucky, you'll encounter the island's one endemic species, the Annobón white-eye, and its two endemic subspecies, 'Fea's' African scops-owl (*Otus senegalensis feae*) and 'Smith's' red-bellied paradise-flycatcher

Conservation in Equatorial Guinea is at a tipping point. The network of protected areas is relatively young, established only in 1988, and little federal infrastructure exists to manage it effectively, and to mitigate the threats to wildlife posed by extensive commercial bushmeat hunting, local timber harvesting, and continued rapid expansion of the country's infrastructure. The National Institute of Forest Development and Protected Area Management (INDEFOR-AP) and the Ministry of Fisheries and the Environment, the federal entities tasked with protected area management, have been active and motivated, despite operating with little support but bureaucratic issues have continued to inhibit their ability to effectively manage protected areas and enforce regulations. Fortunately, there are a number of high-impact research, education and conservation projects operating in Equatorial Guinea, and the overall conservation movement is gaining increasing momentum across the country. Furthermore, multi-national corporations working in Equatorial Guinea, including ExxonMobil, Noble Energy, Marathon Oil, Hess Corporation and Equatorial Guinea Liquid Natural Gas, continue to generously support biodiversity conservation activities. Ultimately, the relative cost of conservation is low, the long-term benefits are great, and the opportunity to reverse the tide of unsustainable exploitation is high. With decreasing revenues from hydrocarbons, it is important for the government to act now to secure the long-term future of the country's ecosystems and the services they provide.

Throughout the 20th century prior to independence, much of Equatorial Guinea's forests were converted for plantation agriculture, such as cacao and coffee. Following independence in 1968, most plantations were abandoned and timber became the primary export leading to heavily logged forests throughout the country. Some of the abandoned plantations were reclaimed by secondary forests, especially on Bioko, where the terrain makes logging difficult. The extent of reclamation became evident with the return of biologists to Equatorial Guinea in the mid 1980s led by the Spanish NGO, Los Amigos de Doñana, and primatologists, Thomas Butysnki and Stanley Koster. Butynski and Koster alleviated fears that a number of primate species might have become extinct during the Macías years, and laid the groundwork for the primate research on Bioko that is still ongoing today. Doñana advised the government of Equatorial Guinea in the design of the country's first protected areas in 1988, and shortly thereafter developed an extensive research and conservation programme, which came to an unfortunate halt in January 1998, after unfounded rumours surfaced implicating Doñana staff as conspirators in an attempted coup d'état. Soon after the departure of Doñana, the Bioko Biodiversity Protection Program (BBPP) was officially formed as an academic partnership between the National University of Equatorial Guinea (UNGE) and Beaver College (later Arcadia University, and now Drexel University). The BBPP, founded by Dr Gail Hearn, is the longest

(*Terpsiphone rufiventer smithii*). The lowlands of both Bioko and Río Muni are home to a wide variety of Lower Guinean birds, and spending time scouring the canopy and hiking through the impressive rainforests may yield such treasures as rufous-sided broadbill (*Smithornis rufolateralis*), lyre-tailed honeyguide

successful conservation organisation in Equatorial Guinea, and is built upon the long-term academic partnership with UNGE. The BBPP helped to form the growing Department of Environmental Studies at UNGE, and has helped to usher in the era of contemporary conservation on Bioko.

In recent years, however, there has been a considerable increase in conservation research and activities throughout the country. Beginning in March 2002, with the 'Bioko Biodiversity Roundtable' in Malabo, Conservation International (CI) has worked with the government of Equatorial Guinea on numerous conservation strategies. The collaboration had some success in Río Muni, with lesser results on Bioko. On Bioko, BBPP has continued to further its education efforts with UNGE, developed the country's first research station in Moka, and expanded its research and monitoring activities in the Gran Caldera de Luba Scientific Reserve; while Ecotono, a collaborative foreign and Equatorial Guinea-based NGO formed in 2014, is developing a comprehensive research and management programme for Pico Basilé National Park.

The Equatorial Guinea Bird Initiative is currently undertaking a project spanning Bioko and Río Muni meant to expand the bird species list for the country to inform both conservation and birding ecotourism, and are training a cadre of UNGE students in the hopes of developing local interest in ornithological research. The Zoological Society of London has maintained an intensive research programme based out of Bata since 1999 which has focused on bushmeat sustainability and alternatives, while the Wildlife Conservation Society has sustained a long-term partnership with INDEFOR-AP to conserve marine turtles along Río Muni's coast, and is in the process of beginning a multi-year project to improve local livelihoods and management of coastal resources in the Río Campo, Punta Ilende, and Corisco and Elobeyes natural reserves. A joint project was originally initiated in 2010 by the United Nations Development Program, the Global Environmental Facility, and CI, as well as a number of other government and non-governmental organisations in Equatorial Guinea in order to strengthen the country's protected area system. The project has been rife with setbacks, however, and has just recently begun to be implemented. Despite these challenges, the prospects for conserving Equatorial Guinea's unique wildlife are not bleak. Non-governmental organisations and companies operating within the country on biodiversity conservation issues, more proactive forest governance by INDEFOR-AP, and higher education initiatives led by UNGE's Department of Environmental Studies have begun to improve the prospects of the wildlife and their habitats by cultivating collaborative public and private partnerships founded upon biodiversity conservation concerns, by increasing federal involvement in managing the existing protected areas network, and by creating a larger population of citizens well versed in environmental issues.

(*Melichneutes robustus*), grey-necked picathartes (*Picathartes oreas*), and forest swallow (*Petrochelidon fuliginosa*).

Further reading on the birdlife of Equatorial Guinea is available from the African Bird Club (*www.africanbirdclub.org*), BirdLife International (*www.birdlife.org*)

and the West African Ornithological Society (WAOS; *http://malimbus.free.fr*). Several guides that cover the region currently exist, but by far the most up-to-date and comprehensive one presently available is *The Birds of West Africa* (2nd Ed) by Nik Borrow and Ron Demey. Those travellers that are seeking island endemics will find Jaime Pérez del Val's *Aves de Bioko* indispensable for learning about the island's birdlife and where to find it (available only in Spanish). Recordings are also a necessity for identifying birds in the dark forests of Central Africa, and Claude Chappuis's legendary *Birds of North, West and Central Africa* will cover almost all of the possibilities. The West and Central half of the collection costs £75 (US$120/68,000CFA). Additionally, songs and calls can be downloaded individually from Xeno-Canto (*www.xeno-canto.org*) for free. Information regarding specific birding sites and species localities can be found on eBird (*www.ebird.org*), and we highly recommend submitting your sightings to help scientists understand the birds of this under-visited region. The birds of Equatorial Guinea are poorly known relative to other tropical nations, but the Equatorial Guinea Bird Initiative (*www.kickstarter.com/projects/1663751187/equatorial-guinea-bird-initiative?ref=discovery*) is seeking to build scientific knowledge about the country's avifauna.

Reptiles The star attraction in terms of reptiles is the turtle population. The beaches of Equatorial Guinea are frequented by a number of marine turtle species, including the green turtle (*Chelonia mydas*), leatherback (*Dermochelys coriacea*), olive ridley (*Lepidochelys olivacea*), and hawksbill (*Eretmochelys imbricata*). For more information on turtles, see TOMAGE information, page 162.

There are also two types of crocodile in Río Muni: the critically endangered African slender-snouted crocodile (*Mecistops cataphractus*), which has not been seen there in the wild for years, and the dwarf crocodile (*Osteolaemus tetraspis*).

There are many species of snake present in the country, including nine venomous snakes. The first seven of the snakes listed have recorded cases of bites causing fatalities in humans. This is not to say that the final two are safe though; in fact, the banded water cobra is the most venomous cobra species in the world, but a combination of being very shy and living mainly in water means that it has so far avoided human contact. Always seek local advice before hiking through an area.

Variable bush viper (*Atheris squamigera*) – Found in Río Muni, especially by the border with Gabon, this green or brown snake prefers to stay at low levels in flowering bushes.

Variable burrowing asp (*Atractaspis irregularis*) – Found across a large distribution through West, Central and East Africa, this dark brown or black snake can grow up to 55cm in length.

West African Gaboon viper (*Bitis gabonica rhinoceros*) – Sluggish and shy, this large, heavy, nocturnal viper has the longest fangs and highest venom yield of any venomous snake. Specimens have been measured at over 2m long. Bites are very rare due to a lack of aggression in the species.

Rhinoceros viper (*Bitis nasicornis*) – Named after the distinctive horns on its nose, this nocturnal viper lives in forests, hiding at ground level. It is one of most dangerous snakes on the list, as its venom is extremely potent, and is both neurotoxic (attacking the nervous system) and haemotoxic (attacking red blood cells).

Jameson's mamba (*Dendroaspis jamesoni*) – This fast moving, tree-dwelling snake is green and can grow up to 2.6m long. Although not aggressive, a bite from this snake can prove fatal in as little as 30 minutes, and untreated bites have a very high mortality rate.

Forest cobra (*Naja melanoleuca*) – This is possibly the largest of all the true cobra species in the world. It prefers a moist habitat and is a good swimmer. Bites are very rare, although it can become aggressive when threatened, showing its wedge-shaped hood.

Forest vine or **twig snake** (*Thelotornis kirtlandii*) – Disguised as a twig, this snake sits in bushes, swaying gently and waiting for prey such as birds. It has fangs at the back of the mouth and is able to inflate its throat to intimidate potential attackers.

Banded water cobra (*Naja annulata*) – Found in forest freshwater sources, this shy snake feeds on fish and will generally swim away if approached in water.

Goldie's tree cobra (*Pseudohaje goldii*) – At home both in the trees and in the water, this extremely venomous snake is poorly studied and rarely encountered, although some sources note that it can be very aggressive.

If you are looking for endemic reptiles, the best places to head for are the islands of Annobón and Bioko. The reptiles on Annobón are more easily accessible, and you will find Girard's green snake (*Philothamnus girardi*), the Annobón lidless skink (*Panaspis* or *Afroablepharus annobónensis*), Newton's leaf-toed gecko (*Hemidactylus newtoni*), and the Annobón leaf-toed gecko (*Hemidactylus aporus*). On Bioko there is Fea's chameleon (*Chamaeleo* or *Trioceros feae*), and the legless skink (*Scelotes poensis*).

Fish The mainland is home to the catfish *Microsynodontis nannoculus*, which lives in the river Kyé of the interior. Litoral Province is home to numerous small endemic killifish such as *Fundulopanchax avichang*. Annobón has the sleeper goby (*Eleotris annobónensis*) and scorpionfish (*Scorpaena annobónae*).

Amphibians Equatorial Guinea has at least three endemic amphibians: the Insel Fernando Poo Caecilian (*Schistometopum garzonheydti*), the Musole Forest tree frog (*Leptopelis brevipes*), and the Bioko squeaker frog (*Arthroleptis bioko*). The Goliath frog (*Conraua goliath*) occurs only in northern Río Muni and Cameroon, and is the largest living frog on the planet, growing up to 32cm long and weighing in excess of 3kg.

Invertebrates The diverse landscapes of Equatorial Guinea are home to a vast variety of insects, molluscs and spiders. Some butterflies, such as *Cymothoe owassae* are endemic only to Bioko. Others, such as *Epitola insulana* are found regionally, as are the silk moths *Lobobunaea vingerhoedti* and *Goodia canui* and the hawk moth (*Pseudoclanis biokoensis*).

Arachnophiles will be pleased to hear that the rare Bioko baboon spider (*Hysterocrates ederi*), jumping spider (*Tomomingi silvae*) and goblin spider (*Triaeris moca*) are spread across the territory.

Other invertebrates include two types of cricket (*Eulioptera insularis* and *Paragryllodes pictus*), the long-horned beetle (*Acutandra camiadei*), seed bug (*Dieuches annobónensis*), harvestman (*Mbinia xenophora*), land snails (*Ptychotrema malaboensis* and *Gulella pooensis*), and the slug (*Dendrolimax newtoni*).

HISTORY

THE ORIGINS OF THE POPULATION Equatorial Guinea is a Spanish-speaking country made up of several ethnic groups. The main groups are: the Fang, Bubi, Ndowe, Annobónese, Bissio, and the complex Fernandinos and Krumen.

When examining the history of Equatorial Guinea, the issue of what the country is called, and what its constituent parts are called, can get a bit confusing. This is not helped by the fact that even today, some people use certain historical labels interchangeably with newer ones. To clarify:

THE ENTIRE NATION Despite hundreds of years of Portuguese and Spanish control, all of the territories of Equatorial Guinea did not get a collective label until the 20th century. Prior to that each region was labelled separately, either with a Spanish or African title.

Spanish Guinea: In 1926 this administrative region united the three previously separate Spanish territories of Río Muni, Fernando Pó and Annobón.

Overseas Province of Spanish Guinea: From 1959 onwards Equatorial Guinea was given the same status as a metropolitan Spanish province, just overseas.

Autonomous Community of Equatorial Guinea: The name from 1 January 1964, after Spain granted the country internal autonomy.

Republic of Equatorial Guinea: The name from 12 October 1968 onwards, after a referendum on independence.

BIOKO ISLAND

Formosa: Derived from 'Formosa flora' meaning 'beautiful flower', the name given to Bioko by Portuguese explorer Fernão do Pó when he located it in 1471.

Fernando Pó or **Fernando Póo**: Name given to the island by King João II in honour of the Portuguese explorer Fernão do Pó. Used from 1494 to the 1970s.

Genetic sampling shows that Bioko island was first settled around 10,000 years ago, at the end of the last glacial period, by the Bubi ethnic group (page 51). The Bantu-speaking Bubi are the only population native to Bioko, descendants of the original colonisers of the island. There is no clear historical explanation as to why the Bubi chose to make Bioko their new home. Oral tradition contends that it was to escape their enslavement on the mainland by a more powerful ethnic group.

The space now known as Río Muni was most likely first occupied by Pygmy tribes, although there are now only small pockets of them remaining such as the Bakola-Bagyeli, in the north of the country, straddling the border with Cameroon. Migration by Fang and Ndowe (groups of Bantu origin) between the 13th and 19th centuries eventually displaced these native tribes.

The origins of these newer groups is unclear, although Fang tradition traces their ancestry to Nigeria, until they were forced from their land by the eastward expansion of Islamised Hausa groups, making the long migration south into modern day Cameroon, Gabon and Equatorial Guinea. Genetic sampling hints that the Fang are relatively new arrivals to the region, having appeared from the northeastern open grassland plateau during the 17th and 18th centuries. Some contend that their arrival in the territory of Equatorial Guinea was not a forced migration borne of warfare, but a deliberately timed relocation, coinciding with the arrival of the Spanish colonisers with whom they hoped to form a trade alliance.

Ndowe is a collective label for the coastal tribes of the mainland, including the Combes, Bujebas, BaBalengues and Bengas. The traditional demarcation line between the Fang and these coastal tribes was the town of Niefang (meaning 'limit

Masie Nguema Biyogo: The island was briefly renamed after former president Macías in the mid 1970s.
Bioko: The name of the island from the start of President Obiang's rule in 1979 to the present.

MALABO CITY
Port Clarence: The name given by the British while they rented the space between 1827 and 1843. For more information, see *The Arrival of the Spanish and British*, pages 15–16.
Santa Isabel: The Spanish name for the settlement from 1843 until the 1970s.
Malabo: Renamed as part of former president Macías's African authenticity campaign in the 1970s.

ANNOBÓN ISLAND
Annobón: Derived from 'Ano bom' meaning 'good year', the name given to the island by Portuguese explorers Pêro Escobar and João de Santarém on its discovery on 1 January 1473. This is the more common name for the island today.
Pagalu: Renamed as part of former president Macías's African authenticity campaign in the 1970s.

CORISCO ISLAND
Corisco: The name given to the island by Portuguese explorers in the 1470s, and which is still in use today.
Mandji: The Benga (page 52) name for the island.

of the Fang') on the Benito River, around 55km inland from Bata. Historians believe that the Ndowe first arrived in Río Muni from the Upper Ubangi River, which forms the border between the modern day Republic of Congo and Democratic Republic of Congo, at some stage between the 12th and 14th centuries. These groups attempted to flee inland when European slave traders began raiding the coastal region, but they were driven back by the Fang, finally taking up the position of middlemen between the Fang and European traders. The Bissio ethnic group also originates from the mainland but is now located in the coastal region of Equatorial Guinea. In their oral tradition, many trace their roots back to Ebolowa, which is a town in southern Cameroon. This area is now home to the Bulus, whom the Bissio believe displaced them.

Pre-colonial interactions The history of pre-colonial interaction between these African societies is difficult to piece together, but it seems that there was both conflict and co-operation. Warfare between the Ndowe and the Fang was common, but it was limited in scope. There is evidence of Fang and Pygmy groups trading on the mainland, with the Fang providing 'bridewealth', hunting tools and cloths in return for bushmeat from the Pygmies. However, this relationship was not always an equal one, with the numerically and militarily superior Fang sometimes coming into social conflict or even displacing the Pygmies.

Bioko, despite being ethnically homogeneous for much of its history, was also not always a peaceful place. The Bubi migrated to Bioko in several waves, with each group setting up their own enclave, meaning that they were never a single social group until interaction with the Europeans and other outsiders began and forced them into a more unified group in the interior. Bioko appears from the oral histories to have been in an almost constant state of inter-clan warfare, as each group struggled for control of resources on the small island.

Later arrivals to Equatorial Guinea European arrival in Equatorial Guinea caused pronounced changes in the population. The extinct volcanic island of Annobón (known locally as Pagalu) was uninhabited before the 15th century. Sources conflict over when and by whom it was discovered. Limited sources state that it was found in 1470 by Spanish explorer Diego Ramirez de la Diaz. Most claim it was the Portuguese explorers Pêro Escobar and João de Santarém who first found it on 1 January 1473. Regardless, from this point onwards, Portuguese traders took slaves from Angola (via São Tomé) and resettled them on the island to work on plantations.

The Annobónese remained under Portuguese rule until the Treaty of El Pardo in 1778 transferred control of the island over to the Spanish. These people of Angolan origin, named *escravos de resgate* by their Portuguese masters, formed the core of Annobónese society. As in many Portuguese colonial possessions, the European men took local partners. The offspring of these unions, dubbed *forros* ('slaves about to be released'), occupied a higher socio economic position than their fully African cousins, and developed a Creole language called Fá d'Ambô, very similar to the São Toménse language.

On Bioko, the Spanish and British also brought radical change to the Bubi population. The Fernandinos group was introduced; a mixed group of freed slaves from areas such as Sierra Leone, Côte d'Ivoire, Ghana, Liberia, Nigeria and Cameroon. This was then added to through mixed race relations with the Spanish, as well as descendants of the pre-existing indigenous Bioko population and Spanish colonisers (offspring of Spanish males and female Bubi). The Fernandinos gradually came to form part of the *Emancipados* social class, which also consisted of descendants of freed Cuban slaves brought to the island in 1845 and a small number of full-blooded Equatoguineans who had received a Catholic Spanish education.

These Fernandinos are not to be confused with the Creole population of Krumen, who were African immigrant labourers from the Kru Coast (Sierra Leone and the Côte d'Ivoire). The Krumen were also introduced during British rule, with their descendants being called the Krio. Their linguistic footprint can still be heard around Malabo today, with around 6,000 people speaking Fernando Pó Creole (also known as Pichinglis).

DISCOVERING FERNANDO PÓ – EARLY PORTUGUESE AND DUTCH RULE In 1469, King Afonso V of Portugal granted the Portuguese merchant Fernão Gomes a monopoly on trade in the Gulf of Guinea, under the condition that he explore 100 leagues (555km) of uncharted coast every year over the course of five years. At that time the most southerly point reached by European navigators on the African west coast had been Cape Palmas, a headland on the coast of Liberia.

Fernão Gomes's hope in exploring this area was to find a route around Africa to the Far East, and all the spices, silks and precious gemstones available for trade there. At the time it was believed that Africa was a large oval-shaped island on an east–west axis. This is how it was shown on the famous Fra Mauro world map of 1450, a copy of which was sent to Portugal in 1459 for King Afonso V to view.

To help him with his endeavour, Fernão Gomes recruited a crack team of navigators, including Fernão do Pó, Pêro de Sintra, Lopes Gonçalves and Pêro Escobar. By 1471 Fernão do Pó (sometimes referred to as Fernando Pó) had discovered that the African coast began to curve southwards after Nigeria, rather than continuing eastwards towards India as they had first hoped. In the same year Pó became the first European to sight Bioko, which he named Formosa Flora ('beautiful flower'). In 1494, the name was changed to Fernando Pó in his honour. While Fernão Pó was busy with the islands, between 1473 and 1475 his fellow navigator Lopes Gonçalves sailed along the African coast from Ghana down to Cape Lopez (modern day Port-Gentil in Gabon), likely making him the first European explorer to visit Río Muni.

The first 350 years of European interaction with Equatorial Guinea revolved around trade, with a focus on slaves, palm oil and sugar. In the second half of the 16th century, when Portuguese Brazil's larger, more efficient and better-located plantations came online, the sugar plantations of Bioko and Annobón slowly shut down, shifting their focus to other forms of agriculture.

In 1641, the Dutch established trading posts on Río Muni, and the following year on Fernando Pó, without Portuguese consent. This incursion formed part of the Dutch–Portuguese War, which lasted for much of the first half of the 17th century. On Bioko, many of the Bubi managed to remain undisturbed for quite a while, their reputation for savagery keeping European slavers and explorers at bay. However, with the gradual encroachment of Europeans on the island, many clans began to move away from their exposed coastal settlements and into the safer interior. As if violence from the native population was not enough, there was also a very high mortality rate on the island for Europeans, caused by diseases such as yellow fever, sleeping sickness and malaria. This meant that the Portuguese never attempted to settle there in great numbers, although in 1648 they did set up their own trading base on Corisco, building the Ponta Joko fort. In collaboration with the local Benga population, they used this island to manage slaving operations on the mainland.

While the Europeans were establishing themselves in the region, the Bubi clans were slowly coalescing and forming the core of a Bubi kingdom on the island of Fernando Pó. Leaders such as Chief Mölambo (1700–60) contributed to the Bamöumá dynasty and his successors helped to unify the Bubi in the face of later Spanish imperialist intrusion.

THE ARRIVAL OF THE SPANISH AND THE BRITISH Spanish colonialism was established by the Treaties of San Idelfonso in 1777 and El Pardo in 1778, under which Portugal ceded Fernando Pó, Annobón and the mainland coastal areas to Spain in return for recognition of their dominion over much of modern day Brazil. Things did not start well for the Spanish and the first official expedition to Equatorial Guinea in 1778 from Montevideo (modern Uruguay), ended with the death of the expedition leader, Felipe de Santos Toro, the Earl of Argelejo. Spanish sources state that he died from fever while in transit, although other historians claim he died at the hands of the Annobónese, and his killing was covered up. From then on, Spain had little interest in Equatorial Guinea as a colonial possession before the late 19th century, instead preferring to focus their overseas efforts (and budget) on Morocco and Cuba.

In 1801, the Spanish built a small fortress on Annobón and the same year gave the British permission to use the island as a resupply point for their ships to collect fresh water on their Atlantic journeys. Also during that year, an entire English crew was killed by a Batété Bubi tribe upon landing on the island of Bioko, which further added to its savage reputation, and encouraged Europeans to stay away. Fernando Pó lay unoccupied until 1827 when the Spanish leased Malabo (then known as

Port Clarence) to the British for 50 years as a base for anti-slaving operations. The British also used a second port, San Carlos, for anti-slavery patrols.

Vice Admiral William Fitzwilliam Owen was tasked with creating a British colony on Fernando Pó in 1827. By October 1828, Port Clarence had a registered population of 747 inhabitants. Owen spent just under three years on the island, and during this time he focused most of his efforts on the anti-slavery patrols. His forces managed to detain 20 ships and liberate around 2,500 slaves. A Court of Mixed Commission, jointly run by Britain and her European allies for the prosecution of foreign nationals involved in the slave trade, was even set up in Port Clarence. Prior to this the nearest court had been in Freetown, Sierra Leone, which significantly slowed the legal process.

The year 1828 was also marked by the arrival of Owen's friend, James Holman, on the Royal Navy frigate HMS *Eden*. Notable for being the first blind man to circumnavigate the globe, James's published writings about the journey did not help Owen in his task of encouraging settlers: James wrote that of the 135 men who sailed on the HMS *Eden*, only 12 survived the expedition, with many dying of malaria and other fevers while in Port Clarence.

Perhaps due to the inherent health risks, Owen refused the post of Superintendent of Fernando Pó in 1829, so it was handed over to General Sir Edward Nicolls. Nicolls worked tirelessly to suppress the slave trade in the region, causing great tension with the Portuguese governor of nearby São Tomé and Príncipe. The governor accused him of encouraging slaves from his colony to run away to Fernando Pó and then of refusing to return any of them (as this was against British law). Nicolls countered that if the Portuguese governor could persuade any of the newly escaped slaves to voluntarily return to a state of slavery on São Tomé, he would not impede them. Unsurprisingly, no slaves were returned. As well as battling slave traders and antagonising Portuguese diplomats, Nicolls was often very ill during his time on Fernando Pó. In April 1830, he was forced to leave the island for health reasons, handing over to the Master of Works at the time, a man named John Beecroft. Nicolls's departure was not unusual, as most early European settlers to the island suffered from serious health issues such as malaria and yellow fever. Only five of the original 47 Royal Marines that Nicolls brought to the island when he took over survived their two-year tour of duty.

THE DEPARTURE OF THE BRITISH The British government finally decided to evacuate the island of Fernando Pó on 29 August 1832, and shut down its anti-slaving operations base. From this time onwards, John Beecroft had de facto control of the island, first in the role of acting governor conferred on him by Spain, and then more formally as governor, from 1843 to his death in 1854.

In 1840, the Spanish offered to sell Fernando Pó and Annobón to the British for £60,000 but the deal fell through (some say because the asking price was too high, others that public opinion in Spain prevented it). Regardless, in 1843 the British officially ended their use of Bioko, preferring to base their ships in Freetown, Sierra Leone. Port Clarence was left with a population of around 900 people. The Spanish re-established their presence on the island, with Juan José Lerena raising the Spanish flag in Port Clarence in March 1843, renaming it Santa Isabel (a monument to this event can still be seen in Malabo; see page 131). The British lease was officially revoked in 1855, but by this time they had long since departed.

The Spanish quickly signed agreements with the Benga king, Bonkoro I to continue the commercial collaboration on the island of Corisco that had begun under the Portuguese. This indirect rule lasted a few decades until the end of King

Munga II's rule (1859–75), when the role of Governor of Corisco was taken up by a Spanish representative. During this time an American Presbyterian mission also set up on Corisco.

SPANISH CONTROL OF RÍO MUNI WEAKENED Meanwhile, on mainland Río Muni, both Europeans and Americans were encroaching. Between 1842 and 1890, buoyed by successes in the freed slave colony of Liberia, American Presbyterian missionaries set about establishing the United States of the Ndowe. This stretched from Banôkó (modern day Kribi, southern Cameroon) to Mponggwé (modern day Libreville, Gabon). In theory, this unification was designed to help combat the transatlantic slave trade still occurring in the area. Various stations were set up along the coast, and some African pastors were trained to help spread the gospel. Unfortunately, this effort was short-lived, as the 1884 Berlin Conference saw the coastline divided between German, Spanish, French and Belgian colonies.

One of the first Westerners to record contact with the Fang was American missionary William Walker in 1848, while working for the American Board of Commissioners for Foreign Missions. He was soon followed by his Franco-American friend Paul Belloni Du Chaillu. Unlike Walker, Du Chaillu was more interested in hunting gorillas than spreading the gospel. Between 1855 and 1859, he explored equatorial Africa under the patronage of the Academy of Natural Sciences in Philadelphia, claiming to be the first European to see a live gorilla. His first journey departed from the Muni River and crossed the first ranges of the Monts de Cristal in the north of Gabon. He did little to change Victorian attitudes towards Central Africa, filling his books with grizzly tales of barbarity and Fang cannibalism:

> I perceived some bloody remains which looked to me human but I passed on, still incredulous. Presently we passed a woman who solved all doubt. She bore with her a piece of thigh of a human body, just as we should go to market and carry thence a roast or a steak.
> Paul Belloni Du Chaillu, *Explorations and Adventures in Equatorial Africa*, 1861

On a subsequent expedition, between 1863 and 1865, he also became the first European to have a documented encounter with Pygmy groups, confirming their existence. He wrote three main books about his travels, published between 1861 and 1872. These experiences are said to have inspired the Tarzan story, first published in a pulp magazine in 1912.

In the mid 19th century, while these early explorers were pushing back the frontiers of continental Africa, the Spanish began to focus on occupying their land lest it be encroached upon by other European powers. The Spanish authorities tried many initiatives to populate the territory with settlers. On 13 September 1845, Queen Isabel II authorised the voluntary transfer of black and free *mulattos* (*mulatto* was the Spanish term for people of mixed European and African ancestry) from Cuba to Equatorial Guinea. These arrivals made up part of the *Emancipados* social class on the island of Bioko. However, given the appalling mortality rate on the island and the mainland, the Spanish struggled to encourage migration to this colonial possession. By 1856 there were only 13 white settlers recorded in the main town of Santa Isabel.

To try to boost immigration figures, on 13 December 1858 the Spanish government passed the Organic Statute, promising free passage to the colony for willing settlers. This was renewed in the Royal Decree of 24 December 1894. Land was offered free of charge to those willing to build on it or farm it, and five-year tax exemptions were given out. Grants of 3,000 reales (the former Spanish currency) were also offered. As white Spaniards were still not choosing to relocate, on 20 June 1861, by order of the queen, Fernando Pó was designated a Spanish military prison site, hosting exiled politicians from Spain known as the *Represaliados*. The Spanish government's efforts to significantly increase the population and build an economically viable colony were so unsuccessful that by December 1873, Ignacio García Tudela, the governor of Fernando Pó, wrote to Madrid advising a complete withdrawal from all possessions in the Gulf of Guinea. However, his advice was ignored. His successor, Diego Santisteban, persuaded the Spanish government that the colony had great potential through a series of 14 photos stressing the economic opportunities available. Despite his enthusiasm, by 1877 there were still only around 1,100 registered inhabitants in Santa Isabel, very few of whom were European.

By the late 19th century, the 'Scramble for Africa' was truly in effect, with imperial European powers racing to explore, annexe and colonise new areas. At the Berlin Conference (1884–85) agreements were hashed out amongst the European powers relating to claims on the continent. Spain, with such a small foothold in the Gulf of Guinea and so few Spanish colonists, struggled to make a strong argument for claiming much territory. Sandwiched between the stronger imperial powers of France and Germany, Río Muni ended up a rather truncated 26,000km^2, despite the Spanish arguing for a claim of 180,000km^2. The situation was formalised in the Treaty of Paris in 1900. This left the Spanish negotiator and governor general of Río Muni, Pedro Jover y Tovar, so bitter that he described the treaty as '*un verdadero despojo a un pais desmoralizado*' (the true pillaging of a demoralised country) and said that Spain '*ha salido del Continente negro del modo mas cursi posible*' (Spain had left the 'Dark Continent' in the shabbiest way possible). He committed suicide in 1901 whilst sailing home to Spain.

THE ARRIVAL OF COCOA Despite the efforts of the Spanish government to expand their colony, both geographically and demographically, the dominant cultural paradigm on Fernando Pó remained English, centred on the main town of Santa Isabel. This settlement was the engine of the colony's economy, fuelled by palm oil trading between the European–Fernandino partnerships and the inland Bubi. One Spanish Catholic missionary even complained in the 1890s that Fernando Pó had been 'captured by the English blacks of Sierra Leone… they have herded the Bubis, the natives of the island, into the interior'.

This economic focus shifted in 1854, and along with it, the ethnic make up of the country. Following the successful transplant of cocoa pods from Brazil to São Tomé a few decades earlier, cocoa cultivation took root on Fernando Pó. Successful palm oil traders shifted their focus to this new crop, with its promise of greater returns. This rapid shift to cocoa is attested to in Mary Kingsley's book *Travels in West Africa*, published in 1897 (page 225). In 1889, records show that only 474kg of cocoa was produced on the island. This reached over 1.4 million kilos by 1899, and doubled over the next ten years.

Migrant labour, exploitation and the economic boom The expansion of the cocoa industry on Fernando Pó led to a shortage of labourers on the island at the turn of the 20th century. The Bubi, with their numbers declining due to disease and social division, were not able to make up the shortfall. By 1901 the number of white settlers recorded on the island had only increased to 445, and European settlers were very unlikely to come to the island to work as manual labourers anyway. More workers had to be found.

A solution to this problem was to bring in migrant labour. In 1898, a total of 1,937 contract labourers were brought in from Liberia. Three years later, another 993 immigrants arrived directly from Monrovia. From 1897 onwards the Liberian government was supposed to receive a US$150 bond for each of these exported workers, and a fine of US$100 for each worker that died while abroad. In practice, it was easy for African recruiters in the Liberian interior to smuggle the workers out of the country without paying these fees. Many companies made side agreements directly with the Liberian government to avoid paying duties. All workers were supposed to be hired for a maximum of two years and then returned to Liberia upon completion of their contract but in practice many stayed for much longer.

This labour system was rife with abuse, and public opinion soon became critical of African labour conditions across the continent. In 1904, British diplomat Roger Casement wrote a report that exposed slave-like labour conditions in the Congo Free State, causing scandal back in Europe. On 26 September 1908, the British newspaper *The Evening Standard* published an article accusing English chocolatier Cadbury Brothers Limited of exploiting forced labourers (*serviçaes*) in Portuguese West Africa (in particular, men taken from Angola to work on cocoa plantations in São Tomé). This led to a much-publicised lawsuit against the newspaper, which Cadbury won. They did not deny the conditions of the workers on the islands, but did successfully rebut the accusation that they had not taken any action to improve the situation.

WAR IN EUROPE AND THE UNIFICATION OF SPANISH GUINEA Concerns over labour abuses took a back seat to the growing political tensions in Europe, which resulted in the outbreak of World War I in July 1914. While Spain remained officially neutral throughout the four years of the conflict, their colony in Africa was heavily affected due to fighting in neighbouring Cameroon. Starting in September 1914 and running throughout 1915, 3,000 men from the German army fought a combined British and French force for control of German Cameroon. By February 1916, 1,000 Germans, 6,000 African troops (mainly Beti of Yaoundé) and 7,000 African civilians crossed Spanish Guinea's northern border to escape into internment before their colony was overrun. The Spanish crown, under Alfonso XIII, spent a great deal of money caring for these prisoners until they were returned to their homes once the war in Europe had ended.

After World War I ended in November 1918, the focus once again turned to European imperialism and its role in Africa. By the mid 1920s public outcry regarding the treatment of African labourers was too widespread to ignore, and politicians in Europe were forced to act. Between 1923 and 1930 the League of Nations investigated the abuses of migrant labourers transported between Liberia and Fernando Pó. Its conclusions, published in the Christy Report in September 1930, noted:

> The Commission finds that a large proportion of the contract labourers shipped to Fernando Pó and French Gabon from the southern counties of Liberia has been recruited under conditions of criminal compulsion scarcely distinguishable from slave raiding and slave trading, and frequently by misrepresenting the destination.

Following an intervention by the International Labour Organisation as a result of the Christy Report, the labour supply from Liberia to the island of Fernando Pó was cut off. The Spanish authorities had already begun taking steps to insure against such an eventuality after Liberia briefly renounced the treaty in 1926, which led to an immediate labour shortage on the island. In that year the Spanish responded by uniting the three disparate territories of Río Muni, Fernando Pó and Annobón into one administrative region of Spanish Guinea. Under the new unified governor, General Miguel Nuñez del Prado, the Spanish authorities set about militarily occupying Río Muni in search of a new labour source.

THE GREAT DEPRESSION AND THE RISE OF THE *RECLUTADORES* Before the Spanish military occupation, Río Muni had seen little development from the colonial authorities. Control was limited to the coastal towns, where there were only 100 European residents; most of whom were not even Spanish but German traders looking for rubber, wood and ivory. From 1926 onwards, General del Prado's troops press-ganged upwards of 4,000 Fang men at a time into unpaid public works projects, mainly building bridges and roads into the interior. Rather conveniently, those found guilty of disobedience could be shipped off to work on Fernando Pó. By the harvest season of 1926 over 4,500 *braceros* (agricultural contract workers) had been sent over to Fernando Pó, many under duress, thereby helping to avert the complete collapse of the cocoa industry. In 1928, the 'Patronato de Indígenas' was set up, charged with enforcing these controversial laws on the native population through the promotion of Spanish morality and culture.

The Spanish state at the time had a protectionist policy of guaranteeing to buy Fernando Pó's cocoa exports, often at up to three times the global market rate. This, combined with the history of exploitative labour practices, guaranteed huge profits for a minority of traders. Just as Liberia was winding down its provision of labour to Fernando Pó, others moved in to exploit this new opportunity.

During the 1920s there was an economic boom on the island, which attracted many unsavoury types from the Spanish mainland, intent on seeking their fortune. Owing to the sheer lack of European settlers, there were no laws (as in other European colonies) to filter the quality of European emigrants. Many Europeans became *reclutadores* (professional recruiters) who used Mafia-like tactics such as bribery, coercion and outright violence to sign up *braceros* from the mainland for work on the cocoa plantations. Sizeable *regalos* (literally a gift, but actually a wage advance) were offered to those who volunteered to sign up.

The *reclutadores* used African *ganchos* (runners) who could act as interlocutors between those hiring, and the village chiefs who had manpower to offer. Lies were told to those signing up about the location, length and conditions of their work. Village chiefs were given cash bonuses, alcohol and even guns for their help. Documents were forged, and people were smuggled. After completing a tour of Africa to review the status of native teacher training, educational writer Albert Victor Murray commented in 1929 that Equatorial Guinea had become 'A landfill site for the worst class of Spaniards who wish to get rich quickly and easily'.

The Great Depression, which began with the Wall Street Crash of October 1929, coincided with the Christy Report, and heralded a period of decline on Fernando Pó that lasted until after World War II. There was a steady reduction in the wealth and influence of the Fernandinos plantation owners as a growing number of Spanish and Portuguese entrepreneurs, *reclutadores* and planters made their way to Fernando Pó. Spanish government records show that in 1930, 18,000ha of arable land belonged to Africans, while 21,000 belonged to Europeans. Given that the population split was around 22,000 Africans and 1,000 Europeans on the island, this was not an equitable distribution of resources.

In the late 1920s there were only around 100,000 Fang in Río Muni. Republican Spanish colonial officials began to realise that the work of the *reclutadores* was extremely damaging, both to the demographics of their African colony, and also in terms of the development of the colonial economy, as not enough native workers were being left in Río Muni for the burgeoning logging industry. As with the Liberian solution at the turn of the century, once again workers were sought from abroad. Nigeria seemed the ideal candidate.

The arrival of the Nigerians From 1930 until the end of World War II, the colonial economy of southeastern Nigeria was in continual decline, mainly due to a collapse in the global price of palm oil. This left communities of over three million people destitute, mainly the Owerri Igbo and Southern Ibibio from Oweri and Calabar provinces. The British colonial authorities had ruled it illegal in 1929 for anyone to recruit Nigerian subjects for work overseas, but the rewards offered by desperate plantation owners on Fernando Pó proved too tempting. Igbo and Efik Nigerian recruiters soon moved in, transporting agricultural labourers across the Bight of Biafra to work on the plantations. This coincided with a period of renewed economic interest in Spanish Guinea from the authorities in Madrid, as a series of governor generals continued to turn the colony into a site of forced labour, with many native inhabitants coerced into working 14-hour days cultivating cocoa or lumber. By 1935 there were 5,000 Nigerians on the island and by 1945 there were 20,000, a staggering number considering the total population of Fernando Pó was 40,000 at the time.

THE SPANISH CIVIL WAR (1936–39) There was relatively little fighting over Equatorial Guinea during the Spanish Civil War. However, investment in controlling the colony seemed worthwhile for both sides in the conflict, as its supplies of cocoa, coffee and tropical hardwood could be used to fund the war effort, and it was a net exporter of food, which always proves useful in wartime.

The situation for most Equatoguinean subjects at the outbreak of the war was a poor one: most were in forced labour, they were not allowed to purchase property, alcohol was forbidden and they lacked any rights or legal status as Spanish citizens.

In July 1936, when the war broke out, the Spanish naval cruiser *Méndez Núñez* was stationed off the island of Fernando Pó, giving the Republican government a seemingly strong hold over the island. During this time the colonial administration of Spanish Guinea remained loyal to the republican cause. However, the warship soon returned to take part in fighting in European waters, and on the morning of 19 September, the island of Fernando Pó joined the nationalist side after Lieutenant Colonel Serrano, commander of the Colonial Guard, led a coup and declared a state of war on the island. A few days later, there was a skirmish in Río Muni between nationalist rebels from Kogo and forces loyal to the republicans. In Bata, the deputy governor Miguel Hernández Porcel (who was a member of the Popular Front) refused to join the rebellion, leaving Río Muni cut off from the rest of the colony, in republican hands.

This situation was reversed on 14 October when 500 nationalist reinforcements from the Canary Islands arrived in Bata. This force was made up of two companies of infantry, a section of machine guns, a battery of artillery and a group of snipers from Spanish Sahara. They sailed in on the newly armoured *Ciudad de Mahón* (sailing under the false name *Ciudad de Macao*), briefly bombarded the mainland, sinking the mail ship *Fernando Póo* (which they claimed was hiding militiamen), and quickly took control of the colony. The deputy governor of Bata fled inland with his men, towards Cameroon and Gabon, and was sentenced to death *in absentia* by the nationalist Franco regime. Franco's victory marked a new period in Spanish Guinea's history, characterised by greater metropolitan interest in the colony, increased investment and an expansion of racist colonial control.

WORLD WAR II AND THE ORIGINS OF JAMES BOND The Spanish Civil War ended in April 1939 with a nationalist victory. Barely six months after General Franco had taken power, World War II erupted in Europe. General Franco declared Spain a non-belligerent nation, a vague term that meant they stayed out of direct fighting, but were still able to materially support their favoured participants (initially the Axis powers of Italy and Germany). Franco wanted to expand Spain's small footholds in the Gulf of Guinea, imagining a larger territory comprising chunks taken from British Nigeria and French Equatorial Africa. However, German leader Adolf Hitler was not keen on entertaining these ambitions, which is one of many reasons that Franco never actually joined the Axis cause and declared war on the Allies.

World War II had a mixed impact on Spain and her African colony in Guinea. There was no fighting but plenty of intrigue, and economically there were difficulties as well as new opportunities. The Allies used their naval power to threaten Franco with economic collapse, as they had the power to blockade fuel and food imports from overseas but they did not actually do so. Instead, they kept the pressure on by allowing imports from her African possessions for internal use only, badly impacting the Spanish treasury. Spanish Guinea's plantations of tropical okoumé timber, previously exported to Germany for aircraft manufacture, were simply left to grow unharvested.

In response to the difficulty of bringing in imports from the rest of Europe, the Spanish government went to great efforts to increase colonial production of required raw materials, for use back in Spain. Cocoa traders in Spanish Guinea, now no longer allowed to export their product overseas, switched rapidly to coffee production in order to sell successfully to their domestic market back in Madrid. Rough wood was harvested and by 1945 provided for almost all of Spain's needs. Likewise, palm oil, copra, dried bananas and rubber were soon being imported from Spanish Guinea in hitherto unseen quantities. In 1934, only 3% of Spain's imports came from its overseas colonies but by 1942 this had rocketed to 21%. While some Africans benefited from this economic expansion, many were exploited in order to achieve it. In 1939, the inhabitants of Spanish Guinea had to dedicate one day in four to forced labour for the state in lieu of military service.

There were likely only ten military casualties in Spanish Guinea throughout World War II. On 3 June 1944, a Royal Air Force Sunderland Flying Boat crashed on Bioko island, *en route* from Lagos in Nigeria to Libreville in Gabon. Nine of the ten crew members died on impact, with one crash survivor, William Best, dying shortly thereafter. The aircraft, which was part of 302 Flying Training Unit, went down near Laka Baney, around 16km east of Malabo. There are competing stories as to the cause of the crash and a few claim it was shot down while observing German U-boat movements, but most accounts now accept that it was brought down by bad weather. John E Bennett, the US ambassador to Equatorial Guinea from 1991 to 1994, was accused of practising witchcraft at the graves of the airmen, which are still maintained in Malabo's main cemetery. There is a Commonwealth remembrance service for the fallen airmen every year.

The only other event of note during the hostilities was a secret British Special Operations Executive raid on the port of Santa Isabel on 14 January 1942. The British government was concerned that the neutral Spanish port was being used by German and Italian forces to spy on British naval movements in the region and also as a hub for the transshipment of arms. Of particular concern was the 8,600-tonne Italian merchant vessel *Duchessa d'Aosta*, which was believed to be carrying weapons, as well as two German vessels, the *Likomba* and the *Bibundi*.

The plan was simple: Major Gus March-Phillipps would set out from Poole harbour with his highly trained force of only 15 men. They would make their way down the coast of Africa and secretly enter Santa Isabel harbour in two tug boats. While the officers from these Italian and German ships were distracted at a pre-arranged dinner party onshore, March-Phillipps's men would sever the anchor chains, take any men onboard hostage, then tow the three ships out into international waters and captivity. All of this was to be achieved without alerting the Spanish authorities. Amazingly, the plan was a success in the face of overwhelming odds, although it did cause a serious diplomatic incident between Britain and Spain. Major March-Phillipps and his men are said to have been the inspiration behind Ian Fleming's famous fictional spy James Bond.

THE GROWTH OF NATIONALISM Perhaps sensing the wind of nationalist change that World War II was generating in many of Europe's African colonies, in 1944 Spain introduced a complex series of assimilation laws, defining two kinds of 'semi-emancipated' Africans as well as a 'fully emancipated' category. Very few Equatoguineans ever achieved this designation, as it involved a number of difficult steps including completing a Spanish-Christian education and learning to speak Spanish fluently. Fully emancipated Equatoguineans would enjoy almost all of the same rights as white Spanish citizens. On the ground in Spanish Guinea, this meant that they could now apply for loans from the bank, buy and sell property, act as witnesses in court, buy olive oil and wheat bread in the shops and go to white European bars to drink alcohol. Despite this, laws remained in place forbidding sexual relations between white European women and black African men in the colony. This concession to nationalist feeling may have actually helped to stoke the fire of independence, as the first generation of Equatoguineans to benefit from these laws included independence leaders such as Acacio Mañé Elah, Bonifacio Ondó Edú, Enrique Nvó Okenve and the first president of independent Equatorial Guinea, Francisco Macías.

This newly emancipated class of Equatoguineans was helped by a positive economic climate. Migrant labour arrangements with Nigeria, which had begun in the late 1920s, continued to be key to economic growth in Spanish Guinea after World War II, leading it to become one of Africa's most productive agricultural areas. However, the Spanish state was still struggling to encourage European immigration. According to the official census of Fernando Pó on 15 December 1942, there were 2,693 white men and 375 white women on the island. By 31 December 1950, this had only grown to 2,493 men and 1,102 women. Racial divisions within the colony were still acute, and in 1947 Governor General Juan Maria Bonelli Rubio was removed from his position for daring to suggest reforms to the extremely low wages paid to Equatoguinean teachers. That same year, King Santiago Uganda, the last king of Corisco, gave visiting Spanish ministers a list of political and economic grievances against Spanish rule. Most of the *Emancipados* who had signed the list were either deported to Annobón or thrown in prison. The king was stripped of his authority.

On Fernando Pó in December 1950 the first organised nationalist movement was founded: the National Liberation Crusade of Equatorial Guinea (Cruzada Nacional de Liberacion de Guinea Ecuatorial; CNLGE). As with many other African independence movements, this group was made up of educated individuals who had (to varying degrees) been accepted into European society through the emancipation systems. Acacio Mañé Elah, one of the key founders, received an education at a Catholic mission school in Bata and even worked on the 'Patronato de Indígenas', charged with the promotion of Spanish morality and culture. He and Enrique Nvó Okenve were also wealthy planters, who could use their money to finance these early independence struggles.

Unfortunately for the independence leaders, throughout this period (1949 to 1962) the governor general of Spanish Guinea was Admiral Faustino Ruiz Gonzalez, who was strongly opposed to any notions of independence. As with the dictatorship in mainland Spain, there was little tolerance for political opposition or protest.

Acacio Mañé Elah, who had always refused to go into exile despite being an outspoken critic of the regime, was arrested in Bata by the Civil Guard in November 1958. He was killed by Spanish authorities around 28 November, allegedly by being thrown overboard whilst *en route* to imprisonment on Bioko. After the CNLGE collected the signatures of tribal chiefs on a petition to the UN to change the status of Spanish Guinea, 24 key leaders were arrested by the Spanish authorities in November 1959. Enrique Nvó, who had been in Cameroon on his way to the UN in New York, was murdered on 21 November 1959. Many feel this killing was carried out by the Spanish authorities. With the death of their leaders and imprisonment of key members, thousands of nationalists fled abroad and the movement almost collapsed.

Guinean nationalists now chose to wage their struggle from outside the country, fearing for their safety. The National Movement for the Liberation of Equatorial Guinea (Movimiento Nacional de Liberación de Guinea Ecuatorial; MONALIGE) was begun in 1959 by Torao Sikara (a prominent Bubi leader), Samuel Ebuka Besebo and Atanasio Ndongo Miyono (composer of the national anthem) in neighbouring Gabon. Another group, called the People's Liberation Union of Equatorial Guinea (Union Popular de Liberacion de Guinea Ecuatorial; UPLGE) was formed by exiled primary school and religious studies teacher Bonifacio Ondó Edú in Libreville, Gabon in October of the same year.

Some members of MONALIGE, led by Luis Maho, then relocated to Douala, Cameroon, as they felt that the government there was more supportive of their cause. Other exiled nationalists, led by Kose Perea Epota, also set up a base in Cameroon, this time in Ambam. Perea, a relative of the deposed king of Corisco, called their movement Idea Popular de la Guinea Ecuatorial (IPGE). This group was distinct as it called for an eventual union or federation with Cameroon upon independence.

Also in 1959, the status of Spanish Guinea was changed and it was designated the Region Ecuatorial de España, essentially an overseas province. It was divided into Fernando Pó and Río Muni and each area was placed under the control of a civil governor. This was bad news for the nationalists, as it signalled a complete unwillingness on the part of the Franco regime to envisage a time when the colony might become independent.

There is much debate over the efficacy of these domestic struggles for independence, versus the impact of pressure from the UN and the general trend towards independence spreading across West and Central Africa. In any event, the Spanish chose to respond in a similar manner to the French: by sowing division amongst the different regional, ethnic and political groups; investing in development; making small concessions to political freedoms; and by offering autonomy rather than independence. In this way it was hoped that a leader would emerge who was pro-Spanish and who could be influenced to keep ruling in the interests of the European colonisers.

In 1956, only around 4% of Equatoguineans spoke Spanish, with illiteracy rates at between 75% and 80% according to UNESCO. Through a combination of paying artificially high prices for cocoa and coffee exports, forced labour on public works projects, and investment in education and healthcare, over the next decade Equatorial Guinea would come to have one of the highest literacy rates and per capita income rates in sub-Saharan Africa (US$170). The number of schools doubled between 1950 and 1968, with attendance rates hitting 90%. The economy grew at 7.56% per year in the four years before independence. In 1961, infant mortality was 40.1 per thousand, compared with an average of between 150 and 200 per thousand for the rest of Africa. By 1962 the country was also top of the table for per capita exports, with US$332 of exports per head.

This economic development was coupled with political concessions. By 1960 Fernando Pó was allowed to elect one European and two African deputies to the Spanish Cortes Generales (the legislature). Río Muni was allowed one African and two European deputies. The constitutional distinction between natives and *assimilados* was also abolished. More senior administrative roles were opened up to locals, paving the way for Francisco Macías Nguema (the future president of Equatorial Guinea) to become mayor of Mongomo in 1960.

However, many nationalists would not be bought off by these changes. In December 1962, the various opposition groups managed to join forces and create the National Liberation Front, to co-ordinate all of their nationalist activities. The group presented a petition to the 17th General Assembly of the UN in New York on the status of their country, and denounced the Spanish government for its policy of assimilating it into metropolitan Spain as provinces without consultation. Their case was strongly supported by the African nations present, especially Gabon and Cameroon.

The early 1960s saw a proliferation of political parties and coalitions emerge, such as the Movement for the National Unity of Equatorial Guinea (Movimiento de Union Nacional de Guinea Ecuatorial; MUNGE), which was established in November 1963 with Bonifacio Ondó Edú as its leader. This was an attempt to unite all the moderate nationalists under one banner. Ethnic differences became politicised as groups such as the Bubi Union, led by Edmundo Bosió Dioco and Enrique Gori Molubela, the Democratic Fernandino Union and the Ndowé Union sprang up, all aiming for control of the autonomy or independence process, and reliant on purely ethnic support bases.

AUTONOMY AND INDEPENDENCE On 15 December 1963, a referendum on autonomy from Spain was held. Just under 95,000 votes were cast representing a large proportion of those eligible to vote (although exact figures are unavailable), In the end 62.5% of Equatoguineans voted in favour of autonomy. The autonomous regime came into being on 1 January 1964, with Bonifacio Ondó Edú leading and Francisco Macías Nguema as vice president. If requested, they could achieve independence in four years, which is exactly what happened, although this was by no means a foregone conclusion at the time. Spaniard Pedro Latorre Alcubierre was also appointed as high commissioner of the new Autonomous Community of Equatorial Guinea.

Some political groups were successfully co-opted by the Spanish government by being given limited access to the resources of power. However, MONALIGE did not feel this autonomous system went far enough, and immediately agitated for full independence. They were wary, having seen the fate of former French colonies in West Africa, whose affairs had remained tightly intertwined with those of Paris after choosing autonomy within the new Communauté française in the French Fifth Republic. Under this arrangement, France retained close control over key areas such as defence, financial and foreign policy.

Those calling for full independence were successful in publicising their cause. On 16 December 1965, the UN General Assembly reaffirmed:

The inalienable right of the people of Equatorial Guinea to self-determination and independence; [and] Requests the administering Power to set the earliest possible date for independence after consulting the people on the basis of universal suffrage under the supervision of the United Nations.

In a further bid to pressure the Spanish government, civil servants in the Autonomous Community of Equatorial Guinea went on strike on 21 April 1966. Three years after its formation, the Organization of African Unity (OAU) also declared its support for the independence of Equatorial Guinea on 6 November 1966. The following month, the UN General Assembly repeated its calls upon Spain to organise elections in Equatorial Guinea.

In Madrid on 30 October 1967, the Constitutional Conference on Equatorial Guinea was convened. Most of the discussion revolved around the nature of independence: whether Río Muni and Fernando Pó should become two separate independent nations, or one united one, or enter into some form of federal arrangement with one another, or possibly even with Cameroon. Ultimately, the proposal put forward by the Spanish Ministry of Foreign Affairs was selected, which called for a single federal republic with two autonomous provinces, and the constitution they had drafted.

Many Bubi were unhappy with this arrangement, seeing this not as a recipe for independence, but as the substitution of a Spanish colonial governor for a Fang colonial governor. The Spanish countered that their proposed constitution gave the Bubis and Fernandinos the vice premiership, a veto over financial legislation and 12 parliamentary seats out of 35. Despite these measures, many of the Equatoguinean representatives, internally divided throughout the negotiations, were very unhappy and expressed this dissatisfaction on the global stage. Macías Nguema's faction went so far as to ask the UN to condemn the conference. The Spanish were not keen on dragging out the discussion, and announced that independence would be granted on 12 October following a referendum on the constitution that August.

On 11 August 1968, there was a UN-supervised referendum on the constitution. The nationalists were split over this issue: Bonifacio Ondó Edú and Atanasio Ndongo Miyono pushed for acceptance of the constitution, perhaps signalling their willingness to work with the Spanish in the future, whereas Francisco Macías Nguema and his supporters (including those who wished to see Fernando Pó become independent separately from Río Muni) wanted to reject the constitution. In the end the vote only narrowly passed on Fernando Pó, with 4,763 votes in favour versus 4,486 against. The nationwide vote resulted in 63% of participants voting to approve the constitution.

Immediately after this vote, preparations for the general elections began. They were held on 22 September with a second round a week later, in which the underdog Francisco Macías Nguema defeated Bonifacio Ondó Edú to become the first president of an independent Equatorial Guinea (likely to the frustration of the Spanish government). The UN certified that the elections had been free and fair. On 12 October 1968, Equatorial Guinea finally gained its independence.

EARLY INDEPENDENCE AND THE START OF MACÍAS'S REIGN OF TERROR President Macías had a difficult task in front of him. While the Spanish had certainly made some positive economic changes to their colony in the last decade of control,

Equatoguineans faced many problems. There were few paved roads and a lack of public transportation. There was no industrial production base, and consumer goods were hard to find. Electrical coverage was also poor outside the three main towns. However, the main issue was the simmering ethnic tensions, mainly between the Fang and other groups such as the Bubi, which the Spanish had systematically entrenched through deliberate colonial policy. In the run up to independence, these ethnic differences had become politicised, and would soon lead to bloodshed on an unprecedented scale.

President Macías began his rule on a positive note, giving rival Atanasio Ndongo Miyono the position of foreign minister in what many saw as a conciliatory move, and Edmundo Bosio Dioco, head of the Bubi Union, was made vice president. Unfortunately, the optimistic mood did not last long.

In March 1969, Ndongo was accused of launching an abortive coup with Spanish complicity. In response, on 5 March 1969 President Macías declared he was assuming absolute power. He also declared that all Equatoguineans studying abroad had to return immediately or face loss of their citizenship. There followed numerous violent incidents against Spanish citizens in Río Muni, who were accused by the president of trying to undermine the new republic including the killing of a Spanish national at the Spanish consulate in Bata. This prompted, on 22 March, the departure of almost all of the remaining 7,000 Spaniards who had been in the colony before independence. British and American employees of Mobil Oil were also evacuated.

On 2 February 1970, President Macías combined all political groups to form the Partido Unico Nacional de los Trabajadores (PUNT), creating a one-party state. He also created a paramilitary youth wing, the Juventud en Marcha con Macías. The constitution was reformed, freedom of movement and expression were curtailed and a national assembly was set up, with all members appointed directly by the president. On 14 July 1972, Constitutional Decree No 1 proclaimed Macías President for Life, Commander in Chief of the Army, and Grand Master of Science, Education and Culture. These events marked the end of the fledgling democracy.

A wave of arrests followed as President Macías consolidated his position. Atanasio Ndongo Miyono, Torao Sikara and Armando Balboa (mayor of Santa Isabel) were all rounded up. Atanasio Ndongo Miyono was said to have committed suicide by jumping out of a window (despite the claims of eyewitnesses that both his legs were broken before the 'jump'). Equatorial Guinea's delegate to the UN, Saturnino Ibongo, was recalled to the country and immediately executed behind a bush at Malabo airport. Macías's main competitor in the first presidential elections, Bonifacio Ondó Edú, died in Malabo prison under mysterious circumstances; Torao Sikara, a key Bubi politician and president of the National Assembly, died from lack of water in a Bata prison; and Enrique Gori Molubela, a key figure in the Bubi Union, died of gangrene after having his eyes gouged out. His compatriot in the party, Edmundo Bosio Dioco, was tortured and then shot in February 1975, apparently because the official picture of the president hanging in his office was torn at the corner. The wives and children of most of these politicians were also killed.

Between 1968 and 1975, two-thirds of the original 1968 parliament were either executed or went missing. Over 300 individuals, mostly key figures in the government, civil service, army and police, were killed by order of President Macías. The first public executions occurred in 1972, and at Christmas in 1975, 150 prisoners were executed in the national stadium while loudspeakers played 'Those Were The Days' to the spectators. The UN also later reported that executions were often carried out using iron bars, or in the case of 36 unfortunate victims, by being buried up to their necks and left to be eaten by red ants. One former inmate of the notorious Black Beach prison outside Malabo reported that between 1971 and 1975 he counted 157 prisoners beaten to death with metal rods outside his cell.

The dwindling expatriate community (mainly diplomats) was also affected by this atmosphere of violence and paranoia. On 30 August 1971, Alfred Erdos, the US chargé d'affaires in Santa Isabel and the most senior US diplomat in the country at the time, stabbed his administrative officer Donald Leahy to death with a pair of scissors after accusing him of being involved in a communist plot. At his trial back in the US the following year, Erdos entered a defence of insanity, detailing a deliberate policy of harassment and intimidation from the Macías regime, which included seeing the embassy's cook (an Equatoguinean national) flayed alive in full view of his residence, and having the screams of tortured prisoners deprive him of sleep for weeks on end. Within the Cold War context, President Macías's actions were not challenged for fear of him siding with the Soviet Union, so these events were not publicised in the West.

THE TERROR SPREADS By 1975 the country was emptying out. From a total population of 400,000, 60,000 had fled to Gabon, 30,000 to Cameroon and a further 5,000 to Spain and the rest of Europe. During the year, seemingly overcome with paranoia and weakened through illness, President Macías relocated from Malabo to his hometown of Nsangayong, south of Mongomo on the mainland. He took the entire national treasury with him, having had the director of the National Bank publicly executed.

From 1975 to 1979, President Macías widened the focus of his terror campaign as he increasingly lost touch with reality. He smoked the local intoxicant *bhang* and took a stimulant called *iboga*, with effects similar to LSD. He issued decrees based on imagined conversations with spirits, and many close to him suspected mental instability. Whereas he had previously only trusted his own ethnic group, the Fang, with positions of responsibility, he now narrowed his requirements for entrusted power further and only promoted those from his specific clan, the Esangui. His violence was now directed towards the Bubi minority of Bioko and the thousands of Nigerian contract labourers working on the plantations. Nigerian workers suffered extortion, brutal beatings and executions at the hands of the security services. In January 1976, 11 Nigerian citizens were even killed within the grounds of the Nigerian embassy, leading the government of Nigeria to evacuate all 40,000 of its citizens on boats and military transport planes.

This sudden labour shortage almost led to economic collapse in the country. In response, the Macías regime arrested thousands of men and children in Río Muni (some as young as seven) and shipped them over to Bioko as forced labourers for the plantations. Fishing was banned on the island in order to prevent potential escapes. In Mongomo, near the mainland hometown of the president, girls between the ages of 14 and 20 were forced to work without pay on his private farms and coffee plantations. Some were also raped by members of the Presidential Guard.

In 1975, state schools across the country were closed and there was widespread persecution of anyone seen as an intellectual. The president introduced an authenticity campaign, seeking to divest Equatorial Guinea of the trappings of colonialism. Laws were passed forcing people to change their European names to African ones, with the president himself changing his name from Francisco Macías Nguema to Masie Nguema Biyogo Ñegue Ndong. Priests were even punished for baptising babies with European names. This quest for authenticity also covered medicine, with Western products shunned in favour of traditional African remedies. Certain foods, such as bread, tomatoes, sugar and milk were also banned for being too Western.

The Roman Catholic Church, viewed by Macías as an instrument of Spanish imperialism, was blamed for many of the problems in the fledgling independent state. It was also a rival power structure that could not be tolerated. Macías first demanded that all their services began with the words 'in the name of President Macías and his son'. Soon this was not enough, and all Catholic schools were closed, clergymen were imprisoned, and finally, in early 1978, all Catholic Church activities were made illegal.

THE COUP – 3 AUGUST 1979 By early 1979, President Macías had driven around a quarter of his country's citizens into exile and killed between 35,000 and 80,000 people, a shocking statistic considering that the total population at the time was under 400,000. A media blackout on the former colony in Spain meant that few reports on this tragedy were released. The economy had also collapsed, with public sector wages going unpaid and electricity unavailable even in the capital city. All the while though the president's official annual salary sat at over US$10 million.

At the time of President Macías's retreat to the mainland, his nephew Teodoro Obiang Nguema Mbasogo was military governor of Bioko island and acting head of the armed forces, giving him effective control of the country. He had also previously acted as director of the notorious Black Beach prison. In the spring of 1979, a six-man delegation of senior military officers, including Obiang's brother, travelled to Mongomo to request that the president release some funds from his treasury to enable them to pay the army. Convinced that they were plotting against him, Macías had them all executed.

In what was possibly a pre-emptive strike, Obiang evacuated his family and then on 3 August 1979 led a coup against the president, a coup that some have alleged received tacit Spanish support. Macías and some loyal supporters managed to hold out for two weeks, during which time over 400 people died in heavy fighting. Finally, on 18 August Macías was captured in the jungle. A quick show trial began on 24 September, in which Macías and ten co-defendants were charged with genocide, mass murder, embezzlement of public funds, material injury, systematic violations of human rights and treason. Many other crimes of the regime, including mass killings, were ignored, as these could have implicated some of those behind the coup.

Within five days Macías was found guilty of most offences and handed a death sentence. He was executed by firing squad at Black Beach prison at 18.00 on 29 September 1979.

A NEW LEADER... Obiang initially installed himself as provisional head of state under a military council, and was then inaugurated as president on 11 October 1979. As with his uncle a decade earlier, Obiang's rule began on a positive note. One of his first moves was to release all political prisoners, and invite those in exile to return to the country. Obiang also tore down the 4m-high security wall that Macías had installed around his palace in central Malabo, which had cut off numerous houses and the cathedral from public access. In April 1980, Obiang restored the independence constitution. The following year, the joint Spanish–Equatoguinean company GEPSA was given permission to start oil exploration in a bid to revive the flailing economy.

Equatorial Guinea, for many years a pariah state, was back on the international scene. King Juan Carlos of Spain dined with the new president on his first official visit to Spain in May 1980. In February 1982, Pope John Paul II visited Malabo.

That same year discussions began to integrate Equatorial Guinea into the Central African Franc Zone (CFA), something that was achieved by 1985.

... IN THE OLD STYLE Not every Equatoguinean was happy with Obiang's rule. Opposition groups abroad remained sceptical, and international observers struggled with Obiang's credibility given his closeness to the previous regime, and the continued undemocratic dominance of the Fang ethnic group in government and economic spheres. In August 1982, a new constitution was promoted and Obiang's term as president was extended by seven years. May 1983 saw the first well-publicised coup attempt, with one conspirator, Sergeant Venancio Mico, seeking refuge in the Spanish embassy before being turned over for imprisonment. A more serious coup attempt by Obiang's former minister of defence, Fructoso Mba Onana, was put down in July 1986. This pattern of violent uprisings against the government would continue for the next 20 years, culminating in the infamous 2004 Wonga coup (pages 38–9).

By the mid 1980s the economy of Equatorial Guinea had shown few signs of recovery, and President Obiang was under increasing pressure from groups such as the International Monetary Fund (IMF) to improve his state's governance and accountability before any financial assistance would be rendered. In 1985, the average Equatoguinean could expect to live 44.7 years, over four years less than the average sub-Saharan African. They could also expect to earn the equivalent of US$415.71 per year, making them some of the poorest citizens on the planet according to the IMF. Persecution of political opponents continued, with many finding themselves either imprisoned or exiled.

In this climate of economic stagnation, the first parliamentary elections were held in August 1983, providing a civilian governing structure to replace the previous military council. These elections were based on a single list with no political parties, where around 50,000 registered voters chose 41 members to sit in the House of Representatives of the People for a five-year term. Shortly after this, in 1984, following four years of exploration, GEPSA recorded its first hydrocarbon discovery at the Alba field, located 32km northwest of Bioko island. However, this was a gas and condensate field (as opposed to an oilfield), which would take seven years to come online, meaning it had very little impact on the economy at the time.

In 1987, Obiang created the first official political party since Macías's reign: the PDGE (Partido Democrático de Guinea Ecuatorial). Opponents to his regime attempted to legalise their own party, the Progress Party of Equatorial Guinea (PPGE), however, this request was rejected in June 1988, meaning the parliamentary elections a month later featured only one party. With his party having won all 60 seats in parliament, Obiang was then re-elected unopposed in the June 1989 presidential elections with 99% of the vote, beginning a pattern of political dominance and incredible election results that continues to this day.

In 1991, a constitutional referendum was passed by 98.4%. The new constitution implemented a multi-party democracy to replace the single party state. This led to the legalisation of numerous opposition political groups such as the Popular Union, the Union for Democracy and Social Development, the Progress Party, the Demo-Christian Alliance and the Social Democrat Party. It also paved the way for the return of numerous political exiles, the most famous of whom was Severo Matías Moto Nsá, leader of the Progress Party. He had been an active opposition leader in Spain, where he had sought asylum in December 1981. Upon his return in 1996, however, Moto soon found the political climate unwelcoming and was arrested for defaming the president, plotting a coup and trying to corrupt a policeman. Other opposition figures brave enough to come back faced the daily risk of arbitrary detention, torture and sometimes death at the hands of the security forces.

The second set of parliamentary elections since independence were held in November 1993. This was the first time voters were given a choice of parties. Several countries, including France, Spain and the USA, criticised the organisation of the elections and refused to validate them by sending observers. A coalition of opposition parties named the POC (Joint Opposition Platform) called for a boycott amid allegations of intimidation and electoral register irregularities. As a result, some claim the abstention rate was around 80% of eligible voters. In the end the ruling PDGE party took 68 of the 80 available seats, with the CPDS and two other smaller parties sharing the remaining 12.

THE DISCOVERY OF OIL AND OBIANG'S CONTINUED ELECTORAL SUCCESS In 1995, the US embassy in Malabo closed, after Ambassador John Bennett received death threats. Stationed there since 1991, Bennett was critically outspoken on the issues of human rights abuses and the endemic corruption of the regime. Commenting on the situation, he stated: 'There is not really a government. There is an ongoing family criminal conspiracy. That's what runs the country.' This was also the year that Equatorial Guinea struck oil. ExxonMobil and Ocean Energy discovered the Zafiro oilfield, located around 68km northwest of Bioko island, adjacent to the Nigerian international border. This field was exploited immediately and was the main driver behind the massive economic expansion of the following years.

With a flow of oil wealth secured, on 25 February 1996 Obiang won another seven-year term in the presidential elections, receiving an incredible 97.85% of the vote. Before the discovery of oil, politicians were vying for control of one of the smallest national economies on the planet. By the second multi-party elections of March 1999, the economy had increased in size almost tenfold, with the promise of further expansion to come thanks to the oil industry. Thirteen parties contested the 80 available seats, with the ruling regime winning a landslide 75 seats. The remaining five seats were split between the Popular Union (UP) and Convergencia para la Democracia Social (CPDS) parties. The validity of these elections was disputed, both internally and internationally, due to the incredibly high recorded turnout (95%) and the lack of international electoral observers.

The terrorist attacks of 11 September 2001 saw a marked change in US foreign policy towards Equatorial Guinea. The architect of this change was Walter Kansteiner, assistant secretary of state for African affairs under the Bush administration. He spearheaded a diversification drive away from Middle Eastern oil, and towards the Gulf of Guinea. In 2002, the African Oil Policy Initiative Group described the area as of vital interest to the USA, advising that a military base be set up in the region to protect future investments. That same year Obiang had breakfast with President Bush at the White House.

On 15 December 2002, presidential elections delivered Obiang another seven-year term, after he won 97.1% of the vote amid an opposition boycott. In 2003, the USA announced the reopening of its embassy in Malabo (page 71). This was the same year that President Obiang announced to his citizens via state radio that he felt compelled to take full control of the national treasury, to protect the money from corrupt civil servants. To this end, around US$700 million of national wealth ended up in 60 accounts in Riggs Bank, Washington DC, held by government entities, family members of the president and senior officials. Suspicions of money laundering led a US Federal Court to fine the bank US$16 million in 2004.

From 2004 to 2009 there was a series of literally unbelievable electoral successes for the President's PDGE ruling party. These began with the April 2004 parliamentary election with the PDGE and a group of eight allied parties (known as the Electoral Coalition) taking 98 of the available 100 seats. The Convergence for Social Democracy (CPDS), the only party opposing the government, took the remaining two seats. In the May 2008 parliamentary election the ruling PDGE did even better, winning 99 of the available 100 seats with Plácido Micó Abogo, leader of the CPDS handed the difficult task of becoming the sole opposition representative in parliament. The Progress Party had been banned from participating after its leader, Severo Moto, had been sentenced *in absentia* to 62 years in prison for alleged involvement in the failed 2004 Wonga coup (pages 38–9).

Finally, the November 2009 presidential elections delivered Obiang another seven-year term, after he won 95.36% of the vote amid widespread criticism from opposition figures and international observers. The US State Department noted 'raised suspicions of systematic vote fraud'.

PRESIDENT OBIANG REBRANDS HIMSELF – 2010 ONWARDS Tiring of the constant international criticism, from 2010 onwards President Obiang made a concerted effort to rebrand himself, his rule and his country. Such a decision was not made overnight. The regime had been paying DC lobbying firm Cassidy and Associates at least US$120,000 a month since 2004 to try and improve its image in the USA. But in May 2010 the government subcontracted a further US$55,000 a month to the public relations firm Qorvis Communications to supplement this advocacy work. They also signed a contract worth over US$2 million with Lanny Davis, a former special counsel to President Bill Clinton, to help implement 'a comprehensive reform program', in the hopes of turning Obiang's legacy into one of 'change and reform'. Davis was handed the difficult task of helping Equatorial Guinea enter the Extractive Industries Transparency Initiative, which is designed to prevent corruption by having leaders publicly disclose payments made to them by natural resource extraction companies. Unfortunately, Equatorial Guinea was rejected for membership in April 2010, and their relationship with Davis soon turned sour when he sued the regime for unpaid legal fees in 2011.

Setbacks aside, Equatorial Guinea's relationship with the West was slowly improving thanks in part to this advocacy work. International oil companies bolstered these efforts by also investing in lobbying on Equatorial Guinea's behalf in Washington. In June 2010, Equatorial Guinea drew closer to the US establishment by signing a US$250 million maritime security contract with American private security firm Military Professional Resources Initiative. In September, at the 65th session of the UN General Assembly, Equatorial Guinea's minister of foreign affairs, Pastor Micha Ondo Bile, explained to the world the numerous initiatives the government was undertaking while implementing its Horizon2020 development plan, which was first outlined in 2007. This billion-dollar plan is aimed at turning Equatorial Guinea into an emerging economy by 2020, through investments in health, education, infrastructure and industrial development. The plan also includes many of the benchmarks set out in the UN Millennium Development Goals relating to poverty reduction, healthcare improvements and educational reform.

In October 2010, the rebrand hit another roadblock. A few years previously the Obiang government had donated US$3 million to UNESCO to set up the UNESCO–Obiang Nguema Mbasogo International Prize for Research in the Life Sciences. The prize, awarded for research aimed at improving quality of life, was severely criticised by human rights groups and African scholars, including former archbishop Desmond Tutu, author Chinua Achebe and Nobel laureate Wole Soyinka, who took issue with the opaque source of the prize funds. In the end, UNESCO was forced to act, suspending the prize, then finally renaming it as the UNESCO–Equatorial Guinea International Prize for Research in the Life Sciences, with the first awards given in 2012.

Around this time the president also began collecting honorary degrees from universities in Venezuela, Costa Rica, Russia, Chile, Benin and, of course, the National University of Equatorial Guinea. In 2011, Obiang took up the prestigious position of chairperson of the African Union (AU), with Malabo hosting the 17th Ordinary African Union Summit in June of that year. Delegates were housed in a purpose-built luxury city called Sipopo, situated 20 minutes outside the capital. It featured 52 presidential villas, and cost a total of US$830 million according to Human Rights Watch.

Equatorial Guinea found itself in the international spotlight again in 2012 when it co-hosted the Africa Cup of Nations football tournament with Gabon, and also hosted the Leon H Sullivan Foundation summit on human rights and African development. With President Obiang as the official host of the summit, a stated aim was to create 'an atmosphere of open dialogue about the state of human rights and the interconnected issues of modern Africa'. Organisations such as The Human Rights Foundation were very critical of the choice of venue, in light of the regime's human rights record.

Criticism notwithstanding, President Obiang oversaw another landslide victory in the 2013 legislative elections when 54 of the 55 contested senate seats were won by the PDGE, with only one going to the CPDS. The final 15 senators were directly appointed by the president. Likewise, 99 of the 100 seats in the lower house went to the PDGE, with one going to the CPDS.

In February 2014, a conference entitled 'Emerging Equatorial Guinea' was held in Malabo, to showcase the country's investment opportunities for an international audience. During the event President Obiang complained that his country was 'not being shown for what it is' and that negative media coverage was one of the biggest obstacles to international acceptance and progress. Gregor Binkert, World Bank Country Director for Equatorial Guinea, also noted that: 'Statistics about Equatorial Guinea are very much outdated, particularly poverty numbers. Some of the figures [cited in public sources] are from as far back as '05 or '06.' In June, the 23rd Ordinary Session of the African Union was successfully held in Malabo, this time focusing on agriculture and food security. Discussions also centred around the proposed African Court of Justice and Human Rights, which would serve as an alternative to the International Criminal Court. Notably, discussions at this summit produced the 'Malabo Protocol' in which AU leaders voted to grant themselves immunity from prosecution before their as yet unestablished new human rights court.

THE FUTURE OF EQUATORIAL GUINEA The 29 August 2014 marked a key development in Equatorial Guinea's politics, and surprised many observers. In a routine speech from his palace in Malabo, President Obiang called on all Equatoguinean political leaders, including those living in exile, to convene that November in Sipopo for a national political dialogue. This was the result of several months of back room negotiations and meetings in Madrid, where opposition groups had united and signed the 'Madrid Manifesto' on 22 March, outlining their grievances and what format a national dialogue should take.

The national dialogue took place as announced, between 7 and 15 November, reviewing numerous issues such as the laws governing political participation, expression and organisation. Some political groups hailed this as a step in the right direction, whereas others denounced it as a masquerade with few long-lasting effects. As of 2015, it is unclear how much longer President Obiang intends to remain in power. He is in his seventies and is now Africa's longest serving head of state, having been in power over 35 years (narrowly beating President Dos Santos of Angola by one month and President Mugabe by eight months). Many see the appointment of his son Teodorín as second vice president in 2011 as an attempt to groom him for succession in the future. The next presidential elections are due to be held in Equatorial Guinea at some stage between November 2015 and December 2016. Whatever happens, the international community will be hoping for a peaceful transition and a more effective redistribution of the oil wealth amongst the general population.

GOVERNMENT AND POLITICS

Equatorial Guinea is a presidential republic. President Teodoro Obiang Nguema Mbasogo is Africa's longest continuously serving head of state, having been president of his country since 3 August 1979. Many Equatoguineans continue to live in exile in Spain, the USA and other nations, voicing their criticism of the Obiang regime and setting up parallel political structures that question the legitimacy of the government in Malabo. Notable political figures in exile include Dr Adolfo Obiang Biko, president of MONALIGE (page 24) and Severo Moto (page 30).

Resources within the government are not equally distributed, and there is a lingering element of Spanish bureaucracy in some of the ministries and departments. Nepotism and cronyism within government also mean that some elements of the public sector are not run as efficiently as they could be. There were 13 recognised, legal political parties in Equatorial Guinea as of September 2014; however in a speech on 3 September, President Obiang invited political forces both inside and outside the country to converge for a national dialogue (pages 33–4), implying further efforts at democratic reform and inclusiveness were underway.

THE GOVERNMENT STRUCTURE The government of Equatorial Guinea is divided into identifiable executive, legislative and judicial branches, although there is not full separation of powers.

Executive branch This branch of government is headed up by the president as the head of state. According to the August 1982 constitution, the ruling terms are seven years. In 2011, following a referendum, a limit of two seven-year terms was put in place, although President Obiang has announced these limits will not apply retroactively. The president has extensive powers, including legislating through decree and is the commander in chief of the armed forces. He also directly appoints governors to all seven of the country's provinces (page 35).

After the 2011 referendum, the posts of first and second vice president were created. Since 22 May 2012, these have been occupied by Ignacio Milam Tang and Teodoro Nguema Obiang Mangue (Teodorín) respectively. The head of government is the prime minister, who is directly appointed by the president. Vicente Ehate Tomi has occupied this post since May 2012. The Council of Ministers is made up of representatives from the Chamber of People's Representatives who are selected by the president to manage the government, in particular monetary policy and the annual budget.

The State Council also occupies an important role in the administration. It includes the president of the National Assembly, the prime minister, the minister of defence and the chairman of the Social and Economic Council, and is designed to act as a caretaker government should the president be rendered incapable of ruling.

Equatorial Guinea's provinces The country is divided into seven administrative provinces, each with a governor appointed directly by the president. Each province also has a capital city. The divisions are as follows:

Mainland provinces (Río Muni)

Centro Sur Province (Evinayong)   Litoral Province (Bata)
Kié-Ntem Province (Ebebiyín)   Wele-Nzas Province (Mongomo)

Island provinces

Annobón Province (San Antonio de Palé)   Bioko Sur Province (Luba)
Bioko Norte Province (Malabo)

The legislative branch

This branch traditionally consisted of the Chamber of People's Representatives but after the 2011 referendum, a senate was added as an upper house of the parliament, to form a bicameral national assembly system.

There are 100 seats available in the Chamber of People's Representatives, with members directly elected by popular vote in a closed-list proportional representation system, to serve five-year terms. The next elections are due to be held in 2018. There are 70 seats available in the senate. Fifteen of these seats are appointed by the president and 55 are directly elected by popular vote to serve five-year terms.

The legislature has been dominated by President Obiang's political party the PDGE since it was officially created in 1987. In the May 2008 parliamentary election they took 99 of the available 100 seats with the CPDS taking the one remaining seat. The 2013 legislative elections featured another PDGE landslide victory, with 54 of the 55 contested new senate seats won by the PDGE (with one going to the CPDS), and 99 of the 100 seats in the lower house going to the PDGE (with one going to the CPDS).

The judicial branch

The Supreme Court of Justice is the highest ranking body in the judicial branch of government. Supreme Court judges are appointed by the president for terms of five years.

Equatorial Guinea also has a constitutional court, a court of guarantees, military courts, two courts of appeal and several tribunals. Although the constitution recognises the principle of judicial independence, President Obiang is named as Chief Magistrate of the Nation, meaning that he chairs the Supreme Council on Judicial Power and is able to influence the appointment and career paths of judges. The president is also able to appoint Supreme Court justices without parliamentary approval. These issues led the International Bar Association to comment that: 'The courts are not independent and impartial. The range of external pressures flows from both systemic difficulties and from direct intervention from the President in order to protect his personal interests.' On 20 May 2015, President Obiang issued Decree 36/2015, which summarily dissolved the entire judiciary. At the time of writing no new appointments had been made, leaving Equatorial Guinea effectively without a judiciary.

SECURITY AND COUPS The territory of Equatorial Guinea does not have a good track record of the democratic transfer of power. Historically, Spanish, British and Portuguese rule was maintained through coercion rather than legitimacy, a pattern that has repeated itself throughout independence. The current president came to power as the result of a military coup in 1979. It is therefore understandable that his administration is preoccupied with the threat of violent regime change (whether real or imagined).

In March 1969, when independent Equatorial Guinea was not yet six months old, Atanasio Ndongo Miyono, then foreign minister, was accused of launching an abortive coup, with Spanish complicity. The resulting security crackdowns led to the departure of most remaining Spanish nationals, and the beginning of Macías's decade-long reign of terror (pages 26–9). Macías alleged numerous other attempts against his rule in subsequent years. How much of this was truth and how much paranoia is open to debate, although a British police report from Gibraltar in January 1973 sheds some light on the threats to Macías's rule.

Fred Llambias was head of Special Branch in Gibraltar, the tiny British Overseas Territory at the southern tip of the Iberian Peninsula. In January 1973, he filed a four page report titled 'Re: Possible armed invasion of Fernando Pó by mercenaries sometime after the 20th January, 1973'. In this report, now available at the National Archive in London, he detailed how boat owner George Allan had approached the police with some information. Allan had chartered his boat, the *Albatross*, for an oil survey in West Africa to a man named Harry Greaves. Allan became suspicious when Mr Greaves and his men began loading the *Albatross* with military equipment, rather than survey gear.

It turned out that Harry Greaves was in fact Alexander Ramsay Gay, a well-known Scottish mercenary who had fought for the Biafran rebels in the Nigerian Civil War. He was joined by a small group of British, French and Canadian mercenaries. Gay claimed later that the plot was carried out with the 'full knowledge of the Spanish Foreign Minister, Senor Lopez Bravo'.

Their plan was to ship arms from Hamburg for collection off the coast of Malaga, sail to Portugal to collect more European mercenaries, head south to refuel in Cape Verde, and then finally collect another 50 African mercenaries (possibly Nigerian) from an undisclosed location before the assault. Maps found in the cabin showed that the port of Fernando Pó was their final destination.

Llambias's report sparked a flurry of diplomatic cables between Spain and Britain, which resulted in the arrest of the mercenaries in the Canary Islands on 23 January 1973. Nobody thought to inform the Macías regime, however, which eventually heard of the plot and put the city on high alert one week later, sparking widespread panic.

In 1978, *The Sunday Times* alleged that the mastermind and financier behind this coup attempt was none other than novelist Frederick Forsyth, then famous for his first novel *The Day of the Jackal*, about a plot to assassinate French president Charles de Gaulle. In a bizarre case of art imitating life, Forsyth's 1974 book *The Dogs of War* featured a small group of European mercenaries attempting to depose the dictatorial government of the mineral rich, fictional West African island nation of Zangaro. There are numerous similarities between the characters and events in the book, and the 1973 coup attempt. During his research for the book Forsyth even posed as a South African arms dealer and met with mercenaries and other men who could help to organise a coup. In a 2006 interview, Forsyth admitted to financial involvement in the coup attempt, but stated that this was for research purposes only.

Leaving aside Forsyth's level of involvement, the 1973 coup did not end the way it did in his book, and President Macías remained in power. In 1975, he even relocated from Malabo to his hometown of Nsangayong, south of Mongomo for the increased security it provided from amphibious assault. Despite the relocation, Macías did not achieve the security he desired. On 3 August 1979, Obiang led a coup against his uncle, a coup that some have alleged received tacit Spanish support (pages 40–1).

Like his uncle, President Obiang has faced numerous threats to his rule. May 1983 saw the first coup attempt (page 30), and a more serious coup attempt by Obiang's former minister of defence, Fructoso Mba Onana, was put down in July 1986. The next 18 years saw a series of plots discovered, opposition members jailed, and order restored. Sometimes alleged plotters were executed, but more often than not they were released into exile or received a pardon from the president. Notable amongst the coup attempts of this period was the 1997 effort by Severo Moto from Luanda, Angola. Although the plotters managed to fill a boat with weapons it never left the harbour as it was discovered by the Angolan authorities. The attempt resulted in a 121-year sentence handed down *in absentia* to the ringleader. Moto did not let this deter him, however, and in 2004 he found himself at the centre of a plot which posed a much more serious threat to the Obiang regime (pages 29–34).

The 2004 Wonga coup (pages 38–9) was the most famous attempt, but it was certainly not the last aiming to remove President Obiang from power. Early on the morning of 17 February 2009, the presidential palace in Malabo was attacked by two speedboats filled with heavily armed assailants. President Obiang was not in the palace at the time, however, but over on the mainland in Bata. The Obiang government initially claimed the attackers were Nigerian militants from the MEND (Movement for the Emancipation of the Niger Delta) group, although the group's representatives in the Niger Delta denied this. In August 2010, four men, Jose Abeso Nsue, Manuel Ndong Anseme, Alipio Ndong Asumu and Jacinto Micha Obiang, were executed for their role in the plot. Amnesty International claimed that the men played no role in what occurred and were in fact kidnapped from exile in nearby Benin in January 2010 by Equatoguinean security forces.

As with his uncle before him, President Obiang has decided to seek improved security inland, away from the amphibious assault threats of Bioko. He told the BBC in December 2012 that one of the reasons for constructing Oyala – a new capital city – was because, 'We need a secure place for my government and for future governments… to guarantee the government of Equatorial Guinea.' Due for completion in 2020, it remains to be seen whether the relocation of the seat of government from Malabo to Oyala will spell an end to the threat of coups.

FOREIGN RELATIONS

Relations with the Soviets and Cuba Under President Macías, Equatorial Guinea was aligned with the Soviet Bloc and Cuba. Macías allowed the Soviet embassy in Malabo to expand greatly, increasing its capabilities to co-ordinate spy trawlers throughout the Atlantic. In return for this concession, he was given some technical and financial assistance, as well as the use of around 200 Cuban soldiers and advisors, responsible for training his bodyguard and paramilitary forces. Cuban doctors, teachers and other skilled professionals were used to fill the gaps left by the departing Spaniards in the 1970s.

Relations with China Quickly isolated from Western support due to an appalling human rights record, Macías could offer the Chinese little more than his UN vote for support. In return, in 1971, they signed an economic and technical co-operation agreement which saw technicians, medical teams and road builders

On 7 March 2004, a chartered Boeing 727 flew from South Africa to Zimbabwe and was impounded at Harare International Airport while trying to load up assorted weaponry. Seventy men on board were arrested, the majority of whom were South African. Two days later, 15 men, also mainly South African, were rounded up and arrested in Equatorial Guinea. Over the next few months, details emerged of a daring coup attempt and an incredible conspiracy, stretching from Africa across Europe, America and the Middle East.

The leader of the men on the plane in Zimbabwe was Simon Mann, an ex-SAS officer and private military contractor. His previous connections to companies such as Executive Outcomes and Sandline International had led to him selling his military skills in conflicts as diverse as the Angolan Civil War, the Bougainville Uprising and the Sierra Leone Civil War throughout the 1990s.

In late January 2003, it is alleged that Simon Mann met with a Lebanese business tycoon named Ely Calil and began plotting what would later be dubbed the 2004 'Wonga coup', named after the list of financial backers discovered by the authorities. Over the next 14 months a plan was hatched to violently overthrow President Obiang using retired elite South African and Angolan troops from 32 Battalion (the same men who had fought for Executive Outcomes and Sandline International in the past).

A small advance party of men, led by former 32 Battalion officer Nick du Toit, would infiltrate the country under the guise of legitimate businessmen. Meanwhile, the main assault group would set off from South Africa, collect weapons in Zimbabwe under the pretence of needing them for a mine security job in the Democratic Republic of Congo, and then head to Equatorial Guinea. At the appointed time the advance party would seize the airport, allowing the main contingent of heavily armed men to land in Malabo, overpower the security forces and storm the presidential palace. The plan was then to fly in Severo Moto, an exiled Equatoguinean politician living in Madrid, and install him as the new president. Once the coup was successful, the plotters would be rewarded with multi-million-pound defence, mineral and oil contracts by the new government.

The plan failed spectacularly, partly due to disorganisation and lack of funding, but mainly due to a lack of operational secrecy. South African, Zimbabwean, American, French, Spanish and British intelligence agencies all seemed to have varying degrees of prior knowledge of the coup attempt before it occurred. As

sent to the country. Four hundred Chinese workers headed to Río Muni to improve the dilapidated colonial road and telecommunications networks. By 1978, there were also around 100 military specialists, although they chose to support the wrong side in the 1979 coup which led to a frosty five-year interruption of Chinese and Equatoguinean relations.

President Obiang reinstigated relations with China in 1984 with a state visit. This was at a time when relations with the West were still strained, as the IMF and World Bank were struggling to implement aid programmes due to corruption and mismanagement in the country. Most aid was finally cut off in 1993. Bilateral trade with China slowly grew until 2005 when, after returning from another Chinese visit, President Obiang announced that China was Equatorial Guinea's main development partner. China had opened up a US$2 billion line of credit to them. Analysts have commented that some of the growth in this relationship with China

with the 1973 plot against President Macías, Western intelligence agencies failed to alert the authorities in Equatorial Guinea.

Simon Mann was given a seven-year prison term in Chikurubi prison in Zimbabwe, while most of the men with him spent around 14 months behind bars. In South Africa, Mark Thatcher, son of former British prime minister Margaret Thatcher, was arrested for financially supporting the coup. He eventually negotiated a plea bargain – claiming that he believed he was financing the purchase of an air ambulance – and was forced to leave his Cape Town home to relocate outside South Africa. Other figures implicated in funding the mission included British author Jeffrey Archer and numerous British, South African and Lebanese businesspeople.

After nearly four years in a Zimbabwean prison, Mann was illegally extradited to Equatorial Guinea on the night of 31 January 2008. He joined Nick du Toit and the rest of the advance party in the notorious Black Beach prison outside Malabo. Conditions there were poor, with one coup plotter, German national Gerhard Eugen Nershz, having already died in captivity from alleged torture and lack of access to medical facilities. In July 2008, after a show trial in which Mann implicated other co-conspirators including Ely Calil and Mark Thatcher, he was handed a 34-year jail sentence and a fine of nearly US$24 million.

In November 2009, Mann and his co-conspirators were given presidential pardons after a series of back room negotiations with the Foreign Office and various other public and private agencies. Most of the freed men went straight home. It is believed that their freedom came at the price of helping to implicate those who President Obiang believed were really behind the plot: the alleged financiers such as Ely Calil. Beginning in 2010, Simon Mann returned to Equatorial Guinea on a number of occasions to do consultancy work for President Obiang, and has been actively involved in a lawsuit brought in Lebanon against Ely Calil by the Equatoguinean government. President Obiang has also alleged that there was tacit support from Western intelligence agencies. In particular, that the Spanish authorities under President José Maria Aznar had not only known about Mann's attempts, but sent two naval vessels (the *Patino* and the *Canarias*) loaded with 500 marines on board, for an exercise down in the Gulf of Guinea to help secure Moto's government once it was put in power. The Spanish government continues to deny these claims.

came as a result of the failed 2004 Wonga coup, which President Obiang believed Western authorities tacitly supported.

In 2007, the Chinese foreign minister opened the new state radio and television buildings in Malabo, both built by Chinese construction companies. By 2008 China's imports from Equatorial Guinea stood at US$2.3 billion, and were mainly oil and timber – approximately 70% of Equatorial Guinea's timber is exported to China. That year there were clashes between 200 striking Chinese construction workers and Equatoguinean security forces, which resulted in the deaths of two workers, causing tension in the relationship and the repatriation of 400 workers. Despite this, President Obiang travelled to China six times between 1984 and 2010, and the relationship remains strong.

Commenting on the influx of Chinese investment and workers into Equatorial Guinea in a 2012 BBC interview, President Obiang noted: 'I am a realist when it comes to political life. I go where the offers are. I am going with China because China gave me a two thousand million dollar loan that others did not give me… We don't have any concerns when China is helping us economically as we know they do not interfere in our political problems.' The Chinese principle of non-interference in internal affairs, first espoused in 1954, has proven attractive to many African leaders who struggle to secure funding from the IMF, World Bank or Western donors due to the conditions placed on the funds (such as respecting human rights and good governance requirements).

Relations with the USA Despite increasing Chinese influence, especially after the 2004 coup attempt, the USA is still dominant on the Equatoguinean oil scene. Today, the USA is one of Equatorial Guinea's key trading partners. In 2013, a total of US$1.6 billion in goods was traded between the two countries, with the USA consistently one of the top five importers to Equatorial Guinea.

Relations between Equatorial Guinea and the USA have not always been good. In 1995, the US embassy in Malabo closed, after Ambassador John Bennett received death threats for his outspoken criticisms of the Obiang regime's human rights record. The rapid development of the oil industry, coupled with the increased strategic importance of non-Middle Eastern oil supplies after the events of 11 September 2001, changed this. In 2002, President Obiang had breakfast with President Bush at the White House, and in 2003 the US announced the reopening of its embassy. In 2006, whilst she was secretary of state, Condoleezza Rice called Obiang a 'good friend' and he has since met President Obama on a number of occasions, most recently in August 2014 at the US–Africa Leaders Summit.

Relations with Spain The Spanish ruled Equatorial Guinea for almost 190 years. It is believed that descendants of Spanish settlers today make up 5% of the country's population, so there are strong historic, cultural and linguistic ties. Relations with Spain are often tense, although today Spain (along with China) is the dominant importer in the country and hence plays a key part in the economy. Under President Macías, relations with Equatorial Guinea were poor, with Spanish engagement limited to issuing muted criticism of human rights violations, accepting exiles and (according to some sources) conspiring to have Macías replaced in a coup.

Things were initially little better under President Obiang, who complained of the legacy of colonialism and refused to grant Spanish companies concessions in the mid 90s oil bonanza. Relations were not helped by the political asylum granted to Severo Moto in Madrid (page 30). A change of government to the PSOE (Spanish Socialist Workers' Party) in 2004, however, led to a great improvement in relations. In a mark of how times had changed, during an official visit to Madrid in 2006, President Obiang was granted full state honours and had an audience with both King Juan Carlos and Prime Minister José Luis Zapatero. In February 2013, Equatorial Guinea even handed management responsibilities for their national football team to Spanish coach Andoni Goikoetxea Olaskoaga.

Since 2004, Spain has had the uneasy balancing act of on the one hand encouraging democratic reform, hosting exiles and speaking out against human rights abuses, and on the other, working to protect Spanish interests in Equatorial Guinea. This has not always been possible, resulting in some highly publicised diplomatic spats. There was controversy in November 2013 when the Spanish national football team was criticised by the Equatoguinean opposition in exile for playing a friendly in Malabo. In both April and August 2014, the government of

Equatorial Guinea reacted angrily to criticisms regarding human rights levelled against it in Spanish parliament.

Despite these issues, Spanish businesses occupy a prominent position in the development of Equatorial Guinea, and Spanish politicians continue to try and improve relations. The 23rd AU Summit, held in Malabo in June 2014, marked the first time that a Spanish head of government had visited Equatorial Guinea since 1991. Prime Minister Mariano Rajoy was invited to speak to the 54 country representatives in support of Spain's candidature for the UN Security Council. A week later, José Luis Rodríguez Zapatero, who led the government of Spain from 2004 to 2011, also visited Malabo, in a show of strengthening relations.

Relations within Africa Relations between Equatorial Guinea and her African regional neighbours are mixed. There have been maritime boundary disputes with Nigeria, Cameroon and Gabon. The issue with Gabon over Mbañe (see *Geography*, page 3) and other lesser islets is problematic as there are thought to be hydrocarbon reserves in the waters surrounding the disputed area. However, the two governments are working to resolve the dispute amicably through international mediation. The Fang ethnic group's homeland extends southwards into Gabon as well as northwards into Cameroon, so there are trade and cultural links across these porous jungle borders. Equatorial Guinea imports some food products from Cameroon, and exports their Alba condensate crude oil for the Cameroonians to use in the Sonara Limbe Refinery. There is a strong link between Equatorial Guinea and Nigeria due to historic ties related to the cocoa industry, and trade between the two countries is growing.

In terms of regional co-operative bodies, Equatorial Guinea is a member of the Central African Economic and Monetary Union (CEMAC) and the CFA Franc Zone. In 2014, Equatorial Guinea joined the Community of Portuguese Language Countries (CPLP), based on its historic ties as a Portuguese colony, and the fact that some of its citizens speak Portuguese-based Creole languages (such as the Annobónese language). Links with Angola are strengthening, with numerous official state visits between Malabo and Luanda in 2014, as the Angolans assist with the development of the Equatoguinean security forces.

Regional relations were strained, however, by the 2014 Ebola epidemic. Although Ebola did not reach Equatorial Guinea, in August 2014 the government cancelled regional flights by its national carrier Ceiba Airlines to and from Cameroon, Nigeria, Gabon, São Tomé and Príncipe, Côte d'Ivoire, Ghana, the Republic of Congo, Benin and Togo as a preventative measure. The government also temporarily halted issuing visas for travel from West and Central African countries. These services were resumed a few months later once Ebola prevention measures had been put in place, such as medical screening at all ports of entry.

HUMAN RIGHTS The constitution of Equatorial Guinea enshrines respect for human rights as a fundamental principle of the state. Article 1 recognises political pluralism and multi-party democracy, stating that the supreme values of the state shall be unity, peace, justice, freedom and equality. Article 9 further highlights the right to free association within a democratic framework, and that political parties should not be based along ethnic or tribal lines. Article 2 guarantees elections by universal suffrage. Article 5 details the fundamental principles at the foundation of Equatoguinean society, which include: 'respect of [the] individual, his dignity, freedom and other fundamental rights.' Article 13 outlines a number of individual rights and liberties to all citizens including: respect for life, freedom of expression, gender equality, freedom of movement, residence, religion and worship, the right to a fair trial and to hear the charges brought against them, freedom of association and no arbitrary detention.

Article 8 states that it shall endeavour to respect the principles of international law and confirms its commitment to the rights and obligations that are set down by the charter of the international organisations to which it has become a member. Equatorial Guinea is a signatory of a number of human rights conventions. In particular, the Geneva Convention, Universal Declaration of Human Rights, International Covenant on Civil and Political Rights, Convention against Torture and Other Cruel, Inhuman or Degrading Treatment or Punishment, Convention on the Rights of the Child, Convention on the Elimination of all Forms of Discrimination against Women, as well as the International Covenant on Economic, Social and Cultural Rights. On 20 August 2012, Malabo hosted the ninth biennial Leon H Sullivan Foundation Summit on Human Rights, reaffirming its commitment to safeguarding human rights. In February 2014, President Obiang announced a moratorium on the death penalty nationwide, as one of the conditions to joining the CPLP.

Despite these commitments, in practice, since independence the government of Equatorial Guinea has shown little respect for the human rights of its citizens, or foreign nationals within its territory.

Since 1972, Freedom House has consistently rated Equatorial Guinea as having some of the poorest political rights and civil liberties in the world. In 2013, it ranked Equatorial Guinea alongside Eritrea, North Korea, Saudi Arabia, Somalia, Sudan, Syria, Turkmenistan, and Uzbekistan in its 'Worst of the Worst' category. Their political rights ratings are based on an evaluation of three sub-categories: electoral process, political pluralism and participation, and functioning of government. Civil liberties ratings are based on an evaluation of four sub-categories: freedom of expression and belief, associational and organisational rights, rule of law, and personal autonomy and individual rights. While most commentators would agree that the human rights outlook has certainly improved since the rule of President Macías, this is not a ringing endorsement of the current regime, considering that Macías was a genocidal dictator who managed to kill a larger proportion of his own population than any other leader in modern history.

Freedom House are not alone in their criticism of President Obiang's human rights record. Other organisations such as Amnesty International, Human Rights Watch, the US State Department and the UN High Commissioner for Human Rights have all denounced Equatorial Guinea for a swathe of human rights violations. The 2013 US State Department Country Report on Human Rights Practices in Equatorial Guinea noted the following:

The most significant human rights abuses in the country were disregard for the rule of law and due process, including police use of torture and excessive force; denial of freedom of speech, press, assembly, and association; and widespread official corruption. Other human rights abuses included: inability of citizens to change their government; arbitrary and unlawful killings; abuse of detainees and prisoners; and poor conditions in prisons and detention facilities. Arbitrary arrest and detention, incommunicado detention, harassment and deportation of foreign residents without due process, and lack of judicial independence were problems.

The government restricted the right to privacy, freedom of movement, and political party activity. Restrictions on domestic and international nongovernmental organization (NGO) activity, violence and discrimination against women and children, and trafficking in persons occurred. Societal discrimination against persons with disabilities; ethnic minorities and immigrants; the lesbian, gay, bisexual and transgender (LGBT) community; and persons with HIV/AIDS was a problem. Labor rights were restricted. The government did not take steps to prosecute or punish officials who committed abuses, whether in the security forces or elsewhere in the government, and impunity was a serious problem.

These violations have not been limited to Equatoguinean citizens. Famous examples include the torture and lack of medical care for detainees from the 2004 Wonga coup case and the shooting of Chinese workers on strike in Mongomo in 2008. More recently, Italian businessman Roberto Berardi has been arbitrarily detained in a Bata prison since February 2013 after a dispute with his business parter, Teodorín Obiang, over a suspicious bank transfer from one of their joint ventures. He alleges mistreatment and torture during his detention, and was not released following the completion of his 28-month prison sentence in May 2015. Likewise, South African businessman Daniel Janse van Rensburg was held in Black Beach prison from December 2013 until March 2014 following a contractual dispute. In January 2014, the Africa editor of the *Financial Times* was arrested in Malabo and had his computer equipment confiscated before being deported.

ECONOMY

Before the end of Spanish rule in 1968, the main focus of the economy was cocoa and coffee exports, up to 80% of which were sent back to the Spanish metropole. There was also timber, mainly in the form of okoumé, exported from Río Muni. Per capita exports were some of the highest in Africa, standing at US$332 per head in 1962. Areas that had not seen Spanish investment, such as Annobón or the inland Río Muni region, continued to rely on subsistence fishing and farming respectively.

Citizens of the newly independent Equatorial Guinea were relatively wealthy by African standards, with a per capita income of US$170, and high literacy thanks to 90% school attendance. The economy had also grown at a consistent 7.56% per year in the four years before the Spanish left. This situation was quickly reversed under the misrule of President Macías, with the departure of both skilled Spanish labour and Nigerian contract labourers. Likewise, much of the local working age population fled the country, was imprisoned or was killed. By the time the coup took place in 1979 Equatorial Guinea was one of the poorest countries not only in Africa, but in the world.

The discovery of oil completely changed this situation in only a generation. Today, Equatorial Guinea is the third largest oil producer in sub-Saharan Africa after Nigeria and Angola, and the second largest gas producer. These abundant offshore oil and gas reserves account for around 90% of the GDP and almost all of the country's export earnings. Farming, fishing and forestry also contribute a small share.

Accurate economic statistics on Equatorial Guinea are difficult to obtain due to the secrecy surrounding state enterprises and inconsistent monitoring by international financial institutions. However, in terms of GDP per capita, the citizens of Equatorial Guinea today are some of the richest in Africa. The economy of Equatorial Guinea was valued at US$15.57 billion in 2013, while the population was estimated to be just over 750,000. Using these figures, the IMF ranked Equatoguineans above both Portugal and Poland in terms of each citizen's average annual income. The World Bank went further, ranking the country among the 30 richest nations (per capita) on the planet, with an income exceeding citizens of South Korea, Israel and Spain, and just below New Zealand and Italy. Real GDP growth between 1995 (when oil was discovered) and 2008 (before the Global Financial Crisis struck) averaged an incredible 23% per year. Equatoguineans went from earning an average of US$321 per capita in 1995 to US$23,432 in 2008.

The Global Financial Crisis had a serious impact on the oil-dominated economy of Equatorial Guinea, immediately leading to a negative growth rate in 2009 of –8%. Equatorial Guinea's economy again went into recession in 2013, with growth estimated at –1.4% GDP with further negative forecasts for 2014 and 2015. This was the result of a change in oil prices, as well as an overall reduction in gas and oil production as the Zafiro oilfield gradually runs dry (production peaked in 2004) and newer finds fail to make up for the shortfall.

In a bid to diversify the economy, 2013 saw the second phase of the Horizon2020 plan (also known as the PNDES or the Plan Nacional de Desarrollo Económico y Social) rolled out. Five priority sectors of the economy were identified for development: tourism, fisheries, agriculture and livestock farming, petrochemicals and mining, and financial services.

Anyone who visits Equatorial Guinea will be struck by the pace of construction, with brand new hotels, office blocks and public works springing up all over the place. It is clear that oil wealth is leading to rapid changes within the country. However, the economic windfall has not been distributed evenly. Equatorial Guinea ranked 144th out of 187 countries in the UN Human Development Index ranking in 2013. Life expectancy is a very low 54 years. Poverty is widespread, with estimates ranging from 60% to 75% of the population living below the poverty threshold. The World Bank also ranked them 166th of 189 countries in their Ease of Doing Business Index, which judges how conducive the regulatory environment is for doing business. In short, while a small elite has profited greatly from the oil boom, this windfall is not being effectively distributed or invested in long-term growth.

GOVERNMENTAL CORRUPTION Many international organisations have accused the leadership in Equatorial Guinea of endemic corruption. Equatorial Guinea also ranked 163rd of 175 surveyed nations on Transparency International's Corruption Perceptions Index in 2013, which ranks countries based on how corrupt their public sector is perceived to be. The perceived levels of corruption in Equatorial Guinea are worse than in Zimbabwe, Venezuela and Myanmar.

The Riggs Bank scandal in July 2004 (page 31) led a US Senate investigation to conclude that:

> Riggs Bank serviced the E.G. accounts with little or no attention to the bank's anti-money laundering obligations, turned a blind eye to evidence suggesting the bank was handling the proceeds of foreign corruption, and allowed numerous suspicious transactions to take place without notifying law enforcement.

A 2009 leaked US embassy cable from Malabo noted that: 'Suddenly rich, the country's over-reliance on now-defunct Riggs Bank, a lack of conflict-of-interest rules and a legacy of moonlighting further complicate EG's record.' It went on to discuss the minister of justice running his own law firm, as well as the minister of transportation being a director of the parastatal airline. More recently, there have been legal cases in both France and the USA against Teodorín, eldest son of the president, who is both the minister of forestry and owner of a timber company operating in Río Muni (pages 46–7).

In an October 2012 interview on CNN, President Obiang commented on these corruption allegations and stated:

> The government has actually established laws that prohibit corruption and I believe that in Equatorial Guinea we are very serious about prosecuting anyone involved in corruption. So, no, it's not a problem in Equatorial Guinea.

He also responded to accusations of corruption against his son due to suspicions about his wealth:

> He did not achieve all this as a minister. He was a businessman before he became a minister. He has his own businesses in Equatorial Guinea. And he has some companies in Malaysia as well. He has his personal finances that he manages, but there are no signs, or any proof that he had actually embezzled any in government property or government money.

These denials were repeated in a December 2012 interview with the BBC, in which the president emphasised that his family 'is not involved with oil resources. We have genuine management here, the oil revenues are managed through commissions'.

Those wishing to do business in Equatorial Guinea should be aware that foreigners entering into disputes with local business partners have been detained in the country, and even pulled off planes at Malabo airport, until the problems have been resolved (page 43).

NATURAL RESOURCES
Oil and gas
Oil The waters around Equatorial Guinea were known to contain oil even before independence. Exploration rights for both the shelf off Río Muni and the shelf around Bioko were offered for international tender in 1965, with Spanish Gulf Oil and Mobil exploring without success.

In 1981, a consortium of Elf Aquitaine and the Gabonese state oil company Petrogab began prospecting for oil around Corisco Bay. However, disputes between Equatorial Guinea and Gabon over ownership of the small islands of Mbañe, Cocotiers and Conga in this area have made it impossible for maritime boundaries to be drawn up, so the oil in this region has yet to be fully exploited (although joint exploration was ongoing as late as 2004). Until this dispute is resolved, the current focus for Equatoguinean oil extraction is around the island of Bioko.

In 1984, following four years of exploration, GEPSA recorded its first undisputed hydrocarbon discovery with the Alba field, located 32km northwest of Bioko island. This offshore field came online in 1991, with liquified natural gas (LNG) being produced from 1997.

In March 1995, ExxonMobil and Ocean Energy discovered what is now known as the Zafiro field complex, located around 68km northwest of Bioko, adjacent to the Nigerian international border. This area was exploited immediately and was the main driver behind the massive economic expansion of the following years, producing up to 100,000 barrels of oil per day.

Additional discoveries were made near Zafiro and included the Serpentina, Jade, Amatista, Topacio and Rubi fields. In 1999, La Ceiba deepwater field was discovered 35km offshore, with reserves estimated at between 300 and 500 million barrels. Okoumé field was discovered in June 2001 near the Ceiba field, and went online

No discussion on corruption in Equatorial Guinea would be complete without mentioning President Obiang's eldest son, Teodoro Nguema Obiang Mangue (nicknamed Teodorín). Teodorín was educated privately in France before finishing his studies in California. Returning home to go into politics, he took up the position of foreign minister, then minister of forestry and agriculture in 1997, with an official salary of US$6,799 per month (around US$80,000 per year). In May 2012, he was promoted to second vice president of Equatorial Guinea by his father.

Teodorín is famous for his extravagant lifestyle and the controversies surrounding the source of his wealth, which have made media headlines in the past few years. In 2004, Teodorín purchased a flat on Clifton Fourth Beach in Cape Town for 23.5 million rand. He also bought a property in Constantia for 26 million rand. In 2006, after a commercial dispute with a South African company relating to the construction of an airport on Annobón, Teodorín's South African property assets were seized in relation to debts. During this case, in a sworn affidavit filed with the South African court, Teodorín attempted to explain how he could afford such expensive properties on his public servant salary:

> Cabinet Ministers and public servants in Equatorial Guinea are by law allowed to owe [sic] companies that, in consortium with a foreign company, can bid for government contracts and should the company be successful, then what percentage of the total cost of the contract the company gets, will depend on the terms negotiated between the parties. But, in any event, it means that a cabinet minister ends up with a sizeable part of the contract price in his bank account.

Teodorín allegedly supplemented this income from government contracts by charging illegal rents to international timber companies for access to logging concessions. US prosecutors state that he was able to abuse his position as minister of forestry to charge fees to timber companies looking to export wood using the port of Bata. In some cases, exporters claim he was personally paid US$27 per log, sometimes in suitcases full of cash. Companies who refused to pay faced expensive delays in exporting their products, having their equipment confiscated or were even sometimes banned from operating in the country. Such revelations help to explain how despite a relatively modest official income, the US Department of Justice believes that Teodorín managed to spend US$315 million between 2004 and 2011, leading an extravagant international lifestyle.

Until 2012 Teodorín owned a five-storey town house at 42 Avenue Foch, in the exclusive 16th *arrondissement* of Paris, with an estimated value of between €100 and €150 million. There he kept his collection of luxury cars, which included two Bugatti Veyrons, a 2007 Maserati MC 12, a 2010 Ferrari 599 GTO, a Rolls Royce Phantom, two Bentleys, a Mercedes Maybach 62 and a Porsche Carrera 980 GT. The collection was valued at €3.21 million. The walls of his home were filled with artworks by Chagall, Degas, Matisse, Monet, Renoir and Toulouse-Lautrec, valued at over US$100 million.

To celebrate the Christmas and New Year period in 2005, Teodorín paid over US$1 million to rent a luxury yacht in St Barthelemy for 11 days. In June 2006, he purchased a US$30 million mansion at 3620 Sweetwater Mesa Road, Malibu, which at the time was the sixth most expensive sale in the USA that year. His neighbours included Britney Spears and Mel Gibson. That same year he also purchased a US$38.5 million Gulfstream V jet.

In 2008, Teodorín purchased a US$15 million home in São Paolo, Brazil. A year later, he commissioned Germany's Kusch Yachts to draw up designs for a US$380 million super yacht codenamed 'Zen', although at the time of writing construction had not yet started. This is probably for the best, as in autumn 2009, Teodorín managed to capsize one of his Nor-Tech 5000 speedboats on a trip to Maui, leading to a salvage bill of US$400,000.

From June 2010 to June 2011 Teodorín went on a Michael Jackson memorabilia spending spree, paying US$275,000 for a glove worn on the *Bad* tour, US$140,000 for a jacket and shirt, and US$245,000 for a basketball signed by Michael Jackson and Michael Jordan.

This extravagant lifestyle has been the focus of other legal cases, beyond the 2006 Cape Town trial. In March 2007, the financial crimes organisation SHERPA, in association with Survie and the Fédération des Congolais de la Diaspora filed a complaint with the public prosecutor in Paris. In this complaint, they alleged that the ruling families of Angola, Burkina Faso, Republic of Congo, Equatorial Guinea and Gabon owned considerable assets on French soil that could not have been obtained through legitimate business activities and their official salaries. They must therefore be the proceeds of embezzlement. Transparency International France became involved in the case a few years later.

These allegations caused a storm of political controversy when they were first released, with the French Supreme Court eventually becoming involved. It appears now that Teodorín's playboy lifestyle is no longer welcome in France. His Paris mansion was raided in February and September 2011 by French authorities, with numerous items confiscated as embezzled public funds and auctioned. That same year on the other side of the Atlantic, the US Department of Justice filed civil forfeiture complaints against around US$70.8 million of Teodorín's assets, which the government alleged were the proceeds of foreign corrupt practices and money laundering.

Two weeks after the September raids, President Obiang appointed his son Permanent Assistant Delegate to UNESCO, and designated his Paris mansion part of the Equatoguinean embassy in Paris. When, in July 2012, the Paris property was seized and France issued an arrest warrant for Teodorín on charges of money laundering, the Equatoguinean authorities argued that both Teodorín and the space should enjoy diplomatic immunity, and that the raids and confiscations were therefore illegal under international law. Equatorial Guinea took their case to the International Court of Justice in September 2012, and it is still ongoing.

With regards to the US corruption case, in July 2014 federal prosecutors stated that they had reached a tentative deal to settle the matter out of court, and in October Teodorín was asked to pay US$30 million to settle the case. Commenting on the settlement, Assistant Attorney General Caldwell noted:

Through relentless embezzlement and extortion, Vice President Nguema Obiang shamelessly looted his government and shook down businesses in his country to support his lavish lifestyle, while many of his fellow citizens lived in extreme poverty... This settlement forces Nguema Obiang to relinquish assets worth an estimated US$30 million, and prevents Nguema Obiang from hiding other stolen money in the United States'

Teodorín's official response to these allegations can be found on his Vice Presidential webpage: http://equatorialguineavp.com/press/.

in December 2006. Aseng oilfield was discovered off Bioko in 2007 and brought online in November 2011. It has an estimated yield of 120 million barrels. The Alen field was discovered in 2005 and came online in 2013.

Oil production hit a peak of 376,000 barrels per day in 2005 and has since declined, with six oilfields (Alba, Zafiro, Ceiba, Okoumé, Jade and Serpentina) having matured (already passed peak output) and not enough new finds being brought online to make up the shortfall. Oil production in 2013 was around 270,000 barrels per day, with the Republic of Congo now likely to leapfrog Equatorial Guinea into third place on the list of sub-Saharan Africa's top oil producers by 2017. The country has 1.1 billion barrels of proven oil reserves, meaning around ten years' production at the current rates before the oil runs out. These reserves are managed by the national oil company GEPetrol.

In the future, there are plans to build a new petrochemicals complex at Riaba, along with a refinery in Mbini in partnership with Sinopec (China Petroleum & Chemical Corporation). This will have the capacity to refine 22,000 barrels of oil per day. Part of the Horizon2020 plan is to diversify the economy away from oil export dependence. However, these abundant offshore oil and gas reserves account for around 90% of the country's GDP and almost all export earnings, so it appears that in the short term Equatorial Guinea will remain highly dependent on its oil. This has recently caused serious financial difficulties for the Equatoguinean state, as the global price of oil more than halved between June 2014 and January 2015.

Gas Proven natural gas reserves in Equatorial Guinea were 1.3 trillion cubic feet as of January 2013. Most of these are found in the Alba gas field. The gas reserves are managed by state gas company, Sonagas. Most of the gas today is exported to Asia, with South Korea and Japan consuming the bulk of it.

In 2004, British BG Group signed up to buy all of Equatorial Guinea's LNG for the next 17 years (3.4 million tonnes until 2024) at a fixed discount, pegged to costs in the US market (as this was where it was all intended to end up). Owing to fluctuations in the LNG markets since, BG Group have been able to get the LNG at very low prices, then divert it all to Asia where prices are much higher, making huge profits, with no legal obligation to share them with the Equatoguinean government. There is also no renegotiation clause in the contract, which serves as a warning to other potential African gas exporters to be wary of the long-term arrangements they enter into. In 2009, after public objections from the deputy energy minister, BG Group agreed to pay 12.5% of their profits or US$20 million (whichever was higher) each quarter, made from selling the LNG in Asia.

In 2007, a liquefied natural gas terminal was built at Punta Europa, near Malabo by Marathon Oil and its partners. This is capable of producing 3.4 million metric tonnes of LNG per year, with an expansion of the terminal planned for 2016, which would increase capacity by 4.4 million metric tonnes.

Minerals In pre-colonial times there were accounts of Equatorial Guinea producing both gold and iron. However, mining was never really pursued under Spanish rule.

After independence, both Soviet and French geological teams conducted systematic geological surveys in the 1970s and 80s, finding little to arouse international interest. More recently, groups such as GEMSA (a Spanish–Equatoguinean joint venture), UMCEG (a US company), and Exploration Consultants Limited (a British company) have explored the country looking for bauxite, columbo-tantalite (known as Coltan, used in the manufacture of electronic goods), diamonds, gold, iron ore and molybdenite (used in steel manufacture). The focus of these efforts has been in Río Muni, specifically around Coro, Mongomo and Aconibe, where artisanal miners have been successfully panning for gold in the rivers for many years. Historical records indicate that 2.3 tonnes of gold were found in this area in the mid 1970s. In 2006, the US Geological Survey reported that miners had recovered around 200kg of gold that year.

Beginning in November 2010, Brilliant Resources Inc (a Canadian company) in conjunction with Fugro Airborne Services (a Dutch company), carried out a US$10 million airborne mega survey of the whole of Río Muni. In return for funding and completing this survey, Brilliant Resources were promised their pick of 15% of the Río Muni land area for exclusive mining exploration concessions by the government of Equatorial Guinea. A final report was delivered two years later, but no mining has taken place due to a dispute with the government, which in June 2014 was sent for arbitration at the International Chamber of Commerce.

In Nsork, in the far southeast of Río Muni, there are hopes that diamonds may be discovered, as they have been 50km over the border in Mitzic, Gabon, but commercial diamond mining has not been undertaken yet.

Timber Forests cover around 79% of inland Río Muni and its offshore islands. Wood had traditionally been a profitable export under Spanish rule, but was never as dominant as cocoa exports. The majority of logs harvested went straight back to metropolitan Spain. In 1968, over 360,000m³ of timber were felled in Río Muni and exported to Europe. Under the misrule of Macías, by the late 1970s the timber export industry had collapsed and only 6,000m³ of timber a year was exported.

Under President Obiang, in the years before the discovery of oil, timber soon came to occupy a more important role in the economy than both coffee and cocoa, especially after the collapse of cocoa prices between 1985 and 1991.

Timber became, and still is, Equatorial Guinea's main export after hydrocarbons, accounting for an average of 12.4% of export earnings between 1996 and 1999.

Wood exports reached a record peak of 789,000m³ in 1999, although they have declined since then. Considering that the annual allowable cut for all species has been set at 450,000m³ since the mid 1990s, many environmental groups are concerned that unsustainable logging practices will have long-term adverse effects on the country, especially as the vast majority of the country's population rely directly on the forest for food, fuel, building materials and medicines.

Up until 1992, 85% of Equatorial Guinea's wood exports went to the European Union, with Spain getting the lion's share. The situation is a little different today, with approximately 70% of Equatorial Guinea's timber exported to China, making Equatorial Guinea one of China's top five suppliers in Africa, along with Gabon, Cameroon, Mozambique and the Republic of Congo. Much of this wood is okoumé (*Aucoumea klaineana*), used particularly in the manufacture of plywood.

Management of Equatorial Guinea's forests is the responsibility of the Minister of Agriculture and Forests, currently Francisco Mba Olo Bahamonde. Prior to his May 2012 appointment as second vice president, it was the responsibility of President Obiang's son Teodorín, who was simultaneously owner of at least two construction and timber companies such as Grupo Sofona and Somagui. He has also been linked to the largest logging company operating in the country: Shimmer International, which is a subsidiary of Malaysian logging conglomerate Rimbunan Hijau.

Some positive steps have been taken recently to try and protect Equatorial Guinea's forests, through collaboration with groups such as the World Resources

1

Institute and the Bioko Diversity Protection Program, as well as the implementation of environmental legislation (for more information, see *Flora*, page 6).

However, whether these policy initiatives have translated into effective protection of the forests of Equatorial Guinea is less clear. According to US Department of Justice information, logging companies were able to pay bribes to avoid following any environmental regulations, sometimes directly to former minister Teodorín, and there is minimal oversight or governance over logging activity. Total wood export figures have also consistently been over the internal legal limit of 450,000m³ per year, which itself is well above the 400,000m³ recommended by environmental agencies as being a maximum sustainable harvest.

AGRICULTURE Agriculture represents only 1.1% of the total GDP of Equatorial Guinea, yet it is the main economic activity of around three quarters of the population. Equatoguineans grow plantains, bananas, sweet potatoes, cassava, yams, rice, palm oil nuts and coconuts, many in a subsistence capacity, although some items (such as bananas) are exported in large numbers.

Cocoa Cocoa was a key element in the early development of Equatorial Guinea. It is possible that the Spanish unsuccessfully tried to introduce cocoa to Fernando Pó as early as 1788. In 1822, cocoa seeds were introduced to São Tomé from Brazil by the Portuguese. Seeing their success, they were then successfully transplanted to Fernando Pó in 1854. The first major commercial cocoa producer was Francisco Romera, a naval officer with experience in Cuba. Successful palm oil traders soon shifted their focus to this new crop, with its promise of greater returns. In 1889, only 474kg of cocoa was produced on the island. This reached over 1.4 million kilos by 1899, and doubled over the next ten years. By 1910, Spain's colonial cocoa quota alone was 2,000 tonnes per year.

While the industry was affected by both the *Evening Standard* scandal of 1908 (page 19) and the damning League of Nations Christy Report of 1930, it continued to be a vital part of the Spanish Guinean economy right up until independence. In 1968, Equatorial Guinea was still exporting 36,161 tonnes of cocoa, and the product had a reputation for being high quality.

Under President Macías, a once thriving industry collapsed almost immediately. Production fell to less than 20,000 tonnes at the beginning of the 1970s, then to around 7,000 tonnes by 1976 once all the Nigerian labourers had fled Macías's brutal regime. Another issue to bear in mind is the reduction in the quality of the cocoa beans that were being exported, due to poorer farming practices and a lack of access to imported pesticides.

Equatoguinean cocoa needs to be artificially dried on wood-fuelled dryers due to rains right after the major harvest, which adds to the production costs and puts it at a disadvantage relative to other cocoa producing areas. The industry was never able to recover after Macías, even with a change of leadership, and between 1985 and 1991 there was a collapse in world cocoa prices, with a 68% drop in real terms. The Equatoguinean cocoa industry had an output of only 4,800 tonnes in 2000, 3,000 tonnes in 2006 and 890 tonnes in 2011. Cultivation occurs only on a small scale today, and it is difficult to get hold of locally grown cocoa products without going directly to the plantations.

Coffee Small amounts of coffee are grown in the north of Río Muni, by the border with Cameroon. On independence in 1968 coffee production stood at 7,664 tonnes. As with cocoa, coffee exports virtually disappeared under Macías, with a collapse to under 500 tonnes by 1978. There has been a slow recovery under President Obiang, from a low of 200 tonnes in 1996 up to 4,900 tonnes in 2011.

PEOPLE

Finding reliable statistical information on Equatorial Guinea is difficult, and demographics are no exception. A 2002 census estimated the population at 1,015,000; however, domestic opposition figures claimed that the government had inflated these figures in anticipation of the presidential election that December. The aim is for another census to occur around 2017, but in the meantime observers must rely on other international bodies to estimate the total number of Equatoguineans. The World Bank put the 2013 figure at 757,000, while the *CIA World Factbook* estimated it to be 722,254 in July 2014, and the official website of the Equatoguinean government states that it is a suspiciously round 1,014,999.

The population is not split evenly between the mainland and the islands, with around three-quarters of Equatoguineans residing in Río Muni. The largest city in the country is Bata, with just under 175,000 official inhabitants, closely followed by Malabo with around 156,000 people. The whole island of Annobón has only around 5,000 inhabitants, while some smaller islands and islets remain uninhabited. Population density is a low 27 people per square kilometre, with particular concentrations on the north of Bioko island, the north of Annobón, the coast of Río Muni and around the provincial capitals.

UN-Habitat data suggests that urbanisation in Equatorial Guinea actually decreased between 2001 and 2010, with a slight majority of Equatoguineans living in rural rather than an urban environment. Of those that do live in an urban environment, as many as 60% are thought to live in slums. Equatorial Guinea has a very young population, with 38.9% of citizens under the age of 14.

The majority of citizens of Equatorial Guinea are of **Bantu** origin. Around 80% of Equatoguineans are from the **Fang** ethnic group, and they live chiefly in Río Muni. The **Bubi** are the next largest group, and were originally the sole occupiers of Bioko island. They now make up only around 6.5% of the population, following successive waves of violent persecution under colonialism and then President Macías. Other smaller ethnic groups include the **Ndowe** (or Playeros) of coastal Río Muni, the **Fernandino** peoples concentrated in Malabo and Luba on Bioko, the **Krio** on Bioko and the **Bissio** people of coastal Río Muni. The **Annobón** islanders, with their distinct language and history, are considered a minority ethnic group and make up around 0.5% of the total population. Smaller still, groups of **Bakola-Bagyeli Pygmies** (around 200) are known to reside in the forests of Río Muni, in the north of the country, straddling the River Ntem on the border with Cameroon. The Camp River Delta in the north of Río Muni is also home to small groups descended from Igbo tribes.

LANGUAGE

The official administrative and educational language of Equatorial Guinea is Spanish, with French as a second language. Since 2007, the government has been discussing making Portuguese a third official language, and this was one of the conditions for Equatorial Guinea's entry into the CPLP in 2014, although very few Equatoguineans actually speak Portuguese.

Article 4 of the Fundamental Principles of State in the Equatoguinean constitution states that 'Aboriginal languages shall be recognized as an integral part of... national culture.' Given the diversity of the nation's minority groups, there are a wide variety of non-European languages spoken. The most widespread is **Fang**, with the least common probably the **Bakola-Bagyeli Pygmy** language, which is spoken by only around 200 people in Equatorial Guinea (although more in Cameroon). Other languages include: **Basek Seki** from coastal Río Muni, the **Fá d'Ambô-Portuguese Creole** of Annobón, **Bube**, **Benga**, **Fernando Pó Creole** (Pichinglis), **Kombe**, **Balengue**, **Bissio** (the local dialect of Kwasio), and **Yasa**.

In contrast to other West and Central African nations, Equatorial Guinea boasts a high proportion of proficient metropolitan language-speakers (in this case **Spanish**) thanks to the influence of the Spanish educational system before independence. Some degree of Spanish is spoken by around 90% of people on Bioko, and between 60% and 70% of the inland inhabitants of Río Muni. The inhabitants of Annobón are also proficient in Spanish, although it is rarely used in daily communication. It is of course possible to encounter Equatoguineans who have no proficiency in Spanish, usually in isolated rural communities on the mainland.

Although spoken with a slightly different accent from European Spanish, linguistics professor John Lipski notes that Equatoguinean Spanish 'shares enough internal coherence to be considered a legitimate sub-dialect of world Spanish', as opposed to being a form of Creole or Afro-Hispanic language. While many Equatoguineans speak Spanish perfectly, you may notice some grammatical differences from less-fluent speakers including:

- Frequent use of subject pronoun *usted* instead of *tú*, eg: *usted comes*.
- Common prepositions such as *en*, *de* and *a* are either left out or used interchangeably, eg: *Voy en Malabo*.
- Subject and verb sometimes do not agree, with the third person singular often used as a default option regardless of who you are talking about, eg: *yo tiene* instead of *yo tengo*.

French was made compulsory in the national curriculum in 1988. There are around 100,000 Equatoguineans who can speak French, mainly those who fled to Cameroon or Gabon during the Macías years, or those travelling and trading with neighbouring Cameroon and Gabon. Since 1989, Equatorial Guinea has been a member of Organisation internationale de la Francophonie, which is understandable given that it is surrounded by French-speaking states.

English is not widely understood, even in the capital city.

RELIGION

An estimated 93% of Equatoguineans identify themselves as Christian. Of this group, 6% identify themselves as Protestant, and 83% as Catholic. Only 5% of the population are believed to practise indigenous religious beliefs exclusively. Muslims currently make up less than 1% of the population, although their numbers are increasing due to immigration from the Middle East (especially Lebanon) and West Africa.

Religious freedom and freedom of worship are protected in the Equatoguinean constitution under Article 13. A 1992 presidential decree required that all religious groups be registered and approved before practising, and also noted that the Reformed Church of Equatorial Guinea and the Roman Catholic Church would be given official preference by the state. In practice, this means an exemption for Church officials on airport taxes, and the inclusion of Catholic masses in state ceremonial functions. Religious persecution does not seem to be a problem, and citizens are generally free to engage in their religion without interference from the government.

EDUCATION

During Spanish rule, many Equatoguineans received their education through the mission schools of various Western Christian denominations, first established in the early 19th century. In the 1840s, American missionaries such as William Walker recorded their work with the Fang in Bata for the American Board of Commissioners for Foreign Missions. Likewise, the Spanish Catholic Church was instrumental in spreading both Catholicism and the European education system throughout Spanish Guinea. Many of the early independence leaders, such as Acacio Mañé Elah, one of the key founders of the CNLGE and MONALIGE movements, received an education at Catholic mission schools in Río Muni. Investment in education was high in the final years of Spanish rule, with school attendance rates topping 90%. Upon independence, Equatorial Guinea found itself with some of the highest literacy rates in Africa.

Once elected president, Macías viewed the Roman Catholic Church as a rival power structure and an instrument of Spanish imperialism. He soon closed all Catholic schools and then in 1978 made all Catholic Church activities illegal. Literacy and education suffered severely as a result.

Under President Obiang there has been increased investment in education. Education is free in Equatorial Guinea and compulsory until the age of 14. According to UNICEF, Equatorial Guinea now boasts a 94% literacy rate, which is one of the highest in sub-Saharan Africa. The government notes that since 1979 over 500,000 students have received scholarships to study at universities, as well as to take part in professional and technical training programmes outside the country.

One of the key aims of the Horizon2020 plan is to focus on the education sector. The Program for Education Development of Equatorial Guinea (PRODEGE) features a US$50 million initiative jointly funded by President Obiang and Hess Corporation (an American oil company). This ten-year plan was implemented in 2009 to improve the education of all students in the country. Currently in the second five-year phase (2014–19), they are focusing on education at the junior secondary level, with initiatives being run across the country by the Ministry of Education and FHI360, an education-focused NGO. A new schools plan called Patria Mia has been implemented which encourages more student–teacher interaction, and four new teacher training centres were built in 2010 and 2011.

While these initiatives are encouraging, there are still many areas of improvement in the field of education. A key issue is funding. Figures for total public sector expenditure on education as a percentage of GDP in Equatorial Guinea are difficult to obtain. The World Bank noted in 2008 that the figure stood at 4%, far lower than the sub-Saharan African average of 16.1%. The IMF estimated in 2009 that education accounted for only 1% of all capital expenditure in 2011, substantially below other high-income countries, even those with lower per capita GDP. As part of the National Public Investment Plan 2013–2016, the government committed to investing 47,338 million CFA in education over a three-year period, which represents around 1.8% of government income for 2014. Although investment in education is highlighted as a priority in the Horizon2020 vision, in practice other sectors appear to have received more focus.

UNESCO have highlighted further issues, including inadequate facilities, a high student-to-teacher ratio, low teacher quality and poor nutrition. Around 45% of students on average drop out of primary school and only around 22% receive a secondary education. There is also a disproportionate focus in the education budget on higher education: 50 times more is spent on higher education than on primary education, which is a problem considering that the vast majority of Equatoguineans never access secondary education. Much of this investment has gone on scholarships to study abroad. Although numerous scholarships have been given out, opposition activists and a US Senate sub-committee have noted that access to them can be highly politicised. They are often exclusively disbursed to those connected to the ruling elite, with oil companies such as Hess Corporation and Marathon Oil picking up the tab. Walter International Inc even paid at least US$50,000 for the son of the president, Teodorín, to study at Pepperdine University in Malibu, California.

Many children of the political elite go abroad to study, mainly in Spain and France, but there are tertiary education opportunities in Equatorial Guinea. The main university is the National University of Equatorial Guinea (UNGE) based in Malabo. Medical training occurs at the National Institute for Health in Bata. There is also the National Centre for Proficiency in Teaching (CENAFOD), the Santa Isabel and Bata Institutes for Teachers' Training, the National Institute for Public Administration (ENAP), and the National Institute for Agriculture (ENAM). The Spanish National University of Distance Education (UNED), modelled on the United Kingdom's Open University, has international centres in Bata and Malabo. This institution allows Equatoguineans to study for the same qualifications that are available at metropolitan Spanish universities. Tertiary education also occurs at the Colegio Nacional Enrique Nvó Okenve, which has two campuses: one in Malabo and one in Bata.

Construction of a new UNGE campus began in early 2014 in Basupu, 3km outside Malabo, and is due for completion soon. In 2015, the Ministry of Education also plans to inaugurate the first American University of Central Africa in collaboration with Boston University, in the new city of Oyala in central Río Muni. The university will have capacity for 8,000 students and will feature seven different faculties.

Equatorial Guinea lacks a certified English-language international school, which is surprising considering the large Western expatriate community present in the country. The Nigeria–Equatorial Guinea International School (NEGIS) offers English-language schooling, although not following an international curriculum. The Colegio Español de Malabo offers a Spanish curriculum secondary education. There is also a French school – Lycée français Le Concorde, which follows the French curriculum – and a Turkish International College in Malabo. In Bata there is a French school called Mlf Bouygues and the Colegio Español de Bata.

Colegio Español de Bata Salesian Missionary buildings, just to the south of the old stadium (Estadio La Libertad); ☎ 333 082 610; e espacol@ intnet.gq. This is a large primary & secondary school offering a full primary & secondary education in the Spanish system, with official support from the Spanish government.
Colegio Español de Malabo Calle José Sí Esono, s/n (barrio Elá-Nguema), Malabo; ☎ 333 092 031. Found to the eastern side of the cemetery, this school offers a full primary & secondary education in the Spanish system, with official support from the Spanish government.

Lycée français Le Concorde BP 134 Parques de Africa, Malabo; ☎ 333 092 912, 333 091 416; e ecolefrance-malabo@guineanet.net; http:// www.ecolefrancaisedemalabo.org. This is a French government-run school with around 400 students. One of the best educational facilities in the country.
Mlf Bouygues – SOGEA SATOM Maison Leopold Sedar Senghor, Paseo Marítimo 5, Bata; m 222 609 203; e direction.bata@mlfmonde. org, college.bata@mlfmonde.org; https://sites. google.com/a/mlfmonde.org/ecole-bouygues-sogea-satom--bata/. Created in 2011, this small

school has around 90 pupils aged between 3 & 15.

NEGIS Malabo Calle de Hipólito Micha Eworo; e http://negismalabo.com. Just opposite the cemetery, this primary & secondary school offers an English-language education based around the Nigerian system. After a recent agreement with their host government, NEGIS now also teach Equatoguinean history to all their students.

Turkish International College Ela Nguema Highway, Malabo. Found to the south of the city centre, off the highway linking the airport to Sipopo, this school offers an education in the Turkish system for children aged 3 to 12.

CULTURE

LITERATURE The canon of Equatoguinean literature from Spanish rule and the early years of independence is scarce. Censorship both at home and under General Franco's regime in Spain meant that most literary work was produced underground and not widely disseminated. We thus see a dearth of anti-colonial literature from this small former Spanish colony. Macías's policy of executing anyone deemed to be an intellectual also discouraged the domestic literary scene from growing upon independence, apart from among the exiled diaspora.

Many of the educated elite under Spanish rule contributed to early written works. Some of these, such as Bubi poet **Juan Chema Mijero**, wrote positively of the Spanish colonial experience, whereas others, such as **Donato Ndongo-Bidyogo Makina**, voiced criticism of the inherent racism of the system.

The first notable Equatoguinean novel published in Spanish was *Cuando los combes luchaban* by **Leoncio Evita Enoy**, released while the country was still under Spanish rule in 1953. It tells the story of two American Protestant missionaries working in Punta Mbode during Spanish colonial times, and their interactions with the indigenous people and a local secret society called the Bueti. In terms of the themes of colonialism and conflict between cultures, it is similar to Chinua Achebe's seminal *Things Fall Apart*, although the book did not achieve fame upon publication. In fact, it was so unsuccessful that when **Daniel Jones Mathama** published *Una lanza por el Boabí* from Barcelona in 1962, he mistakenly labelled it as the first literary work from Equatorial Guinea. This second novel has been dismissed by many academics as a simplistic defence of the Spanish colonial project. The titular Boabí is an indigenous leader on Fernando Pó, and the novel follows his life and that of his son as they interact with the Spanish imperial authorities. Towards the end of the story, the son even heads off to Spain to further his studies.

Today, there are a number of notable Equatoguinean authors with a very different view on colonialism. Their works cover many areas, but we see some uniting themes such as Hispanic heritage, the impact of dictatorship on the population, African heritage and discussions on what it means to be Equatoguinean. These foci are epitomised by the works of **Constantino Ocha'a Mve Bengobesama**, a Fang writer who died in 1991.

Raquel Ilonbé is known for a collection of poems called *Ceiba* published in Madrid in 1978. In 1981, she also published the first ever Equatoguinean children's book, called *Leyendas guineanas*, which was a collection of eight traditional tales from Fang, Ndowe and Bubi oral history.

María Nsué Angüe is famous for her 1985 debut novel *Okomo*, which tells the story of an African woman who was educated abroad and dares to break social taboos upon the death of her husband. It is critical of the subservient role African women are cast in while living in a patriarchal society. Angüe later served as minister of culture and women's minister in the government.

Francisco Zamora Loboch is a famous poet and essayist who was outspoken during the Macías years and remains active today. He has published two books: *Cómo ser negro y no morir en Aravaca* (1994), which discusses the frustrations of racism he faced in exile, and *Memoria de laberintos* (1999), also tackling the culture shock faced by Equatoguineans in Spain. Juan Carlos Bueriberi is a modern poet and political activist.

Juan Balboa Boneke was a novelist from Rebola, northern Bioko who died recently (March 2014). He was also a political writer, part of 'La generacion perdida' that lived in exile under Macías, who took up residence in Majorca. He famously mixed Bubi words with Spanish in his poems. His daughter, Concha Buika, is a very successful singer (page 59).

In the mid 1990s, a new generation of young authors began to appear on the Equatoguinean literary scene. Dubbed '**New Guinean Lyricism**' or '*Nuevo costumbrismo nacional*', much of their work focusses on the immediate realities of post-colonial Equatorial Guinea, and includes strong criticism of the political and economic management of the country. One leading representative of this movement is Juan Tomás Ávila Laurel, a playwright, novelist and poet from Annobón, who is now an editor for *El Patio*, a journal published by the Spanish government-funded Centro Cultural Hispano–Guineano and literature magazine *Atanga*. In the same vein, Jose Fernando Siale Djangany, born in Malabo in 1961, is a lawyer and writer whose work is critical of both the old colonising empires and the modern African state. Maximiliano Nkogo Esono's 2006 short novel *Nambula*, covers similar themes in discussing the formation of a new African republic. Inongo vi Makomé, although technically of Cameroonian descent, lived and studied in Equatorial Guinea and Spain, and devotes much of his time to writing about the interaction between Europe and African immigrants.

Many of these writers, whether living in Equatorial Guinea or abroad, are closely involved in the politics of their country. Cesar Mba Abogo is another of the younger generation of Equatoguinean poets who has returned home from a life in Spain. Stating in a BBC interview in 2012 that he intended to open the first bookshop in Malabo, he was recently chosen by the government to help them implement some of the Horizon2020 aims. Juan Manuel Davies Eiso is a writer who has spent much of his life in Spain and the USA, after leaving Equatorial Guinea in 1975. His most famous poetry collection is called *Abiomo*, and he is also involved with the NGO EGJustice. Dr Justo Bolekia Boleká is a scholar, a writer and a politician. Of Bubi descent, his works have been included in numerous international anthologies. He is also a champion of the MAIB – Movement for the Self-Determination of Bioko island, and is vocally opposed to the Obiang regime. Joaquin Mbomio Bacheng is a writer and human rights activist from Niefang. He was imprisoned under Macías and now lives in exile in France.

Much of the **foreign literature** on Equatorial Guinea is published exclusively in Spanish or French. For those who can read these languages, Max Liniger-Goumaz provides numerous historical overviews of the nation, such as *Guinée équatoriale, 30 ans d'État délinquant nguemiste* and *La Guinée équatoriale – un pays méconnu*. Fernando Ballano's *Españoles en África* also gives an excellent historical overview of the Spanish colonial process. Jesus Ramirez Copeiro del Villar has compiled a detailed history of Equatorial Guinea during World War II called *Objetivo Africa: Crónica de la Guinea española en la II Guerra Mundial*. For those more keen on fiction, Fernando Gamboa González's *Guinea: Más allá de la aventura* is an interesting thriller based in the country, written by an author with extensive experience of the region. Carolina Casado's book *Impressions: Dreaming in the*

Midst of Reality is based around her explorations of Monte Alen National Park. *Palmeras en la Nieve* by Luz Gabás is a very popular story about Spanish colonists living and working on a cocoa plantation in Sampaka, Bioko. This is due to be released as a big-budget film on 4 December 2015.

Finding English-language resources about the country is more difficult outside the academic realm. In 1861, Sir Richard Francis Burton, the famous Victorian adventurer, became the British Foreign Office Consul in Fernando Pó. Two years later he published *Wanderings in West Africa*, a series of books about his travels, the second of which discusses his time in Fernando Pó. For a modern English-language overview of the country, try reading the beginning sections of Adam Roberts's *The Wonga Coup*, which focusses on the 2004 coup attempt by Simon Mann (pages 38–9). Another good source of information on this coup is James Brabazon's *My Friend the Mercenary*, which recounts his time spent with Nick du Toit in the jungle during the Liberian Civil War. If you can cope with the *staccato* writing style, then Simon Mann's autobiographical account, *Cry Havoc*, is also worth a read. Brian Lett has written an excellent account of the British covert operation, Postmaster, carried out off Bioko in January 1942, and which served as an inspiration for the character of James Bond. The title is *Ian Fleming and SOE's Operation POSTMASTER: The Top Secret Story behind 007*. For a more dense, academic analysis of the interplay between Equatoguinean and Spanish society, try *Disorientations* by Susan Martin-Márquez. Lastly, World Bank economist Robert Klitgaard wrote the extremely successful *Tropical Gangsters* in 1990, about his 2½-year adventure trying to help the government of Equatorial Guinea sort out their economy. This is probably the most famous English-language book about the country, which is sad as the Equatorial Guinea depicted is very far removed from the reality of today.

For more recommended reading, see pages 223–9.

FILM The first cinema opened in Equatorial Guinea in 1904, but by the early 1990s there were none left in use. Instead, the historic Cine Marfil in Malabo was used by the government for trials against coup plotters.

Filming in Equatorial Guinea has always been a very difficult process. The Committee to Protect Journalists ranked Equatorial Guinea as the fifth most censored country in the world in 2012, and since then there have been numerous cases of film crews being detained, having equipment confiscated, and being deported from the country.

Despite this reputation, two of the aims of the Horizon2020 plan are to boost foreign investment and to expand the tourism industry, both of which require more open access to the country for journalists and film makers. Keen to change their negative image, efforts have been spearheaded by the Department of Culture and Tourism, as well as the Ministry of Information, Press and Radio to expand the film industry in Equatorial Guinea. A Motion Picture Association of Equatorial Guinea (ACIGE) was set up to 'assist foreign film producers in finding talent and locations and in navigating government requirements'.

In 2010, the Spanish cultural centres in Bata and Malabo hosted the first ever African Film Festival, which included entries from Equatoguinean film makers. In 2011, the Cine Marfil was renovated and reopened to cinema goers, the same year that an Equatoguinean documentary about the location was entered into the Córdoba Africa Film Festival (FCAT).

Between 17 and 26 April 2012, the same cultural centres organised the first ever SouthSouth Itinerant Film Festival of Equatorial Guinea (FECIGE), featuring films from Africa and Latin America. The best Equatoguinean film is awarded a 500,000CFA prize and entered into FCAT.

Building on this success, in September 2012 Malabo was used as a location for an international feature film. *Where The Road Runs Out* was directed by South African film maker Rudolf Buitendach and stars renowned Ivorian actor Isaach De Bankolé. The country has yet to produce and export its own international film using local talent.

Equatorial Guinea does have some homegrown talent, however, such as **Emilio Buale Coka**, an Equatoguinean-Spanish actor of Bubi descent, who was a member of the National Classical Theatre Company of Spain for many years. **Gustavo 'Gus' Envela, Jr** is an Equatoguinean-American better known for his exploits on the athletics track and in the political arena, but he has also had a few Hollywood cameo roles. American actress **Tasha Smith** had DNA analysis done as part of the Procter and Gamble *My Black is Beautiful* campaign, and found out that her ancestors were Bubi from Bioko. American comedian and actor **Anthony Anderson** found out the same results in 2012. Equatorial Guinea-based talent includes actor **Oscar Menejal**, who is currently trying to set up an arts centre on Annobón, and director **Bony Obama Nchama**.

Equatorial Guinea has proven a rich subject for international film makers: *The Dogs of War* is a 1980 film based upon the 1974 novel of the same name by Frederick Forsyth; *Coup!* is a 2006 BBC dramatisation of the abortive real-life attempt by Simon Mann to organise a coup to take over Equatorial Guinea in 2004; and *The Prince of Malabo* is a 2014 documentary that explores Equatorial Guinea's economic rise and the challenges it faces as seen through the eyes of Teodorín, the president's son. In December 2015, the high-budget feature film *Palmeras en la Nieve* will be released. It is based on the extremely successful novel of the same name by Luz Gabás and tells the story of Spanish colonists on a cocoa plantation in Bioko Norte.

Numerous wildlife documentaries have also been filmed in the lush jungles of Bioko, such as the 2012 film *The Drill Project*, which features the first ever broadcast images of wild Bioko island drills (*Mandrillus leucophaeus poensis*) and tells about their biology.

ART Much of the mainstream art of Equatorial Guinea is the art of the dominant Fang ethnic group. **Mask making**, a tradition that spans much of Central and West Africa, is an important part of Fang culture, with many masks designed to depict animals. Masks have a variety of uses, from celebratory to religious and funerary. Masks also play an important ceremonial role in some of the secret societies of Equatorial Guinea. Fang artworks are highly prized by collectors, with the Ngil mask from Gabon selling for US$7.5 million in a Paris auction in June 2006. This was a mask said to have inspired Pablo Picasso, and fetched the highest price ever paid for an African ethnographic piece of art.

Sculpture is also a popular medium in Fang artwork, and is just as highly prized by international collectors. A Cameroonian Fang Mabea statue sold for US$5.9 million in a sale of ethnographic art at Sotheby's in Paris in June 2014.

Leandro Mbomio Nsue, likely Equatorial Guinea's most famous artist, died in 2012. He studied in Bata and then Barcelona, living also in the USA, France and Germany at various points. He was a close friend of Pablo Picasso, and has often been labelled 'the Black Picasso' due to the similarity of his abstract style. In 1980, he returned to Equatorial Guinea where he took up numerous administrative cultural functions in the government, and was even designated a 'UNESCO Artist for Peace' in 2007 for his work on 'negritude concepts', contributing to the self-affirmation of black peoples throughout the world.

Annobón has produced some of the most famous **painters** from Equatorial Guinea. **Ghuty Mamae**, graduate of the prestigious School of Crafts and the Armory Arts and Crafts School in Barcelona, is an established oil painter and part of the contemporary African school of painting. **Ricardo Madana Mateo**, who also works with oil paints on canvas, is another internationally acclaimed painter who has worked and studied in Cameroon, Gabon and Equatorial Guinea. In 2013, the president of the Council of Scientific and Technological Research of Equatorial Guinea (CICTE) even suggested the creation of a National School of Fine Arts on Annobón. Beyond Annobón, Bata is home to the Spanish-born **Luis Royo Del Pozo**, a celebrated artist who has produced works exploring subjects as diverse as the city skyline and the magic of the interior forests.

MUSIC AND DANCE Music and dance are an integral part of many of the indigenous cultures of Equatorial Guinea, and also form an important part of the modern artistic landscape.

Bubi farmers carry out the *abira* celebration in order to cleanse their community of evil spirits, offering up a pot of clean water to the good spirits for protection of the village. The *balélé* dance is carried out in coastal communities year-round and on Bioko during the Christmas season and some other holidays. The Bubi also dance the *cachá*. The Fang national dance is known as the *ibanga* and is quite suggestive. Those who perform it often cover their bodies with white powder. A famous Ndowe dance is called the *ivanga* and involves painting the face.

Dances usually have musical accompaniment, including drums, wooden xylophones and the *mbira* or *sanza*, which is a hand-held thumb piano made of wood. The Fang are also known for the *mvet*, which is a stringed instrument sometimes called a zither. Mvet is both the name of the musical instrument, and the folklore tales that are often told to the musical accompaniment. Their music also involves a side-blown trumpet, made either from wood or ivory.

The modern urban music scene in Equatoguinean cities is dominated by imported styles, such as *makossa* from Cameroon and *soukous* from the Democratic Republic of Congo. It is interesting to note the mixed Hispanic and African origins of the *soukous* genre: it is based on Cuban rumba music imported to the Belgian Congo in the mid 19th century, and rumba itself originated through the interplay between Spanish and African slave populations in western Cuba from the 16th century onwards.

The Equatoguinean diaspora has produced a number of well-known music stars. One of the most famous is **Concha Buika**, 'the Queen of Flamenco'. Daughter of celebrated novelist Juan Balboa Boneke (page 56), Buika was born in Mallorca, released her first album *Mestizüo* in 2000, and has since gone on to win a Latin Grammy Award. **Maélé Ndoñg** was also a very famous singer, who was mentioned in the book *Tropical Gangsters*; he died in 2013. **Petit Chabal** is a modern sensation whose music can be heard blasting out of shared taxi sound systems throughout the country.

Equatorial Guinea is also famous for producing hip hop artists, such as **Jota Mayúscula, MC Yuma, Mefe** and Barcelona-based **El Negro Bey**. The group **Hijas Del Sol**, made up of Piruchi Apo Botupa and Paloma Loribo Apo, are a good example of the diversity of Equatoguinean musical talent. They combine Bubi and Spanish lyrical influences with a host of sounds, from West African and Caribbean rhythms to more contemporary influences such as *soukous* and *makossa*. Their work has kept them near the top of the European World Music Charts since 1995.

Other notable popular singers include the Bubi performers Alex Morris and Juana Sineppy, as well as David Bass, Cheri Malé, Mastho Ribocho and Sita Richi. Among the new wave of younger performers are Nene Bantú, Selin Samourai el Curandero, Luis Mbomio, Fifi LaMiré, Majo Star, Sandra Estar and Amistad Internacional.

2

Practical Information

WHEN TO VISIT (AND WHY)

As Equatorial Guinea is so geographically dispersed, it is impossible to visit all of the regions in a short period of time without getting rained on at some point (dry seasons do not sync up between Bioko, Río Muni and Annobón). However, with a bit of careful planning, you can create a comprehensive itinerary that only involves the odd afternoon sitting out the rain storms! Beyond weather considerations, you may also wish to refer to the cultural calendar (page 95) to decide on the most appropriate time to visit.

If you are visiting **Bioko island**, it is best to go during their dry season, which extends from mid-November until February, although be aware that flights around the Christmas holidays face increased demand from expatriate workers heading home and Equatoguineans visiting relatives, so booking in advance is advisable.

Visiting in the dry season will also guarantee you the highest average monthly hours of sunshine. Malabo is consistently warm, with an average temperature that sits around 26°C, with January to May slightly warmer, and July to October slightly colder. Of course, being on a tropical island so close to the Equator, you are unlikely to avoid the rain completely, and the city is often overcast. The south of Bioko is much wetter than the north, with Ureca confirmed as one of the wettest locations in the world.

If you are heading to **Río Muni**, then you will find similar weather conditions but different rainy seasons. Average temperatures in Bata are slightly lower than in Malabo, and there is a noticeable drop in temperature between June and August. Visitors from Malabo will also find Bata to be less humid than its island-based counterpart. The continental region has two dry seasons, from December to mid-February, and again from July to September. It is best to visit in July and August, as these are the driest months, but if you plan to visit the mainland and island regions, then December to February is your best bet. As you travel south along the coast from Bata rainfall levels increase, with the Río Muni estuary by Gabon being the wettest area. Rainfall decreases the further inland you head, although it is often overcast.

Annobón has a similar climate to Bioko, with the dry season running from June to October and a wet season from November to May. However, the busiest period on the island is December, as many families come here to spend the festive season, so ensure you have made accommodation arrangements in advance if you wish to visit then.

If you intend to visit all the provinces of Equatorial Guinea, then heading over in November might work. This puts you at the beginning of the dry season on Bioko, just before the dry season on Río Muni (but remember that heading inland means less rain) and at the very beginning of the rainy season on Annobón – although the start date here is not set in stone. With a bit of luck, you can avoid most of the rainfall!

HIGHLIGHTS

THE MAINLAND Bata has a bustling nightlife and an excellent fresh fish market. Take a stroll down the new **Paseo Marítimo** and enjoy lunch in one of the many waterfront restaurants. Bata cathedral sits proudly on a hilltop, but the skyline today is dominated by more modern architecture, such as the **Torre de la Libertad**. Just outside the capital you can enjoy the shores of **Bomé beach** where there are various waterfront bars and restaurants. Up and down the coast you have the **Río Campo Natural Reserve**, with its abundance of wildlife including hippopotamuses and Goliath frogs. Nearby are the beaches of **Punta Tika** and **Punta Cuche**, with their nesting sea turtles. To the south is the **Río Muni Estuary Natural Reserve**, home to manatees and all manner of birdlife.

Driving inland you will see **Monte Alen National Park** – 1,400km^2 of protected jungle and up to 1,100 elephants. Further inland still you will find **Oyala** (Djibloho), and exploring this new capital city under construction in the middle of the rainforest is easy. Compare it with the president's hometown of **Mongomo** on the eastern border with Gabon, and marvel at the sheer scale and luxury of the building projects, including one of the largest basilicas in Africa.

If you are looking for natural monuments, then you will find these at **Piedra Nzas** between Oyala and Mongomo, and northeast of Oyala at **Piedra Bere**. The **Altos de Nsork National Park** is a 700km^2 area in the very southeast of the country. Here you will see much of the same wildlife that makes Gabon's forests famous, such as common chimpanzees, forest elephants, gorillas, black colobus, mandrill, forest buffalo and red river hogs. The mainland also offers a number of waterfalls such as the Bonsoc Cascades.

BIOKO ISLAND In **Malabo** a walking tour will reveal numerous beautiful examples of colonial architecture (pages 130–1). If you want to head out of the city centre, spend the day at **Arena Blanca**, the island's only white sand beach, and check out the breeding butterflies. Also, try exploring **Horatio's Island in Sipopo**. This is a very small island filled with local artist Charly Djikou's sculptures. There is also a chance for birding and to see the famous 'Horatio Giant', ceiba tree. The eight main points of interest are all well signposted and connected by pathways through the forest.

Exploring the rest of the island, spend a day in the national park hiking up **Pico Basilé** to the volcanic summit for amazing views of the island plus the coasts of Cameroon (including Mount Cameroon) and Nigeria. Further south you have the **BBPP Wildlife Research Center** at Moka. Situated in the southern highlands of Bioko, here you have access to a range of treks across the south of the island, **Lago de Biaó** and the famous **Iladyi Cascades**, as well as the chance of seeing the numerous monkey species that live in the surrounding forest. Down at the southern tip of the island, in the wettest town in the world, you will find the village of **Ureca** – here you can see the waterfalls on the Eoli River and swim in its pools, plus the beaches of Moraka and Moaba which are annually home to nesting sea turtles. West of Ureca along the southern coast of Bioko is **Nacho**, one of the few surf spots identified on the island. **Luba Crater Scientific Reserve**, which dominates the southern portion of Bioko, is home to five very rare primate species: Preuss's monkey, red-eared guenon, black colobus, western red colobus and drill. Tours can be organised through the Bioko Biodiversity Protection Program (pages 142–3).

OTHER ISLANDS If you can make it to **Corisco** (technically a scientific reserve) then you will be rewarded by secluded white sand beaches and stunning views of Corisco Bay, a breeding ground for various sea turtle species. The island is also home to a 2,000-year-old cemetery, one of the oldest in Central Africa. Known as Mandji to local inhabitants, Corisco features some fascinating ruins from colonial times, especially on the nearby islands of **Elobey Grande** and **Elobey Chico**, which you can reach by pirogue. Corisco also offers the rather strange opportunity to walk around a disused international airport, whose runway is almost as long as the island itself!

Although very remote, **Annobón** is home to the stunning Lago Mazafim crater lake and also offers hiking and snorkelling opportunities. Here you will find a number of secluded white sand beaches, and you can almost guarantee you will be the only tourist on the island. With a linguistic and cultural background very dissimilar to anywhere else in the country, this isolated outpost is the least visited part of an already unexplored nation.

For details of events in Equatorial Guinea, see page 95.

SUGGESTED ITINERARIES

ONE DAY OR A WEEKEND

Malabo There is a lot to see and do in the compact city of Malabo. Even without transport, you can complete a **'do it yourself' walking tour** in an hour or two (pages 130–1). Enjoy lunch in **La Luna Restaurant** overlooking the harbour, before spending the afternoon visiting one of the many markets, museums, cultural centres or nearby beaches. If you are feeling really adventurous, you could even take a drive up Pico Basilé. In the evening, don your finery (or at least change out of your flip-flops) and head for dinner in one of the many restaurants Malabo has to offer. Whether you want to eat sushi, paella, grilled fish, French cuisine, *pepe* (pimento) soup or even kebab, this city has you covered. Depending on your energy levels, there is also a bar or club to suit every taste and budget, so the Malabo experience does not have to end until sunrise. Details of the sights in Malabo can be found on pages 129–33.

Bata Start your day with a **'do-it-yourself' walking tour** of Bata (pages 160–2), focusing on the sights along the brand new Paseo Marítimo, such as Bata cathedral, the Torre de la Libertad and Plaza Del Reloj. Enjoy lunch in the waterfront Spanish cultural centre, where you can also pick up a souvenir or two from one of the shops they host. Spend the afternoon relaxing down on Playa Bome to the south of the city, where you can rent a kayak from La Ferme and enjoy some delicious local cuisine for dinner. No visit to Bata would be complete without experiencing the famous nightlife, so get dressed up and head back into the city centre, where you can visit a number of bars in the area around the old stadium (Estadio La Libertad).

ONE WEEK Spend a day or two exploring **Malabo** before arranging a hike up the 3,011m-high **Pico Basilé** for incredible views of the island and nearby Mount Cameroon. Then head south to Bioko for a few days of exploring the spectacular landscapes and wildlife of the island. First stop is the **BBPP Wildlife Research Center** at Moka. After touring their displays, and perhaps picking up a guide, you can hike to **Lago de Biaó** or the **Iladyi Cascades**. Either way, you are sure to see some stunning wildlife in the Luba Scientific Crater Reserve. After all this exertion it's time to drive south to **Ureca** and relax on the black volcanic beaches, complete with waterfalls. For those not so keen on all this exercise, a trip down the west coast of Bioko from Malabo, taking in the white sand beach and butterflies of **Arena**

2

Blanca, and the colonial church in **Batété,** might sound more appealing. You could also visit the cocoa processing facilities of **Riaba,** and the quiet but historic town of **Luba,** with its fascinating linguistic footprint of Fernando Pó Creole, linking back to the time the British ruled the island.

TWO WEEKS After spending five days or so exploring **Bioko,** jump on a Punto Azul flight to Bata (or Ceiba Intercontinental Airlines if you want to save money at the risk of losing your bag). After checking out the newly renovated waterfront, the markets and perhaps even sampling the nightlife, head inland to **Monte Alen National Park.** From the Hotel Monte Alen, with its sweeping valley views, you can organise guided treks along one of the many maintained trails, that offer the opportunity to see all types of wildlife from crocodiles to forest elephants and chimpanzees. For those not so keen on strenuous exertion to see their wildlife, a day on the beaches up by **Punta Tika** near Río Campo provide great turtle-watching opportunities at certain times of year (pages 162–3).

It is possible to do a whistle-stop tour of the whole of Río Muni in only two or three days, thanks to the small size of the territory and the excellent road network. If you head back to Niefang from Monte Alen, you can pick up a taxi to **Añisoc,** from where it is possible to explore the **Natural Monument of Piedra Bere,** as well as the new capital city in the jungle, **Oyala.** You can spend a night and morning exploring **Mongomo** before heading south to **Nsoc** to hunt for forest elephants. Your return trip to the capital will take you through the highlands of **Evinayong.** After getting back to Bata, head down the south coast to Cogo (perhaps exploring the estuary for manatees) and jump on one of the daily boats to **Corisco island** for a relaxing last few days to your trip.

THREE TO FOUR WEEKS If you have a month to spare you should, authorities willing, be able to cover all the provinces of Equatorial Guinea, and still not feel like you are rushing. Start by spending a few days exploring **Malabo** while you get your travel permits and airline tickets in order (which is easier said than done). Once these have been secured, you can head to the south of Bioko to explore the **Luba Scientific Crater Reserve.** There is enough to do here to keep you occupied for four or five days. It makes sense to start with the most distant destination and work back, so next fly to **Annobón** and hike to the beautiful Lago Mazafim. After a day or two of sampling the island life, head back to Malabo before jumping on a plane to **Bata.** From Bata you can travel inland to the northeast, via Ebebiyín and Mongomo to the largely deserted **Altos de Nsork National Park** to view the wildlife. Working your way back towards the coast via **Evinayong** you can take in **Piedra Nzas Natural Monument** and the new capital city in the jungle, **Oyala.** The next stop is **Monte Alen National Park,** with hiking and camping opportunities. After viewing the animals, head south to **Cogo** in the Río Muni estuary and hop on a boat to the secluded **Corisco island,** where you can see a variety of wildlife as well as some fascinating Spanish colonial ruins and pristine beaches. The final leg involves working your way back up the coast to Bata, then returning to Malabo by air.

TOUR OPERATORS

It takes a very specialised tour operator to organise a trip to Equatorial Guinea for you, although getting international flights into the capital Malabo is relatively straightforward. For international flight bookings, try going direct through the airlines (page 72) or compare prices at www.kayak.com or www.skyscanner.

com. Note that sometimes loading up the Spanish version of Skyscanner (*www. skyscanner.es*) gives you a broader choice of connections in Equatorial Guinea than the international version. Also worth noting is that the UK currently has one of the highest air passenger duty taxes in Europe, so if there is any way you can start your journey from another European country, or split your journey into one short-haul flight from London, then a long haul to Equatorial Guinea, you should save money. European cities with direct flights to Malabo include Paris, Madrid and Frankfurt. There are also well-priced options from Addis Ababa and Casablanca.

UK

Native Eye   22 Milton Rd, Lawford, Essex CO11 2EG; ☎+44 (0)20 3286 5995; e info@ nativeeyetravel.com; http://nativeeyetravel.com. This small-group tour operator runs regular tours & tailor-made holidays to some of the most exciting & unusual destinations in Africa, Asia, the Middle East & Europe. They specialise in places that offer something unique, & create pioneering adventure tours designed for the intrepid traveller.

Undiscovered Destinations   PO Box 746, North Tyneside NE29 1EG; ☎+44 (0)191 296 2674; e travel@undiscovered-destinations.com, jim. louth@undiscovered-destinations.com; www. undiscovered-destinations.com. This British operator specialises in small group adventure holidays & tours as well as tailor-made itineraries to destinations considered 'off the beaten track'. They have experience of organising private trips to Malabo, & in 2015 began to offer larger tours, including group departures, to the country.

SPAIN

Jordi Piqué   Barcelona; ☎+34 679 925 337; e jordi.pike2@gmail.com; guiasesorguinea. blogviajes.com. An experienced independent Spanish tour guide with a highly informative website.

Ruta47   Sahel Ruta 47 SL, Can Valent, 2 Marratxí, Illes Balears 07141, Spain; ☎+34 597 157 5886; e africa@ruta47.com, rutacuarentaysiete@gmail. com; www.ruta47.com. This Mallorca-based tour company is highly professional & has experience organising trips to numerous African destinations, including Equatorial Guinea. They have a permanent office in the country & can offer tour packages or create a custom itinerary, with full geographical coverage thanks to their extensive network of in-country contacts. Very helpful & willing to go the extra mile, this company should be the first port of call for anyone looking to arrange a complex itinerary.

EQUATORIAL GUINEA

Unless noted, all agencies follow the Equatoguinean business hours (page 101.)

ATGE Travel Agency   Calle de Nigeria; m +240 222 017 044; e atgeturge@yahoo.com. This business can help with internal flight bookings, hotels & car hire.

Bebotra S L   Barrio Alcaide, Malabo; m +240 222 533 934; e besarib@gmail.com, bbohopo@ bebotra.com; www.bebotra.com. Although officially a translation & services company, the director, Mr Besari Bohopo, is also the first government-certified tour guide in the country. Fluent in English, French & Spanish, he is able to organise itineraries & obtain permits & vehicles. He comes highly recommended by the Bioko Biodiversity Protection Program, & is also a partner to the UK-based Undiscovered Destinations (above).

Guineatur   m +240 222 784 477; e infoguineatur@guineatur.com; www.guineatur. com. Based in Malabo, this is an English-speaking tour operator that can help organise every aspect of your visit including visas, hotel reservations, internal flights & guides. Mrs Catalina Martinez Asumu, who runs the organisation, is very knowledgeable & easy to contact.

Ruta47   Malabo; m +240 222 019 786; e angel@ruta47.com; www.ruta47.com. This highly professional Mallorca-based tour company recently opened a new office in Malabo, headed by Angel Vañó. He is very helpful & can assist with every aspect of a journey. Ruta47 also have a very informative website & Twitter feed, & post lots of useful reviews on TripAdvisor.

Satguru   Calle de Enrique Nvó AP627; ☎+240 333 096 326, 333 090 506; e marketing@ satgurutravel.com; ⏰ 08.00–20.00 Mon–Fri, 10.00–20.00 Sat. Highly efficient travel agency that can deal with both domestic & international flight bookings. They have over 25 locations across Africa. The marketing manager, Mr Sid Kumar, in particular is very helpful & can be reached on m +240 551 000 298.

Viajes Guinea Ecuatorial Av de la Independencia 17, Malabo; ☏ +240 333 092 074; e vguinea_ecuatorial@yahoo.es. Based in Malabo, this tour operator can organise international flights, domestic flights, car hire & hotel bookings but staff are not accustomed to dealing with complex domestic itineraries.

RED TAPE

The Portuguese and Spanish influences have left a legacy of bureaucratic complexity in Equatorial Guinea. Getting things done requires a lot of paperwork, and paperwork takes a lot of time. For those looking to set up a business, Equatorial Guinea was ranked 186th out of 189 countries by the World Bank in terms of the challenges faced in starting a business in 2015. Expect 18 separate procedures and an average of 135 days (and a lot of money) from starting the process to finishing.

Things are not much better when it comes to paying your taxes, and do not hold out much hope when it comes to resolving insolvency: Equatorial Guinea is dead last in the world rankings when it comes to this issue. Luckily, as a tourist you should not have to worry about these issues. Instead, you must face the similarly challenging task of obtaining or renewing your visa.

You must carry either your passport or residence permit with you at all times when in Equatorial Guinea and produce it on request. You will find that you are asked to do this repeatedly while travelling around Malabo or Bata for any length or time, or moving from province to province. It is also important to have all vehicle documentation in order before setting out on a journey, as insurance and registration details can also be requested. In reality though, it is not a good idea to hand over your passport to security officials. Try to carry a laminated colour copy (with visa, entry stamp and ID page clearly shown) instead as this is usually accepted if you reassure them your original is in your hotel. You can quickly and cheaply get one of these made at any of the internet cafés dotted around Malabo or Bata.

Upon receipt of your ID for inspection, police may ask for a bribe in order to return it. They may ask for a *cerveza*, *refresco* (literally a beer or soft drink) or Fanta, which may actually be a request for a drink, or may be a request for some money. See box, pages 82–3, for more details, and advice on how to avoid paying bribes.

Visitors staying longer than 90 days are required to register their presence with their local police station.

VISAS If you are entering Equatorial Guinea for work purposes then usually your sponsoring company will deal with the application. For those visiting as tourists, requirements differ from embassy to embassy so be sure to clarify, but you may be asked for some or all of the following:

- Confirmed hotel reservations
- A detailed itinerary
- A local contact
- A letter from your employer
- An official letter of invitation (either officially stamped or notarised at the Equatorial Guinea end by the Ministry of National Security)
- An unofficial letter of invitation from someone based in Equatorial Guinea
- Return tickets
- Proof of sufficient funds for the trip (recent bank statement)

- Criminal background check
- A certificate confirming that you are HIV negative
- Yellow fever vaccination certificate
- Smallpox vaccination certificate
- Cholera vaccination certificate
- Duplicate copies of your passport and documentation
- Passport photos

Prices for a tourist visa also vary wildly depending on the consulate location. Allow plenty of time for the application and ensure that all your paperwork is in order before submitting. Also note that visas cannot be obtained on arrival for any nationality.

Equatoguinean embassies in other African nations have been known to charge very high fees for issuing tourist visas. Be sure that you are paying the official fee, and that your visa is valid for the means of entry you wish to use. There are reports of large bribes being demanded by immigration officials at the Cocobeach southern border post with Gabon to allow entry.

US citizens are subject to a visa waiver programme, but they are still required to fill out two visa application forms, present two passport photos, a certificate of vaccination for smallpox, yellow fever and cholera, and a recent bank statement to prove that they can fund their visit. Business visitors also require a letter from their employer. In practice, very little of this paperwork is actually asked for, and many US citizens are simply waved in after showing the immigration card their airline gives them on landing.

Established **tour companies** have little difficulty getting visas for the tourists they bring in, so those visiting as part of an official group need not worry. Getting a visa in neighbouring Cameroon or Gabon is a challenge, however, with consular staff sometimes refusing to process applications from people who are not resident in that country. On other occasions though they have processed visas for visiting tourists, but at highly inflated prices (especially in Gabon). For this reason it is probably best to organise your visa in your home country rather than while on the road.

Within **Europe** different Equatoguinean embassies have very different lists of requirements in terms of documents to submit, so be sure to check before submitting your application. The London embassy (page 70) has a very fast turnaround time and is very clear about their documentary requirements (which are unfortunately extensive). The consular staff there are also helpful. It is worth noting that the London embassy has recently made it easier to get a tourist visa by dropping the requirement for an official letter of invitation, making this one of the best places in Europe to apply for your visa.

If you find that you are unable to meet the application requirements (for example, they are insisting on the mysterious letter of invitation stamped by the Ministry of National Security), then tour operators such as **Bebotra S L** (page 65) have a proven track record of success in helping (for a fee). Having a contact on the ground in-country that you can list on your application makes a big difference. Alternatively, the ibis Hotel in Malabo (pages 114–15) can provide letters confirming your booking, which can help with your visa application.

Wherever and however you apply, be sure to allow plenty of time before your trip!

Renewing your visa
Tourist visas are typically valid for a 30-day visit, and expire 60 days after they are issued. It is far easier to persuade your original issuing

embassy to give you a 60 day visa, rather than getting a 30-day visa and trying to renew in-country.

To renew your visa in Equatorial Guinea, you need to head to the Ministry of Interior and Local Corporations (Ministerio del Interior y Corporaciones Locales) in either Malabo or Bata (☎ +240 333 092 683/2688/3406). The process is complex, and you are likely to be asked for numerous pieces of supporting documentation, including a letter from a local hotel or tour operator explaining why you need to stay longer. Fees requested for this service vary greatly, but expect it to cost at least as much as the original visa. Also be sure to start the process early as it may take some time.

TOURISM PERMIT   You would imagine that obtaining a tourist visa would permit you to carry out tourist activities freely in Equatorial Guinea. Unfortunately not. Upon arrival, you will need to go to the Ministry of Tourism and Culture (present in both Bata, page 160, and Malabo, pages 128–9) to obtain a Tourism Permit. Specifically, you need to speak to the Inspecion General de Servicios. Take along a photocopy of your passport and visa, a passport photo and a list of all the places you intend to visit during your stay. They will sign off on it and give you an official-looking permit with a ministerial stamp on it. This includes your photography permit. Be sure to list all the places you wish to visit, as this document will be checked repeatedly and you will get a lot of hassle from the police if you try and visit somewhere not on the permit. If in doubt, get them to write down the names of all seven provinces!

A permit costs 15,000CFA and is good for whatever period you ask them to write on it (their default is to give you two weeks, and they may ask for more money if you want a longer period). Processing takes between one and three days, but you may get it while you wait if you ask nicely. The good news is that once you have your Tourism Permit, there are no admission fees applicable to any of the national parks.

Permission from the military   Obtained your tourist visa and your Tourism Permit? Think this entitles you to drive up Pico Basilé for views over Bioko island? Think again. This is classed as a military site due to the communications installations on top, so you may need permission from the military to head up there. Usually this is as simple as talking your way past the checkpoint on the road at the bottom of the mountain, but sometimes the military may refuse entry, in which case you will need to speak to a superior and show your Tourism Permit (which should have Pico Basilé specifically written on it).

DRIVING   To drive in Equatorial Guinea, you need a local driving licence. Police are not keen to accept EU licences or the International Driving Permit, although these should be accepted for short-term visitors. To obtain your local licence, you need to go to the Ministerio del Interior y Corporaciones Locales in either Malabo or Bata with a copy of your original licence. A six month licence costs 30,000CFA, plus an additional 20,000CFA authorisation fee. The process takes between five and ten working days.

EMBASSIES

Equatorial Guinea has embassies across Europe, North America and Africa. Many foreign nations also have a diplomatic presence in Malabo or Bata. Travel advice for those heading to Equatorial Guinea is available ton the relevant embassy website, or from various Western government sources such as the UK Foreign and Commonwealth Office (*www.gov.uk/foreign-travel-advice/*), the US Department of State (*http://travel.state.gov/*), the French Ministry of Foreign Affairs (*www.diplomatie.gouv.fr/*) or the Italian Ministry of Foreign Affairs and International Co-operation (*www.viaggiaresicuri.it/*). Many embassies also offer an online registration service, which can be useful if something goes wrong during your stay.

For the most up-to-date and detailed travel information, it is recommended that you visit the website of the Spanish Ministry of Foreign Affairs and Co-operation (*www.exteriores.gob.es/*). It might also be worth contacting the Spanish or French cultural centres, who have presences in both Malabo and Bata, for on-the-ground information (*http://ccemalabo.es/* and *www.institutfrancais-malabo.org*).

EQUATOGUINEAN EMBASSIES ABROAD Many of the embassies listed below are very difficult to contact via email. You are advised to phone and make an appointment to visit the embassy in person. Also note that opening times are erratic, especially with some of the embassies in other African countries. An updated list of Equatorial Guinea's embassies and consulates abroad (with opening times) can be found here: http://www.embassypages.com/equatorialguinea.

Ⓔ Angola Rua Pedro Miranda, Luanda; m +244 222 353 939, 222 325 936, 923 403 357, 923 340 357; e embguineequatorial@hotmail.com, embajsecretaria@gmail.com

Ⓔ Argentina (consulate) Gurruchaga 2364, Piso 2'8' 1425, Buenos Aires; ☏ +54 11 4831 9676

Ⓔ Belgium 6 Pl Guy d'Arezzo, 1180 Brussels; ☏ +32 2 346 25 09; f +32 2 346 33 09; e guineaecuatorial.brux@skynet.be

Ⓔ Benin (consulate) Cotonou; ☏ +229 300 51; f +229 300 515

Ⓔ Brazil C/Shis QL 10 conjunto 09 casa 01 – Lago Sul, CEP: 71.630–095, Brasilia; ☏ +55 613 364 4185; f +55 613 364 1641; e embaixada@embrge.brtdata.com.br, lazaro.mokomesangui@hotmail.com, consejeroekua@gequatorial.org.br

Ⓔ Cameroon Quartier Bastos, Yaoundé; ☏ +237 2210804; consulate: Av de la Republique BP 5544, Douala; ☏ +237 343 34 35

Ⓔ Central African Republic Av Abdel Nasser, Bangui; e emolamu@gmail.com, lemolamu@yahoo.es

Ⓔ China Beijing, Chaoyang, Sanlitun East 4th St, (No 2, Dong Si Jie); ☏ +86 10 6532 3679, 10 6532 3709; e equatorialguinea-embbj@hotmail.com

Ⓔ Cuba Calle 3ra No 1001 entre 10 y 12, Miramar, Playa, Havana; ☏ +53 7204 1720, 7204 1808, 7206 9675, 7206 9532; f +53 7204 1724; e embaguineacuatorialcuba@yahoo.es; www.guineacuatorialcuba.com

Ⓔ Egypt 56 El-farik Abd El-moneim Riad St, Mohandessin Zone, 12411, Cairo; ☏ +20 33450945, 33450946, 33450948; f +20 33450497; e embajadadeguineaecuatorial.eg@gmail.com, asmaa_abdelazeem@yahoo.com; ⏱ 08.00–15.00 Sun–Thu

Ⓔ Ethiopia Bole Kifle Ketema, Kebele-03, H No 162, Addis Ababa; ☏ +251 62 62 78, 63 74 24; f +251 61 59 73; e embarge@gmail.com; ⏱ 08.30–16.00 Mon–Fri

Ⓔ France 29 Bd de Courcelles, 75008 Paris; ☏ +33 14 56 19 820, 14 56 19 826; ⏱ 09.30–noon & 14.00–16.00 Mon–Fri

Ⓔ Gabon C/Aut de Qué Qué, Libreville; ☏ +241 751056, 732523

Ⓔ Germany Rohlfsstrasse 17–19, 14195 Berlin; ☏ +49 30 88663877/78; f +49 30 88663879; e konsulat.berlin@botschaft-aequatorialguinea.de; www.botschaft-aequatorialguinea.de/; ⏱ 09.00–noon Mon–Wed, noon–15.00 Thu–Fri

Ⓔ Ghana North Airport Rd, No 70 Kufour Lane, Accra; ☏ +233 24 447 5166, 27 755 6700, 249 737 91; f +233 217 706 30

Ⓔ Hong Kong (consulate) 37th floor, Vicwood Pl, 199 Des Voeux Rd Central; ☏ +852 2543 1943; f +852 2854 1728; e market@vicwoodtimber.com.cn; ⏱ 10.00–13.00 & 14.00–17.00 Mon–Fri

Ⓔ Italy Vía Bruxelles No 59A, 00198 Rome; ☏ +39 068555428; f +39 0685305685; e embaregeitalia@yahoo.es

Ⓔ Morocco Av Rosvelt, C/Rue D'añadir No 9, Rabat; ☎ +212 0377 69454; f +212 0377 69454

Ⓔ Nigeria Corner of 20 Dakala St & Parakou St, off Aminu, Kano Crescent Wuse 2, Abuja; ☎ +234 09 7816867; e egembassyabj@hotmail.com; consulate: C/7 Bank Rood Ikoyi, Lagos; ☎ +234 1 68 49 76, +234 1 2 69 12 11; C/42 Anansa (Mcc), Cross State, Calabar; ☎ +234 87 23 70 71; e consuladogeneralgecalabar@yahoo.com

Ⓔ Portugal Av Vasco da Gama, No 34, 1400–128 Lisbon; ☎ +351 21 301 1493; e okori2001@yahoo.co.uk; ⏰ 09.00–15.30 Mon–Fri

Ⓔ Republic of Congo 206 Rue Eugène Etienne, Centre-Ville, Brazzaville; ☎ +242 06 688 72 90; e embaregecongo@yahoo.es

Ⓔ Romania (consulate) Strada Aniversarii 41/610, Sec 3, 031463, Bucharest; ☎ +40 213233234; f +40 213233234; e consul@ecaligiuri.com; www.ecaligiuri.com/index2.php; ⏰ 09.00–16.00 Mon–Fri

Ⓔ Russia 7 Pogorelskiy Alleyway, Bldg 1, Moscow, 119017; ☎ +7 49 5953 3563; f +7 49 5953 2084; e embajada1968@mail.ru; ⏰ 09.30–16.00 Mon–Fri

Ⓔ São Tomé and Príncipe Rua Ex-Adriano Moreira, São Tomé; ☎ +239 225427, 904023; f +239 221333, 226875

Ⓔ Senegal (consulate) Liberté VI Extension No 58 (Cité ASECNA), Dakar; ☎ +221 338675024; e consuleuato@orange.sn

Ⓔ South Africa 48 Florence St, Colbyn, 0028 Pretoria; ☎ +27 12 3429945, 3427087, 3425076; f +27 12 3427250, 3426469, 3427833, 3426469

Ⓔ Spain Av Pío XII, No 14; 28016 Madrid; ☎ +34 91 35 32 169, 91 35 32 165, 91 35 32 181; e rge@embarege-madrid.com; consulate: José Miranda Guerra, No 1235005, Las Palmas, Gran Canarias; ☎ +34 92 82 44 592, 64 90 19 257; e cggelpa@gmail.com

Ⓔ Switzerland Quai de Cologny 1223, Geneva; ☎ +41 0227008677; f +41 0227008677

Ⓔ Ukraine (consulate) Vozdukhoflotsky Av 90, 03036 Kiev; ☎ +380 44 461 54 37; f +380 44 461 54 87; e roman@avia.org.ua; ⏰ 09.00–18.00 Mon–Fri

Ⓔ United Kingdom 13 Park Pl, London SW1A 1LP; ☎ +44 20 7499 6867; f +44 20 7499 6782; e eguinembassy.uk@gmail.com; www.embassyofequatorialguinea.co.uk; ⏰ 09.00–13.00 & 14.00–15.30 Mon–Fri

Ⓔ United States 2020 16th St, NW Washington, DC 20009; ☎ +1 202 518 5700; f +1 202 518 5252; e eg_africa@yahoo.com; http://egembassydc.com; consulate: 6401 Southwest Freeway, Houston, Texas 77074; ☎ +1 713 776 9900, 713 776 9955; e info@egconsulatehou.com; www.egconsulatehou.com

FOREIGN EMBASSIES AND CONSULATES IN EQUATORIAL GUINEA

Ⓔ Angola Caracolas, Malabo; ☎ 333 099 514, 222 600 406. A 1-month visa costs 50,000CFA. Requirements for applications are changeable & are posted on a noticeboard outside the embassy.

Ⓔ Benin Calle de Enrique Nvó 300, Malabo; m 222 575 766

Ⓔ Brazil Av Parques de Africas, Caracolas, BP 119, Malabo; ☎ 333 099 986, m 222 089 525; f 333 099 987; e brasemb.malabo@itamaraty.gov.br; ⏰ 09.00–17.00 Mon–Fri

Ⓔ Cameroon 37 Calle del Rey Boncoro, Apt 292, Malabo; ☎ 333 093 473; m 222 668 074; f 333 093 413; consulate: just behind the Paseo Marítimo near the French Cultural Centre, Bata; ☎ 333 083 083

Ⓔ Canada (consulate) Carretera del Seminario Mayor, Litoral, Apt 598, Bata; m 222 562 655, 222 621 106; e honconeg@gmail.es

Ⓔ Chad Caracolas, Malabo; m 222 586 870. Occupies a large green complex in the west of the Caracolas neighbourhood, on the same road as the Egyptian embassy.

Ⓔ China Carretera del Aeropuerto, PO Box 44, Malabo; ☎ 333 093 505, 092 239; f 333 092 381; e chinaemb_gq@mfa.gov.cn; consulate: Carretera del Aeropuerto, Bata; ☎ +240 333 093 505; f 333 092 381; e chinaemb_gq@mfa.gov.cn

Ⓔ Cuba Autopista del Aeropuerto, Km2, Malabo; ☎ 333 090 975, 333 099 231; f 333 094 793; e consul@gq.embacuba.cu

Ⓔ Democratic Republic of Congo (consulate) Carretera del Aeropuerto de Bata (near Hotel Carmen), Bata

Ⓔ Egypt Caracolas, Malabo; ☎ 333 096 531; m 222 759 874; f 333 096 531; e embassy.malabo@mfa.gov.eg. Down the road from the Hotel Bahia 2.

Ⓔ France Carretera del Aeropuerto, BP 326, Malabo; ☎ 333 092 005, 333 092 108, 333 093 360;

f 333 092 305; e chancellerie.malabo-amba@ diplomatie.gouv.fr; www.ambafrance-gq.org

E Gabon Paraiso, Malabo; ✆ 333 093 180; f 333 090 057. Be careful that taxi drivers do not try to take you to the old location, on Calle de Argelia, opposite Luna Complex; (consulate) Pl de Ayuntamiento, Bata BP 933; m 222 528 048. Documents can be dropped off between 10.00 & 14.00 Mon to Fri, & collected between 11.00 & 14.00 on Tue, Wed & Fri. Turnover can be as fast as a day. A visa costs 65,000CFA, plus an extra 5,000CFA if you want it expedited (while you wait).

E Germany Edificio Venus, 4° piso, Carretera del Aeropuerto, Km4, Apartado Postal 321, Malabo; ✆ 333 093 117, 333 092 020; e embajada. alemania.malabo@diplo.de

E Ghana BP 289, Caracolas, Malabo; ✆ 333 098 909; f 333 098 882/3; e ghemb.gq@live.com, ghcon14@wanadoo.gq; honorary consulate: on new stadium road, Bata

E Guinea (Conakry) Caracolas, Malabo; ✆ 333 092 725; f 333 092 705

E Italy (consulate) Bata; ✆ 333 082 404; f 333 082 131

E Mali (consulate) Calle del Rey Malabo Vivienda 16, Caydasa, Malabo; m 222 090 742, 222 272 584, 222 096 994; f 090 742; e consmalimalabo@yahoo.fr

E Morocco Av de Enrique Nvó, BP 329, Malabo; ✆ 333 092 650; f +240 092 655

E Nigeria Carretera del Aeropuerto, Malabo; ✆ 333 092 386; f 333 092 578; consulate: on the Radio Bata road, Bata; ✆ 333 082 164; f +240 333 082 157; e nigeriaconbata@yahoo.com; ⊕ 08.30–16.30 Mon–Fri

E Republic of Congo Malabo Paraiso BP 110; m 222 216 972; e ambacomalabo1803@gmail. com; Bata, next door to Cyber Café

E São Tomé and Príncipe (consulate) Caracolas, Malabo; m 222 929 270, 222 180 302; ⊕ 09.00–15.00 Mon–Fri

E Senegal (honorary consulate) Carretera del Mercado, Bata; ✆ 333 082 760

E South Africa Av Parques de Africa, Caracolas, PO Box 5, Malabo; ✆ 333 099 522/523; f 333 099 521; e malabo@foreign.gov.za; www.dirco.gov. za/malabo; ⊕ 08.30–17.00 Mon–Fri, consular hrs 09.00–noon

E Spain Carretera del Aeropuerto, Malabo; ✆ 333 092 020, 333 092 868; f 333 092 611; e emb.malabo@maec.es; Economic & Commercial Office: Calle de Enrique Nvó 178, Malabo; ✆ 333 094 550; f 333 093 140; e malabo@comercio. mineco.es; consulate: Paseo Lumu Matindi, s/n, Paseo Marítimo de Bata; ✆ 333 082 635; e cog.bata@maec.es; www.exteriores.gob.es/ consulados/bata; ⊕ 09.00–13.00 Mon–Fri

E United States Malabo II Highway, Malabo; ✆ 333 095 741, 333 098 895; e malaboconsular@ state.gov; http://malabo.usembassy.gov; ⊕ 08.00–17.30 Mon–Thu, 08.00–noon Fri

E Venezuela Paraiso District, Malabo; ✆ 333 040 090, 333 099 001, 333 099 002; m 222 744 782 e embavenezuelage@yahoo.com

GETTING THERE AND AWAY

BY AIR The majority of Equatorial Guinea's visitors arrive at Malabo or Bata international airports. In fact, given the difficulty of overland crossings from Gabon and Cameroon, these may be your only options.

Malabo's airport is 8km to the west of the capital city and is quick to reach with no traffic. It is used by both military and civilian aircraft. A new international airport has been built in Mengomeyén to service Oyala (the proposed new capital city on the mainland), and there is another on Corisco, but for the time being, Malabo is your best bet for getting into the country. Aircraft arriving here feature an interesting mix of Western oil workers, crew-cut security contractors, diplomats, Middle Eastern businessmen, well-off locals, regional visitors and the odd conservationist.

Arriving or departing from Malabo airport is quite a painless process by regional standards. While you may be required to open your luggage for customs, they are unlikely to confiscate items arbitrarily. You can often get waved through without having to open your bag at all. Given the widespread paranoia about coups, it is best to leave potentially dual purpose items (such as GPS equipment, camouflage clothing, etc) at home. Divers do not seem to have issues bringing in scuba equipment, however. If you do need GPS connectivity, for example, to look for the surf spots listed in the guide, then you are better off bringing a GPS-enabled phone or GPS-enabled watch that will arouse less suspicion.

International airline offices in Malabo

Malabo is well served by international carriers, many of which have offices in town as well as smaller facilities within the airport terminal building. Prices and flight duration quotes are based on an economy return ticket to the hub of that airline, not back to the UK. All ticket office opening times are 09.00–16.00 Monday–Friday and 09.00–13.00 Saturday unless otherwise noted.

✈ **Air Annobón** Calle de Kenia 137; ☎ 333 091 030; m 222 284 191. Currently only fly domestically, but are advertising regional routes coming soon.

✈ **Air France/KLM** Av Parques de Africa, Caracolas, BP 1051; ☎ 333 040 401, 333 094 512; m 222 256 161; www.airfrance.com; ⏰ 09.00–16.00 Mon–Fri. Flights every day from Paris connecting through Douala, flight time is 8hrs 30mins & the cost is approx £850 return. You can save up to £200 at certain times of the year by starting your journey in London.

✈ **CamAir Co** Behind BGFI Bank; ☎ 333 096 326, 333 090 506; m 555 226 022, 222 266 022; e adamou.bello@camair-co.net, customerservice@camair-co.net. Flights from Douala to Malabo are currently suspended, although if they are reinstated, you could get yourself to Douala from Paris daily in 6hrs 25mins for approx £500 return.

✈ **Ceiba Intercontinental Airlines** Calle del Presidente Nasser; ☎ 333 040 922, 333 098 149; m 222 270 168, 222 596 152; e ceiba@fly-ceiba. com; www.fly-ceiba.com; ⏰ 08.30–17.00 Mon–Fri, 09.00–16.00 Sat. Flights from Madrid to Malabo 3 times a week (Tue, Thu & Sat); flight time is 6hrs 15mins; cost is approx £300 return. Also offer flights from São Tomé to Malabo 3 times per week (Mon, Wed & Fri); flight time 1hr 10mins; cost £400 return.

✈ **Cronos Airlines** Calle de Enrique Nvó 178, Malabo; ☎ 333 090 471, 333 096 912; m 222 600 707, 222 600 808, 222 600 909; e ssgc8cto@ cronosair.com, online@cronosair.com; www. cronosair.com. Flights to Douala, Cameroon, Cotonou, Benin & Port Harcourt, Nigeria from

Malabo are currently suspended, although planned to resume in late 2015. Currently only offers internal flights between Malabo & Bata twice daily. Also plan to introduce new routes to Niamey, Niger, Lagos, Nigeria & Yaoundé, Cameroon in 2016.

✈ **Ethiopian Airlines** PDGE building, 2nd floor, Av de la Independencia 493; ☎ 333 090 588, 333 090 593; e teshomeGB@ethiopianairlines. com, mariat@ethiopianairlines.com; www. ethiopianairlines.com. Direct flights 4 times a week from Addis Ababa (Mon, Wed, Fri & Sun); flight time is 4hrs 30mins; cost is approx £750 return.

✈ **Iberia** Calle de Enrique Nvó 178; ☎ 333 093 395, 333 920 000; e ssguz@iberia.es; www.iberia. es; ⏰ 08.30–17.00 Mon–Fri. Direct flights every day from Madrid; flight time 6hrs & cost is approx £600 return.

✈ **Lufthansa** BGFI Bank Bldg, Carretera del Aeropuerto, Km5; ☎ 333 090 353, 333 092 827; e lufthansa.malabo@dlh.de. Flights every day from Frankfurt connecting through Abuja; flight time is 7hrs 45mins & cost is approx £900 return. Office is on the same turn-off as the German embassy.

✈ **Punto Azul** Paraiso District (main street); m 222 605 949, 222 111 100; e reservations@ flypuntoazul.com; www.flypuntoazul.com. Flights twice a week from Accra (Mon & Fri), 3 times a week from Douala (Mon, Wed & Fri) & twice a week from Yaoundé (Mon & Fri). Flight time from Accra is 2hrs & the cost is approx £315 return.

✈ **Royal Air Maroc** Av de Hassán II 135; ☎ +240 333 099 592. Flights 4 times a week (Tue, Thu, Sat & Sun) connecting through Libreville; flight time is 5hrs 20mins & cost is approx £680 return.

International arrivals

Malabo's airport is quite small but relatively well maintained. The facilities for processing arriving passengers struggle to deal with high volumes of people, so you are liable to be queuing for a while if you land at the same time as another flight. To speed things up, sit near the front of the plane when landing in Malabo, rush to get to the front of the queue for immigration, and ensure you have all your paperwork available in your hand luggage (such as yellow fever vaccination certificate, letter of invitation, hotel reservation, etc). The odds are they will simply look at your visa, scan your fingerprints and stamp you in, but you may be asked to produce additional supporting documentation at this point, so be prepared.

Baggage claim and customs Bags arrive on the conveyor belt quickly unless you are landing at the same time as another flight. Customs is chaotic: a narrow choke point by the exit door, where passengers are expected to file through and open their bags for inspection by customs officials. Here you may also be hassled by middle men, keen to speed up the process in return for a facilitation fee. You can sometimes get through with only a cursory inspection of your bags (or no inspection at all) if you tell them you are a tourist, and the bags contain only clothes (assuming this is true!).

Taxis wait outside the arrivals hall, and in a time honoured tradition will try to overcharge newly arrived visitors. It should cost no more than 2,000CFA to take one of these taxis (without sharing) from the airport to anywhere in Malabo, regardless of the time of night. Many hotels in Malabo also offer a shuttle service for arriving customers.

International departures
Be sure to reconfirm your flight with the airline a few days in advance of departure and print your boarding pass after checking in online before heading to the airport. The departure service is not too bad as long as you allow enough time. Security checks on departing luggage are worryingly lax. International passengers have their bags scanned and tagged in one area, and are then allowed to carry them out of the building and back in to the bag drop! The departures lounge is large and air conditioned with toilets, seats and a TV. There is also a bar. Many expatriates check in, drop their bags and then wait in the comfort of the Hilton Hotel's bar just down the road, rather than sitting in the airport.

Import and export of currency
As a non-resident, there is officially no restriction on the import of local or foreign currency, provided it is declared on arrival. You may export a maximum of 50,000CFA in banknotes, and only as much foreign currency as you declared upon arrival. In reality there is very little control over currency imports/exports through the airport.

OVERLAND
Overlanders heading down the west coast of Africa tend to skip mainland Equatorial Guinea, choosing instead to cross directly between Cameroon and Gabon. Theoretically, however, there are six official overland border crossing points:

Gabon	Cameroon
Médouneu – Akúrenam	Campo – Río Campo
Oyem – Mongomo	Ambam – Ebebiyín
Kye Effak – Ebebiyín	
Cocobeach – Cogo (by boat)	

In reality, many of these crossing points are for local traffic only, and tourists have been refused entry, fined upon arrival or even deported after entering Río Muni overland. Note that neither the 1926 nor the 1949 International Driving Permit are valid in Equatorial Guinea: you need to obtain a local licence upon arrival in Bata or Malabo (page 109). Also note that the Carnet de Passages en Douane for the temporary importation of vehicles is not officially recognised. The best option is to seek advice locally, or pay a local tour operator to meet you at the border and help manage the crossing process and associated paperwork.

BY SEA Passenger ships do not dock at Equatoguinean ports. Given the history of coup attempts and seaborne attacks, private vessels would be treated with great suspicion in Equatoguinean waters. Around Malabo they would likely be quickly challenged by naval forces. If planning to arrive by sea, you would need to make specific arrangements in advance to ensure all your paperwork was in order. Authorities on Annobón and Corisco islands appear to be far more co-operative and amenable to sea arrivals than those in Bioko or Río Muni.

Visitors arriving in Equatorial Guinea via boat are likely to be treated with suspicion and there are some security issues (page 81). There are reports of travellers arriving via boat from Cocobeach, Gabon to Cogo, Equatorial Guinea, although this point of entry is generally for locals only, and you may be subjected to heavy 'fines' or even deportation upon arrival (page 167). It is also only a short boat ride northwards from Río Campo into Cameroon, although again, this point of entry is generally for locals only (pages 150–1). There are also boats linking Corisco to Libreville, Gabon (page 173) which had been used successfully by expatriates at the time of writing. Those looking for adventure might even be able to hitch a lift on the SOMAGEC supply ship linking Annobón to São Tomé (page 179). At the time of writing there were no commercial ferry services linking Equatorial Guinea to Cameroon, although there is a fair amount of private boat traffic between the two countries (mainly Malabo to Douala), so you could try and hitch a lift from Douala, but be prepared for some hassle from immigration upon arrival!

HEALTH   *with Dr Felicity Nicholson*

Equatorial Guinea, like most parts of Africa, is home to several tropical diseases unfamiliar to people living in more temperate and sanitary climates. However, with adequate preparation, and a sensible attitude to malaria prevention, the chances of serious mishap are small. To put this in perspective, your greatest concern after malaria should not be the combined exotica of venomous snakes, stampeding wildlife, gun-happy soldiers or the Ebola virus, but something altogether more mundane: a road accident. Within Equatorial Guinea, a range of adequate (but well short of world-class) clinics, hospitals and pharmacies can be found around Malabo and Bata, although outside these urban areas you will struggle to secure decent medical care. Doctors and pharmacists generally do not speak English, so unless you have some Spanish you will struggle to make yourself understood. Also worth noting is that consultation and laboratory fees (in particular malaria tests) can be quite expensive by international standards, especially in the clinics frequented by expatriates.

BEFORE YOU GO Sensible preparation will go a long way to ensuring your trip runs smoothly. Particularly for first-time visitors to Africa, this includes a visit to a travel clinic to discuss matters such as vaccinations and malaria prevention at least six weeks before you leave, to ensure there is enough time. For more on travel clinics, see page 76. The Bradt website now carries an African health section (*www.bradtguides. com/africahealth*) to help travellers prepare for their Africa trip, elaborating on the information below, but the following summary points are worth emphasising:

- Don't travel without comprehensive medical travel insurance that will fly you home in an emergency.
- Make sure all your immunisations are up to date. A yellow fever vaccination is advised and you will need to show proof of immunisation upon entry to Equatorial Guinea if you are travelling from another yellow fever endemic area. A valid yellow fever vaccination certificate (within the preceding ten years) will then be required on entry. If the vaccine is not suitable for you then you would be wise not to travel, as West Africa has the highest prevalence of yellow fever and there is around a 50% mortality rate.
- It's also unwise to travel in the tropics without being up to date on tetanus, polio and diphtheria (now given as an all-in-one vaccine, Revaxis), especially as in April 2014 the World Health Organization confirmed a case of wild poliovirus type 1 (WPV1) from Centro Sur Province in Equatorial Guinea (inland Río Muni), believed to have been spread from Cameroon. Equatorial Guinea also has one of the worst polio vaccination rates in the world (sitting at around 39% in April 2014), making future outbreaks more likely.
- Immunisation against rabies, meningitis, hepatitis B, hepatitis A, typhoid and possibly tuberculosis (TB) are likely to be recommended.
- The biggest health threat is malaria. There is no vaccine against this mosquito-borne disease, but a variety of preventative drugs is available, including mefloquine, atovaquone/proguanil (Malarone) and the antibiotic doxycycline. Malarone and doxycycline need only be started two days before entering Equatorial Guinea, but mefloquine should be started two to three weeks before. Doxycycline and mefloquine need to be taken for four weeks after the trip and Malarone for seven days. It is as important to complete the course as it is to take the drug before and during the trip. The most suitable choice of drug varies depending on the individual and the country they are visiting, so visit your GP or a specialist travel clinic for medical advice. If you will be spending a long time in Africa, and expect to visit remote areas, be aware that no preventative drug is 100% effective, so carry a cure too. It is also worth noting that no homeopathic prophylactic for malaria exists, nor can any traveller acquire effective resistance to malaria. Those who don't make use of preventative drugs risk their life in a manner that is both foolish and unnecessary.
- Though advised for everyone, a pre-exposure course of rabies vaccination, involving three doses taken over a minimum of 21 days, is particularly important if you intend to have contact with animals, or are likely to be 24 hours away from medical help (which is quite possible if visiting inland Río Muni or Annobón). If you have not had this and are exposed to rabies then you will almost certainly have to evacuate for medical treatment, as it is very unlikely that Equatorial Guinea will have the necessary treatment. For more information, see page 77.
- Anybody travelling away from major centres should carry a personal first-aid kit. Contents might include a good drying antiseptic (eg: iodine or potassium permanganate), Band-Aids, suncream, insect repellent, aspirin or paracetamol, antifungal cream (eg: Canesten), ciprofloxacin or norfloxacin (for severe diarrhoea), antibiotic eye drops, tweezers, condoms or femidoms, a digital thermometer and a needle-and-syringe kit with accompanying letter from a healthcare professional.
- Bring any drugs or devices relating to known medical conditions with you. That applies both to those who are on medication prior to departure, and those who are, for instance, allergic to bee stings, or are prone to attacks of asthma. Carry

a copy of your prescription and a letter from your GP explaining why you need the medication.

- Prolonged immobility on long-haul flights can result in deep vein thrombosis (DVT), which can be dangerous if the clot travels to the lungs to cause pulmonary embolus. The risk increases with age, and is higher in obese or pregnant travellers, heavy smokers, those taller than 6ft/1.8m or shorter than 5ft/1.5m, and anybody with a history of clots, recent major operation or varicose veins surgery, cancer, a stroke or heart disease. If any of these criteria apply, consult a doctor before you travel.

TRAVEL CLINICS AND HEALTH INFORMATION A full list of current travel clinic websites worldwide is available on www.istm.org. For other journey preparation information, consult www.nathnac.org/ds/map_world.aspx (UK) or http://wwwnc. cdc.gov/travel/ (US). Information about various medications may be found on www.netdoctor.co.uk/travel. All advice found online should be used in conjunction with expert advice received prior to or during travel.

COMMON MEDICAL PROBLEMS

Malaria This potentially fatal disease is widespread in low-lying tropical parts of Africa, a category that includes all of Equatorial Guinea, and while the risk of transmission is highest in the rainy season, it is present throughout the year. Since no malaria prophylactic is 100% effective, you should take all reasonable precautions against being bitten by the nocturnal Anopheles mosquitoes that transmit the disease (see box, page 78). Malaria usually manifests within two weeks of transmission, but it can be as little as seven days and anything up to a year. Any fever occurring after seven days should be considered as malaria until proven otherwise. Symptoms typically include a rapid rise in temperature (over 38°C), and any combination of a headache, flu-like aches and pains, a general sense of disorientation, and possibly even nausea and diarrhoea. The earlier malaria is detected, the better it usually responds to treatment. So if you display possible symptoms, get to a doctor or clinic immediately (in the UK, go to Accident and Emergency and say that you have been to Africa). A simple test, available at even the most rural clinic in Africa, is usually adequate to determine whether you have malaria. You need three negative tests to be sure it is not the disease. And while experts differ on the question of self-diagnosis and self-treatment, the reality is that if you think you have malaria and are not within easy reach of a doctor, it would be wisest to start treatment.

Travellers' diarrhoea Many visitors to unfamiliar destinations suffer a dose of travellers' diarrhoea, usually as a result of imbibing contaminated food or water. Rule one in avoiding diarrhoea and other sanitation-related diseases is to wash your hands regularly, particularly before snacks and meals. As for what food you can safely eat, a useful maxim is: PEEL IT, BOIL IT, COOK IT OR FORGET IT. This means that fruit you have washed and peeled yourself should be safe, as should hot cooked foods. However, raw foods, cold cooked foods, salads, fruit salads prepared by others, ice cream and ice are all risky. It is rarer to get sick from drinking contaminated water but it happens, so stick to bottled water, which is widely available. If you suffer a bout of diarrhoea, it is dehydration that makes you feel awful, so drink lots of water and other clear fluids. These can be infused with sachets of oral rehydration salts, though any dilute mixture of sugar and salt in water will do you good, for instance a bottled fizzy drink with a pinch of salt. If diarrhoea persists beyond a couple of days, it is possible it is a symptom of a more serious sanitation-related illness (typhoid, cholera, hepatitis, dysentery, worms, etc), so get to a doctor. If the diarrhoea is greasy and bulky, and is accompanied by sulphurous (eggy) burps, one likely cause is giardia, which is best treated with tinidazole (four x 500mg in one dose, repeated seven days later if symptoms persist).

Bilharzia Also known as schistosomiasis, bilharzia is an unpleasant parasitic disease transmitted by freshwater snails most often associated with reedy shores where there is lots of water weed. It cannot be caught in hotel swimming pools or the ocean, but should be assumed to be present in any freshwater river, pond, lake or similar habitat, even those advertised as 'bilharzia free'. The most risky shores will be within 200m of villages or other places where infected people use water, wash clothes, etc. Equatorial Guinea is host to the Lower Guinea strain of *Schistosoma intercalatum* (the parasitic worm causing bilharzia). The specific snail that acts as the intermediary host is *Bulinus forskalii*, found especially around Bata.

Ideally, you should avoid swimming in any fresh water other than an artificial pool. If you do swim, you'll reduce the risk by applying DEET insect repellent first, staying in the water for under 10 minutes, and drying off vigorously with a towel. Bilharzia is often asymptomatic in its early stages, but some people experience an intense immune reaction, including fever, cough, abdominal pain and an itching rash, around four to six weeks after infection. Later symptoms vary but often include a general feeling of tiredness and lethargy. Bilharzia is difficult to diagnose, but it can be tested for at specialist travel clinics, ideally at least six weeks after likely exposure. Fortunately, it is easy to treat at present.

Meningitis This nasty disease can kill within hours of the appearance of initial symptoms, typically a combination of a blinding headache (light sensitivity), blotchy rash, and high fever. Outbreaks tend to be localised and are usually reported in newspapers. Fortunately, immunisation with meningitis ACWY vaccine (eg: Menveo, Nimenrix) protects against the most serious bacterial form of meningitis. Nevertheless, other less serious forms exist which are usually viral, but any severe headache and fever – possibly also symptomatic of typhoid or malaria – should be sufficient cause to visit a doctor immediately.

Rabies This deadly disease can be carried by any mammal and is usually transmitted to humans via a bite or a scratch that breaks the skin. In particular, beware of village dogs and monkeys habituated to people, but assume that any mammal that bites or scratches you (or even licks an open wound) might be rabid even if it looks healthy. First, scrub the wound with soap under a running tap for a good 10–15 minutes, or while pouring water from a jug, then pour on a strong iodine or alcohol solution, which will guard against infections and might reduce the risk of the rabies virus entering the body. Whether or not you underwent pre-exposure vaccination, it is vital to obtain post-exposure prophylaxis as soon as possible after the incident. The full post-exposure treatment is unlikely to be available in Equatorial Guinea if you have not had a pre-exposure course of the vaccine. Evacuate as soon as you can. Death from rabies is probably one of the worst ways to go, and once you show symptoms it is too late to do anything – the mortality rate is 100%.

Tetanus Tetanus is caught through deep dirty wounds, including animal bites, so ensure they are thoroughly cleaned. Immunisation protects for ten years, provided you don't have an overwhelming number of tetanus bacteria on board. If you haven't had a tetanus shot in ten years, or you are unsure, get a booster immediately.

HIV/AIDS   Rates of HIV/AIDS infection are high in most parts of Africa, and other sexually transmitted diseases are rife. Condoms (or femidoms) greatly reduce the risk of transmission. The UN estimated that the HIV prevalence rate in Equatorial Guinea was around 6.2% in 2012, slightly higher than in neighbouring Cameroon and Gabon.

Tick bites   Ticks in Africa are not the rampant disease transmitters that they are in the Americas, but they may spread tick-bite fever along with a few dangerous rarities. They should ideally be removed complete as soon as possible to reduce the chance of infection. The best way to do this is to grasp the tick with your finger nails as close to your body as possible, and pull it away steadily and firmly at right angles to your skin (do not jerk or twist it). If possible douse the wound with alcohol (any spirit will do) or iodine. If you are travelling with small children, remember to check their heads, and particularly behind the ears, for ticks. Spreading redness around the bite and/or fever and/or aching joints after a tick bite imply that you have an infection that requires antibiotic treatment, so seek advice.

Skin infections   Any mosquito bite or small nick is an opportunity for a skin infection in warm humid climates, so clean and cover the slightest wound in a good drying antiseptic such as dilute iodine, potassium permanganate or crystal (or gentian) violet. Prickly heat, most likely to be contracted at the humid coast, is a fine pimply rash that can be alleviated by cool showers, dabbing (not rubbing) dry and talc, and sleeping naked under a fan or in an air-conditioned room. Fungal infections also get a hold easily in hot moist climates so wear 100%-cotton socks and underwear, and shower frequently.

AVOIDING MOSQUITO AND INSECT BITES

The Anopheles mosquitoes that spread malaria are active at dusk and after dark. Most bites can thus be avoided by covering up at night. This means donning a long-sleeved shirt, trousers and socks from around 30 minutes before dusk until you retire to bed, and applying a DEET-based insect repellent to any exposed flesh. It is best to sleep under a net, or in an air-conditioned room, though burning a mosquito coil and/or sleeping under a fan will also reduce (though not entirely eliminate) bites. Travel clinics usually sell a good range of nets and repellents, as well as Permethrin treatment kits, which will render even the tattiest net a lot more protective, and helps prevents mosquitoes from biting through a net when you roll against it. These measures will also do much to reduce exposure to other nocturnal biters. Bear in mind, too, that most flying insects are attracted to light: leaving a lamp standing near a tent opening or a light on in a poorly screened hotel room will greatly increase the insect presence in your sleeping quarters. It is also advisable to think about avoiding bites when walking in the countryside by day, especially in wetland habitats, which often teem with diurnal mosquitoes. Wear a long loose shirt and trousers, preferably 100% cotton, as well as proper walking or hiking shoes with heavy socks (the ankle is particularly vulnerable to bites), and apply a DEET-based insect repellent to any exposed skin.

Eye problems Bacterial conjunctivitis (pink eye) is a common infection in Africa, particularly for contact-lens wearers. Symptoms are sore, gritty eyelids that often stick closed in the morning. They will need treatment with antibiotic drops or ointment. Lesser eye irritation should settle with bathing in saline solution and keeping the eyes shaded. If an insect flies into your eye, extract it with great care, ensuring you do not crush or damage it, otherwise you may get a nastily inflamed eye from toxins secreted by the creature.

Sunstroke and dehydration Overexposure to the sun can lead to short-term sunburn or sunstroke, and increases the long-term risk of skin cancer. Wear a T-shirt and waterproof sunscreen when swimming. When walking in the direct sun, cover up with long, loose clothes, wear a hat, and use sunscreen. The glare and the dust can be hard on the eyes, so bring UV-protecting sunglasses. A less direct effect of the tropical heat is dehydration, so drink more fluids than you would at home.

Other insect-borne diseases Although malaria is the insect-borne disease that attracts the most attention in Africa, and rightly so, there are others, most too uncommon to be a significant concern to short-stay travellers. These include dengue fever, Chikungunya and other arboviruses (spread by day-biting mosquitoes), sleeping sickness (tsetse flies), and river blindness (blackflies). Bearing this in mind, however, it is clearly sensible, and makes for a more pleasant trip, to avoid insect bites as far as possible (see box, page 78). Two nasty (though ultimately relatively harmless) flesh-eating insects associated with tropical Africa are tumbu or putsi flies, which lay eggs, often on drying laundry, that hatch and bury themselves under the skin when they come into contact with humans, and jiggers, which latch on to bare feet and set up home, usually at the side of a toenail, where they cause a painful boil-like swelling. Drying laundry indoors and wearing shoes are the best way to deter this pair of flesh-eaters. Symptoms and treatment of all these afflictions are described in greater detail on Bradt's website (*www.bradtguides.com*).

OTHER SAFETY CONCERNS
Wild animals Don't confuse habituation with domestication. Most wildlife in Africa is genuinely wild, and widespread species such as hippo or hyena might attack a person given the right set of circumstances. Such attacks are rare, however, and they almost always stem from a combination of poor judgement and poorer luck. A few rules of thumb: never approach potentially dangerous wildlife on foot except in the company of a trustworthy guide; never swim in lakes or rivers without first seeking local advice about the presence of crocodiles or hippos; never get between a hippo and water; and never leave food (particularly meat or fruit) in the tent where you'll sleep. Equatorial Guinea has a variety of potentially dangerous animals, such as crocodiles, hippos and even leopards in Monte Alen National Park, although you are much more at risk from mosquitoes!

Snake and other bites Snakes are very secretive and bites are a genuine rarity, but certain spiders and scorpions can also deliver nasty bites. In all cases, the risk is minimised by wearing trousers and closed shoes when walking in the bush, and watching where you put your hands and feet, especially in rocky areas or when gathering firewood. Only a small fraction of snakebites deliver enough venom to be life-threatening, but it is important to keep the victim calm and inactive, and to seek urgent medical attention. The World Health Organization identifies nine venomous snakes as present in Equatorial Guinea, including the Gaboon viper which has the worrying distinction of having the highest venom yield of any snake in the world. A list of the snakes can be found on pages 10–11.

Ask for local advice on snakes before hiking in the bush. Some hiking spots, such as those on Annobón, are relatively snake-free, whereas others such as those on Corisco Island are densely populated by snakes.

Car accidents Dangerous driving is probably the biggest threat to life and limb in most parts of Africa. On a self-drive visit, drive defensively, being especially wary of stray livestock, gaping pot-holes, and imbecilic or bullying overtaking manoeuvres. Many vehicles lack headlights and most local drivers are reluctant headlight-users, so avoid driving at night and pull over in heavy storms. On a chauffeured tour, don't be afraid to tell the driver to slow or calm down if you think he is too fast or reckless. Road fatalities in Equatorial Guinea occur at over three times the rate they do in the UK, and the government has estimated that up to 60% of these deaths were attributable to drink-driving, so be especially careful driving at weekends and holidays. In particular, be wary of the road between Arena Blanca and Malabo at the weekend, when it fills up with people driving home after a day of beers on the beach.

SAFETY AND SECURITY

EMERGENCY NUMBERS The phone number for the police in Equatorial Guinea is ✆113. The Gendarmería can be reached on ✆114, and the fire department on ✆115. There is no equivalent number for an ambulance service. These numbers do not always work, and in most cases it is more effective to make your own arrangements to travel to the nearest police station, fire station or hospital. In the event of legal issues, it is advisable to notify your nearest embassy or consulate (pages 70–1), as the Equatoguinean police do not always do this when detaining foreigners.

CRIME AND VIOLENCE The level of violent crime in Equatorial Guinea is relatively low compared with other countries in the region and there is a strong police presence in most urban centres (which is a mixed blessing). It is still important to take security precautions to avoid becoming a victim of crime, as crime levels, especially those targeting expatriates, are reportedly on the rise. These crime levels also increase markedly during the Christmas holiday season. For advice for women travellers, see page 81.

The main issue you may face is extortion by corrupt police officers. Typically, police will claim you have committed a road traffic violation or that your paperwork is not in order. Tourists have also been fined for taking photographs of sensitive buildings, or for not having a photography permit (even though these are no longer required; see page 81). While you are unlikely to face physical violence during one of these 'shakedowns', police officers may be drunk and will sometimes use their position or weaponry to intimidate you into paying an on-the-spot fine.

Theft of unaccompanied items is also a problem, so be sure to secure all your belongings properly, and do not leave anything visible in your car when it is parked. Residential burglary is also common, with at least two home invasions by armed intruders occurring in the expatriate community in 2013. That being said, Equatoguineans are far more likely to be the victims of burglary than foreigners.

Marijuana is prevalent and easily obtained. It is illegal and you should avoid any form of narcotics activity as this may lead to serious problems with the local police authorities.

While the police will generally respond to the report of a crime by a foreigner, you may be asked to pay a substantial fee (between US$50 and US$100) in order for them to file a police report, which you may require for an insurance claim.

Equatorial Guinea is a very low-risk destination with regards to international terrorism. There are no armed insurgent groups anywhere in the territory.

NO-GO AREAS There are few no-go areas in Equatorial Guinea in terms of crime rates. Most areas to avoid are more due to the sensitive nature of the site to the authorities. You may not access the very peak of Pico Basilé as this is a military site. Approaching or photographing the presidential palace is also a bad idea, as is photographing the presidential motorcade as it passes by. In fact, it is best not to go near or photograph any site that has the potential to upset the authorities. This includes prisons, military bases, communications infrastructure, airports, bridges, dams, power plants or government buildings. These are all listed on your Tourism Permit.

It is advisable to stay away from the three small islets in Corisco Bay: Conga, Cocotiers and especially Mbañe. These are the site of a territorial dispute between Gabon and Equatorial Guinea. Likewise, wandering around the interior of Annobón island with camera gear or scientific equipment may land you in trouble, as it is said to house secret government waste dumping sites (page 178).

Do not attempt to cross the southern border of Río Muni from Cocobeach in Gabon to Cogo in Equatorial Guinea without first seeking local advice. Although this is an official border crossing, the immigration authorities have a bad reputation for corruption, and extorted fines from and deported visitors in both 2014 and 2015. Likewise, seek local advice before attempting to cross any of the other land borders with Gabon or Cameroon (pages 192, 197, 207 and 209).

TRAFFIC Traffic incidents are one of the biggest dangers you will face while in Equatorial Guinea (page 80). Many local drivers are unlicensed, and their vehicles unroadworthy by Western standards. Local taxis in the urban centres are especially problematic, as they are often overloaded, drive recklessly and stop erratically to load and unload passengers.

You may be at risk of robbery while waiting in stationary traffic. It is advisable to keep your doors locked, your windows wound up and your seatbelt fastened. Keep valuable belongings such as laptops out of sight. Also be sure to leave enough room between you and the car in front so that you can manoeuvre away if the need arises. Robbers have also been known to set-up obstacles, such as rocks or logs in the road, in order to stop vehicles. If you encounter this, especially at night, either drive around the obstacle or turn around if this is impossible. Do not stop to assess the situation.

WOMEN TRAVELLERS Levels of sexual violence are relatively low, although lone female travellers should still exercise caution. Avoid travelling at night, staying in shared accommodation or travelling in local shared taxis. Security is much better at the higher-end hotels.

Since July 2013, there has been a noted increase in crime directed against women, including expatriate women, by groups posing as taxi drivers and passengers, who will hold people hostage at knife-point and rob them. This is especially a problem in Bata, although it has also occurred in Malabo. Sexual assault directed against foreigners is extremely rare, although recently, a very violent rape of an American energy company employee occurred as she was on her way to board a company shuttle bus.

Not long after arriving in Equatorial Guinea I encountered my first corrupt public official eliciting a bribe. Having heard horror stories about corruption before my arrival, I made sure I was prepared. With lots of patience and a couple of strategies, I found that it was possible to travel throughout the country without engaging in any corrupt practices.

Often a police officer would stop my vehicle and demand payment of a fine for some imagined infraction of road traffic regulations. Official consular advice recommends that visitors do not pay bribes, instead requesting an official citation, to be paid at the local court, police station or bank, which clearly states the violation, amount due and the officer's name. In reality, this request will not get you very far, and neither will threatening to phone your embassy. I found the following approach much more successful:

DO NOT SPEAK THE LANGUAGE Although my Spanish is perfectly functional, for the purposes of my interaction with the police, I did not speak Spanish. I inserted a language barrier by beginning our conversation in a language that the police officer did not speak. In most areas I was safe with English, although this approach did not always work in Malabo or Bata. My aim was to appear friendly, co-operative and keen to assist, but ultimately unable to comply with certain requests due to an inability to understand what was being asked of me. I generally had a clear picture of what was being asked, but was able to selectively misunderstand requests through feigning ignorance of the language.

MAKE A CONNECTION Unsurprisingly, it is a lot more difficult to extort money from someone you get on with. Upon being pulled over, I tried to build up a rapport as quickly as possible. Using a greeting in one of the local languages worked very well (pages 220–1). Even without this, language did not tend to be a barrier here: I was surprised how well a bit of smiling, pointing and a thumbs up went down. Explaining that I was a teacher was also received positively, as certain professions tend to be well respected throughout the continent.

CARRY COPIES Most shakedowns were a simple case of ransom: the police officer wanted to take my documentation and not give it back until I handed over a certain amount of cash. My passport was the jackpot in this scenario, so I always tried to avoid handing over anything that I was not willing to lose or leave behind.

I would always begin by handing over a laminated colour photocopy of my passport, explaining (not in Spanish) that the original was in my hotel. At this stage I would often also hand over more than had been requested, to reinforce the idea that I was attempting to be co-operative: photocopies of visas, driving licences, even random travel insurance documents all got thrust into the unsuspecting hands of police officers. An original International Driving Licence was an excellent addition to my tool-kit, as it only cost me £5.50 from a UK post office, making it official-looking but ultimately disposable (unlike a more expensive EU driving licence or equivalent).

BE PATIENT Most police shakedowns occured not because the policeman was necessarily a bad person, but because they wished to supplement their meagre state salary with additional income. By this logic, they needed to extract a certain amount of money from people per hour of work in order to hit their earnings target. I was clearly singled out as I was visibly foreign, perceived as rich, and they (incorrectly) assumed that I would therefore be more likely to hand over a large bribe to be on my way quickly.

However, I tended to find that the longer the police spent unsuccessfully trying to persuade me to part with my cash, the more potentially easier targets passed them by, and the closer they got to the end of their shift. At a busy road checkpoint with plenty of traffic near Malabo, police invested a maximum of around 20 minutes trying to persuade me to hand over my cash before giving up and moving on. This figure increased exponentially when I was out in rural and isolated areas without many other opportunities for shakedowns. Generally speaking I was not in a rush so I just tried to remember to be patient, as time was on my side, not theirs.

BE STUPID BUT CO-OPERATIVE As I discovered the hard way many years ago, losing my temper and showing a lack of respect does not go down well with corrupt officials and certainly did not speed up my departure from checkpoints. Coming off as a co-operative, smiling foreign idiot usually gets me much better results. If the policeman asked for one thing, I would give him three alternative items. If he asked where I was going, I told him where I had come from. If he asked for my nationality, I told him my name. The list is endless, although it is walking a fine line between building frustration and causing them to lose their temper (which is never a good thing).

CARRY UNWANTED GIFTS When is a bribe not a bribe? Perhaps when they refuse to take it! While this is certainly a moral grey area with regards to encouraging police corruption, I often found that offering a very low-value gift (that the officer did not want) helped to expedite my departure more effectively than an angrily waved US$20 bill. In Equatorial Guinea, a bribe is often referred to as a 'Fanta', ostensibly a drink, but in reality a small amount of cash. I tried apologising for not having Fanta, and instead offered a warm bottle of water (which always got refused). Alternatively, I also carried a packet of the filthiest, cheapest Chinese cigarettes I could find in the local market (we're talking US$6 for 200), which not even the most nicotine-addicted police officers would accept. But hey, at least I was being polite by offering!

IF IT ALL GOES WRONG My rather time-consuming efforts to avoid corruption paid off, as throughout my entire research trip I did not hand over a single illegal payment to the security services. However, in the immortal words of Brian Fantana in the film *Anchorman*: '60% of the time, it works every time', these techniques are certainly not foolproof! In the past I have found myself in situations where trying these techniques would be ineffective or even foolhardy; for example, when someone is pointing a gun at me, I tend to prefer doing exactly what they ask, immediately. Likewise, if officials are drunk or getting aggressive, I try not to test their patience as it often results in more trouble. I find that the best thing about introducing an artificial language barrier at the beginning of the shakedown is that if it all starts going wrong, I can magically regain my ability to speak functional Spanish (or whatever the local language is) and start complying more readily with their demands. Oddly, the police tend not to notice this, or notice and do not care as they are happy you are suddenly doing what they want!

Equatorial Guinea receives very few tourists every year, and the only foreigners that many rural communities have seen tend to be associated with the oil industry (making them predominantly male). This may make you an object of interest in rural areas, but you should still be safe.

TRAVELLERS WITH A DISABILITY There is no legislation in place to ensure that travellers with a disability can access public or private facilities. Such travellers will also struggle to access transportation. Malabo and Bata feature good quality pavements in most parts, making access easier, but outside the provincial capitals wheelchair users will find uneven surfaces and road crossings the norm. The higher-end hotels in Malabo, such as the Hilton or Sofitel, are well equipped to cater for wheelchair users, although those wishing to head out of the regional capitals will need to make special arrangements as none of the national parks or other tourist sites of interest have disabled facilities.

LESBIAN, GAY, BISEXUAL AND TRANSGENDERED (LGBT) TRAVELLERS There are no specific laws to criminalise same-sex sexual activity in Equatorial Guinea (it has been decriminalised since 1931). The age of consent for homosexuals is also the same as for heterosexuals: 18. However, the prevalence of Catholicism and the conservative nature of society mean that homosexuality is not widely accepted, and societal stigmatisation and discrimination is strong, with little effort made by the government to combat it. There are very few openly LGBT individuals in Equatorial Guinea. Within the expatriate-dominated bars, clubs and hotels of Malabo and Bata, openly LGBT travellers are unlikely to elicit much attention, although it is advisable to avoid public displays of affection in more conservative, rural areas.

TRAVELLING WITH CHILDREN Children are a key part of Equatoguinean society. They make up 45% of the population thanks to an average of 4.9 children per woman. You will encounter children everywhere on your travels, and if you are visiting with children they are sure to be made welcome. Given the lack of international schooling facilities in Malabo or Bata, few expatriate families bring their children with them, so travelling around as a foreigner with a child is likely to attract curious attention.

While supermarkets and pharmacies in the urban centres stock a range of Western baby products, it is advisable for those with very young children to bring their supplies with them, as they may find some items unavailable, or more expensive than back home.

WHAT TO TAKE

Lightweight, loose-fitting, washable clothing is recommended for the humid climate. Smart casual clothing will be suitable for most occasions. Ensure that you have closed shoes, long trousers and a collared shirt (a polo shirt will do) to wear when visiting ministries and some foreign embassies, as you may be refused service if you are perceived to be improperly dressed. A waterproof jacket is also recommended as no matter where in the country you go, at some point you are likely to get rained on!

Insect repellent with a high DEET content is essential. This is much easier to bring with you than source locally. Likewise pack high-factor suncream, personal toiletries and cosmetics, and a mosquito net, which is rarely provided in less expensive accommodation.

If you are going hiking in one of the national parks, or anywhere remote, a solid pair of boots that cover the ankle will be useful. They should also give some protection against snakebites. Anybody travelling away from major centres should carry a personal first-aid kit (page 75).

Those hiring a car will require an International Driving Permit, which must then be swapped for a local driving licence upon arrival. In theory, you should be able to drive on your International or EU licence for a short stay, but in practice the police are not keen to accept EU licences or the International Driving Permit (page 109). You should also take multiple photocopies of all your major documentation (passport, visa, etc), and ideally make a laminated, colour photocopy of your passport with the visa, information page and entry stamp clearly shown as soon as you arrive.

ELECTRICALS Ensure that your mobile phone is unlocked so that you can buy a local SIM card. You generally cannot roam with your home SIM card once you arrive, unless you have an Orange SIM bought from within the region (such as in Gabon or Cameroon). GSM coverage is good on Bioko, covering most of the island apart from a southern portion. In Río Muni it is far more patchy, with limited signal outside the provincial capitals. If you are going to be travelling outside these areas and need to stay in touch, consider packing a satellite phone, but be prepared for some suspicious questioning at immigration on arrival, as there is paranoia surrounding potential dual-use equipment (items which can have both military and civilian applications).

If you are taking a laptop or other electronic device which you intend to power or charge from the mains, consider investing in a surge protector. The electricity grid in some areas is unreliable, and when power switches to a generator, this can often cause a power surge which damages any equipment plugged into the mains. You may also need a plug adaptor, as Equatorial Guinea uses plugs with two round pins, as in Spain, running at 220V, 50Hz cycles (page 2). Modem and telephone jacks are European RJ-11 size, so you may need an adapter which will be difficult to find locally.

Memory cards and batteries are available but they may be expensive and difficult to find, so it is perhaps best to bring them from home.

Always bring a torch, as power cuts are frequent.

MONEY

The local currency in Equatorial Guinea is the Central African CFA franc (iso code: XAF). Equatorial Guinea has a predominantly cash-based economy. Only the high-end hotels and restaurants accept credit cards, and there are a small but growing number of ATMs that accept foreign cards both on Bioko and in Río Muni (but not on Corisco or Annobón). Euros are widely accepted and easily converted. US dollars can also be used. It is advisable to take enough cash to cover your entire trip, rather than relying on accessing your funds in-country. Travellers' cheques can be changed at some of the larger banks in Malabo or Bata, but rates are not good. You are better off sticking with cash.

THE CFA FRANC The CFA franc is also used in Cameroon, the Central African Republic, Chad, the Republic of Congo and Gabon. It is pegged to the euro at a rate of 655.957CFA to €1 (accurate as of September 2015). This currency is not to be confused with the West African CFA franc (iso code: XOF), which is used in Benin, Burkina Faso, Côte d'Ivoire, Guinea-Bissau, Mali, Niger, Senegal and Togo, and is also pegged to the euro and is of exactly the same value as the CFA franc.

The CFA franc is available in 1, 2, 5, 10, 25, 50, 100 and 500 franc coins and 500, 1,000, 2,000, 5,000 and 10,000 franc notes.

EUROS AND DOLLARS The euro is king in Equatorial Guinea. Payment in euros is accepted by most businesses, although your change will be given in CFA. In more rural areas though you may struggle to persuade people to accept euros, or agree an exchange rate.

Dollars are also widely accepted, but less popular. All bills must be in good condition, and some vendors may refuse to accept any US$100 bills from before 1996 (with small heads on them), as these are considered easier to counterfeit across Africa.

CASH MACHINES (ATMS) AND CREDIT CARDS Cash machines can be found in most provincial capitals. There are ATMs in both Malabo and Bata that will work with international Visa and MasterCard, distributing CFA notes. You may need to run around a number of ATMs before finding one that still has notes available, especially during the weekend or just after payday, often the last Friday of the month.

You can use credit cards at the higher-end hotels (such as the Hilton and Sofitel), as well as the major airline offices (Air France, Iberia and Lufthansa). Other than that, they are not widely accepted so be sure to check before incurring expenses!

MONEY TRANSFERS Bank transfers within the Economic and Monetary Community of Central Africa are generally a simple affair which can be organised from any bank. Opening an account as a short-term visitor can be a tricky process, and you would be better off having money sent to you via Western Union or MoneyGram if you need cash to arrive quickly. You will need to present your passport to collect money sent via these services. Western Union's local partners are Ecobank and Société Générale de Banque GE (SGBE). MoneyGram use Caisse Commune d'Epargne et d'Investissement (CCEI).

CHANGING MONEY The preferred currencies for exchange at local banks are euros, US dollars and pounds sterling. There is technically no limit to the amount of foreign currency you can bring into the country as a foreign tourist, as long as you declare it upon arrival. The best exchange rates are usually to be found by talking to local businesses that trade overseas, such as importers, although changing your money in this unofficial capacity is of dubious legality.

TIPPING There is not a widespread tipping culture in Equatorial Guinea, although higher-end establishments are used to foreigners leaving a tip. A few euros generally sufficient in restaurants and other settings. Western-style tipping of 10% plus is uncommon.

BUDGETING

Equatorial Guinea is an expensive place to live, work or visit. The US State Department augments their workers' salaries in Malabo to the same extent as those posted in places such as Berlin, Hong Kong or Tokyo. An abundance of oil wealth, combined with a lack of domestic production and a reliance on imports, means consumers face high prices for most goods. In a Malabo supermarket you will often be able to find many of the same brands as back in Europe, but at a premium price. A lack of quality accommodation means that hotel prices are also very high: the cheapest room at the Sofitel or Hilton will set you back €245/US$280 per night. Combined with the frequently high cost of international flights, Equatorial Guinea represents a serious challenge for the budget traveller.

The Equatoguinean consulate in London requires a bank statement showing at least £2,000 in funds before issuing a 30-day tourist visa. This implies that the official recommended daily budget for visitors is set at around £66 (US$105/€90). It is possible to get by on this, or even less, but it requires some careful planning.

Your main expense will likely be the airfare. Direct flights from Madrid or Frankfurt tend to be booked out in advance by business travellers and therefore are the most expensive. Also, try to avoid leaving the UK on a long-haul flight (as opposed to a cheap regional flight), as these incur the highest departure taxes and fuel surcharges. Consider taking a non-direct route via a regional hub such as Addis Ababa or Casablanca for a discounted fare. You might also consider splitting your journey, getting a cheap return on a route like Paris to Douala, then buying a ticket into Equatorial Guinea with a regional carrier such as Ceiba Intercontinental Airlines. Although this is a logistical headache, it could save you a fair bit of money.

Paying for accommodation does not have to be extortionate. One option available is to use CouchSurfing.com, which is a social networking website that allows free hospitality exchanges. Users can give each other public feedback, in much the same way as eBay or Amazon, to ensure that hosts and guests behave according to the terms and conditions. There are numerous active members in both Malabo and Bata, advertising their couches as available for guests. Please note that this online community is reliant on trust and reciprocity: a brand new user with zero reviews is less likely to be hosted than an established user who has themselves hosted visitors in the past and been reviewed. Also, be sure to take sensible precautions before staying in the house of a complete stranger: check to ensure they have positive reviews from previous visitors, make sure someone else knows exactly where you are staying, and have a backup plan: if things do not work out with your host, where can you leave to quickly?

Another option is to try using Airbnb. This is a commercial website that allows people to rent out private lodging. There are whole homes, flats or even individual rooms available in 34,000 cities across 190 countries. Coverage of Equatorial Guinea is currently very limited, but even now their prices offer better value for money than most hotel rooms in Malabo, plus you can find somewhere with a kitchen which enables you to save money by cooking at home. You may also be able to arrange cheaper accommodation through one of the numerous NGOs working in Equatorial Guinea, who sometimes rent out vacant staff accommodation to visitors in order to fund their projects.

If none of these options sound appealing, then there are budget hotel rooms available, sometimes as cheaply as US$25/€20 a night in the capital, but do not expect much in terms of creature comforts in this price bracket!

In terms of your day-to-day shopping expenses, see below for some typical item prices from Malabo in early 2015:

Litre bottle of water	1,000CFA	½ litre of beer (imported)	2,000CFA
Litre of UHT milk	1,000CFA	Loaf of bread	1,500CFA
170g can of tuna	600CFA	Street snack	1,000CFA
Packet of crisps	200CFA	Mars Bar	500CFA
100g of sliced cured meat	750CFA	T-shirt	6,000CFA
100g of sliced cheese	1,100CFA	Litre of petrol	465CFA
500g tub of margarine	600CFA		

BY AIR

Domestic airlines At the time of writing the following airlines were certified by the Equatoguinean authorities for domestic flights (both commercial and charter), although not all were currently active: Ceiba Intercontinental Airlines, Cronos Airlines, Ecuato Guineana de Aviacion (EGA), Guinea Ecuatorial Airlines (GEASA), General Work Aviation, Guinea Equatorial de Transportes Aereos (GETRA), Jetline International, KNG Transavia Cargo, Punto Azul and Star Equatorial AL. Domestic airlines in Equatorial Guinea have a poor reputation for safety by international standards. Since 2006, all air carriers certified by the authorities in Equatorial Guinea are subject to a ban within the European Union. This includes: Ceiba Intercontinental Airlines, Cronos Airlines, Punto Azul and Tango Airways, although it is worth noting that Ceiba Intercontinental does maintain one aircraft that is allowed access to European airspace, and makes the direct Malabo to Madrid run. Other airlines may also follow this pattern of keeping one better-maintained plane for access to Europe.

British government employees do not use Equatorial Guinean-registered aircraft unless it is unavoidable. Some domestic carriers still use old, poorly maintained Soviet Antonov or Yakovlev planes, which tend to be the ones involved in local aviation accidents. In April 2008, an Antonov 32 skidded off the end of the short runway at Annobón while landing in poor weather conditions, killing all 13 people on board. Charter flights are also of variable quality, as exemplified by the plane by the side of the road between Bata and Río Campo (page 162).

If you choose to brave an internal flight, ticketing options are varied. Some airlines require purchase in cash at their office, whereas others (such as Punto Azul) will allow you to buy through their website with a credit card, and even have an online check-in facility. Some travel agencies, both in Equatorial Guinea and abroad, will be able to issue you with a domestic ticket (pages 65–6).

Check-in tends to run right up until the flight is scheduled to depart, and many travellers leave it very late to arrive at the airport. Arriving 2 hours before departure often makes you the first person there. Punctuality and reliability are highly variable and last-minute cancellations are a possibility. However, given the volume of flights moving between the main hubs of Malabo and Bata, you are unlikely to remain stranded for long, provided you do not mind paying for another ticket.

Punto Azul are the best domestic airline, and it is worth paying extra to fly with them rather than the national airline Ceiba Intercontinental Airlines. Punto Azul's punctuality and reliability is superior, and they are less likely to lose your bag.

The domestic terminal in Malabo is attached to the international terminal. It is small, crowded and very poorly organised. Expect chaos while checking in, with hot and crowded bag drop facilities and no information screens. The domestic terminal in Bata is also in the international terminal. It is air conditioned, spacious and has a bar area.

Domestic airline offices in Malabo and Bata Fares vary between airlines but on average you can expect to pay 105,000CFA for a return from Malabo to Bata, and 125,000CFA for a return from Bata to Annobón. All ticket office opening times are 09.00–16.00 Monday–Friday and 09.00–13.00 Saturday, unless otherwise noted.

Malabo

✈ **Ceiba Intercontinental Airlines** Calle del Presidente Nasser, Malabo; ☎333 040 922, 333 098 149; 📱222 270 168; e ceiba@fly-ceiba. com, general@ceibaintercontinental.com; www. fly-ceiba.com; ⏱ 08.30–16.00 Mon–Fri, 09.00–noon Sat. Sell all domestic tickets except those to Annobón, which must be purchased from the Ceiba office in the airport (which is only open when there is a Ceiba flight departing). There are flights from Malabo to Bata up to 3 times a day, Annobón twice a week & irregular flights to Mengomeyén.

✈ **Cronos Airlines** Calle de Enrique Nvó 178, Malabo; ☎333 090 471; 📱222 600 808; e ssgc8cto@cronosair.com; www.cronosair.com. Flights from Malabo to Bata twice daily.

✈ **Punto Azul** Paraiso District (main street) or Av de la Libertad, Centro Comercial La Libertad, Malabo; 📱222 605 949, 222 111 100; e reservations@ flypuntoazul.com; www.flypuntoazul.com. Flights from Malabo to Bata 3 times a day.

Bata

✈ **Ceiba Intercontinental Airlines** Punto de Ayuntamiento, Bata; ☎333 581

027; e verahose@gmail.com, general@ ceibaintercontinental.com; ⏱ 08.00–16.00 Mon–Fri, 08.00–noon Sat. They only accept cash payments for tickets in this office, & do not sell tickets to Annobón, which must be purchased from the Ceiba office at the airport, which opens 2 hrs before flight departures & closes upon flight departure. Queues are often long & customer service poor so it is probably worthwhile heading to the airport to buy your tickets, unless you can find a quiet time.

✈ **Confort Airlines** Calle de Radio Bata, Bata; ☎333 081 087; www.confortairlines.com. Offer freight & charter aviation services from Bata airport.

✈ **Cronos Airlines** Next to Aparthotel Plaza & Discoteca Rolex; ☎333 087 986; e ssgc8cto@ cronosair.com, online@cronosair.com; www. cronosair.com. Currently offers only twice-daily flights between Malabo & Bata. Routes to Douala in Cameroon, Cotonou in Benin & Port Harcourt in Nigeria from Malabo are currently suspended, although planned to resume in late 2015. The company also plans to introduce new routes to Niamey in Niger, Lagos in Nigeria & Yaoundé in Cameroon in 2016.

BY BOAT It is possible to travel both domestically and throughout the region via boat, although this is suggested only for those travellers with a lot of patience and an open ended schedule! For those looking to travel around Equatorial Guinea, there is a domestic ferry service that links Malabo to Bata, and then on to Annobón, but this is highly irregular and seemingly impossible to book (page 150). Much more reliable is the SOMAGEC ferry service that links Cogo to Corisco and Annobón (page 173). It is also possible to hire smaller *pirogues* to travel between Acalayong and Cogo (page 167), Corisco and the Elobey islands (page 170) plus Cogo and Corisco (page 168), although this method of transport is not recommended for longer sea journeys due to safety issues.

BY ROAD There are **no public railways** in Equatorial Guinea, so if you are not flying then you will be using the road network to travel around. The majority of the **roads** in Equatorial Guinea are paved and are of good quality, so you need not be concerned with having a 4x4 to access major towns and settlements. Driving conditions can become dangerous with torrential downpours, however, especially as many vehicles on the roads are poorly maintained. It is best to avoid driving at night or during adverse weather. You will find you need a 4x4 for certain unpaved roads, and the newly completed road from Luba to Ureca on Bioko, which has an extremely steep gradient.

There are a number of **toll booths** on the major roads heading out of provincial capitals. The price of the tolls is very low, at only 100CFA. Ensure you are carrying change, as the booths cannot always break large notes.

The favoured means of getting between population centres in Equatorial Guinea is in **shared taxis** (this is true for Bioko island as well as Río Muni). These can be found in most major towns, usually at the market. Within towns, there are also licenced shared taxis, which will take you from A to B for 500CFA.

Inter-provincial buses are run by companies such as Kassav Express in Río Muni (page 209), and are usually cheaper than taking a shared taxi, albeit less comfortable.

Car hire There are a number of international rental operators in Equatorial Guinea, as well as smaller outfits, often associated with the tour companies. You can pick up rental cars in both Bata and Malabo. Car hire is expensive and requires a large security deposit (page 109). For information on driving licence requirements, see page 109.

Autos Litoral ibis Hotel, Paseo Marítimo de Bata, Bata; ☎666 187 195, 666 162 840; m 222 604 674, 222 604 999; e autoslitoralbata@yahoo.es; www.autoslitoral.com; ⊕ 09.00–20.00 Mon–Fri. Situated in the lobby of the hotel, Autos Litoral has a fleet of over 200 vehicles & offer up to a 40% discount for w/end special bookings. Prices are still very high, with their cheapest vehicle (a Renault Clio) going for 69,000CFA per day, plus a 250,000CFA deposit. It can also organise drivers for sightseeing trips.

AVIS Cfao Motors, Carretera del Aeropuerto, Km4 Sn, Malabo; ☎333 090 769; www.avis.com/car-rental/location/AFR/EQ/Malabo; ⊕ 07.45–12.15 & 14.30–18.00 Mon–Fri

Europcar Malabo airport; ☎333 091 902; or Malabo Downtown, BP 493; ☎333 091 902, 333 091 823; www.europcar.com/location/equatorial-guinea/malabo

GE Leasing Carretera del Aeropuerto, Bata; m 555 782 050. This business mainly deals with commercial construction rentals but can organise 4x4s for customers.

Intercar Fru Hotel Bahia 2, Caracolas, Malabo; ☎333 091 328, 333 250 366

HITCHHIKING In rural areas hitchhiking is a common means of transportation for the local population. There is also a fair amount of construction traffic moving between urban sites, so you will not have difficulty getting a lift in a company 4x4 or on a truck if you are willing to wait for it. In some areas, such as on Annobón or Corisco islands, hitchhiking with construction traffic is the only means of getting around as there are no private vehicles at all!

ACCOMMODATION

Unless you are staying with a contact in-country, or have made arrangements for a place through CouchSurfing or Airbnb, hotels will be your main accommodation option.

The government has invested a great deal of money in high-end accommodation over the past few years, meaning that business travellers and those tourists with a larger budget will find themselves well catered for in Malabo, Bata and Mongomo.

ACCOMMODATION PRICE CODES

Prices are based on a double room per night, including taxes

$$$$$	luxury	100,000CFA+	€150+
$$$$	upmarket	70,000–100,000CFA	€105–150
$$$	mid range	40,000–70,000CFA	€60–105
$$	budget	20,000–40,000CFA	€30–60
$	rock bottom	<20,000CFA	<€30

More luxury accommodation is due to come online soon on Corisco island and in the future capital of Oyala. Prices are very high for this type of accommodation and there is plenty of availability unless your visit coincides with an official function or regional meeting. Note that many of these hotels, and those in the mid-range bracket, are filled with long-term residents who sometimes smoke in their rooms, so be sure to check before accepting your room.

Decent mid-range accommodation is much harder to find, and even more overpriced relative to the quality of services on offer. Unless you speak Spanish, it will be difficult to book these hotels in advance, and they do not always respond to email requests. In this situation, social media is often a more fruitful means of communication than official email addresses or website enquiry forms.

There is a dearth of budget or backpacker accommodation in Equatorial Guinea. At the lowest end of the price range you will find some truly awful places, with no air conditioning, running water or even proper toilet facilities. Some of these places are frequented by prostitutes and have a lot of people coming and going all night. Where this is the case it has been noted in the listing. It is inadvisable for lone female travellers to stay at these locations.

Those wishing to travel around over a longer period on a budget are advised to try and organise accommodation through a local contact, or scout www.couchsurfing.com or www.airbnb.com for non-traditional options. Outside the main cities, camping is often preferable to the low-budget hotel options.

CAMPING There are no formal camping grounds in the country, beyond the official research sites in Bioko Sur run by the Bioko Biodiversity Protection Program (page 143). Despite this, there are some great camping options, especially on the idyllic and quiet beaches of Bioko island and Litoral Province, for example up on the Punta Tika and Punta Cuche beaches in the northwest of the Reserva Natural de Río Campo, on the conservation site run by the TOMAGE Project (page 162). There are also many private spaces where you could camp on both Annobón and Corisco islands. It is a good idea to register your presence with the local village *comisario* or police chief before setting up camp (this is a requirement in some places such as Ureca). Be aware of the potential threat from wild animals, and also the tide lines when camping on the beach. Camping equipment is available to rent from guides at the Monte Alen National Park (page 189), as well as from the BBPP Wildlife Research Center just outside Moka (pages 142–3). Also, try to camp responsibly by taking all of your waste with you when you leave the site, putting out fires correctly and not polluting water sources. This is especially important when camping on beaches with turtles, as plastic litter can kill baby turtles.

EATING AND DRINKING

The food of Equatorial Guinea has much in common with the dishes found in West and Central Africa. Similarities include: widespread (and liberal) use of pimento, the mixing of meat and fish in the same dish, the use of groundnuts or ground pumpkin seeds, and the prevalence of shrimps, prawns and river crayfish (whether dried, smoked or ground). These culinary similarities are not surprising when considering the climate in the areas these dishes are found, and the availability of local ingredients.

The Portuguese introduced food and plants in many of the areas that they colonised. *Malanga cubana* (cocoyam) from the Americas and *malanga bubi* (taro)

TRADITIONAL DISHES OF EQUATORIAL GUINEA

Recipe list courtesy of Dr Igor Cusack, from the *Arizona Journal of Hispanic Cultural Studies*

Dish Name	Description	Origins
Aloso Godo Jojondjo	Rice and coconut pudding	Annobón
Banga Sup	Meat, smoked shrimp and stockfish cooked in a cream of palm oil	Common across West Africa
Bekoka	Smoked fish	Ndowe recipe (coastal Río Muni)
Bita-leef	Greens, meat, *egussi* (made from seeds of a melon-like fruit, sometimes called pumpkin), smoked fish, palm oil, dried powdered prawns	Mixed
Bokaho	Soup made of fish and greens	Bubi (Bioko)
Boll-Miná	Fish balls cooked with greens, pimento and aubergine in a fish stock	Found in Equatorial Guinea, Nigeria and Cameroon
Djom-Anuan (pheasant or toucan), *Djom-Chit* (meat), *Djom-Fuas* (palm tree grubs), *Djom-Kuas* (fish)	All wrapped in banana/plantain or other large leaves, mixed with various seasonings and vegetables and cooked on the fire in sand in a pot, or on charcoal or in a pot with some water in the base	Mixed
Djomba	Fish with spicy sauce (*modika*)	Ndowe recipe (Combe), also found in Cameroon, Nigeria, Liberia, Sierra Leone
Ebafono	Maize, peanuts, freshwater crayfish wrapped in banana/plantain leaves	Fang
Itocod-ja Mepoo	Smoked meat, tomato, dried crayfish, pimento and nuts	Ndowe

from India have since established themselves as staples of local cuisine in very geographically dispersed areas of Africa. In terms of drinks, both palm wine (*tope*) and *malamba* (an alcoholic drink made from sugarcane) are very popular, although imported European alcohols tend to dominate the market today.

One of the more unusual dishes found in Equatorial Guinea was the African brush-tailed porcupine (known locally as *chucku-chucku*, and which was incidentally the 2015 Africa Cup of Nations mascot). This is sometimes baked with a cocoa sauce, giving a distinctive sweet flavour to the fatty meat. In the south of Bioko at Ureca, the local population has a tradition of eating the meat and eggs of marine turtles, preferring those of the green and leatherback turtles over the olive ridley or hawksbill species. Green turtles are typically found for sale in the markets of Bata and Libreville in neighbouring Gabon. They are hunted by the Benga tribe communities around Corisco Bay, as this is a known turtle foraging ground although conservation efforts are helping to reduce this practice. The Annobónese also supplement their diets with whale meat after the annual whale hunt.

Dish Name	Description	Origins
Lomandoha	Homemade chocolate, tomatoes, malanga (cocoyam) leaves, fish or sardines, pimento	Mixed
Mbombi Muadjakasi	Salt fish with lemon and pimento cooked in banana/plantain leaves	Mixed
Mbua Mua Menoni	Aubergine, okra and crab	Mixed
Mendja	Sauce of yuca (cassava) leaves and other vegetables and fruit-small aubergines, fresh maize, malanga, dates, bananas and pimento	Fang
Mendjim Ondondo	Fish cooked in peppery sauce	Mixed
Metonga	Stuffed crab cooked in the shell with lemon and pimento	Mixed
Nsa Nguam	Porcupine, pumpkin seeds, smoked fish, onions, tomato and palm oil	Mixed
Pepe sup	Fresh fish, onion and pimento soup	Common across West Africa
Pishojo Jojond'o	Yuca (cassava) and coconut milk cooked in banana leaves	Mixed
Sup-Oguon	Groundnut soup made from ground roasted groundnuts, fish (fresh or dried), meat (especially chicken), okra, tomato, oil, pimento	Mixed
Tochi Machea	Snails cooked in leaves with pumpkin seeds, onion and palm oil	Bubi
Yeb'e (malanga soup)	With sardines, malanga, dried crayfish	Bubi

Many types of bushmeat are also traditionally consumed. The three most popular species on Bioko are the blue duiker (*Cephalophus monticola*), the forest giant pouched rat (*Cricetomys emini*), and the African brush-tailed porcupine (*Atherurus africanus*). None of these species are endangered, although the Bubi are also keen on the tree pangolin (*Phataginus tricuspis*), while the Fang prefer to eat the giant pangolin (*Smutsia gigantea*), both of which are vulnerable species. You may also find monkey on the menu in certain markets, but since the 2014 Ebola epidemic in West Africa, demand has reduced. The trade in bushmeat in Equatorial Guinea is not effectively regulated, and as such represents risks to both the health of the consumers and biodiversity in the hunting areas. It is not recommended that you support this trade. The Zoological Society of London Bushmeat Research Programme has been monitoring the situation in Equatorial Guinea for the past 15 years. More information can be found at: http://www.zsl.org/science/research/bushmeat.

The cuisine of Equatorial Guinea offers something for all taste palettes. For breakfast, be sure to try a traditional Spanish potato omelette in one of the many cafés dotted about the towns. *Pepe sup* (see above) is a great and widely available

Prices are based on the cost of a main course per person

$$$$$	expensive	30,000CFA+	€45+
$$$$	above average	20,000–30,000CFA	€30–45
$$$	mid range	10,000–20,000CFA	€15–30
$$	cheap and cheerful	5,000–10,000CFA	€7.50–15
$	rock bottom	<5,000CFA	<€7.50

option for lunch, assuming you like spice! For dinner, why not try one of the traditional dishes listed on pages 92–3? Included is a description of their ingredients and the origins of the cuisine (if known).

EATING OUT The most expensive and fashionable locations to eat in Equatorial Guinea tend to be the restaurants in the luxury hotels, especially in Malabo and Bata. These often host buffet lunches and barbecue events at weekends, which are popular affairs offering a wide variety of mainly European cuisine. The cultural centres of France and Spain also have busy restaurants. In the Spanish tradition, people eat dinner late, and smart dress is the norm. A bit of hunting around throws up a wealth of dining options, from Cuban to Chinese or Middle Eastern. Outside the two main cities, your dining options will be much more limited, but it is never hard to find a local joint cooking up some fish. If in doubt, follow the crowds, and try to avoid eating meat of suspect origins, as it may be bushmeat!

The majority of restaurants open noon–22.00, but hours are variable.

PUBLIC HOLIDAYS AND FESTIVALS

The national bank holidays in Equatorial Guinea are:

- **New Year's Day (1 January)** The night before features a gala event and large charity fireworks display organised by the Ministry of Culture and Tourism in Malabo. This is also televised across the country.
- **Labour Day (1 May)** This is an international bank holiday observed in Equatorial Guinea.
- **President's Day (5 June)** Celebrating the president's official birthday. Many cultural events are timed to coincide with this celebration.
- **Freedom Day (3 August)** Also known as Armed Forces Day, this is in honour of the military, specifically their coup that ended the rule of President Macías in August 1979. It invariably involves a military parade and events to commemorate veterans.
- **Day of the Constitutional Chart (15 August)** Celebrating the implementation of the new constitution following a referendum in 1982 after the removal of President Macías.
- **Independence Day (12 October)** Celebrating the end of Spanish rule in 1968. This is a huge event, with the president giving a special nationwide address.
- **Immaculate Conception Feast (8 December)** A Christian celebration commemorating the Immaculate Conception of the Blessed Virgin Mary.
- **Christmas Day (25 December)** A Christian celebration commemorating the birth of Jesus Christ.

Any bank holiday falling on a non-working day is shifted to the next working day. There are also two religious bank holidays with changeable dates:

- **Good Friday** A Christian celebration commemorating the crucifixion of Jesus Christ, falling in either March or April. This is taken very seriously in Equatorial Guinea, with families coming together and attending special church services.
- **Corpus Christi Feast** A Christian feast in honour of the Holy Eucharist, falling in either May or June. A group of children known as Seises sing and dance in the cathedral. Streets are covered in rushes and rosemary.

Aside from these key dates, some other events to look out for include:

- **The Africa Cup of Nations** This huge football event is organised biennially with 16 national teams participating in the finals. Equatorial Guinea hosted it in 2012, and then again in January 2015 after Morocco pulled out unexpectedly. The next event will be held in January 2017. Whether hosting or not, football is a big deal in Equatorial Guinea, and you will be sure to find a screen to watch it on and a carnival atmosphere wherever you are in the country.
- **Francophonie Week** Organised around 20 March which is International Francophone Day, the French cultural centres in Malabo and Bata offer a series of special events highlighting the diversity of Francophone culture, including music, cinema, cuisine, art and theatre.
- **Eco Carnival** Inaugurated in 2012, this event, held in conjunction with the French Cultural Centre, aims to raise awareness among young people of the value of the natural environment on Bioko. The date is variable, with the last event occurring on 15 November 2014.
- **Malabo Hip Hop Festival** A ten-day event held in December, with acts from the hip hop community across Africa, as well as French and Spanish groups. The event was first organised by the Spanish Cultural Centre in Malabo (CCEM) and the Cultural Institute of French Expression (ICEF) back in 2007, and has grown annually to become one of the most successful and popular events on the cultural calendar.
- **Malabo International Fashion Week** Running since 2010, this event features a showcase of local design talent, as well as established names from the French and Spanish fashion world. It tends to be centred around Sipopo, and takes place in the last quarter of the year.
- **Music Day Festival** Hosted by the Ministry of Culture and Tourism and the construction company SOMAGEC to celebrate Equatoguinean musical heritage, this is a large music festival in Malabo. Dates change annually, with events usually held around June/July.

SHOPPING

Finding consumer goods in Equatorial Guinea has become less difficult in recent years, but it will still be expensive and time consuming. If there's something you need, bring it with you from your home country. There is no fixed retail area in either Bata or Malabo, so you may have to scout around more than one location to find what you are looking for. Generally speaking, you should be able to find most electrical items or foods at a large premium, but will struggle to hunt down Western clothing, cosmetics or other luxury items. The supermarkets have an increasing

with Jacob C Cooper and Luke L Powell, Equatorial Guinea Bird Initiative

Birding is easy in Equatorial Guinea, and just driving through the fringes of towns and cities will undoubtedly result in multiple sightings of hornbills and turacos flying by. Roadside birding is extremely productive, and birding forest-agricultural transitions can often result in impressively diverse birding days, regardless of what habitat you are in. Just be sure to check in with the locals before going out – guides are a must in most regions, and government officials can be very sensitive about where you point your camera and binoculars.

BIOKO Arguably the crown jewel of Equatorial Guinea, Bioko hosts a plethora of rare and local species and is often the highlight of any birding trip to the region. In addition to hosting more than 40 endemic subspecies and three endemic species, the island provides an excellent mix of lowland and highland birding opportunities. Regrettably, much of the lowland forest on the northern half of the island has been cleared for development and farmland, but many species can still be found in the forests surrounding the town edges. More adventurous visitors can hike into the pristine lowlands of the southern coast for some of the more local inhabitants, including black-casqued wattled hornbills (*Ceratogymna atrata*) and grey-necked picathartes (*Picathartes oreas*). The three peaks of Bioko all harbour Afromontane species, but visiting at least two (Pico Basilé and Pico Biao) is necessary to get the full suite.

Two must-stop locations are the peak itself and the 'Bosque del 2,000m'. The peak's actual summit is occupied by military towers, but the surrounding elfin forests provide the only habitat in the world for the Bioko speirops (*Zosterops brunneus*) and provide an opportunity to see many other high-elevation forest and grassland species such as African hill babbler (*Sylvia abyssinica*), yellow bishop (*Euplectes capensis*), and oriole finch (*Linurgus olivaceus*). Driving back down the mountain, you will soon find the forest transition to the denser Afromontane forests of the Cameroonian highlands ecoregion, and will know that you are at the 'Bosque del 2,000m' when you reach a giant landslide on the south side of the road with trees on all sides. Walking this stretch of road provides excellent opportunities for encountering evergreen-forest warblers (*Bradypterus lopezi*) and green longtails (*Urolais epichlorus*). Further south, the southeastern flanks of Pico Biao are home to the Bioko Biodiversity Protection Program (BBPP) field station. Home to a bird population programme that has been in place since 2011, the trails behind the station offer an excellent mix of open country and forest birds, and the dawn chorus from the porch is one of the best in the world. The distinctive 'whip-crack' calls of foraging mountain sooty boubous (*Laniarius poensis*) is a constant distraction from the ubiquitous hooting of the yellow-rumped tinkerbirds (*Pogoniulus bilinetus*), and the chatter of grey parrots (*Psittacus erithacus*) often betrays the presence of the large flocks that move across the valley. The fields behind the station often have foraging mountain sawwings (*Psalidoprocne fuliginosa*), and the forest hosts white-bellied crested flycatchers (*Elminia albiventris*), surprisingly tame yellow-billed turacos (*Tauraco macrorhynchus*) and a resident pair of endemic 'Bioko' red-chested goshawks (*Accipiter tousseneli lopezi*).

Those wishing a more unique experience can hike the trail to the summit of Pico Biao, and encounter a wide mix of open, montane and submontane forest birds. The most productive stretches of the trail are usually the forest just above town, which is reliable for the endemic Bioko batis (*Batis poensis*), and the stretch of forest approximately 2km from town that parallels the barbed-wire fence. The fence section is excellent for the black-capped woodland warbler (*Phylloscopus herberti herberti*, the endemic Bioko subspecies) and the Cameroon olive greenbul (*Phyllastrephus poensis*). The summit itself is a stretch of alpine forest and grassland surrounding a large volcanic lake, and is a great place for eating lunch while watching little grebes (*Tachybaptus ruficollis*) swimming far below and large flocks of swifts flying high above you. Several species of swift occur on Bioko, including the exceedingly rare (and aptly named) scarce swift (*Schoutedenapus myoptilus poensis*) and the enigmatic Sladen's swift (*Apus sladeniae*). Most of these swifts cannot be safely identified in the field, so exercise caution when trying to identify them, and don't feel guilty if you have to 'swift spp.' in your notes.

ANNOBÓN Having more in common with São Tomé than with Bioko, Annobón is home to very few species. The largest draw is the endemic Annobón white-eye (*Zosterops griseovirescens*), but the endemic 'Annobón' red-bellied paradise-flycatcher (*Terpsiphone rufiventer smithii*) and 'Fea's' African scops-owl (*Otus senegalensis feae*) should also be sought. Watch the sky for pigeons – the regionally endemic São Tomé pigeon (*Columba malherbii*) can also be found here. Coastal vantage points offer the nation's best opportunity for viewing seabirds.

RÍO MUNI The mainland is home to a large amount of primary rainforest, most of which possesses the same species. The key to lowland birding on the mainland is time; each and every day spent in the lowland forest can be extremely different, so try to find a nice reserve (or two) to spend your time in the lowlands. Excellent locations include Río Campo on the northern coast (which is also home to chimpanzees) and the boulder-studded forests of Parque Nacional de Los Altos de Nsork, home to the shy grey-headed picathartes (*Picathartes oreas*). Learning songs is key in these regions, as greenbuls and nicators call incessantly from thick cover and you'll hear, rather than see, most of the birds you encounter. For those with the patience to scour the dense vegetation, the time and effort put it is worth it: four species of hornbill in a day is not uncommon, and species such as bare-cheeked trogon (*Apaloderma aequatoriale*), chocolate-backed kingfisher (*Halcyon badia*), and lowland akalat (*Sheppardia cyornithopsis*) are just waiting to be found. Those who wish for another taste of the highlands can head to Parque Nacional de Monte Alen, home to the steep and jungle-laden mainland mountains that possess some of the most unique bird communities in the country. Pink-legged puffbacks (*Dryoscopus angolensis*), black-capped woodland warblers and grey cuckooshrikes can all be found here. For those who are becoming claustrophobic from so much jungle birding, Reserva Natural de Punta Llende on the southern coast offers cool ocean breezes and a unique grassland ecosystem surrounded by native forest. Migrant rosy bee-eaters (*Merops malimbicus*) can be found flying over the clearings as long-legged pipits (*Anthus pallidiventris*) run down the road ahead of you. A stop in the nearby city of Mbini is also a must; the town is home to one of the southernmost Preuss's cliff swallow (*Petrochelidon preussi*) colonies in the world and the estuary is home to western reef-herons (*Egretta gularis*) and giant kingfishers (*Megaceryle maxima*).

range of imported fresh goods, and some higher-end hotels feature boutiques with a range of imported items. There is usually a Chinese copy of the thing you are looking for available in one of the local markets (whether this is a drug, electronic item or film). How much you trust the quality is down to your own judgement. The local markets are interesting to walk around, and tend to be a good source of street food. You may also be able to find some local art, carvings or traditional masks to take home as souvenirs, although much of this is generically West African as opposed to specifically Equatoguinean. If you want a distinctive gift, try heading to one of the music shops and picking up a CD or two by local artists.

SPORTS AND ACTIVITIES

There are opportunities for fishing in and around Malabo (page 127). On the mainland, you can go freshwater fishing, especially on the Mbini, Campo and Muni rivers, where it is possible to catch kili, catfish, shad, bonga and jewelfish. If you prefer to get closer to the fish, diving tours can be arranged in Malabo (pages 126–7). The best conditions for diving are from December to March.

SURFING Much of Equatorial Guinea's coastline faces directly out onto the Atlantic Ocean, so there is definitely surf out there. The trick is being able to find it and then access it. June, July and August are your best bets for finding waves, as during this time large low-pressure systems from the south travel up Africa's western coastline and deliver regular southwesterly and westerly swell. Annoyingly, this time of year also features light onshore winds, so you want to head out in the morning. Bioko and Annobón are better positioned to receive swell than the Río Muni region, which can be shielded by the shape of the neighbouring Gabon coastline, as well as São Tomé and Príncipe. Two locations known to the international surf community are **Nacho**, on the very southern tip of Bioko island (⊕ 3°15'19.8"N 8°29'54.0"E), and **Caracas** (⊕ 3°24'00.7"N 8°47'00.7"E), on the east coast just north of Riaba. Both are very isolated, so be sure to take appropriate safety precautions.

PHOTOGRAPHY

No aspect of your visit to Equatorial Guinea is as likely to cause more problems than attempts to record your stay through photography. Remember that the country has a pervasive security apparatus and a (some might say justified) paranoia of foreign spies and coup-plotters. Entering the country with professional photography gear is likely to cause issues at customs, although a single camera with a telescopic lens should not raise eyebrows. If you intend to visit the country for professional photography purposes, make sure you explicitly organise this with the respective visa-issuing embassy: as this will arm you with the paperwork required to get your gear through the airport. Do not try and fly under the radar on a tourist visa.

While things have certainly progressed in recent years, waving a big camera around in public is still likely to draw unwanted police attention very quickly. This is regardless of whether you have the Tourism Permit which entitles you to take photographs. To avoid issues, carry a smaller camera, keep your camera out of sight when around security officials and do not photograph sensitive areas such as bridges, military installations, presidential complexes, power stations, etc. Also be sure to ask permission before taking a person's photograph. Many Equatoguineans are wary of being photographed and may not be happy if you point a camera at them without asking first.

PHOTOGRAPHY PERMITS Up until recently the Ministry of Information and Tourism issued permits to those visitors wishing to take photos. The law has now changed so that no permit is required, but police still sometimes try and fine people for taking photographs, stating the old law. Your Tourism Permit specifically states that it also entitles you to take photographs. Point this out if challenged. To avoid trouble, try to keep your camera out of sight while around security officials, and remember that you are not permitted to take photos anywhere near the presidential palace or other strategically sensitive areas such as government buildings, military bases, bridges, airports or harbours. You are also not permitted to take photos that show Equatorial Guinea in a bad light, such as of slums or street children. Visitors have been detained by security forces in the past, and either had their equipment confiscated or been forced to delete their photos.

MEDIA AND COMMUNICATIONS

MOBILE PHONES Officially, you can roam in Equatorial Guinea with a phone on the Movistar, Vodafone or Orange networks. In reality it is difficult to roam in Equatorial Guinea with most foreign SIMs. You will need to purchase a new local SIM at the central GETESA office in either Malabo or Bata. You will also need to register it, which requires a copy of your passport, a passport photo, your address in Equatorial Guinea and 2,000CFA (which is immediately registered to your account). The process is instant, assuming there is no queue at the office.

There are two mobile network operators in the country: Orange and MUNI, with Orange having far more subscribers. Orange phone credit scratch cards are available all over the country from street traders in values of 2,000CFA, 5,000CFA and 10,000CFA. You can recharge your credit by dialling 222, and check your balance by dialling 333.

DIALLING CODES The international dialling code for Equatorial Guinea is +240. Most fixed-line numbers in Malabo begin with 333, but 666 is also sometimes used. Numbers starting with 222 or 55X indicate mobile phones. There is very low penetration in terms of landlines throughout the country, with most individuals and businesses relying on the mobile phone network. Emergency numbers are:

☏ 113 for police   ☏ 115 for the fire department
☏ 114 for the gendarmería

INTERNET Cyber cafés are difficult to find outside Malabo and Bata but generally charge 1,000CFA per hour of access. The larger hotels provide Wi-Fi for guest use, as do a few high-end restaurants and bars. Outside the main population centres, you will struggle to get online, and some areas (such as Annobón) are completely internet-free. Residents and frequent visitors should purchase a 3G dongle from GETESA or one of the mobile phone shops, but remember that coverage is limited outside the regional capitals. There is currently no evidence of ongoing state censorship of the internet, although there were documented incidences of the government blocking certain websites (such as Facebook or the site of the main opposition party, CPDS) during planned anti-government demonstrations in 2013.

POSTAL SERVICE The postal system is regulated by the public entity GECOTEL (Guinea Ecuatorial Correos y Telecomunicaciones/Postal and Telecommunication

Services of Equatorial Guinea), but it is currently not possible to send private correspondence using the state postal system. Those wishing to send packages and letters internally will need to use a private courier such as DHL, which has locations in Malabo and Bata.

MEDIA In theory there are numerous privately owned independent media outlets in Equatorial Guinea. However, the government practises widespread censorship of all state-owned media, and suppresses criticism in the private sector through a combination of draconian legal powers regarding defamation and extra-judicial intimidation. This encourages many private outlets to self-censor, and the only criticism of the government now comes from opposition websites edited from outside the country, such as Diario Rombe (see *Further Information*, page 228). For example, all mention of the Arab Spring was banned from news coverage on state media in 2011, with one radio presenter detained and suspended for violating this protocol. International media working in the country are also closely monitored by security forces, and face arrest, confiscation of their equipment, destruction of their material and deportation if they fall foul of the censorship requirements. This happened to a German ZDF film crew in June 2011 and a *Financial Times* team in January 2014. For more details of censorship in the country, see page 99.

The state broadcaster TVGE is the source of TV news for most of the population, along with the RNGE state-run radio stations Radio Malabo and Radio Bata. Newspapers and news magazines published in-country include *La Gaceta de Guinea Ecuatorial* and *El Diario de Malabo*. Many people also read the Spanish newspaper *El País*, although print versions are not widely available. Getting hold of English-language publications is difficult, although some of the luxury hotels may stock foreign periodicals. Many expatriates buy subscriptions to the South African satellite service DSTV, meaning that they can watch international news channels such as BBC World and Al Jazeera while in the country.

BUSINESS

Equatorial Guinea is not an easy place to do business. The World Bank placed Equatorial Guinea 165th in their ease of doing business ranking in 2015 out of the 189 countries surveyed. They highlighted particular difficulties with starting a business, paying taxes, registering property and resolving insolvency. A widely corrupt, inefficient and bureaucratic administration, coupled with a volatile oil-dependent economy make Equatorial Guinea a high risk, but also potentially high reward marketplace. The US Department of State's Bureau of Economic and Business Affairs published a 2014 investment climate statement on doing business in Equatorial Guinea which can be read here: www.state.gov/e/eb/rls/othr/ics/2014/228804.htm. It included warnings on the government of Equatorial Guinea's extensive record of expropriating locally owned property, lack of compliance with international agreements and legal decisions and noted that 'bureaucratic procedures are neither streamlined nor transparent, and can be extremely slow for those without the proper connections'.

In stark contrast to the sombre US assessment, the embassy of the Republic of Equatorial Guinea in the United Kingdom released a glossy 17-page investment guide in 2015, which outlined the operating environment, areas of opportunity and the legal framework for those wishing to do business in the country. The PDF can be found here: www.embassyofequatorialguinea.co.uk/opportunities-for-investment/.

BUSINESS HOURS Business hours for most shops are 08.00 to 13.00 and 16.00 to 19.00 Monday to Friday, with some businesses also open from 08.00 to 13.00 on Saturdays. Office hours within the public administration are 08.00 to 16.00 Monday to Friday. Banks are generally open from 08.00 to 14.00 Monday to Friday.

BUYING PROPERTY

Foreign investors are not permitted to own land or property in Equatorial Guinea, but can lease it from the government or other parties (such as local business partners). The World Bank identifies six stages required for those buying property in Equatorial Guinea, taking an average of 23 days and costing around 12.5% of the overall property value. The most time-consuming and expensive element of the procedure is having a notary legalise your sales contract and prepare the public deed (*escritura publica*), the cost of which is linked to the value of your property.

CULTURAL ETIQUETTE

Most urban communities in Equatorial Guinea are accustomed to foreigners, although the children in rural areas may automatically label you as Chinese, given that these tend to be the only outsiders they have seen. The general assumption wherever you go will be that you are able to speak Spanish. In Malabo and Bata, which have large expatriate communities, your presence is unlikely to elicit any sort of interest. People are generally friendly when spoken to but quite reserved in public situations. You should not be hassled while walking down the street, or followed by hawkers, which is a welcome change from some regional neighbours. Be sure to ask permission before taking photographs of people, especially when photographing children, as people may become upset at unsolicited photographs.

Outside the main urban areas, it is advisable to register your presence with the local police chief or *comisario* when arriving somewhere new. This is mainly to show respect, but also to avoid any issues with less senior security personnel. Senior security people tend to react to unsolicited attempts to register your presence either with disinterest or genuine curiosity, so there is little harm in doing so upon entering a new town.

When greeting new people, try to do so in order of seniority, assuming that you can work this out. Also note that smart dress is important in Equatoguinean business culture: you may not be allowed into certain government buildings if you are in shorts and flip-flops. When trying to elicit services from government officials, note that you may be kept waiting for no apparent reason. The official may also publicly berate less senior employees in front of you. Such actions serve to highlight their relative status, and should not be seen as an indication of disrespect.

CORRUPTION Corruption exists at all levels of the economy in Equatorial Guinea. On a day-to-day level, there are regular police and traffic checkpoints, especially when leaving Malabo. If your documentation is not in order, expect to be asked to pay a fine. Be sure to carry your passport or residence permit, driving license and all the registration/insurance documents for the car when driving.

Separate photography permits used to be required for all tourists, although this is no longer the case. Now, your photography permit is on the same document as your Tourism Permit, which you will need to obtain from the Ministry of Culture and Tourism in Malabo or Bata upon arrival.

Even with your permit, do not wave your camera around in front of police, as most have a poor understanding of what is and is not allowed, and may fine you or confiscate your camera. Also, never take photographs of strategic locations (bridges, military installations, the presidential palace, power stations, etc) or the Equatoguinean security forces as this may also lead to the confiscation of your camera (this is clearly explained on your permit)!

Officials will sometimes not consider dealing with you until you have paid a bribe, often referred to as a 'Fanta', to speed up the process. If you are intending to travel outside Malabo or Bata, you used to have to inform the Protocol Division of the Ministry of Foreign Affairs, Co-operation and Francophonie in advance. This is no longer the case, as once again your Tourism Permit covers you for all travel, so do not let police at checkpoints tell you otherwise. There have also been reports of police asking for large payments (of between US$50 and US$100) to file official police reports or give you a copy of a report on file, which may be required for insurance claims back home.

BEGGING Despite Equatorial Guinea having one of the highest GDP per capita ratings in Africa, poverty is widespread, unemployment is high and social support is inadequate. In these circumstances begging directed towards perceived wealthy foreigners does take place, although not nearly as often as in other countries in the region (you are unlikely to be followed down the street by beggars, even in Malabo or Bata). It is unwise to pull out your wallet to hand over cash to people on the streets, especially those who may be under the influence of alcohol or drugs. Likewise, handing over gifts to small children (such as pens or sweets) only serves to promote a state of dependence and makes little positive difference in the long run. If you wish to help those most in need, it is advisable to donate to NGOs or associations that focus on activities carrying a wider benefit (see below).

TRAVELLING POSITIVELY

Despite the oil wealth, Equatorial Guinea has many issues associated with poverty. NGOs must tread a fine line between trying to help improve the situation, without overtly criticising the ruling regime. As such, the NGOs allowed to operate in the country tend to focus on uncontroversial areas such as education and healthcare, as opposed to the more sensitive issues of transparency, good governance and human rights issues. Travellers keen to make a contribution could contact the following organisations:

EGJustice PO Box 57297, Washington, DC 20037, USA; +1 202 643 4345; e mnavia@egjustice. org; http://egjustice.org/. EGJustice was launched in 2008 in the United States (rather than in Equatorial Guinea, as human rights organisations are not permitted to operate within the country) to promote human rights, the rule of law, transparency, & civic participation to build a just Equatorial Guinea.

The Ladybug Project, Inc 50 C/ La Libertdad, Malabo; m 222 144 416; e ladybug.project.eg@ gmail.com; www.theladybugproject.com/get-involved.html. This is a non-profit organisation working to foster education & health infrastructure in Equatorial Guinea. Their website outlines a number of ways you can help, from donations to internships.

Part Two

THE GUIDE

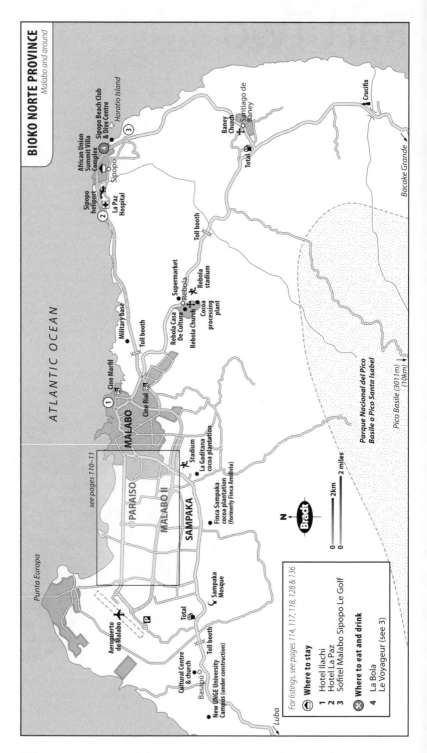

BIOKO NORTE PROVINCE
Malabo and around

ATLANTIC OCEAN

Punta Europa

see pages 110–11

MALABO

PARAISO

MALABO II

SAMPAKA

Aeropuerto de Malabo

Cultural Centre & church

New UNGE University Campus (under construction)

Basapú

Total

Toll booth

Sampaka Mosque

Finca Sampaka cocoa plantation (formerly Finca Amélivia)

La Gaditana cocoa plantation

Stadium

Cine Rial

Cine Marfil

Military base

Toll booth

Rebola Casa De Cultura

Supermarket

Rebola

Rebola Church

Cocoa processing plant

Rebola stadium

Toll booth

La Paz Hospital

Sipopo heliport

African Union Summit Villa

Complex

Sipopo Beach Club & Dive Centre

Sipopo

Horatio Island

Baney Church

Santiago de Baney

Total

Crucifix

Parque Nacional del Pico Basile o Pico Santa Isabel

Pico Basile (3011m)

(10km)

Bacake Grande

Luba

N

Bradt

0   2km
0   2 miles

For listings, see pages 114, 117, 118, 128 & 136

Where to stay
1   Hotel Ilachi
2   Hotel La Paz
3   Sofitel Malabo Sipopo Le Golf

Where to eat and drink
4   La Bola
    Le Voyageur (see 3)

104

3

Malabo and around

Whatever you are expecting of Malabo, the city is bound to yield a few surprises. Bioko island is historically the home of the ancient Bubi ethnic group, yet they are in the minority here. Malabo was an isolated outpost of Spanish colonialism, yet many inhabitants speak English Creole in the marketplaces. Today, the economy is dominated by the American oil industry, but you are far more likely to bump into a Chinese person than an American on the streets.

Sitting at the northern end of Bioko island in Bioko Norte Province, Malabo looks out across the Gulf of Guinea towards the shores of Cameroon, 40km away on the African mainland. The pulsing heart of one of the least visited states in modern Africa, this city is still one of the ten smallest capitals on the continent. This may not be the situation for long though, as it is expanding rapidly thanks to an influx of oil wealth, as well as Western and Chinese workers. Touring the centre, you get the impression that this used to be a sleepy little place, perhaps like nearby São Tomé, but when they struck oil two decades ago everything changed, and there are few who would want to go back to that earlier time.

Nobody is sure what the exact population of Malabo is, but at around 100,000 there are not enough people for it to feel crowded (though those commuting through the city centre at rush hour might disagree). As with other oil-rich African states, the capital city is one of stark social contrasts. On the one hand there is evidence of great wealth in the presidential palace, the beautifully refurbished Santa Isabel Cathedral or the ever-expanding luxury hotels, office blocks and high-end villas. On the other hand, many of the citizens are still living in poorly constructed shanty towns with little access to electricity, clean drinking water or sewage treatment. Seeing these two faces of the city jammed up against one another can come as quite a shock, although the government is keen to emphasise that these less positive elements are hopefully not permanent features of the city.

Malabo is compact, logically laid out and made up of numerous distinct areas, each with their own atmosphere. To the north of the airport is Punta Europa, the main LNG terminal and also a home away from home for the thousands of Americans who work on the island. If you manage to get an invite from a resident, expect villas with swimming pools, large security fences and all the trappings of expatriate compound living. The closest most people get to this place is viewing it from above as they make their final approach to Malabo airport.

The airport road which passes through Malabo II is clearly the political and business area. Here you will find the offices of the major oil and construction companies, as well as numerous government ministries and embassies. If you have a shiny new building to put up, it is here that you do it, in the lofty company of the sprawling US embassy compound, overlooking the main highways. The sleepy suburbs of Paraiso and Caracolas, on the outskirts of town, are home to some of Malabo's wealthier residents as well as the rest of the city's embassies. To the south of the centre is Semu, home to the largest market in the country and a large proportion of the city's inhabitants. It is noisy and never boring. The area around the central market (near the National University) is called Los Angeles and is another bustling spot.

The city centre is tiny, barely 800m across, with a wealth of restaurants, bars, shops and hotels to suit most budgets. Despite this density of sites, it still feels quiet, especially if you wander around during the daily siesta, or on a Sunday. Calle de Argelia and the port area offer views of the Atlantic and a constant reminder that you are on an island nation. To the east of the city centre you will find a quiet suburb around Plaza de Fernando and then further on, the upmarket residences of Buena Esperanza.

Visitors should be under no illusions: Equatorial Guinea is not an easy destination in terms of tourism. However, Malabo is definitely the easiest part of the country to visit. The people in Malabo are reserved but friendly once engaged. The police are so used to foreigners that they tend to leave you alone.

It is possible to see all of the major sites in the city on foot in a day. Malabo is small, beautiful and unique due to its Afro-Hispanic heritage, and thanks to a recent new government drive to improve tourism as part of the Horizon 2020 Plan (page 32), there has never been a better time to visit.

HISTORY

Evidence suggests that the Bubi of Bioko have been resident in and around Malabo for around 10,000 years, although the area was not 'discovered' by the Europeans until the arrival of the Portuguese explorer Fernão do Pó in 1471. Even then, it would take another 350 years before a settled European community was established at the site of what we now call Malabo. The Portuguese never settled the island, apart from Ramos de Esquivel's ill-fated attempt to build a sugarcane plantation in 1507, which ended in failure. In 1642, the Dutch set up a trading depot, although they preferred to use the nearby island of Corisco as a base due to the tales of the savage Bubi tribes and tropical diseases on Bioko. The treaties of San Idelfonso in 1777 and El Pardo in 1778 saw Portugal cede control of Fernando Pó, Annobón and the mainland coastal areas to Spain in return for recognition of their dominion over much of modern day Brazil. However, the Spanish, like the Portuguese and Dutch before them, showed little interest in colonising the island.

It was not until 1827 that the area of Malabo (then known as Port Clarence) was leased to the British as an anti-slaving base, along with Luba (then known as San Carlos). Vice Admiral William Fitzwilliam Owen was charged with developing the British settlement, and by the end of his first year the population was 747; an odd mixture of Royal Navy staff, Royal Marines, Fernandinos, Krumen, as well as British and Bubi traders.

In 1843, the British officially ended their use of Port Clarence, preferring to base their anti-slaving ships out of Freetown, Sierra Leone. They left the settlement with a population of around 900 people. The Spanish re-established their presence, with Juan José Lerena raising the Spanish flag in March 1843. They promptly renamed the city Santa Isabel, and, in an attempt to boost numbers, Queen Isabel II authorised the voluntary transfer of black and free *mulattos* from Cuba to Equatorial Guinea. This initiative failed, and by 1856 there were still only 13 white settlers recorded in Santa Isabel. Numerous other royal decrees and tax incentives were put in place, but Spanish settlers were simply not willing to relocate and face the risk of tropical diseases and hostile local tribes. As if Bioko's reputation was not bad enough, in 1861 Irish citizen William Looney made international headlines when he was devoured by a shark in front of shocked onlookers just off the beach in the capital. By 1877 there were still only around 1,100 registered inhabitants in Santa Isabel, few of whom were European.

By the turn of the century, cocoa production had displaced palm oil trading as the chief economic activity carried out in Santa Isabel. The 445 European settlers and the Fernandinos dominated the industry, a famous example being Maximiliano Cipriano Jones, the richest Krio planter on the island by 1929. With the flat land around Santa Isabel being some of the finest for growing cocoa, traders and investors tended to base themselves here.

These groups began bringing in migrant labourers from Liberia to work on their plantations, often in conditions no better than slavery. This influx of workers led to an economic boom on Fernando Pó (the European colonial name for Bioko island), which attracted more Spanish settlers from the metropolis. This growing economy led to an investment in building in Santa Isabel, and many of the most distinctive architectural features of the city today can be traced back to this time: Casa Verde, Santa Isabel Cathedral, Casa Teodolita, the Agricultural Chamber and the National Library are all products of the influx of wealth during this period (pages 130–1).

Coinciding with the global economic downturn of the Great Depression, a growing number of Spanish and Portuguese men moved to Fernando Pó to seek their fortune, leading to a steady reduction in the wealth and influence of the Fernandinos plantation owners, and an influx of Fang and Nigerian migrant workers, something which was actively encouraged by the Spanish colonial authorities. By 1930, Fernando Pó had overtaken São Tomé as the world's largest producer of cocoa, with all exports heading back to the Spanish metropolis at a guaranteed price.

After World War II a series of assimilation laws were introduced by the Spanish colonial authorities, but the contrast between the lives of Europeans in Santa Isabel, who still numbered only 2,493 men and 1,102 women in 1950, and the locals was stark: racial segregation was visible everywhere from the bars people drank in to the jobs they performed and even the foods they were allowed to purchase and consume. Europeans were clustered in the higher-value accommodation overlooking Santa Isabel Bay, around Plaza de España, whereas Equatoguineans were forced out into the peripheries of the city.

By the early 1960s, with nationalist movements across Africa gaining momentum, the Franco regime began a programme of heavy investment in their African colony in a bid to keep them from demanding independence. Santa Isabel was a great beneficiary of numerous public works projects and investments during this initiative, with schools and medical clinics springing up seemingly overnight. Over the next decade Equatorial Guinea would come to have one of the highest literacy rates and per capita income rates in sub-Saharan Africa. Yet this did not stop the Equatoguineans from voting for independence in the August 1968 constitutional referendum.

After independence, President Macías changed the name of Santa Isabel to Malabo, after a former Bubi king of the island. This was part of his Africanisation campaign which saw any remaining Spanish residents quickly flee the country. The city soon fell into disrepair due to his misrule (pages 26–9). By 1974, all print media had shut down, as had the majority of the productive economy and by 1978 there was no electricity in the capital, meaning also no telephone systems. All state and private educational institutions had been closed, and the Catholic Church was banned from operating in the country. Malabo was being reclaimed by the jungle by the time President Obiang launched a coup and took over in August 1979. President Macías's trial was held in Malabo's Cine Marfil, which still stands today and is the focus of the 2011 documentary titled simply *Marfil*.

Although the economic situation immediately improved under President Obiang, Malabo continued to be a small, dilapidated ex-colonial town throughout the 1980s. World Bank economist Robert Klitgaard, author of the *New York Times* bestseller *Tropical Gangsters* (page 57) was in Malabo between 1985 and 1987, and describes an impoverished, backwards city with two hotels, neither of which had a reliable water supply. There was little external investment or foreign interest.

Malabo's fortunes, along with the rest of Equatorial Guinea's, changed in 1995 with the discovery of the Zafiro oilfield, 68km northwest of Bioko island. By 1999 the economy of the country had increased tenfold, with huge multi-national oil companies setting up their bases on Bioko.

As the economy has grown, so too has the city, in a frenzy of construction financed by a US$2 billion credit line from China, opened in 2005. In 2007, a LNG terminal was built at Punta Europa, on the very northern tip of Bioko. Luxury hotels, conference centres, a redeveloped airport and six-lane highways are now the order of the day in Malabo.

Development is currently focused on Malabo II, which is the area between Malabo and the airport. Here in July 2011, the state oil company Sonagas GE opened its new Chinese-built headquarters, and many companies and ministries are expanding westwards into this zone. To the east of the city sits the Buena Esperanza complex, originally intended as social housing but now occupied by some of Malabo's most privileged citizens.

Equatorial Guinea is reportedly home to over 25,000 US expatriate workers, along with thousands of Europeans and other foreigners, mainly involved in the oil and gas sectors. Many of these visitors are concentrated in Malabo. How long the city will continue to expand remains to be seen, given the reducing oil income, and the government's stated aim of relocating the capital to Oyala on the mainland. For now at least though, the Chinese construction crews are still building, and the expats are still arriving.

GETTING THERE AND AWAY

Malabo is the hub for most domestic and international **flights**, although a few also service Bata. Corisco, Annobón and Mengomeyén airports also have the infrastructure in place to serve as international hubs, but do not currently have any international connections. Malabo airport [map, page 104] is around 8km to the west of the city and is quick to reach when there is no traffic. A taxi there will cost between 2,000CFA and 5,000CFA. Allow plenty of time for checking in due to the chaos and disorganisation of getting through customs, security and the check-in desk at Departures. Frequent travellers often check-in early, or get checked in by their drivers, and then wait elsewhere (such as in the nearby Hilton Hotel's bar). Many of the higher-end hotels offer an airport shuttle service.

There is also an irregular **ferry service** between Malabo and Bata which costs 15,000CFA, departing from the main port [110 D1]. The ferry is called the *San Valentin*, and the crossing to Bata takes between 5 and 10 hours, depending on the weather. On departure day (which tends to be once a week) you need to be ready to go at 06.00. Departure days and times are highly changeable, so seek local advice when purchasing tickets.

You are likely to be treated with great suspicion if you arrive on a private boat, and may even be intercepted while in coastal waters by the ever vigilant coastguard.

GETTING AROUND

Malabo is a very small capital city and it is easy to find your way around. The newly built roads are generally signposted, using Spanish-style signage.

Marking the western extremity, there is the **international airport** [map, page 104], with the Punta Europa LNG Plant above it, where many of the US expatriate workers live. As you head into town via the Carretera del Aeropuerto, you will first pass the huge new zoo, then go through Malabo II and then the suburb of Caracolas, which is home to many of the embassy buildings and expatriate compounds. The centre of town can be crossed on foot in 10 minutes, bounded by Calle del Rey Malabo to the south, the presidential palace to the east and the port on the northern shoreline. Roads are built on a grid system orientated to the northwest (the same direction the bay is facing), so if you ever get lost just head northwest and eventually you will come to the seafront.

On the airport road you will find many embassies, hotels and restaurants. Most addresses for this road tell you which kilometre the building is at, but a few useful waypoints are the turn-off for Paraiso district, the turn-off for Caribe, the toll booth and the so-called 'bridge to nowhere' (you will recognise this when you see it!).

The roads across the entire country are excellent and mainly empty but Malabo is one of the few places where you will encounter traffic jams at rush hour. Malabo is small enough to walk around, although doing so late at night is not recommended.

BY CAR If you wish to drive yourself, there are rental agencies based in the capital. A few even have stands at the airport. Renting a car from these places is generally very expensive and requires a massive security deposit. The cheapest car available from the airport costs around 70,000CFA per day (€106) but requires a 250,000CFA security deposit (€380). Ensure that you bring an International Driving Permit, as traffic police often will not accept foreign licences, but be prepared to switch your licence for a local one if you plan to do a lot of driving: although police should accept the International Permit, many will use this as an excuse to impose fines. It is possible to obtain an Equatoguinean licence at the Ministerio del Interior y Corporaciones Locales. The cost is 30,000CFA for a six-month local licence, plus another 30,000CFA authorisation fee. The process takes between five and ten days depending on volume of applications at the time.

Autos Litoral [116 B1] This rental company has a desk inside the ibis Hotel, by reception (pages 114–15); ✆ 666 162 839, 666 591 355; e autoslitoralmalabo@yahoo.es. Autos Litoral have a fleet of over 200 vehicles & offer up to a 40% discount for w/end special bookings. Prices are still very high, with their cheapest vehicle (a Renault Clio) going for 69,000CFA per day, plus a 250,000CFA deposit.

BY PUBLIC TRANSPORT Local taxis and minibus services cover the entire island, with many based in Malabo. They are cheap, crowded and plentiful. When getting a **taxi**, look out for battered old Toyota Corollas with a distinctive blue stripe. If you stand by the pavement, they will beep their horn to indicate that they are accepting passengers. Flag one down, tell the driver where you are going, and if he agrees he will beep again meaning that you can get in. If not, he will just drive away without saying anything (which is apparently not rude). Journeys across the city cost

3

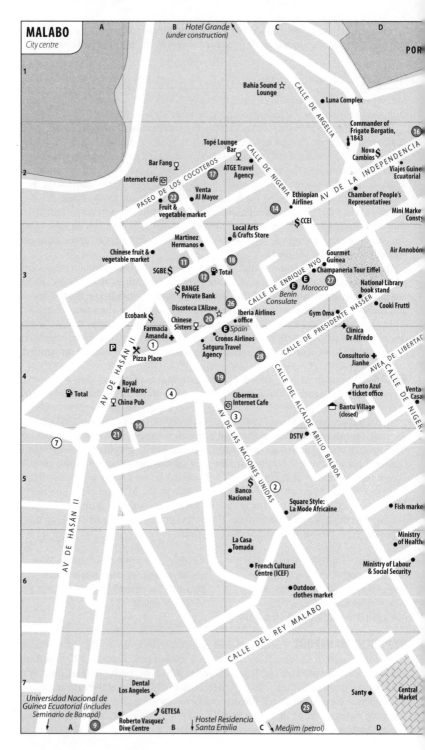

MALABO
City centre

A
B — Hotel Grande ↖
(under construction)
C
D

POR

Bahia Sound ☆
Lounge

CALLE DE ARGELIA

● Luna Complex

Commander of
Frigate Bergatin,
↑1843

16

Nova $
Cambios

Topé Lounge
Bar

CALLE DE NIGERIA

AV DE LA INDEPENDENCIA

Viajes Guine
Ecuatorial

Bar Fang ♀

PASEO DE LOS COCOTEROS

ATGE Travel
Agency

17

Internet café ⓔ

Venta
Al Mayor
22 ●

Ethiopian
Airlines

Chamber of People's
Representatives

Fruit &
vegetable market

14

$ CCEI

Mini Marke
Consty

Local Arts
& Crafts Store

Air Annobón

Martinez
Hermanos ●

Gourmet
Guinea

Chinese fruit & ●
vegetable market

SGBE $

11

18

CALLE DE ENRIQUE NVÓ

Champaneria Tour Eiffel

27

● Total

12

BANGE
$ Private Bank

ⓔ
Morocco

National Library
book stand

26

Benin
Consulate

● Cooki Frutti

Ecobank $

Discoteca L'Alizee

Iberia Airlines
☆ ● office

Gym Oma ●

+ Clinica
Dr Alfredo

Farmacia
Amanda +

①

Chinese
Sisters ♀

20

ⓔ Spain

CALLE DE PRESIDENTE NASSER

Cronos Airlines

AVEA DE LIBERTAE

CALLE DE

P

✕

Satguru Travel
Agency

28

Consultorio +
Jianhe

Pizza Place

AV DE HASÁN II

19

Punto Azul
● ticket office

Venta
● Casa

Total 🅿

● Royal
Air Maroc

④

Cibermax
Internet Cafe

Bantu Village
(closed)

DE NIGE

♀ China Pub

ⓔ
③

21

10

AV DE LAS NACIONES UNIDAS

DSTV ●

CALLE DEL ALCALDE ABILIO BALBOA

⑦

$
②

Banco
Nacional

Square Style:
● La Mode Africaine

● Fish marke

AV DE HASÁN II

La Casa
Tomada ●

Ministry
● of Health

● French Cultural
Centre (ICEF)

Ministry of Labour +
& Social Security ●

● Outdoor
clothes market

CALLE DEL REY MALABO

Dental
Los Angeles +

Universidad Nacional de
Guinea Ecuatorial (includes
Seminario de Banapá)

♪ GETESA

● Santy

Central
Market

25

9

Roberto Vasquez'
Dive Centre

↓ Hostel Residencia
Santa Emilia

C ↘ Medjim (petrol)

A
B
C
D

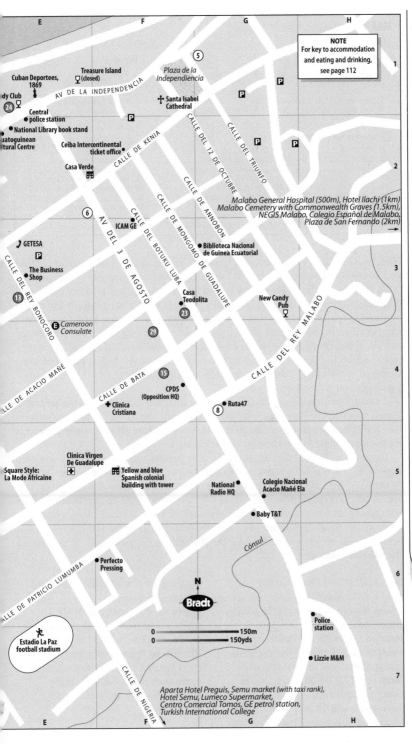

NOTE
For key to accommodation
and eating and drinking,
see page 112

Cuban Deportees,
1869

dy Club
24

Treasure Island
(closed)

Plaza de la
Independiencia

5

AV DE LA INDEPENDENCIA

Santa Isabel
Cathedral

Central
police station

National Library book stand

uatoguinean
tural Centre

Ceiba Intercontinental
ticket office

Casa Verde

CALLE DE KENIA

CALLE DEL 12 DE OCTUBRE

CALLE DEL TRIUNFO

Malabo General Hospital (500m), Hotel Ilachi (1km)
Malabo Cemetery with Commonwealth Graves (1.5km),
NEGIS Malabo, Colegio Español de Malabo,
Plaza de San Fernando (2km)

6

GETESA

The Business
Shop

13

AV DEL 3 DE AGOSTO

CALLE DEL BOTUKU LUBA

ICAM GE

CALLE DE MONGOMO DE GUADALUPE

CALLE DE ANNOBON

Biblioteca Nacional
de Guinea Ecuatorial

3

CALLE DEL REY BONOCORO

Cameroon
Consulate

Casa
Teodolita

23

29

New Candy
Pub

CALLE DEL REY MALABO

CALLE DE ACACIO MAÑÉ

CALLE DE BATA

15

CPDS
(Opposition HQ)

Clinica
Cristiana

Ruta47

8

4

Clinica Virgen
De Guadalupe

Square Style:
La Mode Africaine

Yellow and blue
Spanish colonial
building with tower

National
Radio HQ

Colegio Nacional
Acacio Mañé Ela

Baby T&T

5

Perfecto
Pressing

Cónsul

CALLE DE PATRICIO LUMUMBA

N

Bradt

Police
station

6

Estadio La Paz
football stadium

0   150m
0   150yds

Lizzie M&M

7

CALLE DE NIGERIA

Aparta Hotel Preguis, Semu market (with taxi rank),
Hotel Semu, Lumeco Supermarket,
Centro Comercial Tomos, GE petrol station,
Turkish International College

E   F   G   H

500CFA. Going out of the centre of town (for example, to the Ministry of Culture and Tourism in Malabo II) will cost 1,000CFA, with longer journeys negotiable.

To travel out of the capital, you will need to go to one of the shared taxi ranks, one of which can be found by Semu Market [off map, 111 F7]. Cars generally leave their boots wide open to indicate that they are accepting passengers. Seats are sold at a fixed price and vehicles leave when they are full, so turn up early and be prepared to wait. This is generally the most economical method of getting around. A journey from Malabo to Luba in a shared taxi costs only 2,000CFA, but be prepared to be squeezed in with three other people in the back of a small car, or to share the front passenger seat with a second passenger!

If you are in a rush or want a bit more comfort, you can buy all of the seats in a shared taxi and use it as your own personal rental. You can talk most taxi drivers into giving you some sort of discount as they are heading off more quickly (which means more total fares in the day) and are using less fuel.

There are also local drivers available with **private vehicles** but these are very expensive. Anyone with a decent car and proper paperwork will expect around 80,000CFA per day minimum. Drivers offering day rates cheaper than this are usually unreliable (both in terms of their paperwork at checkpoints, their punctuality and the mechanical performance of their vehicle). Also, going this route makes little sense when you can often just turn a shared taxi into your own rental for a lower price. However, for those feeling brave, you could try contacting the following drivers:

Desi m 222 580 447. Offers return trips to Moka from Malabo for 30,000CFA, including waiting time in Moka. He is friendly & reliable but his vehicle is in poor condition.
Jorge m 222 209 909. Offers transportation around the island for 50,000CFA per day. Speaks Spanish, drives safely & has a decent new car.
Oscar m 551 320 110. Offers transportation around the island for only 40,000CFA per day. Speaks good English & is very friendly & helpful. His prices are low because his Toyota Corolla is on its last legs, & may in fact have exploded by the time this guide is printed.
Romeo m 555 402 053, 222 004 788. A professional driver offering transport around the island starting from 80,000CFA per day in a new Mitsubishi 4x4. Speaks English, drives safely & is very friendly & helpful. Although expensive, Romeo would probably work out cheaper than hiring your own 4x4 for an extended period of time.

LOCAL TOUR OPERATORS

Although it is technically possible to visit the Ministry of Tourism and Culture in Malabo or Bata for travel advice, in practice this is not an efficient way of getting up-to-date information. There are also few travel agents in Malabo, but they are are not accustomed to dealing with foreigners. Your best bet is to contact **Ruta47** [111 G4] or **Guineatur**, who have a proven track record of delivering high-quality custom-designed tours (page 65).

WHERE TO STAY *Maps, pages 110–11 and 116 unless otherwise stated*

There are a variety of sleeping options in Malabo, and the majority of them have one thing in common: high prices. The oil boom has led to massive inflation in the cost of accommodation, especially at the higher end of the spectrum. That being said, the presence of business travellers and expatriate workers also means that you can find some international-quality facilities, as long as you are willing to pay the asking price.

At the top end of the range, many travellers head to the **Sofitel**, which has two locations, one in the centre of town and the other on the outskirts in the Sipopo area. By the airport you will also find the **Hilton**, which is a popular choice with business travellers. These hotels tend to be filled with long-term block bookings from the oil companies and associated industries.

Mid-range hotels will have air conditioning and warm water, with some even offering complimentary Wi-Fi, but you will be shocked at the prices of most of these.

At the lower end of the scale, do not expect more than a bed, a fan and intermittent electricity. It is advisable to bring your own mosquito net as these are rarely provided. Finding decent budget options in the city centre is a struggle but there are a few worth finding. For those on a shoestring budget, you will either need to base yourself well outside the centre or keep your expectations at rock bottom!

LUXURY

Hilton Malabo Hotel (187 rooms) Carretera del Aeropuerto, Km7; 333 096 811; e www3.hilton.com. While it cannot compete with the Sofitel Sipopo in the luxury stakes, the Malabo Hilton has a few things going for it that make it a potential option for travellers with a bigger budget. Firstly, it is extremely close to the airport which is very convenient. It is also at the cheaper end of the luxury options, & has the nicest pool in Malabo, which non-residents can use for 10,000CFA. There is free Wi-Fi throughout the hotel, too (although it crawls to a halt at night). Room windows cannot be opened, so there should be no mosquitoes. There is a good fitness centre, numerous eating options & comfortable rooms with a separate bathtub & shower. On the negative side, while rooms have DSTV, it is only possible to watch one Super Sport channel at a time; you have to phone reception & tell them to change the channel! Many of the long-term residents smoke

in the rooms, & the AC is overly powerful with few options for manually adjusting it. There are also a lot of mosquitoes down by the pool area, so it is not advisable to sit out there at night. Being so close to the airport makes it harder to go out & explore Malabo at night unless you have your own transport, & guarantees that you will head through a checkpoint in the evenings between town & the airport (which can sometimes be a hassle). Despite these issues though, the Hilton has a more upbeat atmosphere than the quiet Sofitel Malabo Sipopo Le Golf & seems less rigidly formal than the Sofitel Malabo President Palace. This, combined with the price tag, makes it a good option. **$$$$$**

Magno Suites (formerly Mango Suites) (15 rooms) Carretera Principal de Paraiso; 333 096 333; e reservas@mango-suites.com; www. mango-suites.com. Website in English & Spanish. This small boutique hotel in the Paraiso district between the airport & the city centre is a good option for those looking for something a little different from the high-end chain hotels. Design was a major focus during construction & it shows: both the rooms & communal spaces are visually impressive. There is a good restaurant & bar which is open until midnight & the majority of the staff are English-speaking. Wi-Fi is available throughout the property & there is a free interactive entertainment system if you want to watch films in your room. The presidential suites offer private parking & even their own pool. What really sets this hotel apart from the others though is the quality of the customer service from the hotel staff. Everyone is very friendly & eager to help. Note that they recently had to change the name from Mango to Magno after a commercial dispute with the Mango clothing company. Accepts Visa & MasterCard. **$$$$$**

🏠 **National Hotel Angue Ondo** (76 rooms) Carretera del Aeropuerto, Km4, near the Paraiso district entrance & the Muankaban Supermarket; m 222 250 768, 222 796 161. This newly opened hotel competes directly with the Hilton for business clients looking for a convenient location. It offers a range of standard rooms as well as business & deluxe suites. Features a conference room with capacity for 180 people, a large pool, spa, sauna & a marquee on the grounds that can host events for up to 500 people. **$$$$$**

🏠 **Sofitel Malabo President Palace** (100 rooms, 3 suites) Pl de la Independencia, Centro Historico, Zona Presidencial, PO Box 383; 333 099 940; m 222 239 357; e H5630@sofitel.com; www. sofitel.com. Website in English, French, German, Italian, Spanish, Portuguese, Chinese & Russian. Adjoining the presidential palace & overlooking the cathedral square, this Spanish-style hotel offers all the amenities you would expect at this price point, including a fitness centre, swimming pool, international satellite TV in the rooms, free airport shuttle & an excellent restaurant (El Basilé). The African art contributes to some beautiful communal spaces. Some of the north-facing rooms feature balconies with sea views. The location is very convenient & it is walking distance from most of the main attractions in the city, although it will take you longer to get to some of the ministries & government offices located over in Malabo II. The hotel also has a great buffet which is popular with expatriates. Given the similarities in price, however, it makes more sense to stay at the superior Sofitel Sipopo & commute into Malabo. **$$$$$**

🏠 **Sofitel Malabo Sipopo Le Golf** (200 rooms, 10 suites) Zona Sipopo, PO Box 209; 350 091 010; e H8212@sofitel.com; www. sofitel.com. Website in English, French, German, Italian, Spanish, Portuguese, Chinese & Russian. By far the best hotel in the nation (for now), this place oozes luxury. Set amidst the manicured lawns of the impressive Sipopo area, the hotel offers sea views stretching all the way to Mount Cameroon, an 18-hole golf course, a spa, swimming pool, numerous restaurants & a private beach with white sand famously imported from Cameroon. The rooms are beautiful, the internet is reliable, the customer service is great & the buffet is plentiful. There is also an airport pickup service & a shuttle bus into town. Great if you can afford it! **$$$$$**

UPMARKET

🏠 **El Complejo Caribe** (24 rooms) Carretera del Aeropuerto, Km5; 666 592 231; m 222 665 874. This large maroon-coloured complex sits on a peninsula to the north of the airport road. It offers a restaurant, disco, hotel, conference room, gym, spa & Go-Go dance strip club. The rooms are spacious & feature large TVs, combined bath/shower, AC & double beds. There are also 3 different tiers of suites available. **$$$$**

🏠 **Hotel Bahia 2** (10 rooms) Av Parques de Africa, Caracolas; m 222 096 609, 222 242 955; e bahia2caracolas@yahoo.es. Rooms come with balcony, AC, bath, shower, TV & desk. The hotel is generally empty apart from a few business visitors milling around. It looks new & clean but is not good value for money relative to other sites in this price bracket. Wi-Fi is unreliable & generally only works in the lobby. The receptionists also need a bit more training on hiding their disdain for newly arrived guests. On the plus side, this is the site for vehicle rental agency Intercar Fru (page 90). **$$$$**

🏠 **Hotel Grande** Calle de Argelia; 333 096 609. Occupying a prime waterfront location on the site of the old Hotel Bahia, upon completion in 2016 this hotel will offer impressive views of Malabo Port, the Enriquez islets, Mount Cameroon & the old city centre. **$$$$**

🏠 **ibis** (130 rooms) PO Box 201, Malabo II; 333 098 965; e H7121@accor.com; www. ibis.com. Website in English, German, Spanish, Portuguese, Italian, Dutch, Chinese, Japanese, Polish, Russian, Swedish & Indonesian. One of the first hotels built in the new Malabo II development, this ibis is well located for quick access to the airport & various government buildings. Rooms are what you would expect from the chain: clean, comfortable & of a practical design. There is an ATM in reception & a car hire company (Autos Litoral, page 109). Be sure to check the room before you accept your keycard as some of the long-term residents, who make up a large proportion of the guests, tend to smoke in their rooms. Restaurant is average. The pool area is great & there are connections to the airport. Overall, this place is not really worth the money, but is the most reliable business option in this bracket. **$$$$**

MID RANGE

Aparta-Hotel Preguis (22 apts) Barrio Alcaide, PO Box 490; 333 040 710; m 222 019 955; e apartahotelpreguis@gmail.com. This big green building on the road south out of town features apartments of 50m² with small terraced areas. Apartments have ovens with hobs, a fridge-freezer & a large counter top for cooking. There are no washing machines. It is located next door to the Iglesia Jesús y María. **$$$**

Apart Hotel Impala (20 rooms) Calle de Enrique Nvó 60; 333 092 492; e mamenus29@hotelimpala.net; www.hotelimpala.net. Has both rooms & apts, which feature a refrigerator, electric cooker & a terrace overlooking the city. Reopened after major renovations in mid 2015, this place has been a feature of the Malabo skyline since the 1980s & was very popular with UN & NGO staff in its day. **$$$**

Apart Hotel Litoral Just off the northeastern-most roundabout on Avenida de los Parques de África, Caracolas. A good location in an area that does not feature many budget options. Closed for refurbishment at the time of writing, with reopening predicted for mid 2016. **$$$**

Bantu Village (16 rooms) Avenida de la Libertad; m 222 121 378, 222 121 379. Currently undergoing refurbishment, this hotel has a popular outdoor sports bar area with large projection screen & a stage for live performances. Seems like it might be a noisy place to try & sleep but well located for access to the city nightlife! **$$$**

Flarex Residential Complex (16 suites) Carretera de Luba, off the Rotonda del Balon (football roundabout) in front of the Estadio de Malabo; m 222 538 332, 222 528 595;

e flarexhotel@yahoo.es. Situated a fair distance outside the town centre, this complex has 16 large suites available, along with a restaurant & spa. Suites include a kitchen area with bar stools, flatscreen TV, sofas, combined bath & shower, & a large double bed. The hotel signs also say it has a gin club, & by this they mean it has a bar that serves gin (amongst other things). **$$$**

Hotel 3 De Agosto (36 rooms) Av de Hassán II; 333 099 915; m 222 174 815. This Canadian-run hotel is conveniently located near a major crossroads which gets you to the airport, the centre of town or Sipopo all within 15mins (with no traffic). It has very generously sized rooms with AC, minibar, combined bath & shower, TV & a big double bed. The downside to being on a major road is the noise from the traffic, so choose your room carefully. Accepts cash payments only. The hotel restaurant is good, especially the fish dishes & the cocktails. You can even cook your own steak or fish on a hot rock. Good value. **$$$**

Hotel Restaurante El Castillo De La Mancha (7 rooms) Av Parques de Africa, Caracolas; m 222 098 836. This small 2-storey hotel is shaped like a castle & is well located in the centre of Caracolas district, near many embassy buildings. The highlight is the roof terrace & restaurant. All rooms are en suite, & have AC & free Wi-Fi but are quite small & dark. B/fast inc. **$$$**

Stella (20 rooms) Calle 3 de Agosto (Jardin); 333 098 052, 333 098 053. Simple rooms in a very central location, with a Middle Eastern-style restaurant downstairs offering grilled meats & salads. All rooms have double beds & either fans or AC, showers or baths. There is quite a discrepancy in size between rooms, & some have balconies with good views, so be sure to inspect the room before agreeing to take it. **$$$**

Tropicana (60 rooms) Av de Hassán II; 333 640 964. Rooms are large, with a fridge, double bed, AC, combined bath & shower & TV. All are en suite. The hotel is walking distance from most major landmarks in the city. There are 2 buildings, try to choose a room in the newer one as the fittings in the old one feel dated & the rooms are musty. Also, there is no lift so try to ensure that you are on the 1st floor (but not the ground floor due to noise). There is an excellent crafts shop outside which sometimes turns into a larger market. Breakfast is included in the price & staff are generally friendly. The restaurant is good with

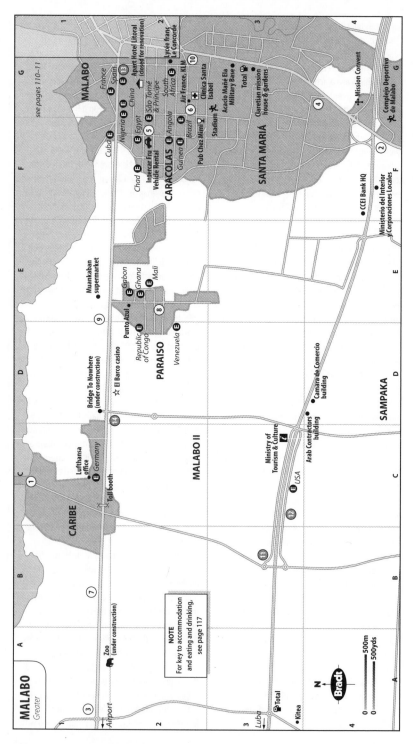

MALABO
Greater

see pages 110–11

MALABO

France 🅴
Spain 🅴 🚢 ⑬

Apart Hotel Litoral
(closed for renovation)

Lycée franç
Le Concorde

China 🅴
Egypt 🅴

São Tomé
& Príncipe

⑩

Nigeria 🅴 🅴

Intercar Fru
Vehicle Rental

⑤ 🅴

Mission Convent ✝

Cuba 🅴

Angola 🅴

South
Africa 🅴

Complejo Deportivo
de Malabo ⚓

Chad 🅴

CARACOLAS

Guinea 🅴

Brazil 🅴

Air France, KLM

Clínica Santa
Isabel ✚

Acacio Marié Ela ●
Military Base ●

Total ⛽

Claretian mission
house & gardens

Pub Chez Mimi 🍴

Stadium 🏟

SANTA MARÍA

④

②

CCEI Bank HQ ●

Ministerio del Interior
y Corporaciones Locales

Muankaban
supermarket ●

Gabon 🅴

⑨

Punto Azul 🅴

Ghana 🅴

Mali 🅴

⑧

PARAISO

Republic
of Congo 🅴

Venezuela 🅴

Bridge To Nowhere
(under construction)

☆ El Barro casino

⑭

Lufthansa
office ●

Germany 🅴

Toll booth ⛽

CARIBE

①

MALABO II

Ministry of
Tourism & Culture ℹ

Cámara de Comercio
building ●

Arab Contractors ●
building

🅴 USA

SAMPAKA

⑫

⑪

NOTE
For key to accommodation
and eating and drinking,
see page 117

Zoo
(under construction) 🦁

⑦

③

Airport ✈

N

Bradt

0 ___ 500m
0 ___ 500yds

🅿 Total
● Kitea

Luba ↓

A   B   C   D   E   F   G

1   2   3   4

MALABO *Greater*
For listings, see pages 113–15 & 118–20

a reasonably priced dish of the day (7,000CFA). Overall, a solid mid-range option. **$$$**
🏠 **Ureca** (20 rooms, 8 suites) Calle Carretera del Aeropuerto, Apd Correos 274; 🖀 333 093 319, 333 093 226. Poorly signposted, this 4-storey structure looks like an ordinary block of flats apart from the big red lettering. Their 12m pool was the site of the nation's Sydney Olympics tryouts in 2000, where Eric Moussambani Malonga qualified to represent Equatorial Guinea despite having no prior competitive swimming experience (page 126). The rooms are a decent size with double beds & AC, although the fittings all seem outdated & the place looks generally shabby. **$$$**
🏠 **Yoly Y Hnos** (13 rooms) Av del 3 de Agosto; 🖀 333 091 895; m 222 099 139; e hotelyoli@ gmail.com, hotelyoly_hérmanos@yahoo.es; www. actiweb.es/hotelyoli. Website in Spanish. Currently open but undergoing renovations, this hotel at the southern end of the town centre has spacious rooms with AC, fridges, satellite TV & free Wi-Fi. There is also limited parking on the forecourt & an internet café & adjoining massage parlour. This is a great location, right on a crossroads making pickups by shared taxis easy. **$$$**

BUDGET
🏠 **Hostal Residencia Chana** (12 rooms) Av de las Naciones Unidas. Down a dark alleyway,

this place has decent-sized rooms with en-suite bathrooms & shared showers. There are fans, no AC & lots of prostitutes. **$$**
🏠 **Hostel Residencia Santa Emilia** (13 rooms) Calle La Ronda s/n, Barrio Los Angeles/ Caidasa. This budget accommodation is right next to the central market, which is great for access to the centre of town, but not so good in terms of noise or security. Rooms are small & stuffy. **$$**
🏠 **Internet Hostal** (15 rooms) Av de las Naciones Unidas 375; m 222 126 653, 222 588 977. Also has an active Facebook page for online contact. Internet Hostal absolutely dominates the budget category in Malabo. It is a great, cheapish hotel in a central location & some rooms have en suite & powerful AC, a computer terminal & complimentary Wi-Fi. If you take a smaller room though & use the communal toilets (which are very clean) you pay half price which is a bargain for the centre of Malabo. They are also open to negotiating much lower rates for visitors staying a week or longer. This should be a first stop for all backpackers & budget overlanders. **$$**
🏠 **Residencial Morenita** (11 rooms) 44 Calle de Mongorno; 🖀 333 091 026; e residenciamorenita@gmail.com. Large clean rooms for variable rates. Top rate gets you a double bed, AC, shower & bath. Not as good as Internet Hostal down the road, but the owner does speak English & maintains a Facebook page you can make reservations through, so a good fallback option. **$$**

ROCK BOTTOM
🏠 **Hotel Ilachi** (15 rooms) Calle del Rey Malabo; 🖀 333 094 836. If you do not mind walking 2 or 3km into the town centre then this is an excellent rock bottom choice, offering much better value for money than the more central budget hotels. Rooms are a bit dark but come with AC, shower, TV & a fridge. All clean & in working order, plus it is only a very short walk to the scenic Plaza de San Fernando. **$**
🏠 **Hotel Semu** (36 rooms) Calle de Nigeria. Another hotel that also rents by the night or the hour, this place has big musty rooms with en-suite showers. It is cheaper to take a room with just a fan, although AC is available. The more expensive rooms also come with a sofa & a bigger TV. There is a bar downstairs. If you will be spending a lot of time travelling in & out of the city this might be a good rock bottom option. **$**

Malabo and around   WHERE TO STAY

3

There are a variety of eating options in Malabo reflecting the international character of the city. Everything from sushi to paella or kebabs can be found if you know where to look. Staples will be familiar to visitors of the Mediterranean: grilled fish, salads, chicken, beef, pasta and rice dishes appear on most menus. Local favourites such as *pepe* soup can also be found everywhere and there are plenty of Senegalese restaurants dotted about town. Reservations are not necessary in most establishments, and restaurants tend to be open well into the night, in keeping with the Spanish habit of dining late. You are unlikely to encounter English-speaking staff at any but the most expensive locations, so a working understanding of Spanish is useful.

Opening hours for restaurants in Malabo are variable, but as a general rule, those located in the higher-end hotels open the longest hours, opening for breakfast at around 07.00 and serving all the way through to final dinner orders at 23.00. Other more expensive restaurants outside the hotels work in line with the mid afternoon siesta, opening from noon to 16.00, and then again from 19.00 to 23.00. Lower down the price range, especially if the restaurant is attached to a bar, opening hours are broadly 09.00 to 23.00 Monday to Saturday. Outside the expensive bracket, many restaurants close earlier on Sundays, or do not open at all.

EXPENSIVE

✘ **El Basilé** Sofitel Malabo President Palace, Pl de la Independencia, Centro Historico, Zona Presidencial, PO Box 383; ☎333 099 940; e H5630@sofitel.com; ⊕ 06.30–22.30 daily. French gastronomy fuses with local flavours in what Sofitel assures us is Malabo's finest restaurant. The name was inspired by the views of Pico Basilé you can enjoy from the dining room, with its panoramic windows & terrace overlooking the pool. This restaurant is able to cater for business lunches & à la carte dinners, but feels quite expensive for the quality on offer. If you are feeling extravagant then they do have a very popular all-you-can-eat buffet at the w/end. $$$$$

✘ **Imagine** Ela Nguema Highway, Malabo II; m 222 518 626; e contacto@restaurante-imagine.com; www.restaurante-imagine.com; ⊕ noon–16.00 & 19.00–23.30 daily. A new luxury restaurant in Malabo II. This white & black cube has some distinctive design features both inside & out. They have a lot of space out in Malabo II & have made the most of it, with a large dining area, outdoor terrace & the ability to set up a massive marquee or greenhouse-like structure to cater for larger parties. The menu is Mediterranean-focused, with beautiful presentation & there is an extensive selection of wines. There is also a barbecue at w/ends. Since opening this place has swiftly

become a favourite for corporate functions in the oil industry. Menu details & a gallery can be found on the website. $$$$$

✘ **La Vie Est Belle** French Cultural Centre, Calle de Acacio Mañé; ☎333 594 544; www.institutfrancais-malabo.org; ⊕ 07.30–midnight Mon–Sat. L'Institut Culturel d'Expression Française (ICEF) has been in Malabo since 1985 & their restaurant has become somewhat of an institution for food lovers & those looking to impress business clients with something different. Specialising (unsurprisingly) in French cuisine with a focus on seafood, it features an outdoor garden dining area which hosts a barbecue at w/ends. There is also free Wi-Fi. Note that although placed in the expensive category, there is a wide range of pricing, especially for lunches. Highly recommended. $$$$$

✘ **Le Voyageur** Zona Sipopo, PO Box 209; ☎350 091 010; e H8212@sofitel.com; ⊕ 19.00–23.00 daily. This restaurant has a menu of mixed French & Equatoguinean dishes. They have an open terrace overlooking Sipopo's floodlit beach. With a great wine selection, a varied menu & an intimate atmosphere, visiting Le Voyageur makes for an enjoyable dining experience. If you are looking for breakfast or lunch, the Sipopo has 2 other restaurants on site that can cater for you (Le 19 out on the golf course & L'Equateur). $$$$$

✕ **Teatro, Gusto & Aqua Bar and Grill** Hilton Malabo Hotel, Carretera del Aeropuerto, Km7; ☏ 333 096 811; www3.hilton.com; ⏱ 06.30–23.00 daily. A selection of eating places in the Hilton Hotel. Breakfast, lunch & Sun brunch are all served as buffets in the Teatro Restaurant. If you wish to dine after 15.30 you will need to head over to the Gusto Restaurant, which is also a buffet dinner. Alternatively, you can order from a limited menu at the Aqua Bar & Grill by the pool (pizza, burgers, etc.). Overall, a good selection of foods & some great options on the drinks menu. $$$$$

✕ **Yutaka** Carretera del Aeropuerto, Km4; m 551 538 415; e yutakamalabo@gmail.com; ⏱ noon–15.30 & 19.00–23.30 Tue–Sun. With a plain interior & a small courtyard seating area, this is the only place in Malabo where you will find authentic Japanese-made sushi, sharing a menu with some Spanish favourites. As such, it is very expensive. Dish of the day is 13,000CFA, but they also offer tapas from 4,000CFA. Sushi starts at 2,500CFA. Menu details can be found on their Facebook page. $$$$$

ABOVE AVERAGE

✕ **Café Malabo** Av de la Independencia 489; ☏ 333 094 049; m 222 086 017; ⏱ 10.00–midnight Mon–Thu, 10.00–01.30 Fri & Sat, 15.00–midnight Sun. This bar tends to be quite quiet during the day, making it a good option for lunch. The menu is simple with the usual favourites of pizza, burgers & salads. However, the exorbitant price of drinks pushes this up into the above-average category. $$$$

✕ **Delice de France** Av de la Independencia, on junction with Calle del Alcalde Abilio Balboa; m 555 555 100; ⏱ 09.00–23.00 Mon–Sat. This French café & patisserie has a wide variety of pastries & sweets. The menu also includes burgers, sandwiches & salads plus there is a kebab stand attached. It is expensive but has nice décor & is a relaxing (& very cool) environment to spend some time in after walking around the centre of town. $$$$

✕ **La Luna** Luna Complex, Calle de Argelia; ☏ 333 096 096; e contact@lalunamalabo.com; ⏱ 07.30–23.00 Mon–Sat, noon–23.00 Sun. This French-run restaurant is situated around a large terrace area, with a pool overlooking the port. In terms of location & views it is hard to beat. The menu is a mixture of European fare with some

excellent seafood. The service is great, making this a very popular spot for business lunches & expatriate diners. La Luna rightly has a reputation as one of the best restaurants in Malabo. Be sure to try the French onion soup. It is also possible to use the pool during the day. The cost is 7,500CFA for adults & 6,000CFA for under 16s. $$$$

MID RANGE

✕ **Bantu** Calle Mongomo; ☏ 333 090 738; m 222 280 160, 222 272 283; e ninazengmin@yahoo.com.cn; ⏱ noon–22.00 daily. Probably the best Chinese restaurant in town. A lot of old favourites on the menu & great service from the Chinese waitresses. The prices are not unreasonable either. This place also has a crafts market in the entrance selling carvings & other African goods. Lastly, it is open on Sun which is a rare treat for Malabo! $$$

✕ **Bidji Biña Pizza Restaurant** Av de la Independencia 359; m 222 111 999. A great Italian restaurant that serves good thin crust Italian pizzas & a selection of pasta dishes. There is a terrace upstairs, & they also have a buffet. $$$

✕ **Cachirulo** Calle de Bata. Sporting a large painted motif outside which proclaims 'See and Feel the Difference', this black & yellow tiled restaurant is a Malabo institution. It served as a voting booth during the Mar 1999 elections, & was even mentioned in Robert Klitgaard's book *Tropical Gangsters* (page 57). Prices are reasonable & the menu is the usual blend of Mediterranean & African. $$$

✕ **Candy Irish Pub** Av de la Independencia; m 222 254 473; e tom.tom21@hotmail.com; ⏱ 11.00–02.00 daily. This pub is an expatriate favourite, with a great selection of burgers, club sandwiches & juicy steaks. Can get busy at w/ends, especially when there's live music playing. In late Jul 2015 the building housing the pub was demolished. It is unclear whether the pub will return when the new building is completed. $$$

✕ **Da Vinci's Cuban Restaurant** Km4, Ela Nguema Highway, Malabo II; m 222 539 063; e hav6610@gmail.com; ⏱ noon–22.00 daily. This place is excellent. They have a varied selection of Cuban food, Cuban drinks & Cuban salsa music, all served up by real-life Cubans! Also, they host a poker night on Fri from 20.00 onwards. It is a second-chance Texas Hold'em tournament with a 30,000CFA buy-in which usually attracts around

30 players. If that isn't manly enough, ask owner Davide nicely & he might even be able to rustle up some authentic Cuban cigars for you. $$$

✕ **Don Faustino's Gourmet Tapas & Grill** Calle Mongomo (in front of IPRO SL business building); m 222 096 389; e donfaustino@gmail.com; ⊕ 11.00–midnight Mon–Sat. A tiny authentic Spanish tapas restaurant in the heart of the city with a mixed clientele. The paella here is excellent, as are the cheeses & imported hams. It is a small space & always seems to be busy so arrive early, especially for dinner. Menus & sample dishes can be viewed on their detailed Facebook page. $$$

✕ **ibis Restaurant** PO Box 201, Malabo II; ☏ 333 098 965; www.ibis.com; ⊕ 06.30–10.00 & noon–22.30 daily. The restaurant in the ibis Hotel serves an all-you-can-eat breakfast & then lunch & dinner à la carte. The restaurant is clean, the service is fast & there is a reasonably priced dish of the day. $$$

✕ **L'Entrecôte** Hotel 3 de Agosto (page 115), Av de Hassán II; ☏ 333 099 915; m 222 174 815; ⊕ 07.00–22.00 daily. This Canadian-run hotel has a good restaurant. Fish dishes & the cocktails are recommended, plus there is a good variety of meats, with beef tenderloin imported from Canada. You can even cook your own steak or fish on a hot rock, & they have a Sun barbecue by the pool (weather permitting). There is sometimes even sushi on the menu! Well worth a visit. $$$

✕ **Restaurante AC** Calle del Alcalde Abilio Balboa; ⊕ noon–23.00 daily. Large Chinese restaurant. Good food at reasonable prices but the main attraction is probably the convenience of their take-away service. $$$

✕ **Restaurant Pizza Place** Av de la Independencia 319; ☏ 333 093 450. Another Lebanese pizza restaurant offering a mixture of European & Middle Eastern food. With great views of the ocean, free Wi-Fi & an excellent buffet this place is also reasonably priced as a lunch or dinner option. If you want to eat outside try and arrive earlier as this tends to fill up with groups wanting to sit & smoke *shisha*. The T-bone steaks here are expensive but highly recommended. There is also a branch on Avenida de Hassán II (☏ *333 093 450, 333 095 718*). This also has a covered balcony area, which is great for smoking *shisha* or having a beer. $$$

✕ **Spanish Cultural Centre** Carretera del Aeropuerto; ☏ 333 092 186; e info@ccemalabo.es; http://ccemalabo.es/; ⊕ 10.00–16.00 & 19.00–23.00 daily. The Centro Cultural de España en Malabo (CCEM) has a restaurant that serves traditional Spanish cuisine at reasonable prices. The dining space is great if you want Spanish food but do not want to crowd into Don Faustino's. $$$

CHEAP AND CHEERFUL

✕ **Abuin-asi** Calle del Rey Malabo; ⊕ 10.00–22.00 Mon–Sat. Good-value local restaurant with a very distinctive garden & outdoor seating area. Also does take-away. This is a nice quiet spot for such a busy part of town. $$

✕ **Keur Senegalese** Calle Mongomo; m 222 259 704. This is a big restaurant by the university. It has a covered outdoor area & serves budget Senegalese food. Try the peanut stew with chicken. $$

☕ **Tamara Patisserie** Calle de Nigeria 242. Café serving delicious fresh fruit juice & pastries. $$

✕ **Café Kristiana** Calle Av de la Libertad – Apdo 123; ☏ 333 091 330. Café serving tortillas, sandwiches, burgers, tapas, soup & salads. Their pastries are the real attraction though. Dishes average around 3,000CFA. Grab a seat outside to avoid the blasting AC & enjoy the sights & sounds of central Malabo. $–$$

✕ **Restaurant Betty Dougans** Casa Teodolita, Calle del Botuku Luba; ⊕ 18.00–22.00 Mon–Sat. Hidden behind a blue gate in an unmarked courtyard to the side of Casa Teodolita is this quiet family-run establishment. Calling it a restaurant is slightly overstating it: there is an outdoor grill, a couple of plastic chairs & only one thing on the menu – ribs. Run by an English-speaking Equatoguinean family with links to London, this is a great place to relax in the evening & their ribs are amazing (3,000CFA per portion or 7,000CFA for a whole rack). They also do take-away. $–$$

✕ **Salam** Calle de Enrique Nvó. Great Middle Eastern restaurant that serves Halal meats. A whole rotisserie chicken will only set you back 5,000CFA. Cheap & delicious with a large covered seating area. $$–$

ROCK BOTTOM

☕ **Café Bonjour** Av de la Independencia. This small new café is part of the Total petrol station. Has good coffee & pastries. $

✖ Dabakh Paseo de los Cocoteros. This tiny Senegalese restaurant offers tasty food at low prices in a tiny dining room. A main here is only 1,200CFA. $

✖ Friendship Pizza Queen Calle de Enrique Nvó. Offers a mixture of traditional & Spanish foods (tapas, *djomba*, *pepe* soup, etc). Cheap & cheerful with an amazing name! $

✖ Restaurante Plaza II This place is hard to miss with its Art-Deco green ski slope-esque monument. Local foods & lots of beers are served here, & it gets busy (& rowdy) at night. $

✖ Terraza Betty At junction of Calle del Alcalde Abilio Balboa & Calle Mongomo. Offers a mix of cheap local & Spanish cuisine. Good value. $

⌷ Yogui Av del 3 de Agosto 390; m 555 848 654; ⊕ noon–20.00 Tue–Sun. This brightly decorated café offers an assortment of frozen yoghurts, hot & cold drinks, & sweet & savoury pastries. The large beef samosas are great value at only 1,000CFA & very filling. They can also do birthday cakes to order. $

ENTERTAINMENT AND NIGHTLIFE

The great thing about the city centre being so compact is that you can easily do a night out entirely on foot, although most embassies would advise against this for security reasons. Malabo is small but there is enough going on to keep you occupied if you know where to look, regardless of whether you will be stumbling around in flip-flops or being chauffeured in a company vehicle.

CINEMA Cine Rial [map, page 104] over by the Buena Esperanza housing complex on the east side of town is the only modern cinema in Malabo, and it opened in 2011. There are 280 seats on offer, with tickets starting from 5,000CFA for weekday performances, and 10,000CFA at the weekend. It is open from 09.00 to 23.00 daily.

LIVE EVENTS If you are looking for live music or live theatre then your best bet is to check the listings at the **Spanish Cultural Centre** [116 G2] (pages 130–1), the **French Cultural Centre** [110 C6] (pages 131–2) or the **Equatoguinean Cultural Centre** [111 E2] (pages 129–30). Occasionally the embassies also host cultural events so it is worth getting on the mailing list for these or making friends with someone who knows the scene. The **Candy Irish Pub** [110 D2] (page 119) also has live bands and advertises the acts outside the entrance. For Equatoguinean music, check out the fly-posters all over town, or head to Discoteca L'Alizee's. Check out their Facebook page to see who will be performing that weekend (*https://es-es.facebook.com/mico1mico*).

NIGHTCLUBS AND BARS Malabo is full of bars of varying descriptions, with most of them playing very loud music. Things generally do not get going until late (as in after midnight), however, many of the drinking establishments also serve food, or are attached to restaurants or cafés, meaning that they are open from around 19.00 onwards. If you are looking for a drink in the afternoon (around siesta time) you will need to head to one of the expatriate hangouts such as Candy Irish Pub, one of the hotels, or one of the cheap and cheerful local drinking dens.

Make sure you check the price of drinks before ordering them, as prices vary enormously depending on the location. Also note that Equatoguineans tend to get very dressed up to go out, so you might look a little out of place in a T-shirt and jeans. A few of the more popular spots also have door policies such as no flip-flops and no shorts. Some bars are free, but most charge an entry fee, which can be up to 20,000CFA.

☆ **Bahia Sound Lounge** [110 C1] Calle de Argelia 86; m 222 540 382; e Bahiasoundlounge@hotmail.es; ⏱ 17.00–05.00 Thu–Sun. Hidden on a northern peninsula of the city, just past Luna Complex, you would not expect to find a nightclub in this otherwise residential area. However, behind the innocuous façade is a bar with an open-air dance floor facing out over the waterfront, which offers views of Punta Europa at night. Prices are high & parking is a nightmare but with an eclectic mix of music, a friendly crowd & the occasional live band this place is very popular.

🍷 **Bar Fang** [110 2B] Paseo de los Cocoteros; ⏱ noon–02.00 daily. This cheap local bar has a terrace area overlooking the sea. A nice spot for sundowners, but fills up with prostitutes during the evenings.

🍷 **Café Malabo** [110 C2] Av de la Independencia 489; ✎ 333 094 049; m 222 086 017; ⏱ 10.00–midnight Mon–Thu, 10.00–01.30 Fri & Sat, 15.00–midnight Sun. This colourfully painted space has a cosmopolitan atmosphere & is a surprising find just off the main street. They serve decent bar food including pizzas, burgers & salads. Drinks are very expensive, although they have a dangerous offer on a Thu involving buying 5 mojitos & getting the 6th free. The lounge has Wi-Fi & there is a stage which often hosts live acts. This is a popular spot with the local elite & gets busy at w/ends.

🍷 **Candy Club** [111 E1] Av de la Independencia 825; ⏱ 21.00–late daily. Situated above Restaurant Pizza Place in the centre of town is the black-&-white-painted Candy Club. In the cold harsh light of day it looks like a sleazy dive bar & things do not improve much at night, when the place is overrun with ageing oil men who should know better, & overly friendly young local women. It's not big, & it's not clever.

🍷 **Candy Irish Pub** [110 D2] See page 119; m 222 254 473; e tom.tom21@hotmail.com; ⏱ 11.00–02.00 daily. This pub is an expatriate favourite. The wooden interior, bench seating, cluttered walls, flags & port holes overlooking the ocean make you feel like you are drinking on a boat. The dizzying array of spirits on offer might add to this effect. There are drafts on tap, & the bar food is not bad either (especially the steaks). Good service, but prices are relatively high. There is a pool table & a big flatscreen TV for sports events. This place is packed at w/ends, often with a live band playing in the corner. In late Jul 2015 the building housing the pub was demolished.

It is unclear whether the pub will return when the new building is completed.

☆ **Caribe Gogo Dance** [116 C1] Inside El Complejo Caribe, Carretera del Aeropuerto, Km5; m 551 681 521/522. The enterprising owners of Malabo's only strip club offer a free shuttle service, so you may see their minibuses zooming around town, filled with drunk or slightly embarrassed-looking patrons.

🍷 **China Pub** [110 4B] Av de Hassán II. A shady Chinese-run establishment filled with drunken expats and the occasional prostitute. It has a tiny bar with seating spilling out on to the pavement. Expect friendly service from waitresses with bunny ears, loud music & crowds in the evenings. Great fun.

🍷 **Chinese Sisters** [110 4B] Calle de Enrique Nvó. Another entertaining Chinese-run bar, with a similar crowd to China Pub. Chinese Sisters has an outdoor seating area & reasonably priced drinks, plus they are open to suggestions for the playlist. Great fun, if a little chaotic, & it stays open very late. You will not be meeting any of Malabo's high society here, but it is a popular expatriate hangout.

☆ **Luna Club** [110 C1] Luna Complex, Calle de Argelia; m 222 519 835; e contact@lalunamalabo.com; ⏱ 23.00–05.00 Thu–Sun. Sharing the same grounds as one of the most popular restaurants in Malabo, this nightspot gets crowded at w/ends & is the place to be seen for local music lovers. Entry is 10,000CFA & things do not usually kick off until gone 01.00 so expect a long night.

🍷 **New Candy Pub** [111 G3] Continuing the confusing tradition of calling everything they build 'Candy', this location is run by the same management as the popular Irish pub. Another good spot for a drink if you are in this part of town.

🍷 **Pub Chez Mimi** [116 F2] Caracolas; m 222 250 589, 222 564 585; ⏱ 19.00–midnight Mon–Sat. Lively Chinese bar in the Caracolas neighbourhood. Serves draught beers & also has a barbecue.

🍷 **Topé Lounge Bar** [110 C2] Passeo de los Cocoteros; ✎ 333 094 770; ⏱ 20.00–midnight Mon–Sat. With a garish gold colour scheme, this bar offers cocktails & tapas. Best not to go stumbling around this part of town late at night though, so bring your own transport.

🍷 **Treasure Island** [111 E1] Av de la Independencia. Currently closed for renovation, this combined bar, restaurant & casino is situated overlooking the port by the cathedral. Due to reopen in mid 2016, it offers magnificent views across the harbour.

CASINOS Those looking to gamble in Malabo will have to be quite creative. There are a few slot machine houses dotted around, such as Game VIP and Game King, but until Treasure Island reopens there are currently only two places to play:

☆ **Da Vinci's Cuban Restaurant** [116 3B] Km4, Ela Nguema Highway, 10244; m 222 539 063; e hav6610@gmail.com; ⊕ noon–22.00 daily. Once you get sick of playing Hold'em blackjack at the El Barco Casino (which you inevitably will), why not try a proper live poker tournament over at Malabo's only Cuban restaurant? They host a poker night on Fri from 20.00. It is a second-chance Texas Hold'em tournament with a 30,000CFA buy-in which usually attracts around 30 players, meaning you could be playing for over €2,500. And if that wasn't manly enough, ask owner Davide nicely & he might even be able to rustle up some authentic Cuban cigars for you.

☆ **El Barco Casino & Bar** [116 D2] Carretera del Aeropuerto, Km4; ☎ 333 093 507; ⊕ 07.00–03.00 daily. Inaugurated in Jun 2013, this casino is shaped like a big boat, & is situated on the airport road. It has 6 tables: 3 roulette & 3 card games – as well as 44 slots & poker machines. For some reason staff do not seem to mind players showing each other their hands on the Hold'em blackjack tables, which can make for a profitable night on a busy table! Expect to meet an interesting cross-section of Malabo society in here, from Chinese business owners to US oil workers & everything in between. Drinks are free while you are playing, which is either a really good thing or a really terrible idea.

SHOPPING

The usual business opening hours are 08.00–13.00 and 16.00–19.00 Monday to Friday, with some businesses also open 08.00–13.00 on Saturdays. There are few businesses that do not take a siesta in the afternoon, so be sure to factor this into your shopping plans. Generally speaking, opening hours seem to be quite erratic in Equatorial Guinea, so do not rely on places opening at the advertised times.

BOOKSHOPS Former president Macías's campaign against intellectualism left Malabo without any functioning bookshops, a situation that was highlighted as still prevalent in an early 2012 BBC News article. However, by Christmas of that same year Malabo got its first private bookshop, **La Casa Tomada** [110 C6] (*Plaza Ewaiso Ipola, opposite ICEF*; m *222 047 206*; e *librerialacasatomada@rocketmail.com*). The colourful yellow and pink mural outside draws your attention to this small but well-presented bookshop. Inside, there are a number of genres on sale, with a focus on African authors and educational texts. There is also a small café. The owner is very friendly, so be sure to stop in during your visit to Malabo, but call or email to check if they are open first!

You can also purchase a limited range of books at one of the National Library book stands dotted about town, or from the French and Spanish cultural centres.

MARKETS Informal street vendors can offer you everything in Malabo, from cigarettes to smartphones. Fresh produce is often much cheaper in the markets, rather than buying imported produce in the supermarkets. Plus, you are helping support local agriculture. There are a number of markets scattered around town. Their hours can be irregular so check locally, but your best bet is to visit between 10.00 and 16.00 on a weekday.

🛒 **Central market** [110 D7] Backing on to the football stadium on Calle de Patricio Lumumba the central market is chaotic. If you are in need of batteries, fried chicken, hair curlers, used clothing, dog collars, fruit, vegetables, alcohol, cigarettes or dangerously wired Chinese electronic items then you are in luck! Many of the stands stay open quite late.

🏛 **Chinese fruit and vegetable market** [110 B3] Corner of Avenida de las Naciones Unidas. This indoor space sells a lot of fruit and vegetables.

🏛 **Fish market** [110 D5] Calle de Bata. Hidden down a side street in the southern section of town, this market sells a variety of fresh produce. Do not be put off by the urban location; some of this stuff is delicious, as long as it is fresh.

🏛 **Fruit and vegetable market** [110 B2] Paseo de los Cocoteros. There are lots of street vendors down here.

🏛 **Outdoor clothes market** [110 C6] Calle del Rey Malabo. Local clothes vendors gather here. Not much on offer in terms of traditional clothing but OK if you need a cheap pair of trainers or a rain jacket for your travels.

🏛 **Semu market** [111 G7] Calle Nigeria; ⏲ 10.00–16.00 Wed–Mon. This is the largest market in the south of the city. It has a varied selection of fresh goods as well as a wide variety of other products. You will also find a taxi rank here for heading out of town.

SUPERMARKETS The selection of goods in Malabo's supermarkets is quite good and improving every year. The main issue is price. You could stock your kitchen as if you were in Europe but you will pay a high premium, especially when it comes to fresh, perishable produce.

🏛 **Gourmet Guinea** [110 C3] Calle de Nigeria 22–4; m 222 164 043; e guinespa@hotmail. com; ⏲ 09.00–13.00 & 16.00–19.00 Mon–Fri, 09.00–13.00 Sat. This is a high-end delicatessen stocking imported cured meats, pâtés, cheese, chocolate, wine & other luxury items. Frustratingly, none of the chocolate they stock is local, so do not head here if you are looking for an authentic gift for the family back home.

🏛 **Lumeco Supermarket** [111 F7] Calle de Nigeria; ⏲ 09.00–13.00 & 16.00–19.00 Mon–Sat. Small shop but good-quality items.

🏛 **Martinez Hermanos Supermercado** [110 B3] Av de la Independencia; ⏲ 09.00–13.00 & 16.00–19.00 Mon–Fri, 09.00–12.30 Sat. This company has been present in Equatorial Guinea since 1927 & offers one of the best supermarkets on the island. Prices are generally higher than in Europe, & you need to look carefully at the labels in order to avoid being stung (especially with fresh goods). However, this place offers a good selection of Western produce, mainly imported from Spain, in a large central location. The Martinez brothers seem to take shoplifting very seriously, as you will notice a lot of employees floating around keeping an eye on the shoppers.

🏛 **Mini Market Consty** [110 D2] Calle del Rey Boncoro; ⏲ 09.00–13.00 & 16.00–19.00 Mon–Sat. Small supermarket offering a limited selection of refrigerated & frozen goods, along with the usual selection of canned & dry goods.

🏛 **Muankaban** [116 E1] Carretera del Aeropuerto; e supermercadomuankaban@gmail. com; ⏲ 09.00–16.00 Mon–Fri, 09.00–12.30 Sat. This supermarket opened in late 2012 to much fanfare, promoted by the First Lady, Constancia Mangue de Obiang. The red, orange & yellow building is hard to miss on the airport road. It offers a good variety of produce with fresh meat, fruit & vegetables, a fishmongers & a bakery.

🏛 **Santy Supermarket** [110 D7] Av de las Naciones Unidas; ⏲ 09.00–16.00 Mon–Fri, 09.00–12.30 Sat. Opposite the central market is Santy, a large supermarket with a variety of imported produce, much of it Spanish. They have a decent enough frozen food section & some chilled goods such as cheeses, cured meats & fruit (although prices are high).

🏛 **Venta Al Mayor** [110 B2] Calle del Alcalde Abilio Balboa; m 222 786 668; ⏲ 09.00–19.00 Mon–Sat. This is a large Chinese-run supermarket with a wide selection of non-perishable goods.

OTHER GOODS

🏛 **Bioko Heirloom** Contact Dr Shaya Honarvar; ☏ +1 215 895 6906; e sh333@drexel.edu or Sally Vickland; m 222 565 788; e svickland@gmail. com. The Bioko Biodiversity Protection Program co-ordinated by Drexel University have teamed up with artisanal jewellery makers in Ureca to offer genuine Equatoguinean jewellery & hand-woven baskets for sale in Malabo. Locations vary, so contact the organisers to find out where you can get hold of some of these great gifts! These goods can also be purchased in the BBPP fieldhouse in Moka (page 143).

The Business Shop [111 E3] Calle del Rey Boncoro; ☏ 333 098 586; ⊕ 08.00–13.00 & 16.00–18.00 Mon–Fri, 10.00–13.00 & 16.00–19.00 Sat. This shop features computer, printer & office supplies. Well stocked & has English-speaking staff.

Centro Comercial Tomos [111 F7] Calle de Nigeria. A retail park to the south of town with a variety of stores, including a baby shop & electronics.

Cooki Frutti [110 D3] Calle De Presidente Nasser 44; m 555 628 686. Sells an assortment of children's sweets and party gear.

Champaneria Tour Eiffel [110 C3] Calle de Enrique Nvó; m 222 512 624. Seemingly out of place down a quiet side street, this shop stocks Dom Pérignon and various other types of expensive champagne & wines.

DSTV Retailer [110 C5] Calle del Alcalde Abilio Balboa 472. Your first stop if you want to watch South African satellite TV whilst in Malabo.

Kitea Malabo [116 A3] Malabo II. This is a Moroccan-owned IKEA copy. They are a successful chain in the Middle East.

Lizzie M&M [111 H7] Av del 3 de Agosto; m 222 259 578, 222 298 946. This children's party supplier is situated on the road just south of Police Station Lampert, & has all the balloons, party hats & confetti you could ever need.

Local Arts and Crafts Store [110 C3] Av de la Independencia. Situated in an opening opposite Delice de France, this store has carvings, paintings & jewellery.

Square Style: La Mode Africaine [110 C5] Calle de Bata; m 222 749 648, 222 065 801. This tailor has a fantastic assortment of fabrics & can rustle up a shirt & matching trousers for 45,000CFA or a waistcoat for 7,000CFA. They can turn just about anything into clothing for you. A great place for gifts. They also have a location on Avenida de las Naciones Unidas & other outlets in Bata. Highly recommended.

Ventage Casa [110 D4] Calle de Nigeria; ☏ 333 090 553; e ventage@hotmail.com. Department store selling kitchen goods, cleaning products, bicycles, etc.

SPORTS AND ACTIVITIES

The national sport of Equatorial Guinea is undoubtedly **football**, and there are plenty of opportunities to watch it in Malabo. Equatorial Guinea co-hosted the 2012 African Cup of Nations with Gabon, and stepped in as a last-minute replacement for Morocco to host the 2015 tournament, too. The national team, nicknamed Nzalang Nacional ('National Lightning'), were excluded from the 2015 tournament for fielding an ineligible player, before being reinstated as the host nation. The well-known player Rodolfo Bodipo has now retired, but some of the squad's most famous players include Emilio Nsue López (Middlesbrough) and Javier Ángel Balboa Osa (G D Estoril Praia).

The Equatoguinean women's football team is very successful, having won the 2008 and 2012 African Women's Championship, as well as finishing as runners-up in the 2010 tournament. Their star player and captain is Genoveva Añonma Nze, who in 2011 became the first African woman to be included in the FIFA World Cup All-Star Team.

Besides football, **swimming** has become oddly synonymous with Equatorial Guinea, despite the lack of national facilities to practise it. This is mainly due to the headline-grabbing efforts of wild-card Olympic swimmer Eric Moussambani, whose story went viral during the 2000 Sydney Olympic Games. His claim to fame? Recording the slowest 100m freestyle time in Olympic history, amidst some very unusual circumstances (page 126). You can follow in Eric the Eel's footsteps and go swimming in the 12m Hotel Ureca pool for a small fee (page 117), or the Hilton also has a pool which non-residents can use for 10,000CFA. You are unlikely to be allowed to use other hotel swimming pools without being a resident.

It is not uncommon to see an informal **basketball** game taking place as you wander around towns in Equatorial Guinea. The National Basketball League was inaugurated in 2013, co-ordinated by the Equatorial Guinean Basketball Federation

Eric had been unable to swim eight months before the 2000 Olympics, but Equatorial Guinea was allowed to send a competitor under the wild-card entry system established to give athletes from developing countries the opportunity to compete. After qualifying to represent the country in trials held in the 12m Hotel Ureca pool in Malabo, Eric spent most of his time training in lakes and rivers, with the occasional foray into a hotel swimming pool. To make matters more difficult, Eric thought he was training for the 50m freestyle event and was not informed that he was competing in the 100m event until he arrived in Sydney. His arrival in Australia also marked the first time Eric had seen or set foot in an Olympic size swimming pool.

On the day of Eric's race, 17,000 spectators packed into the Sydney International Aquatic Centre to watch the Equatoguinean athlete compete against Tajikistan's Farkhod Oripov and Karim Bare of Niger. Both Oripov and Bare made a false start, meaning instant disqualification. This left the 22-year old Eric to swim the two lengths on his own against the clock. After making a quick start, it soon became clear to the crowd that Eric was struggling, with BBC commentator Adrian Moorhouse saying at the one-minute mark 'this guy doesn't look at though he is going to make it'. However, Eric did make it, finishing at 1 minute 52.72 seconds, marking both a personal best and the new Equatoguinean national record at this distance. The world record currently stands at 46.91 seconds.

Dubbed 'Eric the Eel' by commentators around the world, Moussambani achieved international fame and has since gone on to improve his 100m freestyle time to under one minute. His glorious failure, although initially a source of embarrassment to his home government, was held up as the embodiment of the games' spirit by many commentators. In March 2012, he was appointed national swimming coach for Equatorial Guinea.

(FEGUIBASKET) and currently has six teams in Division I, with the Malabo Kings leading the pack. Equatorial Guinea has yet to compete on the international stage in this sport, but it is gaining in popularity.

GYMS All of the higher-end hotels in Malabo have gyms, with some scattered among the mid-range accommodation too. Policies about non-residents using them are varied, so try contacting places such as the Sofitel or Hilton for more details. The Hotel de Federaciones (*Ciudad Deportiva, Estadio Malabo;* m *222 760 209; www.hotelfederaciones.com*) may also be able to help you arrange use of the facilities at the Complejo Deportivo de Malabo [116 F4]. Outside these hotels, there are few dedicated gyms but you could try **Gym Oma** [110 D3] (*Calle Mongomo 423;* ⊕ *07.00–11.00 & 16.00–20.00 daily*). This gym has resistance machines and free weights and offers martial arts classes including Brazilian jiu jitsu.

DIVING The organised dive tours on the island are run by Spaniard, **Roberto Vasquez** (m *222 274 323, 555 274 323;* e *pescaybuceoge@yahoo.com, robertohevia@yahoo.com*). Roberto has a small air-conditioned container in front of the Sipopo Beach Club (page 136). He has been working in Equatorial Guinea as a coffee exporter for over 25 years, and charges 25,000CFA for a one-tank dive. He can also rent other necessary equipment. Roberto has two boats;

a smaller rigid hulled inflatable for short trips, and a larger, faster fishing boat which can accommodate more divers. His base in Malabo can be found on Calle del Rey Malabo 113 [110 A7].

GOLF There is an 18-hole golf course at the Sofitel Sipopo Golf (page 114). This plays host to the annual Mobil Classic Golf Tournament as well as other corporate golfing events. Rounds can be arranged through the hotel. There is also a clubhouse that offers food and drinks.

FISHING If you wish to fish offshore, you will need to organise this in advance with a private boat, either by asking at one of the high-end hotels, through a tour agency or by hanging around down at the port. Also note that permits are required for any fishing other than in a pirogue, and that the coastguard may board your vessel to check your paperwork. The exact permits required for fishing change often, so be sure to ask at the Ministry of Culture and Tourism (pages 128–9) before heading out. Expatriates who have brought their own fishing equipment into Malabo report that there are a variety of delicious fish including huge barracuda to be caught.

OTHER PRACTICALITIES

BANKS AND FOREIGN EXCHANGE There are numerous bank branches spread across Malabo, many in the centre of town around the intersection of Avenida de las Naciones Unidas and Avenida de la Independencia. They are all willing to exchange euros and US dollars, although you may have to queue. Also take note of the limited opening hours (page 101). You will struggle to change money around siesta time in the early afternoon or at weekends. If you cannot use a bank, you can change your foreign currency at the Nova Cambios money exchange opposite the Chamber of People's Representatives in the centre of town.

It is not advisable to change money on the street, and there is little advantage in doing so with regards to the exchange rate. Most businesses engaging in foreign trade will happily change your foreign currency, offering rates similar to, or better than, the banks. This is a very convenient and quick way of changing money, although this practice is of questionable legality.

$ **Banco Nacional** [110 C5] Avenida de las Naciones Unidas; 333 099 571/576; ⊕ 07.00–15.00 Mon–Fri, 09.00–13.00 Sat. Has an ATM which accepts Visa & MasterCard.
$ **BANGE Bank** [110 B3] Av de la Independencia 312; ⊕ 08.00–14.30 Mon–Fri, 09.00–12.30 Sat. Has an ATM but no Visa symbol.
$ **CCEI Bank** [110 C2] Av de la Independencia; 333 092 910, 333 092 203; ⊕ 08.00–14.30 Mon–Fri, 10.00–13.00 Sat. Has an ATM which accepts Visa.
$ **Ecobank** [110 B3] Av de Hassán II; 333 098

271; m 555 300 203; ⊕ 08.00–14.30 Mon–Fri, 10.00–13.00 Sat. Has an ATM which accepts Visa & MasterCard.
$ **Nova Cambios** [110 D2] Av de la Independencia 677; ⊕ 09.00–12.00 & 14.00–18.00 Mon–Fri. Foreign exchange.
$ **Société Générale de Banque GE (SGBE)** [110 B3] Av de la Independencia 245; 333 093 337; ⊕ 08.00–14.00 Mon–Fri, 08.00–noon Sat. Has an ATM which accepts Visa & MasterCard. Well stocked, best bet for getting out money & the ATMs are accessible 24/7.

HEALTHCARE Visitors are advised to avoid public hospitals due to a lack of equipment, medicines and qualified staff. This includes the **Malabo General Hospital**. The only healthcare facility recommended for medical and dental needs by expatriate employers in Malabo is the **La Paz Hospital** over in Sipopo. However, for minor ailments or repeat prescriptions, you may save time and money by going to one of the following:

➕ **Clinica Cristiana** [111 F4] Calle de Bata; ☎ 333 099 201. Headed by Dr Juan Chaveco, this general clinic is identifiable by its beautiful green garden. Keeps irregular hours so be sure to call ahead.

➕ **Clinica Dr Alfredo** [110 D4] Calle Mongomo 440; ☎ 333 098 361; ⏱ 08.30–13.00 & 16.30–20.00 Mon–Sat. This is a Chinese-run general clinic.

➕ **Clinica Virgen De Guadalupe (Hospital)** [111 E5] Calle del Rey Malabo; ☎ 333 099 013, 333 096 956. This is a large white building with distinctive red cross insignia. Able to handle walk-in cases recommended by the US Department of State.

Clinica Santa Isabel [116 G2] Av Parques de Africa, Caracolas; ☎ 333 092 666, 333 094 504; 🅼 222 636 266, 222 536 973. Offering paediatric & emergency care.

➕ **Dental Los Angeles** [110 D7] Calle del Rey Malabo; 🅼 +227 111 098 638; ⏱ 09.00–15.00

Mon–Fri. Dentist surgery run by Nigerien Dr Yassine. Much cheaper than heading to La Paz, but lower-quality dental care.

➕ **La Paz Hospital Malabo** [map, page 104] Sipopo; 🅼 556 666 160, 556 666 156; 🅴 info@lapazmalabo.com; http://lapazmalabo.org; ⏱ 24/7. This is the top medical facility on Bioko & probably the best hospital in the entire country. It has an emergency & trauma centre, as well as a number of other specialist centres such as surgical, orthopaedics, paediatrics & gynaecology. It is the only place recommended by Western embassies if you need a dentist. La Paz employs a number of specialist expatriate medical practitioners including Spaniards, Cubans & Israelis. The centre also has a pharmacy, hotel & other healthcare facilities. Prices are very high, especially for emergency care, so be sure to consult with your insurance provider before incurring costs.

PHARMACIES There are numerous pharmacies throughout the city of varying quality. Many of them are run by Chinese doctors. Be sure to take along the generic name of any drugs you are looking for (rather than the brand name) and be prepared to do some hunting around before you find everything you are looking for. For **baby supplies**, your best bet is to bring everything you need from your home country. However, there are a few specialist baby stores dotted around town which may be able to help you.

➕ **Baby T&T** [111 G5] Calle del Emperador Haile Salassie 138, Colasesga, Malabo; 🅼 222 664 566; 🅴 telma2teresa@gmail.com; ⏱ 09.00–noon & 14.00–18.00 Mon–Fri. Stocks a selection of Western baby brands (milk powder, supplements, vitamins, bottles, etc).

➕ **Consultorio Jianhe** [110 D4] Calle de Nigeria; 🅼 222 005 898, 222 159 988; ⏱ 09.00–18.00

Mon–Sat Chinese-run so they do not take a siesta, they have a variety of generic drugs on offer here.

➕ **Farmacia Amanda** [110 B4] Av de la Independencia 245; ☎ 333 093 337; ⏱ 09.00–14.00 & 16.00–19.00 Mon–Fri, 09.00–14.00 Sat. Very large & well stocked. This should probably be your first port of call when looking for drugs outside the La Paz hospital pharmacy.

MINISTRY OF TOURISM AND CULTURE Every tourist that visits Bioko island will need to pay a visit to the Ministry of Tourism and Culture [116 D3] (*ask the taxi driver to take you to: Viviendas Sociales, en frente de la Camera de Comercio, Malabo II (this is the unmarked social housing block in front of the clearly marked Camara de Comercio building);* ⏱ 08.00–16.00 Mon–Fri). This ministry is hidden in a social housing block in Malabo II, just off the roundabout with the Arab Contractors building and the Camara de Comercio building on it. There is a sign outside but it is very easy to miss. Taxi drivers tend to have no idea where it is, or will try and take you to the Ministry of Information, Press and Radio where it used to be. They have a better idea of where the Arab Contractors and Camara de Comercio buildings are, so use these as waypoints. For more information on obtaining your Tourism Permit, see *Other practicalities*, page 68.

MOBILE PHONES To buy a new SIM card, head to **GETESA** [111 E3] at the junction of Calle del Rey Boncoro and Calle de Presidente Nasser (\ *333 093 313*). You will need one passport photo and a copy of your passport (plus visa page). The cost is 4,000CFA. There are other GETESA shops spread around town which will sell you credit, but you must come to this central one as a foreigner to buy your SIM.

INTERNET Cibermax Internet Café [110 C4] can be found on Avenida de las Naciones Unidas 375 (🕓 *09.00–19.00 Mon–Sat*) and is attached to the Internet Hostal. It is bright, clean and has a reliable connection and also sells drinks.

OTHER USEFUL ADDRESSES

ICAM GE Film Studio [111 F3] Av de la Libertad 635; m 222 013 302. For those arriving to work in the burgeoning film industry, this may be your first port of call. This studio is able to offer assistance with a whole range of shooting needs, including aerial photography, underwater filming & 3D animation.

Perfecto Pressing Agencia Ibadan [111 F6] Calle del Rey Malabo; m 551 549 552/542; e perfectopressing@yahoo.fr. Good-quality dry-cleaning company able to turn over items quickly, but quite expensive at around €5 for a pair of trousers & €3 for a shirt.

WHAT TO SEE AND DO

There is much to see in the nation's capital and things are generally very close together, so you can walk, take short 500CFA taxi rides or use a private vehicle.

CULTURAL CENTRES
Equatoguinean Cultural Centre (Centro Cultural Ecuatoguineano) [111 E2] (*Av de la Independencia;* \ *333 091 032;* m *222 110 450;* e *ccegmalabo@hotmail. com;* 🕓 *09.00–22.30 Mon–Fri*) Any visitor to the capital should immediately head to the Equatoguinean Cultural Centre to find out what their programme is during your visit. The centre has the mission of co-ordinating and disseminating the traditions and customs of the people of Equatorial Guinea, and they have an amazing space to do it in. Situated on Avenida de la Independencia in the centre of town, this two-storey structure is built around a large atrium. Young people are often attracted in by the free Wi-Fi on offer, but once inside can choose from free indigenous language courses, art exhibitions, workshops and an impressive museum display of local artefacts. Whether you are interested in learning to cook *pepe* soup or exploring the timeline of Equatoguinean independence, this centre has something to offer. At the moment there are free beginners' language classes in Bubi, Fang, Bissio and Fá d'Ambô. Adjoining the main building is a large covered outdoor area used to stage theatre, music and dance productions. Timetables of events are available on the centre's Facebook page, and are also displayed on the walls to the right as you enter the building.

While on the Avenida de la Independencia you can also check out the monument to the Cuban deportees brought to Malabo by boat in 1869, as well as the **monument** to the commander of the frigate *Nervión* who arrived in Malabo in 1843 down at the entrance to Calle de Argelia (page 131). Both of these spots offer beautiful views

There are a number of colonial gems hidden in the side streets of Malabo, many now overshadowed by the high rises springing up in the town centre. They are easy to miss and are not always marked, so follow this route to be sure to take them all in. The walk should take between one and two hours.

This walking tour starts on the southern outskirts of the town centre, and we will work our way in. The first stop is the **Seminario de Nuestra Señora del Pilar de Banapá** [off map, 110 A7], a Catholic boarding school and church built in 1884. It is now on the site of the Universidad Nacional de Guinea Ecuatorial (UNGE), at the intersection of Avenida de Hassán II and Calle Del Rey Malabo. From here if you walk the width of town eastwards along Calle Del Rey Malabo, you will approach the hotel Yoly y Hnos. One hundred metres south of here on Avenida del 3 de Agosto you will see the **National Radio Headquarters** [111 G5], which is another impressive late colonial-era building, soon due to be replaced by a Chinese-built modern facility. If you then head north up the side street, Calle del Botuku Lubá, towards the coast you will pass the bright-yellow **Casa Teodolita** (111 F3). This is one of the oldest residential buildings in Malabo, and dates back to 1902. It is now also the site of one of the tastiest ribs restaurants in the city! The building is marked with a plaque commemorating the date of construction.

Continue northwards for one block and look to your right down Calle de Acacio Mañé and you will see the **National Library (BNGE)** [111 G3], which is a former Spanish private residence completed in 1916 and refurbished in 2009. It is also the former residence of famous Equatoguinean sculptor Leandro Mbomio Nsue. Be careful taking photos here as you are very close to the presidential palace.

Your next stop is in the very northeastern tip of the city. Continue walking north until you hit Calle de Kenia. Tucked into the junction with Avenida del 3 de Agosto, to your left you can see the most celebrated of all Malabo's historic buildings – **Casa Verde** [111 E2]. An early 19th-century colonial structure, it was prefabricated in Belgium and once served as the Portuguese consulate. Renovated in 2014, it is now greener than ever, making it difficult to miss in the Malabo skyline, and upon completion the interior will house a museum of the city. Once you have had a look at the outside (it is still not open to visitors), continue eastwards on Calle de Kenia past the Ceiba Intercontinental Airlines ticket office. Opening out to your left you will see a quaint square and fountain. You are now in the centre of the old

out over the port, although if you want the best photo opportunities (without fear of police hassle), head to **La Luna Restaurant** (page 119).

Spanish Cultural Centre (Centro Cultural de España en Malabo (CCEM))

[116 G2] (*Carretera del Aeropuerto;* 333 092 186, 333 093 275; e info@ccemalabo. es; http://ccemalabo.es/) Further to the west you will find the Spanish Cultural Centre, which has been around since February 2003, with the stated aims of fostering awareness of both Spanish and Equatoguinean culture and empowering artists through co-operation with cultural institutions and the community. The centre wishes to help artists and cultural managers advance and enrich the cultural landscape of Equatorial Guinea. In practical terms, this translates as hosting activities centred around arts, cinema, music, theatre and practical training. The centre has a library, café and internet room. They also have a fortnightly TV show called *Malabeando* which is broadcast on the national TVGE channel. All of their activities are free and

town, and at the steps of **Santa Isabel Cathedral** [111 F1] which was begun in 1897, with input from Antonio Gaudí. The structure was completed in 1916, and in 2014 it underwent a major renovation which included adding a 24-hour clock face to the spire. It is still very much a functional space for worship and visitors are welcome for Sunday services or those on special occasions.

If you walk to the coastal wall on Avenida de la Independencia, you get an excellent view over Malabo Bay. To your left is the Calle de Argelia peninsula, home to expensive bars, restaurants and (soon) a new hotel. To your right is Punta Unidade Africana, hidden behind the presidential complex, which includes the infamous Black Beach prison (page 28). Down the cliff face is the new port facility, with its expansive stretches of tarmac and queue of international ships waiting to unload. Head west down the road and beside the Candy Club on Avenida de la Independencia, you will find a **monument** to the Cuban deportees brought to Malabo by boat in 1869 [111 E1]. These 250 unfortunate souls joined a long list of Spanish political troublemakers who were banished to the island in the 1860s.

One hundred metres further along, on the other side of the road you will see the **Equatoguinean Cultural Centre** [111 E2], which was built in the 1950s as a Spanish religious archive, library and museum. A brief stop here does not do it justice – you could spend a good few hours exploring everything this place has to offer (pages 129–30). The penultimate stop on the tour, slightly to the west is the **Chamber of People's Representatives** [110 D2]. The building which today houses the Cámara de los Representantes del Pueblo was used by the Spanish from 1906 onwards as the colonial **Agricultural Chamber**. Be careful taking pictures here as it is still a functioning government building.

The final stop on the walking tour is a **monument** to the commander of the frigate *Nervión*, who arrived in Malabo in 1843. Captain Juan José de Lerena Barry, representative of the Spanish crown, officially took control of the island after the British relinquished it on 27 February of that same year (page 16).

Although a little out of your way, the **Cine Marfil** [map, page 104] over by Plaza de San Fernando in the east of the city is worth visiting. It has been the site of a cinema in various guises since 1904, and also served as the location for numerous public trials, such as that of former president Macías in 1979.

usually start in the evenings around 18.00 although there are sometimes daytime events from 11.00 onwards. The two highlights of the cultural calendar here are the FECIGE Festival (pages 57–8) and the Malabo Hip Hop Festival (page 95), which is run in conjunction with the French Cultural Centre. It's a great space, easy to find, and all the details of what's on are on their website and Facebook page.

French Cultural Centre (L'Institut Culturel d'Expression Française (ICEF))

[110 C6] (*Calle de Acacio Mañé;* \ *333 093 732;* e *directeur@icef-malabo.org, secretariat@icef-malabo.org; www.institutfrancais-malabo.org;* ⊕ *09.00–noon & 14.00–18.00 Mon–Sat; library & children's library noon–19.15 Mon–Fri, 10.00–18.30 Sat*) Southeast of the Spanish Cultural Centre you will find the French Cultural Centre, which has been in Malabo since 1985. It offers French-language courses as well as all sorts of exhibitions, displays, performances and workshops themed around the Francophonie. Monthly programmes are published on their website, and they have a slot on national television every Friday between 09.00 and 09.30 when they update the city on the latest events. The centre is also home to one of the best restaurants in the city, La Vie Est Belle (page 118). Very close by is La Casa Tomada, the only private bookshop in Malabo (page 123).

If you head through town from here, you will see the **Estadio La Paz**, the old stadium (*Calle de Patricio Lumumba & Calle de Nigeria Junction*). While the national football team have now relocated to the Neuvo Estadio de Malabo in Banapá, some of the National League First Division teams, such as Club Atlético de Malabo, still play their games here. This area also houses the **central market** (page 123).

CONVERGENCE FOR SOCIAL DEMOCRACY (CPDS) HEADQUARTERS [111 F4] (*Av del 3 de Agosto 72, 2nd floor, flat 1*) As you head east through town and cut across Avenida del 3 de Agosto, you should spot the Convergence for Social Democracy Headquarters. While not a particularly impressive building, spare a thought for the occupant, Mr Plácido Micó Abogo, who has one of the most difficult political roles anywhere in the world. In the May 2008 parliamentary elections he became the sole elected opposition representative in the 100-member Chamber of People's Representatives.

CEMETERIES AND PLAZA DE SAN FERNANDO Once you exit the city centre you will find the **Commonwealth Cemetery** [111 H3]. If you follow Calle del Rey Malabo for about 1.5km (and up quite a steep hill) you will find the town cemetery [111 H3]. Here, there is a small section dedicated to the ten crew members of a Royal Air Force Sunderland Flying Boat who died after a crash landing on Bioko island, *en route* from Lagos, Nigeria to Libreville, Gabon on 3 June 1944 (page 22). A little further east from Malabo cemetery is the beautiful Spanish square **Plaza De San Fernando** [111 H3], with its accompanying church. Inside there is an entire wall dedicated to a fresco of Jesus facing the congregation.

MISSION CONVENT [116 G4] If you have access to a car or taxi you can visit the **Mission Convent** on Avenida de Hassán II. Located at the very southern end of the street, before you hit the main road to Luba, this beautiful missionary building is an impressive example of Spanish colonial architecture. Be sure to explain that you are a tourist upon entry as they are not accustomed to strangers wandering around. Slightly further north on the other side of the road you will find the associated **Claretian mission house and gardens** (*Av de Hassan II, Santa Maria region*), where there is a small archaeological-ethnographic museum, which is intermittently open to the public.

MALABO ZOO [116 A1] (*Carretera del Aeropuerto, Km7*) This zoo is currently under construction on the airport road. Once finished, it will be one of the main attractions in the city. As with many government projects in Malabo, this one is shrouded in secrecy. Some sources implied it would be a natural park, while others claimed a zoo, complete with exotic animals from around the world. An opening date of 12 October 2014 was rumoured, but then plans were delayed until 2015. The most current source of information is probably the reception at the neighbouring Hilton Hotel. It is likely to open in time for independence day celebrations in October 2015.

CULTURAL DISPLAYS There are not currently any large, dedicated museums in Malabo, but with a little hunting you can find a number of historical and cultural displays. At the time of writing, the **Museum of Modern Art** (*Centro de Artes de Malabo;* \ *+27 082 781 3891;* e *ms@momart-eg.com; www.momart-eg.com*) was in

the process of selecting a site for construction in Malabo. The impressive collection of African modern art currently tours international galleries around the world. Once it has a permanent home in the capital, this museum will be an essential part of any cultural tour. In the meantime, **Horatio Island** [map, page 104] (*offshore from Sofitel Malabo Sipopo Le Golf*) is an al fresco art gallery filled with local artist Charly Djikou's sculptures. It also has great birding opportunities and the famous 'Horatio Giant' ceiba tree.

For local historical artefacts, try the **Equatoguinean Cultural Centre** (pages 129–30), which has a dedicated display room off the main atrium. The collection features a selection of artefacts from across the territory, including masks, carvings, weaponry and even a stuffed crocodile. The **Claretian mission house** [116 G3] (*Av de Hassan II*) has a library with over 4,000 volumes relating to Africa and Equatorial Guinea, as well as an archaeological-ethnographic display with artefacts of the Bubi culture of Bioko island. Be sure to check locally before visiting, as opening times are erratic.

DAY TRIPS FROM MALABO

Bioko island is very small and the main road around it is of good quality. It is only 70km down the east coast to Riaba or 50km down the west coast to Luba. A large proportion of Bioko Sur, the part that bulges, is taken up by the Luba Crater Scientific Reserve (Reserva Científica de la Caldera de San Carlos), meaning that there is little transport infrastructure. The furthest you can travel on the island is to drive all the way south from Malabo to Luba, then up the very steep new Chinese road to Ureca on the south coast, and even then your journey will be less than 100km in total (clocking in at around 3½ hours with no delays). This leaves all of the island open for potential day trips from your accommodation in Malabo, assuming you are able to organise your own transportation. Below are three suggestions for trips out of Malabo.

PICO BASILÉ AND REBOLA The first one-day trip takes in **Pico Basilé** and Rebola but will involve some planning, as you need a special permit to be able to hike up the mountain. Make sure that your Tourism Permit (page 68) specifically states that you can hike **Pico Basilé**, otherwise the security forces near the entry to the road may not let you pass. There is a well-paved access road that heads to the top of the mountain, due to the military communications station up there, so how long you choose to spend hiking (as opposed to driving) is entirely up to you. From the main road up to the top is an ascent of around 2,700m. The road is long, winding and has some breathtaking views. It is also possible to leave the road and follow trails, although this is only recommended with a guide. There is a Bubi statue near the top of the mountain, dated 1968.

Once you've conquered Pico Basilé, your route back into Malabo takes you through **Rebola**. While here you can walk around one of the numerous cocoa drying facilities and even sample some of the pods (if you ask nicely). There is also a beautiful church here. If you arrive in the late afternoon or early evening, there may also be an event happening at the Casa De Cultura, Rebola's very own cultural centre. Their programme includes theatre, local language presentations, musical recitals and film screenings. From Rebola it is only a 20-minute drive back into Malabo, so staying late is not an issue. For more informaton about Rebola, see page 136.

A CIRCUIT OF THE ISLAND RING ROAD The second one-day trip involves a counter-clockwise circuit of the island ring road, taking in Basapú, Luba, Batété, Moka,

Riaba and Santiago de Baney. Be sure to start your road trip early as you do not want to be driving out in the countryside in the dark, or worse yet in the dark during a rain storm. Start your journey by heading to the green-roofed **La Gaditana** building near the new stadium in the Banapá district of Malabo. It is a 19th-century structure and was formerly the home of the mayor of Malabo. This coffee and cocoa estate is currently owned by a Spanish exporter. Expanded in 1918, it is said to have been the first location on the island to receive electricity.

From here, travel southeast out of town to **Sampaka**. You will know you are on the correct road when you pass the huge, newly constructed Sampaka mosque on your left (this is very difficult to miss). Here you will find Finca Sampaka (once known as Finca Amilivia), a working cocoa plantation founded in 1906, which is the setting for the Spanish novel *Palmeras en la Nieve*, due to be released as a major film in December 2015 (page 58). Tours of the property can be organised through Ruta47 tour agency in Malabo (page 65).

Once out of Malabo, the first stop on the itinerary is **Basapú**, a small town to the west on the main road. Here you will find a small colonial church as well as a cultural centre, with a small selection of local artefacts and displays. You may have to ask around to get someone to open the church or cultural centre for you, especially if you arrive early, as it is sometimes locked.

Continuing along the main road you will pass the impressive **new UNGE campus** on your right, which is still under construction. Just before you reach **Luba**, you will see a billboard for La Guineana beer on your left, and a turning on the right to **Arena Blanca** beach. This is a good photo opportunity, as the beach offers stunning views of the coastline both north and south. At the entrance to Luba you will also see a large obelisk monument, commemorating the arrival of Spaniard Captain Felipe de Santos Toro from Montevideo, who landed in the bay on 24 October 1778 and laid claim to the whole island in the name of the Spanish crown following the Treaty of El Pardo.

A walk around the historic town of Luba will reveal a Spanish church, La Parroquia Nuestra Señora de Montserrat, which is over 100 years old, and the Iglesia Metodias del barrio de Las Palmas. This dates back to when the British had control of the island in the mid 19th century. Near the lighthouse you will see the colonial La Barcelonesa house, constructed in 1913 and the former home of Maximiliano Cipriano Jones (1871–1944). Jones was famous as the richest Fernandino planter on the island in the 1920s and 1930s. Up on a hill overlooking the bay you can also see the Colegío Claret, which has a very impressive collection of colonial-era books in the library.

The next stop is **Batété**, a very small settlement just to the west of Luba. Here you will find the former property of José Vidal Ribas, a wealthy Barcelonian industrialist who in 1856 famously had one of his slaving ships intercepted and confiscated by the Royal Navy, operating from Port Clarence, causing him serious financial difficulties. Batété is also home to the Iglesia de San Antonio María Claret de Batété, a church built in 1887 almost entirely out of wood. Recently refurbished, this yellow structure still has some of its original stained-glass windows.

After retracing your steps to Luba, you will need to cut across the inland hills, eastwards towards Riaba. This green and typically wet journey will take you past the turn-off for **Moka**, a winding 20km ascent which when completed offers some breathtaking views of the island and surrounding coastline. While in Moka you can grab lunch at the Hotel Moka, and check out the informative displays at the Bioko Biodiversity Protection Program Research Station. On the outskirts of town you will see an impressive palace, allegedly belonging to Teodorín (pages 46–7), complete with two helipads.

After lunch, the next stop is **Riaba** (page 145) on the east coast. There is not much to see here apart from the remains of the old lighthouse (Faro de Riaba), but be careful taking photos of it as the police station and army base are nearby. The main attraction is the black sand beach on the edge of town, which is a favourite weekend spot for expatriates from Malabo.

The drive from Riaba up the east coast to **Santiago de Baney** is scenic and there are a number of large modern bridges to be seen *en route*, as well as the ruins of a colonial bridge just after the village of Bacake Grande. The town of Santiago de Baney is an interesting mixture of old and new, with the colonial Iglesia de Santiago de Baney sharing the civic space with an international conference centre (although what international conferences occur in this sleepy town is a mystery). When you are finished in Santiago de Baney it is a short drive back into Malabo, either via Rebola, or the impressive new business district of Sipopo. If you have the funds, dinner in the Sofitel Malabo Sipopo Le Golf would be an excellent end to the day.

A DAY IN URECA Ureca is one of the wettest places on the planet, so be sure to check the weather report before setting off. You do not want to be rained on for the whole time you are there!

The quickest way to drive from Malabo to Ureca is via Luba, down the west coast of Bioko. Your aim should be to get down as quickly as possible, to allow for plenty of time to explore. It should be possible to do this in around 3½ hours, assuming there are no delays. If you do not have your own vehicle, you can always take a shared taxi to Luba, and then hitch a lift with one of the many Chinese construction trucks or 4x4s heading along that route. The drive from Luba to Ureca involves steeply ascending nearly 3,000m, and then dropping back down equally fast to the southern coastline.

Once you arrive in Ureca make sure you register with the *comisario*. He will also want to keep a copy of your Tourism Permit. There are no tourist facilities in Ureca as yet, so make sure you bring everything you need (including drinking water). You could spend the day enjoying the southern beaches, or hike along the coastline to one of the other locations such as Moaba or Moraka. It takes about an hour of hiking to get to the nearest turtle beach. You should be able to arrange a guide in town, or you can co-ordinate your activities through the Bioko Biodiversity Protection Program (page 143), which has a large presence on the southern coastline. Just remember that if this is going to be a day trip, you want to be back in Luba before nightfall: driving up and down the hills in the dark is not particularly safe. For more on Ureca, see page 145.

AROUND MALABO

BASAPÚ The small town of Basapú is the first place you pass through while driving west out of the capital (see *A circuit of the island ring road*, page 134).

SANTIAGO DE BANEY At the road junction between Rebola and Sipopo lies the settlement more commonly known as Baney. Aside from an ostentatious palace for the local PDGE bigwig and a small church, there is not much to see here. The Total petrol station serves as a useful refuelling stop for trips around the island if you do not want to face the queues in Malabo.

REBOLA The inland road heading east out of Malabo takes you through Rebola. Only around 10km from the capital city, Rebola is definitely worth visiting if you have a few spare hours. Here you will find a number of functional **cocoa processing** facilities, easily identifiable through their distinctive smoke stacks. The local workers will happily let you taste a few of the drying pods, and this is a great opportunity to buy some cocoa pods to take home, as they cannot be found in Malabo. Rebola also has a very attractive **church** with stained-glass windows. In the centre of town is the **Casa De Cultura**, Rebola's cultural centre. A gaudy yellow mural featuring a bell and elephant tusks marks the location. This is the centre of community life with numerous activities such as theatre performances and music recitals occurring throughout the year. The centre publishes an up-to-date monthly programme of events on their Facebook page. There is also a small shrine to Rebola's patron saint housed in one of the palm-thatched huts. It is easily identifiable by the long parallel wooden benches outside, and the cleanly swept exterior.

SIPOPO Fifteen kilometres east of Malabo is Sipopo, the luxurious new business resort catering to international visitors. Driving along the eerily empty coastal motorway from Malabo, you can tell that this area was designed to impress visiting dignitaries and potential investors. A small army of gardeners armed with strimmers do battle with the encroaching jungle to keep the landscaped roadside gardens looking pristine. On your way in you will pass a ghost town of 52 massive villas, built to house the June 2011 African Union Summit leaders at a total cost of US$830 million. On the coastal side of the road, the private beaches are well maintained (some with imported sand from Cameroon), and those wishing to relax can spend time sipping cocktails at the Sofitel **Sipopo's Beach Club** beach bar. Here you can enjoy traditional Spanish seafood and a few local favourites in a relaxed atmosphere by the water. It has a well-stocked bar and covered decking overlooking the Atlantic (⊙ *10.00–18.00 Fri–Sun;* $$$) and this is also the location of **Roberto Vasquez's dive centre** (pages 126–7). The place is quiet most weekdays, but can be busy at weekends during special events.

On the same coastline you will find **La Bola Restaurant**, which looks like a large white radar installation. With a fantastic oceanfront location, this expensive restaurant is a favourite of Malabo's elite, and often serves as a location for official banquets following bilateral talks, such as after the November 2014 visit of Turkish president Recep Tayyip Erdoğan. It also hosts events for Malabo International Fashion Week (page 95), which tend to occur between September and December. At the easternmost point of Sipopo you will find the Sofitel Malabo Sipopo Le Golf hotel and golf course.

SAMPAKA A north–south road joins the peninsula of Paraiso with Malabo II and finally Sampaka. What is striking here is the dense collection of unofficial shack dwellings, the growing pains of Malabo. Many illegally built houses bear painted crosses on their wooden sides, marking them out for demolition. This area is a centre for Malabo's Muslim community, and includes the newly built **Sampaka mosque**.

Sampaka is also home to **Finca Sampaka** (formerly known as Finca Amilivia), which used to be one of the biggest cocoa producing farms on Bioko. Built in 1906, this farm is still fully functional, with workers picking, sorting and drying beans before bagging them up for export. Locals say that the farm got its title from a mispronunciation of the original owner's name, Sam Parker. It is also the setting for the romantic novel *Palmeras en la Nieve* by Luz Gabás, which is set to be released as a big-budget film in December 2015.

4

Bioko Sur Province

Bioko Sur puts all of the wild elements of Equatorial Guinea on your doorstep. A short drive from Malabo will bring you to a region of black volcanic beaches, nesting turtles, coastal waterfalls and dense jungle filled with high concentrations of endemic wildlife. If you are fit and able, this is also one of the most accessible wildernesses in Equatorial Guinea, with established trails, campsites and forest guides. The traditional homeland of the Bubi people, this ancient landscape gives you a glimpse of what things might have been like across the whole island before the Europeans arrived.

HISTORY

A history of the south of Bioko island (or Fernando Pó as it was known until the mid 1970s – see page 3) is a history of the Bubi people. The southern parts of Bioko have been occupied for just as long as the north, originally by the Bubi and then by subsequent waves of migration from Portuguese, Spanish, Fernandino, Krio and Fang groups.

The first Bubi to migrate from mainland Africa are believed to have been the Biabba Bubi, who settled at modern day Riaba on the southeast coast. Some of the last to arrive settled on the opposite coast, in places like Batété and Bokoko. The Bubi initially lived in coastal communities (although they did not generally rely on fishing). The village and town names used on the island still reflect the subgroup occupying them today.

Despite the island being discovered by Europeans in 1471, the Bubi managed to resist colonisation for the first three centuries of the transatlantic slave trade. This successful resistance is not to imply that the Bubi were a unified political force at this time; there were huge divisions between northern and southern Bubi tribes, and frequent inter-clan warfare. The first attempt at European settlement came at the beginning of the 16th century. The Portuguese trader Ramos de Esquivel tried to set up a sugarcane plantation in 1507 near Riaba on the east coast, but this ended in failure due to disease and the hostility of the Bubi. Between 1641 and 1648 the Dutch frequently raided the coasts of Bioko for slaves, which encouraged some Bubi communities to move further inland.

The Bubi were helped in their quest to remain isolated by another group of African islanders, the Annobónese. In 1778, the Spanish launched an abortive attempt at laying claim to their newly negotiated territory after the Treaty of El Pardo. Captain Felipe de Santos Toro sailed over from Montevideo, landing in a bay on the western shores of Fernando Pó on 24 October 1778. He named the area Bahia de San Carlos after the Spanish king at the time and erected a monument, which still stands today, laying claim to the whole island in the name of the Spanish crown. Unfortunately

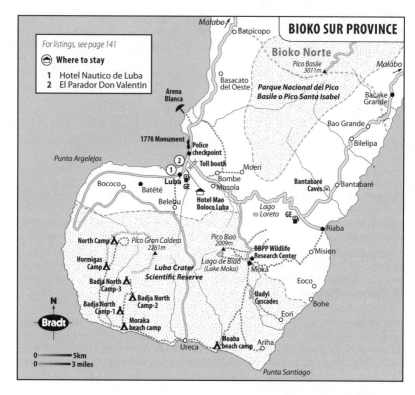

BIOKO SUR PROVINCE

Malabo
Batoicopo

Bioko Norte
Pico Basile 3011m ▲
Malábo

Basacato del Oeste

Parque Nacional del Pico Basile o Pico Santa Isabel

Bacake Grande

Arena Blanca

Bao Grande

Bilelipa

Punta Argelejos

1778 Monument
Police checkpoint
Toll booth
Moeri

Bococo
Batété
Luba
GE
Bombe
Musola
Belebu
Hotel Mao Boloco Luba
Lago Loreto
GE
Riaba

Bantabaré Caves
Bantabaré

North Camp ▲
Pico Gran Caldera 2261m ▲
Pico Biaó 2009m ▲
BBPP Wildlife Research Center
Misión

Hormigas Camp ▲
Lago de Biaó (Lake Moka)
Moká

Badja North Camp-3 ▲
Luba Crater Scientific Reserve
Eoco

Badja North Camp-1 ▲
Badja North Camp-2 ▲
Iladyi Cascades
Bohe

Moraka beach camp ▲
Eori

N
Bradt
Moaba beach camp ▲
Ariha
Ureca

0 ▬▬▬ 5km
0 ▬▬▬ 3 miles
Punta Santiago

for him, he then sailed on to Annobón where he was unceremoniously killed by the local population, which somewhat cooled Spain's enthusiasm for settling any of their new territory. Not to be outdone, the Bubi gained a reputation for savagery in 1810 when a Batété Bubi group slaughtered an entire English crew on the southern shores of the island.

In 1827, the British leased the island of Bioko from the Spanish to use as an anti-slaving base. Their main focus was Port Clarence in Bioko Norte; however, they also set up another base in San Carlos in Bioko Sur (called Luba today). The effects of the gradual expansion of European and African immigrant activities were felt across Bioko. For the first half of the 19th century, the main economic activity on the island was palm oil trading, between European–Fernandino partnerships and the Bubi (who by this stage had been slowly displaced by migrants and forced into the centre of the island). The Bubi's numbers were also declining due to disease and social divisions caused by the introduction of foreign influences such as alcohol.

With the departure of the British and the reintroduction of Spanish rule, the second half of the 19th century saw the arrival of cocoa from São Tomé and with it, an influx of labourers from Liberia. The majority of the land on Bioko is suitable for cocoa cultivation, apart from the overly wet southern section of the island near the Luba Crater Scientific Reserve, and the high ground around Pico Basilé. This meant that immigrant labour spread out across much of the island, and most of the cultivatable land was monopolised by Europeans. The Bubis were put under increasing pressure from immigrant palm oil traders and runaway migrant labourers (both of which groups had firearms), who worked and traded in centres around San Carlos Bay in the west and Melville (Concepcion) Bay in the east.

In response to this challenge, a High King of the Bubi arose in the southern highlands of Riabba by the 1860s, an area that was more isolated from foreign encroachment. His name was Buadjamitá (Moadyabitá), and he was the first of the Bahftaarí dynasty who ruled the Bubi until 1952. Malabo is even named after one of these kings, who ruled from 1904 to 1937. The most famous of the Bubi kings was Moka (c1875–99), who unified and led the Bubi in an unsuccessful attempt to resist Spanish imperialism, through isolationist policies rather than direct force of arms. The gradual expansion of European imperialism can be seen in the historic architecture scattered around the south of the island, such as the wooden church at Batété, dating to 1887, or the lighthouse at Punta Barceloneta, near Luba.

Sadly, the Bubi kings were unable to save their people. It is estimated that from an original population of 30,000 in the 1820s, the Bubi were reduced to around 6,800 by 1912 as the new arrivals introduced smallpox, whooping cough, dysentery and trypanosomiasis (sleeping sickness) into the Bubi communities. By 1917, the Spanish colonial authorities, with the assistance of Claretian missionaries, had succeeded in disarming and concentrating the Bubi into official settlements. They were able to use them as forced labour, while at the same time implementing a policy of Hispanicisation.

The economic boom of the 1920s was of little benefit to the Bubi in the south of Bioko. Great wealth was accumulated by Europeans and some African immigrants, such as Maximiliano Cipriano Jones, who was recorded as the richest Krio planter on Bioko in 1929. His home can still be seen by Luba Bay. The 1930s saw an influx of Nigerian labourers to the island, with World War II expanding the economy further as Spain strove for self-sufficiency by increasing imports from her colonies. This expansion came at a price and in 1939, the inhabitants of Spanish Guinea were forced to dedicate one day in four to labour for the state in lieu of military service.

Bioko Sur saw little development in the last decades of Spanish rule, with colonial and economic activity concentrated in the north of the island, and over in Río Muni. A hospital was built in Luba as was the Nautical Club, but the wet climate in the south of the island discouraged much European settlement.

Upon independence, the Bubi suffered particularly badly under the rule of President Macías. In a move reminiscent of the Khmer Rouge in Cambodia, many were singled out as 'intellectuals', possibly due to their political activism in the run up to the end of Spanish rule, and their threatening stance on Bubi independence for Bioko. Among the most prominent Bubi killed were Torao Sikara (President of the National Assembly), Expedito Rafael Momo Bokara (Minister of Justice), Gori Molubuela (President of the General Assembly of the autonomous region of Equatorial Guinea), Boricho Toichoa (Minister of Labour), and Bosio Dioco (Vice President).

That is not to say that ordinary Bubi or those not involved in politics were spared. Leaked US diplomatic cables at the time show that the diplomatic community on Bioko in the 1970s was aware of the targeting of the Bubi based on ethnicity, in areas such as Basacate Del Este. The disproportionate level of killing of this group led some experts (such as Paul R Bartrop) to label it a genocide.

With the removal of Macías in 1979, the situation for the inhabitants of Bioko Sur immediately improved. Coastal communities, who had been banned from using boats by Macías since 1976 to avoid escape attempts, were able to start fishing again. In 1988, President Obiang laid down laws regarding forest wildlife and protected areas, and with the help of NGOs such as the Asociación Amigos de Doñana (AAD), the unique flora and fauna of Bioko began to enjoy some protection after years of illegal exploitation under Macías.

Today, Bioko Sur is the second least populated province after Annobón. The largest city is Luba on the west coast, with an estimated 24,000 inhabitants. After this comes

Riaba on the east coast, which is much smaller. Beyond these two areas there are very few concentrated settlements, with most of the population dispersed and rural.

GETTING THERE AND AWAY

There are no international points of arrival or departure in Bioko Sur Province. For most visitors, if they do not have their own vehicle, getting to Bioko Sur is a simple case of jumping in a **shared taxi** from Malabo. The roads down the eastern and western coasts are well-maintained asphalt and are passable even in heavy rains.

Head down to Semu market on Calle Nigeria in the southern part of Malabo and look out for cars with their boots wide open (indicating available seats). Seats are sold at a fixed price and vehicles leave when they are full, so turn up early and be prepared to wait. A journey from Malabo to Luba in a shared taxi costs only 2,000CFA, but you will be squeezed in with three other people in the back of a small car, or have to share the front passenger seat with a second passenger. Fewer vehicles ply the route down the east coast from Malabo to Riaba, so if you wish to travel clockwise around the island, you may have to jump from town to town, starting by heading out of Malabo to Rebola or Baney.

Some **boats** ply the route between Malabo and Luba, but they are not regular passenger services, and you are likely to be treated with suspicion if you arrive in Bioko Sur by sea.

GETTING AROUND

Shared taxis, **hitchhiking** and **walking** are the preferred means of transport for locals moving around Bioko Sur. The island ring road, passing from Malabo through Luba, Moka, Riaba, Baney and finally Rebola, is in good condition and does not require a 4x4 for access. However, if you wish to drive from Luba down to Ureca on the south coast, you will require a **4x4** to tackle the extremely steep inclines on the new road (or you could hitch a lift with the construction crews on this route). Likewise, most inland exploration off the main road, such as heading southwest from Luba or heading into the Luba Crater Scientific Reserve, will require a 4x4. For 4x4 hire, see page 90 or page 109.

It is also possible to charter a **boat** from Luba to take you to the southern coast to visit Ureca or Moaka (*3 hours*), but this is expensive at around €700. The boat owner, who is often used by the BBPP, is called Loriano (m *222 246 143*).

ARRANGING TOURS

There are no tour operators based in Bioko Sur. You are advised to make arrangements for visiting the area through companies based in Malabo before your arrival (page 113). However, the Bioko Biodiversity Protection Program run the **BBPP Wildlife Research Center** just outside Moka (page 143), and are able to arrange various activities across the south of the island through their network of research camps which are staffed between October and March.

LUBA

Luba is a quiet seaside town with a long colonial history a short drive to the southwest of Malabo. As a natural harbour it has attracted seafarers for hundreds of years and even today you will find ships lining up to enter the small docks.

Luba is officially the second-largest settlement on Bioko, but do not visit expecting something similar in size to Malabo. It is a very small town with a picturesque beach that can be traversed on foot in 5 minutes.

WHERE TO STAY   *Map, page 138.*

🏠 **El Parador Don Valentin** This new hotel on the northern outskirts of Luba (just after the checkpoint on the main road into town) was closed at the time of writing, but advertises a waterfront restaurant & AC. **$$$**

🏠 **Hotel Nautico de Luba** Av M C Jones. At the southwestern end of town, the entrance to this hotel is adorned with anchors. It is quiet, & has a 2nd-floor restaurant with views of the port. Rooms are bright & have AC, double beds & running water. There is ample parking outside. Definitely the best hotel in town. **$$$**

🏠 **Hotel Jones** Av M C Jones; ☎ 333 094 591. Located on the main road through town, here you get a bed, a fan & a shared bathroom. Oh, & swallows nesting in most of the communal areas. **$$**

WHERE TO EAT AND DRINK   *Map, page 138.*

✗ **Hotel Nautico de Luba** (see above) The restaurant here is the best place to enjoy fresh seafood with great oceanfront views. **$$**

✗ **La Hababa** In front of the ferry docks. Offers a range of grilled meats & fish, with chilled beers. **$$**

🍷 **Pub Cleopatra** Close to the town square. This dubious-looking place offers cheap enough beers & you can watch football on the large public LCD screen.

SHOPPING
There are no shopping options in Luba. Your nearest source of gifts and souvenirs is to the east in Moka at the **BBPP Wildlife Research Center** (page 143). The centre has a gift shop which offers various locally produced goods such as jewellery and art from the Bioko Heirloom range.

OTHER PRACTICALITIES

$ **BANGE Bank** Calle Maximiliano Jones, Apdo 430; ☎ 333 099 572. Has an ATM but no Visa symbol.

GE Petrol Located just after the police checkpoint as you drive south into town from Malabo.

📧 **Luba Internet Café** Calle Maximiliano Jones; 🕐 noon–18.00. Just to the east of Hotel Jones, this café offers the only internet connection in town. You may have to ask around to get the owner to open up for you as it is usually empty.

WHAT TO SEE AND DO
Luba has enough sights to keep you occupied for an hour or so of touring. Beginning at the entrance to town (assuming you've arrived from Malabo) you will see the **1778 Monument**. This monument commemorates the establishment of Spanish colonialism in Equatorial Guinea following the treaties of San Idelfonso of 1777 and El Pardo of 1778, under which Portugal ceded Fernando Pó, Annobón and the mainland coastal areas to Spain in return for recognition of their dominion over much of modern day Brazil. The date on the plaque (24 October 1778) is the date of arrival of the Spanish expeditionary leader from Montevideo, Felipe de Santos Toro, the Earl of Argelejo. Less than a month later he would be dead, either from natural causes or at the hands of the Annobónese depending on which historical account you believe. Also visible upon entering the town is the **Colegio Claret**, which sits on a hill overlooking the bay and has a very impressive collection of colonial-era books in its library.

In the centre of Luba is the **Parroquia Nuestra Señora de Montserrat**. This colonial church is a few hundred metres inland from the Hotel Jones, and is over 100 years old. Nearby is the dilapidated **Iglesia Metodias del barrio de Las Palmas**, a Methodist missionary church building dating back to when the British had control of the island in the mid 19th century. It was one of the first buildings constructed in the Las Palmas region of the settlement. The most historically significant building in town is probably the former **home of Maximiliano Cipriano Jones** (1871–1944), still standing and located at the end of the street with his name. This imposing three-storey structure with Doric columns at the entrance is currently in a sad state of disrepair. Jones was famous as the richest Fernandino planter on the island in the 1920s and 1930s (page 107).

At the other (western) end of town you will find **Casa La Barcelonesa**. Sitting on a point, this 1913 colonial building still sports some original iron trellis work. Next door is the **Punta Barceloneta lighthouse**. This 16m-high striped red and white lighthouse features on the 550CFA Equatoguinean postage stamp. It does not appear to be in active use.

AROUND LUBA

From Luba you can access the west, south and east coasts. A few kilometres to the west you will find Batété, the small settlement which is home to the Iglesia de San Antonio María Claret de Batété. This place of worship dates back to 1887 and is made entirely of wood, making it likely the oldest church on Bioko island and one of only three examples in the world of this type of church construction. It also still features original stained-glass windows. It has been recently refurbished to a high standard, helping to avoid imminent collapse, but beware: it is often filled with mosquitoes!

MOKA Thirty kilometres inland from Luba is Moka, and the town is named after a 19th-century Bubi ruler. Whether you arrive from Luba or Riaba, the views are stunning as you climb into the interior, and on a cloud-free day you can take some very clear photographs of Pico Basilé. On the way in from Luba, you will pass through Musola, which is home to the 1903 Parroquia de San José Church.

Moka itself is clean, quiet and full of children. Visitors wishing to stay here or hoping to eat should head to the **Hotel Moka** (*26 rooms;* m *551 954 714;* **$$$**). Rooms are good quality and have flatscreen TV, air conditioning, a double bed and combined bath and shower. The hotel also offers a transfer service to Malabo for 15,000CFA. Hotel Moka also has a fully stocked restaurant, serving European and Middle Eastern staples as well as great pastries. They are used to catering to day trippers from Malabo, and can put on a great spread if arranged in advance. Their Sunday buffet lunch is an absolute feast! The hotel also maintains a very active Facebook page which you can contact them on.

Travellers on a tighter budget could stay with **Mama Rosa**, an 88-year-old woman who rents out part of her home to travellers for around €20 per night. Her daughter, also called Rosa, lives just down the road and handles payments. She is very well known, so if you ask around town people can direct you to her house. Meals are also available for €7.50 each.

Apart from the town **church**, the most imposing building is the huge **palace** belonging to members of the presidential family. This sprawling structure, complete with security walls and a helipad, is perennially empty and seems very out of place in this otherwise undeveloped town. On the plus side, the local children now have a good flat spot to play football on.

Also in Moka is the **BBPP Wildlife Research Center**, which serves as the gateway to the south of the island. It is the starting point for a number of hiking trails around Bioko Sur. The BBPP Wildlife Research Center is known to the local population by its original colonial name, Casa Risiiti. It is made up of a two-storey staff house and a one-storey building currently being renovated into an education centre and research lab. It is outfitted with indoor plumbing, electricity generators and the only satellite internet connection on the southern half of the island. There is a 1.5km nature trail that loops around the centre with information plaques about all the wildlife in the area. Visits to the research centre can be organised through BBPP's in-country manager, Tonnie Choueiri (m *222 190 369;* e *tonnie. bbpp@gmail.com*). Alternatively, you can contact the director of the Moka Wildlife Center (Bryan Featherstone) directly (m *551 984 049;* e *feath016@gmail.com, mokawildlifecenter@gmail.com*). Between October and March each year the BBPP also maintains a presence on the southern coasts of Bioko, at their research field camps in Moaba and Moraka.

Hiking trails   In addition to the walks outlined below, you can walk north to **Lake Loreto** (✪ 3°24'24.3"N 8°40'21.9"E) from the road that connects Moka with Riaba. Ideally, pick up a guide in Moka first from the BBPP.

The Lago de Biaó Trail   This is an uphill climb to the larger of the two lakes on Bioko island. Wildlife on the route includes egrets and dabchicks (little grebes), palm nut vultures, turacos, chameleons, duikers, and many of the seven monkey species found on the island. This 8km round trip takes about 6 hours to reach the rim of the crater lake, or 7 hours if you wish to climb down to the water's edge. The lake has special religious significance to the Bubi people in the area.

Iladyi Cascades Trail   This 6km round trip along the Moka–Eori trail takes between 3 and 4 hours. After a 3km hike, the jungle trail emerges to a breathtaking view of three separate branches of the Iladyi River plunging over the edge of a 250m canyon. Short sections of this trail are very steep, and there is a river crossing which can be knee-deep in the wet season.

Moka–Moaba Trail   This strenuous 8-hour trek takes you to Moaba on the south coast, home to BBPP's Moaba Beach Camp, used for leatherback turtle research. Visitors can be accommodated here (in tents) through prior arrangement between October and March, although December and January is the best time to visit in terms of weather. Apart from turtles and other wildlife you can also see the Heart

RESEARCH STATION LODGING AND SERVICE RATES

Note that rates were correct at the time of writing.

Service	Daily Rate	Included
Room	25,000CFA	Single bed and bedding
Board	20,000CFA	Two daily meals provided by BBPP staff
Tent space	15,000CFA	Tent space on property and bathroom access
Tent rental two–four person	12,500CFA (plus 50,000CFA refundable deposit)	Daily four person tent rental
Tent rental six person	17,500CFA (plus 50,000CFA refundable deposit)	Daily six person tent rental
Facilities access	7,500CFA per day 75,000CFA per month	Research/storage space and computer/internet access
Guide (4 hours or less)	5,000CFA per day for groups of up to three, then 5,000CFA per additional visitor	BBPP trained local guide
Guide (over 4 hours)	15,000CFA per day for groups of up to three, then 5,000CFA per additional visitor	BBPP-trained local guide
Porter	10,000CFA per day	20kg maximum cargo weight
Cook	10,000CFA per day	Local cooks to prepare two to three meals per day

of Moaba, a natural feature where waves are funnelled into a cave, leading to a rhythmic vertical surge of water. There is also a large rock obelisk standing isolated on the beach.

From Moaba, it is possible to walk along the coast to Ureca in around 2 hours. From Ureca, you can hike west to Moraka Beach Camp through forest and across the beach in about 5 hours, dependent on tides and weather. Far more isolated than Ureca or Moaba, the BBPP have built thatch huts over their tents at Moraka Beach Camp, along with some wooden benches and tables, making the site feel a little more permanent. Apart from offering stunning walks along the black volcanic beaches, this camp is on the edge of forest filled with rare primate species such as Pennant's red colobus.

Moraka–Hormigas–North Camp Trail This hike takes a full day, with the last 3km being very strenuous. Hormigas Camp sits right on the edge of the Caldera de Luba. Another day of hiking brings you into the crater itself, where the BBPP carry out primate surveys.

Moraka–Badja North Camp trails These areas are used by the BBPP for undertaking transects of the forest. As with all the other trails, you are welcome to use them but it is advisable to hire a local guide to avoid getting lost.

Moka–Ariha and Moka–Eori trails These are local bushmeat hunting trails not frequented by the BBPP. As with all the other trails, you are welcome to use them but it is advisable to hire a local guide to avoid getting lost.

URECA Bioko Sur is generally much wetter than Bioko Norte and nowhere is this truer than in Ureca. This southern coastal village receives a record-breaking 10,450mm of rainfall per year, making it the wettest place in Africa and one of the wettest in the world. Ureca used to be extremely isolated but now thanks to a road running from Luba through Belebu, it is connected to the outside world and can be reached from Malabo in a matter of hours. This is great news for the local population in terms of access to government services and economic development, but is also likely to have a serious negative impact on the delicate ecosystem in the area.

If you decide to visit Ureca, be sure to bring everything with you including drinking water, as there are no shops and there is no accommodation available. The road from Luba is incredibly steep so a 4x4 will be required, preferably one with a recently serviced clutch and handbrake. The road is usually empty so if you break down you will need to be able to fix the problem yourself.

Upon arrival you need to register with the *comisario*, who will note down your information in his ledger and also require a copy of your Tourism Permit (so be sure to bring spares). Also, if camping or hiking on the beach, be very careful as at high tide the sea covers the entire beach up to the treeline in most areas.

The beaches around Ureca are breathtaking, composed of black volcanic sand. Here you will also see the **waterfalls** of the Eola River, dropping out of the jungle and straight on to the beach. It is also possible to **hike** east to the turtle-filled beaches of Moaba or west to the BBPP Moraka Beach Camp (page 143), and then onwards into the Luba Crater itself. The jungle in this area is filled with wildlife, including many of the endangered primates that Equatorial Guinea is famous for. The southern coast also receives some of the biggest swell, so intrepid **surfers** could use Ureca as a base to head to the Nacho left-hand point break over by Moraka (✪ 3°15'19.8"N 8°29'54.0"E). For more on surfing in Equatorial Guinea, see page 98.

RIABA AND AROUND The town of Riaba is located on the east coast of Bioko island, around 70km from Malabo. It is much smaller than its western neighbour of Luba, and has historically seen less development, likely due to the logistical difficulties of building transport infrastructure down the east coast. Simply driving from Riaba back up to Malabo involves crossing six large bridges, including the dizzying colonial Puente Cope from 1973. There are plans to build a new petrochemicals complex at Riaba, but until then it will remain a sleepy seaside town with a black sand beach that is popular with the Malabo expat community who visit at weekends. There is no restaurant or hotel in town, but you can stock up on drinks for the beach at the Bar La Buena Madre, which is situated very close to the old lighthouse. In terms of colonial architecture, there is not much to see here apart from the remains of the old **lighthouse** (Faro de Riaba), but be careful taking photos of it as the police station and army base are behind it when facing the sea.

The villages of **Bombe** and **Moeri** can be reached using a signposted turn-off on the road from Luba to Riaba. From Moeri there is a trail which leads to the summit of Pico Basilé, although this is not frequented by foreigners. A guide is advised.

The village of **Bantabaré**, northeast of Riaba along the eastern coastal road, is home to a complex set of limestone caves. One of the caves is said to house a statue of the Virgin Mary taken in there by a Spanish expedition in 1962.

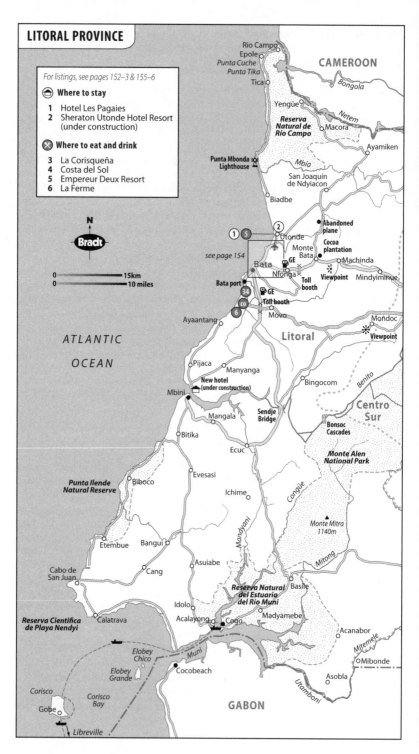

LITORAL PROVINCE

For listings, see pages 152–3 & 155–6

🛏 Where to stay
1 Hotel Les Pagaies
2 Sheraton Utonde Hotel Resort
   (under construction)

✖ Where to eat and drink
3 La Corisqueña
4 Costa del Sol
5 Empereur Deux Resort
6 La Ferme

N

Bradt

| 0 | 15km |
| 0 | 10 miles |

ATLANTIC

OCEAN

CAMEROON

Rio Campo
Epole
Punta Cuche
Punta Tika
Tica

Yengüe
Netem
Bongola

*Reserva
Natural de
Río Campo*
Macora

Ayamiken

**Punta Mbonda
Lighthouse**
Mbía

San Joaquín
de Ndyiacon

Biadbe

● **Abandoned
plane**

② Utonde
**Cocoa
plantation**

Monte
Bata
Machinda

① ⑤

see page 154

Bata
GE
Nfonga
**Toll
booth**
Viewpoint
Mindyiminue

Bata port
③④
GE
Toll booth
⑥ co
Movo

Ayaantang

Pijaca
Manyanga

Bingocom

Litoral

Mondoc

Viewpoint

Benito

**New hotel
(under construction)**

Mbini

Mangala

**Sendje
Bridge**

*Centro
Sur*

Bitika

Ecuc

**Bonsoc
Cascades**

*Monte Alen
National Park*

**Punta Ilende
Natural Reserve**
Biboco

Evesasi

Ichime

Congüe

▲
*Monte Mitra
1140m*

Etembue
Bangui

Asuiabe

Mitong

Cabo de
San Juan

Cang

*Reserva Natural
del Estuario
del Río Muni*
Basile

Idolo

Acalayong
Cogo
Madyamebe

Acanabor

*Reserva Científica
de Playa Nendyi*
Calatrava

Muni

Mitemele

Mibonde

*Elobey
Chico*

Cocobeach

Asobla

*Elobey
Grande*

Corisco

*Corisco
Bay*

Utromboni

Gobe

GABON

Libreville

5

Litoral Province

Litoral Province occupies the entire coastal strip of Río Muni. It is sunny, sandy and by Equatoguinean standards, densely populated, with a range of different ethnic groups brought here by the fishing and trading opportunities. Litoral has traditionally been home to the Ndowe ethnic groups, including the Combes, Bujebas and Bengas, however, there was a lot of Fang migration to this area throughout the 20th century.

The province stretches inland and is 100km at its widest point, which is down by the Río Muni estuary, on the border with Gabon. Other notable settlements in Litoral include Mbini, which sits on the Benito River south of Bata, and Cogo, the remote southern border town. It borders Centro Sur Province to the east (pages 183–92). Crossing the border in the north you will enter Cameroon's South Province. In the south, you head into Gabon's Estuaire Province.

HISTORY

The area around Bata has been occupied since Neolithic times, originally by Pygmy tribes of hunter-gatherers. It is possible that the Carthaginian explorer Hanno the Navigator reached the shores of Río Muni in the 5th century BC. This interpretation is based on a translation of a tablet Hanno wrote about his journey (the only surviving source), describing him seeing a high peak that could have been Mount Cameroon at the southernmost extent of their sailing. Although debate still rages to this day, the account was enough to convince Victorian explorer Sir Richard Francis Burton and a number of modern scholars.

The indigenous tribes were displaced by Ndowe migration between the 12th and 14th centuries. Although their origins have not been definitively traced, many historians believe that the Ndowe first arrived in Río Muni from the Upper Ubangi River, which forms the border between the modern day Republic of Congo and the Democratic Republic of Congo.

Between 1473 and 1475 Lopes Gonçalves, one of a team of Portuguese navigators that included Fernão do Pó, sailed along the African coast from Ghana down to Cape Lopez (modern day Port-Gentil in Gabon), likely making him the first European explorer to visit Río Muni. There was no attempt to settle here by the Portuguese, although there was some trading and slaving done in the area, managed from the nearby islands of Fernando Pó (today's Bioko island), Annobón and Corisco. The area around Bata saw little other European interaction for the next 150 years.

In 1641, the Dutch took control of Río Muni after the famous pirate Cornelis Corneliszoon Jol (nicknamed Pé de Pau by the Portuguese, due to his wooden leg) won them control of Fernando Pó, Luanda and Annobón as part of the Dutch–Portuguese War, which ran for much of the first half of the 17th century.

Although the Portuguese wrested back control in 1649, they still preferred to manage their slaving operations from the fort of Ponta Joko on Corisco, in collaboration with the local Benga population, rather than attempt to settle on the mainland. Throughout the 17th century, the Portuguese exported vast quantities of goods (both human and material) from the area by the Muni estuary, as well as Corisco and Elobey islands.

Spanish control of Río Muni was officially established by the treaties of San Idelfonso of 1777 and of El Pardo of 1778; however, they invested little energy or money into exploring and occupying the area until the late 19th century, preferring instead to focus on colonies such as Morocco and Cuba. When the Spanish were present on the mainland, they tended to be found around Río Muni in the south, rather than up at Bata.

Numerous Spanish explorers, missionaries and officials visited mainland Río Muni in the 19th century during the surge of European neo-imperialism at the time. The first to arrive was the botanist and medic Marcelino Andrés Andrés in 1831. Navigator José de Moros followed soon after, but left no written record of his trips, apart from of his time on Annobón. Spanish official Juan José Lerena toured the coast in 1842, and then in 1845 Capitain Nicolás de Manterola and Consul Adolfo Guillemar de Aragon visited the area to negotiate with the French.

Some of the first missionaries, such as Spaniard Jerónimo M Usera Alarcón, began arriving in the late 1840s. During this time American Presbyterian missionaries set about establishing the United States of the Ndowe in the region to help combat the slave trade. There is an excellent written account of this period by American missionary William Walker who penned *The French at the Gaboon*, while working for the American Board of Commissioners for Foreign Missions.

Spanish explorer Julio Pellón toured the Río Muni coast in 1860, producing detailed maps. Numerous other scientists and adventurers followed in his footsteps, such as Manuel Iradier (1875), Amado Osorio (1884), Luis Sorela (1887) and José Valero (1890). There is no mention at this time though of Bata as a single developed settlement. In 1885, following the Berlin Conference, Río Muni officially became a protectorate of Spain, although it was not until the disastrous Treaty of Paris in 1900 that the borders were officially finalised. As late as 1907, Bata was little more than a military garrison with around 237 inhabitants, of whom 37 were European. The central focus of European activities was to the south.

Throughout the 19th century, expanding European maritime commerce led to competition on the shores of Río Muni. Surveying Corisco, Elobay and the Muni estuary you could find *factorias* representing British, Spanish but predominantly German commercial interests, such as the Compañía Transatlántica, E H Moritz, Woermann Company, Lieb & Friedrich, John Holt or Hatton & Coockson. One survey from 1859 recorded between 50 and 100 British and American ships per year trading in the region for ivory and ebony. Today, anyone exploring the Cabo De San Juan on the mainland, or Corisco or Elobey islands, will find traces of European commercial activity all around them: ruined military outposts, a German lighthouse, abandoned sawmills, a palm oil factory and a Claretian mission house.

The outbreak of World War I in July 1914 had a serious impact on Spain's African colony, despite the fact that Spain remained officially neutral throughout the conflict. Between 1914 and 1915, Germany fought a combined British and French force for control of German Cameroon (*Kamerun*). By February 1916, 1,000 Germans, 6,000 African troops and 7,000 African civilians had crossed Spanish Guinea's northern border to escape into internment before their colony was overrun. This was the biggest influx of Europeans Río Muni would see for almost half a century.

In 1926, the political status of the territory changed again, with the administrative region of Spanish Guinea being set up, uniting the three previously disparate Spanish territories of Río Muni, Bioko and Annobón. This was the same year that the Spanish government began a military occupation of Río Muni, aimed at the forceful recruitment of indigenous labourers for use in the plantations of Bioko, following the departure of Liberian migrant labourers. This led to a temporary expansion of settlements around Bata. Before this occupation, Río Muni had seen little development from the Spanish colonial authorities. Control was limited to the coastal areas, and Bata was little more than a village. There were only around 100 European residents spread across the whole mainland, most of whom were not even Spanish but German traders looking for rubber, wood and ivory.

During the Spanish Civil War there was a skirmish in Río Muni between Nationalist rebels from Kogo and forces loyal to the Republicans. In Bata the deputy governor (who was a member of the Popular Front) refused to join the Nationalist rebellion, leaving Río Muni cut off from the rest of the colony, in Republican hands. However, this only lasted a few weeks until Nationalist reinforcements arrived from the Canary Islands and took control of the city with minimal loss of life. The 1930s also saw an influx of European workers, keen to escape the Great Depression back home and get rich quick in the cocoa business.

There was no fighting in Río Muni during World War II, but it did lead to changes and expansion within the colonial economy. The Allied navies kept financial pressure on General Franco by allowing imports from Spain's African possessions to be for internal use only, meaning the country could no longer export valuable timber and cocoa to the rest of Europe and the Americas. Instead, Río Muni began to cater to many of Spain's other needs: forced labour for the state replaced military service; cocoa traders switched rapidly to coffee production in order to sell successfully to their domestic market back in Madrid; and rough wood, palm oil, copra, dried bananas and rubber were soon being imported from Spanish Guinea in hitherto unseen quantities, increasing the colony's share of the Spanish import market from 3% in 1934 to 21% in 1942. The economy expanded over the next few decades, although standards of living and development were still low for the average Equatoguinean on the mainland. The number of Europeans living in Bata increased from 477 in 1942 to 1,426 in 1960. This was helped by greatly improved transport links, as before the airport was built in 1949 the only way to travel between Spain and mainland Spanish Guinea was on a boat called *Domine* that sailed from Cádiz to Bata. The journey took 25 days, and the boat stopped at Las Palmas, Santa Cruz de Tenerife, Monrovia, Lagos and Santa Isabel. In June 1949, Bata airport was finished and the airline Aviación y Comercio (AVIACO) began monthly flights back to Spain. Taking 12 passengers at a time, the journey took two days as the plane had to land every four hours to refuel. This period of expansion also saw the construction of Bata cathedral (1954) and numerous other civic buildings.

While other European powers were considering granting independence to their African colonies, 1959 saw the status of Spanish Guinea changed and it was designated the Region Ecuatorial de España (essentially an overseas province). In conjunction with efforts on Bioko, by the early 1960s the Franco regime began a programme of heavy investment in Spain's African colony in a bid to keep the population from demanding independence. Over the next decade Equatorial Guinea would come to have one of the highest literacy rates and per capita income rates in sub-Saharan Africa.

Although the communications infrastructure was not well developed, Bata, along with many other parts of Río Muni, had great potential for growth when the

Spanish relinquished control in 1968. Unfortunately, as in Malabo, the city of Bata quickly suffered under the misrule of President Macías. Transport infrastructure disintegrated, the cocoa plantations fell into disrepair, and thousands of inhabitants fled south to Gabon or north to Cameroon. In some respects, the inhabitants of the mainland were luckier than their cousins on Bioko as they had overland routes they could use to escape, and up to 90,000 had fled by 1976. In the last three years of his reign, President Macías forcefully rounded up inhabitants on mainland Río Muni and shipped them to Bioko as labourers, to shore up the failing agricultural sector over there. Many thousands were killed in detention facilities such as the Central Prison in Bata, which was originally a Spanish colonial facility used to hold political prisoners such as Acacio Mañé Elah, who was killed while in custody in 1959.

The beginning of President Obiang's rule saw marked improvements in the human rights situation on the mainland, but it was not until the Zafiro oilfield came online in 1995 that Bata began to change. Like Malabo, Bata boomed with the influx of oil money. Over the last two decades the port in the south of the city has been extended, the airport has grown and Bata is now the largest city in Equatorial Guinea.

BATA

The capital of Litoral Province is Bata, which is also the largest city in Equatorial Guinea, home to around a quarter of the Equatoguinean population. It sits on a narrow coastal plain, with hills and mountains to the east. The city is a favourite of the nation's elite and it is not hard to see why, as the climate is great, the African influences are varied, and the city architects have done a great job sculpting the waterfront into a modern, enjoyable place to spend time.

Average temperatures in Bata are slightly lower than in Malabo, sitting at 25°C, and it is generally wetter, but if you visit in the dry season it can feel very Mediterranean in terms of weather and appearance. Bata is a beautiful city with a renovated waterfront walkway, Paseo Marítimo, that is currently being expanded to the south. The coastal skyline is dominated by the Torre de la Libertad (Tower of Freedom) which was inaugurated on 12 October 2011 to celebrate Equaotguinean independence. The city serves as a gateway to the landlocked interior provinces and also to the region, through the busy international airport and the main highway which takes you all the way to the border with Gabon at Mongomo.

GETTING THERE AND AWAY There are daily **flights** to Bata from Malabo, taking 45 minutes. The airport [151 D1] also has international arrivals from Cotonou in Benin, Libreville in Gabon and Douala in Cameroon. These were all temporarily suspended in August 2014 due to the Ebola crisis but have since been reinstated. There are plans to introduce new routes (via Malabo) to Niamey in Niger, Lagos in Nigeria and Yaoundé in Cameroon in 2016. There is an irregular **ferry** service (the *San Valentin*) that runs from Malabo to Bata, and another that occasionally calls at Annobón from Bata (the *Djiblooh*).

It is possible to **drive** into Litoral Province from Centro Sur at numerous points, although the most used road is the Bata–Niefang Highway, which was upgraded in 2013. This road also forms the main link between the coast and the three inland provincial capitals of Ebebiyín, Mongomo and Evinayong, as well as the future capital Oyala.

There is an official **border crossing** point from Cocobeach in Gabon to Cogo in the south. There is also a border crossing into Cameroon at Río Campo in the

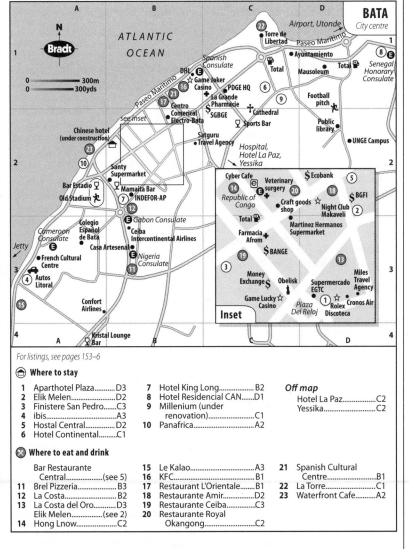

BATA
City centre

ATLANTIC
OCEAN

Airport, Utonde

For listings, see pages 153–6

🛏 **Where to stay**

1	Aparthotel Plaza	D3	7	Hotel King Long	B2
2	Elik Melen	D2	8	Hotel Residencial CAN	D1
3	Finistere San Pedro	C3	9	Millenium (under	
4	ibis	A3		renovation)	C1
5	Hostal Central	D2	10	Panafrica	A2
6	Hotel Continental	C1			

Off map

Hotel La Paz C2
Yessika C2

🍴 **Where to eat and drink**

	Bar Restaurante		15	Le Kalao	A3	21	Spanish Cultural
	Central	(see 5)	16	KFC	B1		Centre	B1
11	Brel Pizzeria	B3	17	Restaurant L'Orientale	B1	22	La Torre	C1
12	La Costa	B2	18	Restaurante Amir	D2	23	Waterfront Cafe	A2
13	La Costa del Oro	D3	19	Restaurante Ceiba	C3			
	Elik Melen	(see 2)	20	Restaurante Royal				
14	Hong Lnow	C2		Okangong	C2			

north. Both of these borders were closed in August 2014 as a preventative measure against the spread of Ebola but have since reopened. Even when they are open, however, foreign nationals are often blocked from using them, or charged exorbitant 'registration fees' upon crossing, so be sure to check locally before attempting the journey.

GETTING AROUND Bata is a long, thin city, stretching for 10km from the airport in the north to the bridge over the river Ekuku in the southern port district. You will find the majority of hotels, shops, bars and restaurants concentrated in the area around the Plaza de la Liberdad.

As in Malabo, the favoured means of transport around Bata is **shared taxi**. Short trips around the town centre will cost 500CFA, with longer journeys negotiable.

Litoral Province   BATA

5

151

Be sure to agree a price to or from the airport before jumping in, to avoid being overcharged.

LOCAL TOUR OPERATORS The majority of the tour operators present in Malabo (page 113) will be able to organise the logistics of travelling across Río Muni. In addition, the following companies or organisations have locations in Bata:

INDEFOR-AP [151 B2] (Instituto Nacional de Desarrollo Forestal y Gestión del Sistema de Áreas Protegidas) Calle Jesus Bacale s/n; m 222 025 154; e krol888@hotmail.com, ayetebemme@yahoo.es; ⏰ 08.00–16.00 Mon–Fri. Your contact should be Carolina Martinez. This government department is responsible for many protected areas on the mainland. If you wish to go camping at any of the TOMAGE Project turtle sites, you must obtain permission from here before going.
Miles Travel Agency [151 D3] Next to Aparthotel Plaza & Discoteca Rolex, 45.21;

m 222 716 212; ⏰ 08.30–14.00 & 16.00–18.30 Mon–Fri, 09.30–14.30 Sat. Excellent customer service. The best travel agency in town for booking international flights & some internal flights.
Satguru Travel Agency [151 B2] Calle de la Libertad; ☎ 333 096 326, 333 090 506; e marketing@satgurutravel.com; ⏰ 08.00–20.00 Mon–Fri, 10.00–20.00 Sat. Highly efficient travel agency that can deal with both domestic & international flight bookings. They have over 25 locations across Africa.

 WHERE TO STAY *See maps, pages 151 and 154, unless otherwise stated.*
There are a number of luxury hotels under construction in and around the city although none of them were complete and accepting guests at the time of writing, which is surprising given that Bata is the largest city in Equatorial Guinea and hosts many business travellers. A huge hotel on the waterfront is being built by the Chinese state construction company, and it aims to be the largest in Bata when it opens in late 2016. It has yet to be officially named, and is rumoured to be supported by the son of the president. The new beachfront **Hotel Miramar** (*63 rooms; Punta del Aeropuerto*) is also in the preliminary stages of being built and does not have an announced opening date yet.

Luxury

🏠 **Media Luna Hotel** Carretera del Aeropuerto; ☎ 333 082 119, 333 082 939. Situated by the roundabout for the airport, this hotel was undergoing major expansion work by SOMAGEC construction company at the time of writing. Prior to closing it had a reputation as one of the best high-end hotels in Bata, & is due to reopen in 2016. **$$$$$**

🏠 **Sheraton Utonde Hotel Resort** [off map, page 154] (216 rooms, 6 villas) Opposite the Empereur Deux Resort, Utonde; ☎ 333 098 129. When it opens in 2016, this is likely to be the most luxurious beach resort in the greater Bata area. Set on a secluded stretch of beach, no expense is being spared during the construction. The white sand on the beach is being imported from Cameroon, & there will be a sunken pool with a bar, a massive patio area & an open-air restaurant. Visitors will stay in private bungalows. Facilities will include 3

event venues, a country club, a spa/fitness centre, restaurants, sports courts, a private beach, marina & heliport. **$$$$$**

Upmarket

🏠 **Villa Celotti** (60 bungalows) Carretera del Aeropuerto; m 222 562 094, 222 252 248; e info@generalwork.biz. The closest accommodation to the airport, this Italian-run complex is actually designed for long-term General Work company residents, but are willing to rent out bungalows on a weekly basis (with discounts if you rent longer term). Each bungalow has 2 bedrooms & a fully fitted kitchen & living room. There is also a large canteen which serves food & drinks. There is a good daily buffet with an assortment of meats & fish, pizzas for 5,000CFA & a meal deal (pizza, chips & a beer) for 8,000CFA. There is a large projector screen for watching football. Tends to be quite busy with long-term residents. **$$$$–$$$$$**

🏠 **Hotel La Paz** (50 rooms) Centro Médico La Paz; ☎ 333 084 829; 📱 222 633 344; http://lapazge.org/. It is expensive & miles out of Bata but the hospital complex also has a 4-star hotel on the grounds if you really want to stay there. Rooms are spacious & clean with satellite TV. There are also suites available. **$$$$**

🏠 **Hotel Les Pagaies** [map, page 146] (7 bungalows) Utonde, Apdo 934; ☎ 333 566 237; 📱 222 545 032, . 10min north of the airport you will find this luxurious & secluded set of colourful wooden bungalows on the beach. Each bungalow comes with a fridge, TV, AC, double bed & (rather bizarrely) your own rowing machine! There is a stunning pool area & the seafood is great. This is a very popular spot, especially at w/ends when they have a large seafood grill, so be sure to book in advance. **$$$$**

🏠 **Hotel Carmen** (40 rooms) Carretera del Aeropuerto; ☎ 333 080 126. Things have certainly improved here since the Zambian squad checked out after 24hrs during their Africa Cup of Nations stay in 2012, although it is still hard to argue that this place deserves a 4-star rating. Rooms are spacious & offer a mainly French satellite TV package, fridge, TV, double bed, AC, intermittent Wi-Fi & there is a pool outside by the sea. Ocean-facing rooms have balconies. This is not good value for money compared with some of the other options in this bracket, due to outdated rooms & furnishings. **$$$–$$$$$**

🏠 **ibis Hotel** (120 rooms) Paseo Marítimo; ☎ 666 187 195, 666 162 840; e H7122-FO@accor.com; www.ibis.com. Website in English, German, Spanish, Portuguese, Italian, Dutch, Chinese, Japanese, Polish, Russian, Swedish & Indonesian. Wi-Fi & en suite in all rooms. There is a restaurant, bar, terrace, 2 meeting rooms, an outdoor swimming pool & a free private car park. Autos Litoral also have a car rental desk by reception (page 90). Breakfast costs an additional 7,000CFA, but is an extensive continental buffet. Rooms are generally quite small & the bathrooms are tiny, but everything is clean & as you would expect from the ibis chain. Ideally you want to be high up on the beach side for the views & to avoid the noise from the generator. **$$$$**

Mid range

🏠 **Aparthotel Plaza** (21 rooms, 28 suites & 14 royal suites) Edificio 3 de Agosto, BP 269; ☎ 333 080 253/54/55; e info@hotelplaza.com, info@aparthotelplazabata.com; www.hotelplaza.com. Website in English. Hotel with sea views if you are on the higher floors. Offer airport transfers, car rentals, a conference room with a sea & city view, Wi-Fi, currency exchange, private phone service, satellite TV, AC, room service & laundry service. Sadly, the receptionists do not offer much in the way of a welcome & appear actively annoyed at being solicited for help. The rooms are discounted on w/days, with w/end rates higher. Rooms are large & suites are huge but check before you accept keys as many long-term residents smoke in the rooms & they smell. This is good value considering the room quality & location. Try not to choose a room lower down as there may be issues with noise from the neighbouring Rolex Discoteca. **$$$–$$$$**

🏠 **Elik Melen** (45 rooms) Junction of Patricio Lumumba & Calle 3 de Agosto; ☎ 333 088 166/67. Clean, spacious rooms with free Wi-Fi & a decent restaurant make this a good choice in the price range. Be sure to book in advance as this place gets busy, often with long-term company bookings. The club in the basement has now closed, which is good news for ground-floor residents! **$$$–$$$$**

🏠 **Hotel King Long** (20 rooms) On the road between Pl Del Reloj & Pl de Ayuntamiento roundabout. This Chinese hotel offers rooms with keycard access for variable rates depending on whether you want a balcony or not. The rooms are musty & dark but of acceptable quality, with a large TV, AC, shower & a double bed. Access to a balcony is what sets these rooms apart, but for this price you could be staying in the Panafrica Hotel with a sea view. There is an attached Chinese restaurant that does good food. **$$$–$$$$**

🏠 **Hotel Continental** Carretera de la Libertad, Bata; ☎ 333 084 357, 333 081 718. Closed at the time of writing, although slated to reopen Christmas 2015, this used to be a popular mid-range hotel with international visitors, & is in a convenient central location. **$$$**

🏠 **Panafrica Hotel** (30 rooms) Paseo Marítimo de Bata; ☎ 333 083 239/40; 📱 222 642 553. Situated overlooking the waterfront, the Panafrica has been in Bata since the 1970s & even gets a mention in Robert Klitgaard's *Tropical Gangsters*. It is conveniently situated near the Santy Supermarket. The building is currently undergoing renovation

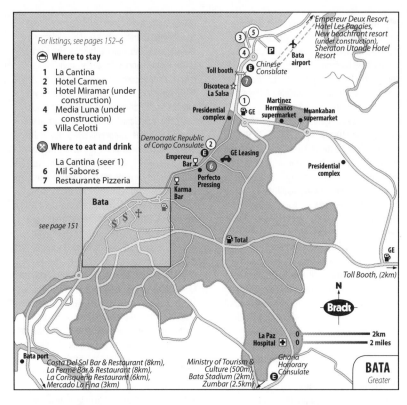

For listings, see pages 152–6

Where to stay
1 La Cantina
2 Hotel Carmen
3 Hotel Miramar (under construction)
4 Media Luna (under construction)
5 Villa Celotti

Where to eat and drink
La Cantina (seer 1)
6 Mil Sabores
7 Restaurante Pizzeria

Empereur Deux Resort, Hotel Les Pagaies, New beachfront resort (under construction), Sheraton Utonde Hotel Resort

Bata airport
Toll booth
Chinese Consulate
Discoteca La Salsa
Martinez Hermanos supermarket
Muankaban supermarket
Presidential complex
GE
Democratic Republic of Congo Consulate
Empereur Bar
GE Leasing
Perfecto Pressing
Karma Bar
Presidential complex
Bata
see page 151
Total
GE
Toll Booth, (2km)
N
Bradt
La Paz Hospital
0 — 2km
0 — 2 miles
Bata port
Costa Del Sol Bar & Restaurant (8km),
La Ferme Bar & Restaurant (8km),
La Corisqueña Restaurant (6km),
Mercado La Fina (3km)
Ministry of Tourism & Culture (500m), Bata Stadium (2km), Zumbar (2.5km)
Ghana Honorary Consulate
BATA
Greater

work & the newly refurbished rooms are excellent & are all finished in a modern style. They come with large bathrooms, sea views & comfortable beds. Hopefully they will refill their beautiful pool with the elephant sculpture by the beach. This represents excellent value in Bata. **$$$**

Budget
Finistere San Pedro (8 rooms) El Cruce Santy; 333 081 838. Good value for money for this location. Cheapest rooms have an en suite with bath or shower, & a double bed, AC & free Wi-Fi. An extra 10,000CFA gets you a bigger room with a nicer bathroom. Friendly receptionists who speak Spanish & French. Highly recommended. **$$**

Hostal Central (14 rooms) El Cruce Santy; 333 274 307; m 222 272 138. This Lebanese hotel is above a restaurant. Rooms are small & clean with strong AC, a tiny TV & a dodgy-looking bathroom but the shower & toilet work. Good price for the central location. **$$**

La Cantina (2 rooms) Paseo Marítimo de Bata; m 222 773 838. This Spanish-run bar &

restaurant on the road to the airport (page 150) also has 2 simple rooms at the back which can be rented for accommodation. The owner Rafael is a great guy & is sure to help out travellers passing through. **$$**

Millenium Hotel (15 rooms) Apdo 512, Bata; 333 082 508, 333 083 146. This hotel was closed for renovation at the time of writing. The Pub Obsession bar next door also appeared closed. In the past this has been an average budget option in an excellent location. **$$**

Rock bottom
Hotel Residencial CAN (8 rooms) Carretera del Mercado (Mondouasi); m 222 270 471. A great budget option for travellers looking to save money. The cheapest nightly price in town gets you a double bed with a fan in a small room with a shared bathroom. You can pay extra for a much larger room with TV, AC, bath, shower & your own toilet. The place is clean, tucked away on the 3rd storey of a residential housing block, but is in a noisy location with the market just outside. **$**

🏠 **Yessika** (12 rooms) Gran Mercado Central; m 222 083 974. Also confusingly listed in various guides as the Hotel Yesika, Yesica, Yesicca or Jessica, this run down budget option was not open at the time of writing, but is well located near the centre of town. You will not get much more than a bed & a communal toilet for your money, & expect only intermittent electricity. **$**

❮ **WHERE TO EAT AND DRINK** *See maps, pages 151 and 154 unless otherwise stated*

Above average

✗ **La Corisqueña Playa Bome** [map, page 146] Matransa; m 222 299 972, 222 588 676; ⏲ noon–23.00 daily. On the road south of Bata before La Ferme or Costa Del Sol you will find the bright-red La Corisqueña complex. It has 4 areas: the main Restaurant Elobey, the pool area Punta Hoco, a disco called Say & a VIP area known as Rey Uganda. This is a modern, luxurious & surprising find in this part of town. The decked pool area is a great place to relax at the w/end enjoying one of the many cocktails on the drinks menu. The food is also delicious & there is an eclectic mix of national & international dishes. Be sure to check their Facebook page to stay up to date on special events. They offer a buffet most w/ends. **$$$–$$$$**

✗ **La Ferme** [map, page 146] Playa de Bome; m 222 257 333; ⏲ noon–23.00 daily. This hidden gem is the best place in Bata to enjoy a drink or a meal by the seaside. Drive as if you are heading to the Costa Del Sol but continue south briefly & you will see the entrance, surrounded by trees. There are caged birds in the car park. The main dining area is decked & under a thatched roof, with steps leading down on to the beach. The menu features a mixture of Spanish & French food as well as some local favourites (try the *pepe* soup but be warned; it is very spicy!). Service is good & prices are reasonable considering the excellent location. They also have kayaks for rent. It gets very busy at w/ends so be sure to book. **$$$–$$$$**

✗ **La Torre** Torre de la Libertad; ⏲ noon–15.00 & 18.00–midnight Mon–Sat, 18.00–midnight Sun. This Italian restaurant is usually empty at lunchtimes but boasts the best views in the city. It is unclear whether the restaurant was supposed to rotate originally but don't worry, it is stationary at the moment. The menu is typically Italian & there are some good seafood dishes. The restaurant is linked to the bar in the basement by 2 lifts. **$$$–$$$$**

Mid range

✗ **Bar Restaurante Central** El Cruce Santy; ☎ 333 274 307; m 222 272 138. This Lebanese-run restaurant is clean, has good Wi-Fi & offers a mixture of Middle Eastern, Italian & Spanish dishes. They also have an open terrace area where you can smoke *shisha*. Upstairs is their hotel/hostal, run by the same management (page 154). **$$$**

✗ **Brel Pizzeria** Calle de Radio Bata. Another good Italian restaurant with a more formal setting than La Costa down the road. Offers typical Italian dishes as well as take-away pizza. **$$$**

✗ **Le Kalao** ⏲ noon–22.00 daily. At the quiet southwestern end of the Paseo Marítimo de Bata, past the ibis. A great restaurant that serves a mixed menu of European & Brazilian food. **$$$**

✗ **Restaurante Ceiba** In front of Edificio Abayak; m 555 029 363. Good restaurant with chicken & fish dishes in a green open-air seating area. Also sell good pastries for breakfast but food is generally quite expensive. **$$$**

✗ **Spanish Cultural Centre** Paseo de Lumu Matindi s/n; ☎ 333 084 940; e cceb@ccebata.es; http://ccebata.es/. The restaurant in the Spanish Cultural Centre on the Paseo Marítimo offers European cuisine with sea views & is very popular with European expatriates, especially for lunch. **$$$**

✗ **Empereur Deux Resort** [map, page 146] Opposite the Sheraton Utonde Hotel Resort, Utonde; A 10min drive north of the airport brings you on to the spit by the river Utonde. You can see the estuary here & the bridge under construction as you land at Bata airport. The Empereur Deux is a newly built resort on the river-facing side of the sand bar. They will soon have bungalows for hire & already offer a variety of aquatic activities such as fishing & jet skiing. There is currently a good restaurant & bar here with a pool. This is a good option if you want to get out of the city quickly. **$$–$$$**

✗ **La Cantina** Paseo Marítimo; m 222 773 838; ⏲ 07.00–23.00 Tue–Fri, 08.00–01.00 Sat, 09.00–22.00 Sun. Possibly the only authentic, Spanish-run bar in all of Bata, this is a great spot for relaxing with a beer & interacting with the Spanish community. It is a simple setup: Spanish football on the TV, Spanish beers in the fridge &

various tapas on the menu, as well as a dish of the day. There is also a private room at the back which can cater for larger groups or parties. Open all day, this place offers breakfast, lunch & dinner. Things get lively in the evenings when the sound system is turned up. Great fun, great value & highly recommended. They also have 2 rooms for rent at the back (page 154). $$–$$$

✖ **La Costa Del Oro** 📞666 184 821; ⏱ 13.00– 22.00 daily. Traditional Chinese restaurant. The proprietors of this place speak their own distinctive brand of Spanish. The food is quite good. $$–$$$

✖ **Restaurant L'Orientale** Paseo Marítimo de Bata. A sprawling Lebanese restaurant occupying the ground floor of a high rise overlooking the Atlantic. Good food with access to a *shisha* terrace. Try the hummus. $$–$$$

Cheap and cheerful

✖ **Elik Melen** Junction of Patricio Lumumba & Calle 3 de Agosto, Bata 16345; 📞333 088 166/67; ⏱ 15.00–23.00, but limited menu available all day. There are 2 restaurants in the hotel (page 153), both serving good-quality food but the service can be slow at times. $$–$$$

✖ **La Costa** Pl de Ayuntamiento; ⏱ noon– 22.00 Mon–Sat. This is a very popular Italian pizza restaurant on the roundabout. Serves great wood-fired pizzas. $$

✖ **Restaurante Amir** Av Mbogo Nsogo BP 94; 📞333 082 900; ⏱ 10.00–23.00 daily. Offers rotisserie chickens, kebabs & pizzas. It also serves dangerously luminous ice cream. $$

✖ **Restaurante Royal Okangong** Av Mbongo Nsogo; 📱 222 115 554, 551 352 727; ⏱ noon– 23.00 Tue–Sat. Offers barbecue food to the crowds out on the street, or in its hall. Good value & smells great! $$

✖ **Hong Lnow** Just off Paseo Marítimo de Bata; ⏱ 11.30–21.00 daily; Recently refurbished, this

Chinese restaurant offers very reasonably priced mains in a clean environment. $–$$

✖ **Restaurante Pizzeria** Carretere del Aeropuerto; ⏱ 12.30–22.00 Mon–Sat, 13.00– 20.00 Sun. This small pizza restaurant can be found by the side of the road to the north of town, just by the airport. Quite easy to miss as it's near the toll booth, this place does an excellent buffet. $–$$

Rock bottom

✖ **Costa Del Sol** [map, page 146] Playa de Bome; 📱 222 151 887; ⏱ 16.00–23.00 Tue–Sat. If you drive south out of town, through the port, you will eventually pass a large residential compound for the expatriate Hess Corporation oil workers. Keep going on the dirt road & on your right you will see a collapsed wall & a shipping container. Down here is a small wooden beach bar. They serve a limited menu of mainly grilled foods & plenty of beers. A cheap spot to relax by the sea. $

✖ **KFC Restaurant** Paseo Marítimo de Bata; ⏱ 17.00–midnight daily. Fans of Colonel Sanders's secret recipe will be sadly disappointed by this Chinese restaurant. It seems that international copyright laws haven't quite reached Bata yet. Putting that aside, what you have here is a great-value Chinese place that also serves burgers, open all week long. $

✖ **Mil Sabores Bar and Restaurant** Carretera del Aeropuerto; ⏱ 12.30–22.00 Mon–Sat. This new restaurant on the road to the airport has an excellent bar & some good quick snacks, but for a full meal there are better eating options nearby. $

🍵 **Waterfront Café** Paseo Marítimo de Bata; ⏱ 09.00–18.00 daily. This cheap & cheerful open-air café is a great place to enjoy the sea views on the Paseo Marítimo. It offers hot & cold drinks, fruit & a variety of pastries. You can also buy fresh Middle Eastern flat bread here. Highly recommended. $

ENTERTAINMENT AND NIGHTLIFE Bata is famous in Equatorial Guinea for its nightlife. Many people spend the day on the beach, either by driving to a secluded stretch or by heading to La Ferme or La Corisqueña, before returning to the city for a night out. Things do not tend to get going until late, but no matter what the time, you are sure to find a watering hole to suit your tastes and budget.

Bars and clubs For those looking for a beach setting within the city, **Karma Bar** [map, page 154] (*Paseo Marítimo;* 📱 *222 249 965;* ⏱ *18.30–02.30 Tue–Sun*) is a very popular beachfront bar and nightclub which fills up at weekends. Whatever you do don't order their Chinese spirits though! Nearby you will also find the much cheaper **Empereur Bar** [map, page 154], which also serves drinks with a sea view.

For a more cosmopolitan scene, be sure to dress up smartly and bring your francs, as things in Bata can get expensive. **Kristal Lounge Bar** [151 A4] (*Calle de Radio Bata; ⊕ noon–late daily*) is situated upstairs in the Radio Television de Asonga building, and is an intimate but popular venue with a great bar, some outdoor seating and live music at weekends. It also serves food. The place to be seen, however, is **Rolex Discoteca** [151 D3] (*Next to Aparthotel Plaza, 45.21; ⊕ 22.00–05.00 Thu–Sun*), the undisputed premier nightspot in Bata, allegedly owned by one of the president's offspring. It is loud, dark and there are mirrors everywhere. Avoid if you are epileptic or in any way upset by lasers or expensive prostitutes. Open late, this place is can prove costly at 10,000CFA entry and 5,000CFA a drink. A popular expatriate spot.

When all else fails (ie: you have been kicked out of the other clubs because it is 05.00), then you have three options. The first is to head to the centre of town and **Night Club Makaveli** [151 D2], which has an odd looking woman and a saxophone painted on the wall outside. Hard to miss at weekends, with music blasting out until the early hours, this is a local favourite but visiting is likely to lead to permanent hearing damage. Your second option is **Mamaita Bar** [151 B2] (*Next to Santy Supermarket; ⊕ 19.00–late daily*). This sleazy dive bar is a favourite among ageing Spanish construction workers who come for the loud music, cheap beers and ridiculously late opening hours. Oh, and the prostitutes. So many prostitutes. Last on the 'late' late-night list is **Discoteca La Salsa** [map, page 154] (*Carretera del Aeropuerto; ⊕ 22.00–08.00 Thu–Sun*), a gargantuan nightclub on the road to the airport. Drinks here are expensive and the toilets are a disaster, but it is one of the most popular spots in the city and often hosts famous local acts such as Petit Chabal. If you want to party well into the early hours, this place has an open door policy after all the other clubs have closed.

Sports bars
Equatoguineans love their sports and most drinking establishments will have the football playing. **La Cantina** (pages 155–6) is guaranteed to be showing La Liga if it is on, as is **Sports Bar** [151 C2] (*⊕ noon–late daily*) over by the cathedral. **Bar Estadio** [151 A2] (*⊕ noon–late daily*), situated at the entrance to the old stadium, on the junction with the Panafrica Hotel and Santy Supermarket, is also a lively nightspot with a few screens. It is a good place to meet the locals while enjoying a cold San Miguel but it is completely open air so bring your mosquito spray. **Zumbar** [off map, page 154] (*⊕ 13.00–23.00 daily*), out on the ring road by the stadium, is a sports bar that is a bit of a trek from town but good fun. It has a projector and large screen showing sports, a table tennis table, a pool table, table football and a wide variety of drinks, plus outdoor seating. **Elik Melen Pub** [151 D2] is situated in the basement of the Hotel Elik Melensh-style pub with wooden panelling everywhere. A very strange find but always a friendly crowd when the sport is on.

Gambling
There are two places to go and gamble in Bata (excluding Mamaita's Bar; see above). The main casino is **Game Joker Casino** [151 B1] (*Paseo Marítimo de Bata; ✆ 333 081 310; e remi@gamesworlduae.com; ⊕ 19.00–03.00 daily, bar open from 11.00 daily*). Owned by the same United Arab Emirates management as the Barco Casino in Malabo, this place features live gaming tables with American roulette with racetrack, blackjack with Perfect Pairs bonus game, Oasis Stud Poker, Ultimate Texas Hold'em and Treasure Poker. There are 38 gaming machines in addition to the live tables, and drinks are free for those who are gambling. The

minimum buy-in is 20,000CFA and flip-flops are not allowed, nor are shorts. A more budget option is **Game Lucky Casino** [151 C3] (*Calle Juan Pablo II, Pl Del Reloj;* \333 081 310; ☉ *noon–03.00 daily*). Situated on the corner of Plaza Del Reloj, this casino has 30 gaming machines and a bar.

SHOPPING The usual shopping hours are 09.00–13.00 and 16.00–19.00 Monday to Friday, and 09.00–12.30 Saturday. Note that some foreign-run businesses (particularly those owned by the Chinese or Lebanese) do not take a siesta. However, some Lebanese-run businesses are closed on Fridays.

Bookshops These are few and far between in Equatorial Guinea, even in its biggest city. In 2013, Bata got its first dedicated bookshop, set up in the **Spanish Cultural Centre** [151 C1] (*Paseo de Lumu Matindi s/n;* \ *333 084 940;* e *cceb@ ccebata.es; http://ccebata.es/*) by the la Asociación Literaria Página de Luz, so be sure to head there if you are hunting for Spanish-language literature. There is also a **public library** [151 C1] in Bata (*opposite the UNGE university campus;* ☉ *08.00– 20.00 Mon–Fri, 10.00–16.00 Sat*), which was inaugurated in March 2012. It features a small but well-organised collection of reference works and free Wi-Fi, and the librarian does not seem to mind foreign visitors. Beyond this you will struggle to find any books for sale, but try checking some of the **informal markets**, such as the one near the Senegalese honorary consulate in the north of town.

Markets The best informal market in town is probably **Mercado La Fina** [off map, page 154], on the eastern outskirts of the city. Here you will find a mad assortment of fresh produce and manufactured goods, as well as shared taxis to other parts of the country. If you jump in a shared taxi from the centre of town and ask them to drop you at 'Fabrica de Ladrilla, Colombo' they will know where to go. There are also a number of **street vendors** situated at the northern end of town, on the same road as the Senegalese honorary consulate.

Gifts and souvenirs If you are looking for gifts, there is a group of local traders selling craft goods from a garage lockup **Craft goods shop** [151 C2] (or *Casa Artesanal* in Spanish) opposite the Martinez Hermanos Supermarket. A good place to start if you are looking for masks, paintings, jewellery, carvings, etc. You will also find the **Casa Artesenal** [151 B3] (*Calle de Radio Bata;* m *222 242 478*) on the same road as Radio Bata, which has a great selection of paintings and carvings, including some huge wooden gorillas. Note that although labelled differently on the map, these two shops have exactly the same name in Spanish, so if asking to be taken there by a taxi driver, be sure to clarify which one you mean. **Street vendors** also display numerous carved and painted goods outside the Santy Supermarket entrance (page 159), hoping to target the numerous Western clients shopping there.

Music and electricals Music is a popular commercial item and can be purchased from many informal stores by the side of the road. There are CDs available all over Bata, or you can purchase a Chinese-made mp3 player pre-loaded with local tunes which plugs into a car cigarette lighter and plays through your radio. Ask around the local shops or any taxi driver and they will point you in the right direction.

There are few decent quality electrical goods for sale in Bata. If you need something specific it is best to import it, but **Centro Comercial Electro-Bata** [151 B2] (*Paseo Marítimo, Thomas Ngono Ncogo, 037 Bata;* \ *333 083 261;* m *222 274 480;* e *electrobata@hotmail.com;* ☉ *08.00–19.00 Mon–Sat*) is a white goods store in the centre of town. You could also try some of the supermarkets such as **Santy** or **Martinez Hermanos** (see below) for household electrical items.

Supermarkets
Supermarkets in Bata tend to stick to the regular hours of 09.00–13.00 and 16.00–19.00 Monday to Friday, and 09.00–12.30 Saturday. You will struggle to find fresh produce for sale outside these times, although some of the street market traders will keep selling into the early evening.

Martinez Hermanos Supermercado [151 C3] Calle Mbogo Nsogo; ✆333 082 881; e mhnos@intnet.gq, information@martinezhermanos.com. Very similar to the Malabo branch, prices are generally higher than in Europe, & you need to look very carefully at the labels in order to avoid being stung (especially with fresh goods). However, this place offers a good selection of Western produce, mainly imported from Spain. There is also another branch out on the road to the presidential complex, Mayor Ngolo. It is slightly smaller & has the same opening hours as the one in the centre, but is less crowded.

Muankaban Supermarket [map, page 154] Mayor Ngolo; e supermercadomuankaban@gmail.com. This bright orange & red building is hard to miss on the highway east out of town, past the Martinez Hermanos location. It offers a good variety of produce including fresh meat, fruit &

vegetables, & there is a fishmongers & a bakery but it is probably not worth visiting if you compare their selection of goods with the closer Martinez Hermanos or Santy supermarkets.

Santy Supermarket [151 B2] No 10 Calle Camaron; ✆333 082 686, 333 088 694; e santy@iintnet.gq. One of the best supermarkets in Bata, this is a very large shop with a variety of imported produce, much of it Spanish. There is a good frozen food section & some chilled goods such as cheeses, cured meats & fruit (although prices are high). Lots of alcohol plus some domestic & electronic goods are on offer, too. Outside there are street vendors selling carvings, jewellery & African paintings.

Supermercado EGTC [151 D3] Pl de la Independencia; ✆333 082 956/58; e info@EGTC.com. Stocks a good variety of fresh, chilled & frozen goods & has an extensive alcohol selection.

SPORTS AND ACTIVITIES
The **Paseo Marítimo** [151 B2] serves as a very popular running track and is a great way to see the shoreline. Most other activities available in Bata are also ocean-related. You can take part in **watersports** at a number of the beachfront restaurants to the south of town on Bome beach (such as La Ferme; page 155) and also to the north of town on the Utonde spit (Empereur Deux Resort; page 155 or Hotel Les Pagaies; page 153). These locations can organise kayak and boat hire, and the Empereur Deux Resort in particular is great for **fishing** on the river.

The majority of the higher-end hotels have **swimming pools** and **gyms** and you may be able to pay for access as a non-resident or get signed in as a guest, for example at Villa Celotti.

Over by the UNGE campus there is a dirt **football pitch** with nets, where there's always a game going. A few of the expatriate compounds also have tennis courts and astroturf football pitches, but you will need a local contact to access these. The Old Stadium by Santy Supermarket also has an attached **boxing and martial arts club**, complete with outdoor ring and punchbags.

OTHER PRACTICALITIES
Banks and foreign exchange
$ **BANGE Bank** [151 C3] Av Mbogo Nsogo, Apdo 781; ✆333 082 721; m 222 082 744; ◷ 08.00–14.30 Mon–Fri, 09.00–12.30 Sat. Has an ATM which accepts Visa & MasterCard.

$ **BGFI Bank** [151 D2] Calle de Patricio Lumumba

BP 533; ✆333 081 764/68; e agence_bata@bgfi.com; ◷ 09.00–14.00 Mon–Fri, 09.00–noon Sat. Has an ATM outside but no Visa symbol.

$ **Ecobank** [151 D2] Av Mbongo Nsogo; ◷ 09.00–17.00 Mon–Fri, 09.00–14.00 Sat. Has ATMs outside which accept Visa.

$ **Money Exchange** [151 C3] Av de S S Juan Pablo II; m 222 080 807/58; e continentalcaja@yahoo.es. Change most currencies. Their euro rate is no better than you will get from any other business in town.

$ **SGBGE** [151 C2] Av Mbogo Nsogo, Apdo 781, BP 781; ✆ 333 082 721/724; ⊕ 08.00–14.00 Mon–Fri. Offers Western Union services & has well-stocked ATMs which accept Visa & MasterCard.

Healthcare

➕ **Bata General Hospital** [151 C2] ✆ 333 082 101, 333 082 290; ⊕ 24hrs. Although undergoing refurbishment, this hospital is not recommended by Western embassies, who favour the La Paz hospital further out of town.

➕ **Farmacia Afrom** [151 C3] ⊕ 09.00–16.00 Mon–Fri. A large & well-stocked pharmacy in the centre of town.

➕ **La Grande Pharmacie** [151 C1] ⊕ 08.30–13.00 Mon–Fri, 10.00–13.00 Sat. Small but well-stocked pharmacy.

➕ **La Paz Hospital** [151 C2] ✆ 333 083 515/518; m 222 633 344; e recruit@lapazge.org; ⊕ 24hrs. This is the top medical facility in mainland Equatorial Guinea, with over 120 beds & a number of specialist expatriate medical practitioners from Israel. The centre also has a pharmacy, hotel & other healthcare facilities. Prices are very high especially for emergency care, so be sure to consult with your insurance provider before incurring costs.

Ministry of Tourism and Culture [off map, page 154] This should be your first port of call as soon as you arrive in Bata (unless you already have a permit from Malabo). As with its counterpart in Malabo, this ministry is hidden in a social housing block well outside the city centre (on the same road as the new Bata Stadium). There is a sign outside but it is very easy to miss. Taxi drivers tend to have no idea where it is, or will try and take you to the old site of the Ministry of Tourism, which is a yellow building in the centre of the city near the PDGE Headquarters (both marked on the map). Use the stadium as a waypoint to guide unsure drivers, and ask for the Delegacion Regional De Cultura Y Turismo. For more information on obtaining your Tourism Permit, see page 68.

Other useful addresses

Canal+ distributor Calle de la Juventud Guineana, Cerca Antanio; ⊕ 09.00–16.00 Mon–Fri. If you are moving to Bata longer term, head here to arrange European satellite TV at home.

Cyber Café [151 C2] Opposite Total petrol station; m 222 034 021; ⊕ 09.00–19.00 Mon–Sat. Lots of computers available with headsets for only 1,000CFA/hr. Also sell drinks.

DHL Office [151 B1] Paseo Marítimo de Bata; m 551 665 259; ⊕ 08.00–18.00 Mon–Fri, 09.00–13.00 Sat. This is the only way of getting things into, out of & around the country.

Perfecto Pressing [map, page 154] Calle Iyubu Jesus Bacale; ✆ 333 083 773, 333 612 973; e perfectopressing@yahoo.fr. Good-quality dry-cleaning company able to turn items around quickly, but quite expensive.

WHAT TO SEE AND DO The airport marks the northernmost extremity of Bata. Beyond this you have the resort area of Utonde and little else. A do-it-yourself walking tour of the city, starting at the airport, can be completed in around an hour. The route is outlined below.

As you drive (or walk) south into town the first noteworthy building is the sprawling oceanfront **presidential complex** [map, page 154], rumoured to be home to the president's eldest son, Teodorín Obiang. You cannot see much because the walls are so high but the sheer size of the complex is breathtaking and it occupies a prime section of waterfront real estate. Next, you will pass the bright-white **Nuevo Ayuntamiento** (Town Hall) [151 C1]. At the time of writing it had yet to be inaugurated. Nearby there is also a **mausoleum** under construction.

If you head inland at the next roundabout (by the Total petrol station), you will soon pass the **UNGE university campus** [151 D2] which is currently being upgraded, specifically the Instituto Tecnico Modesto Gene. This is where the **public library** can be found. To the west of here is Bata cathedral, officially known as the **Catedral de Santiago Apóstol y Nuestra Señora del Pilar** [151 C2]. Built by the Spanish in 1954, it was brainchild of the Italian architect Nino Monti. It took three years to complete. While often locked outside official service times (*irregular w/day mornings from 08.00 & Sun from 09.00*), the cathedral still makes for good photos from the outside because of its beautiful stained-glass windows.

Continuing back towards the well-landscaped **Paseo Marítimo**, you will immediately note the **Torre de la Libertad** (Tower of Freedom) [151 C1] which dominates the Bata waterfront skyline. Inaugurated on 12 October 2011, this futuristic structure was built to celebrate Equaotguinean independence from Spanish rule. Standing at over 60m tall, it houses a restaurant in the upper section with a bar in the basement (page 155).

Slightly further south but still facing the ocean is the **Spanish Cultural Centre** [151 B1] (*Paseo de Lumu Matindi s/n;* \ *333 084 940;* e *cceb@ccebata.es; http:// ccebata.es/;* ⊕ *08.30–15.00 Mon–Fri, library 09.00–21.00 Mon–Fri, 09.00–14.00 Sat*). Around since July 2001 and spread across three floors and over 2,500m^2, the centre is home to an auditorium, classrooms, rehearsal space, a theatre, a library, offices, a craft shop and a bookshop, as well as a popular restaurant (page 155). A timetable of activities can be found on their website or on their Facebook page.

Soon the road curves inland slightly, and you pass the Santy Supermarket, before continuing on past the **French Cultural Centre** [151 A3] (*Paseo Marítimo de Bata;* e *yannick.cornette@gmail.com;* ⊕ *09.00–noon & 14.00–18.00 Mon–Sat*). Opened in December 2009, the Institut Culturel D'Expression Française (ICEF) de Bata boasts six classrooms, a conference room and an exhibition hall. It offers French-language courses as well as all sorts of exhibitions, displays, performances and workshops themed around the Francophonie. Programmes of events are posted in the centre, but are difficult to find online as it does not maintain a website like the ICEF in Malabo. This is about as far south as you ever need to go, unless you are staying at the ibis Hotel or are heading to one of the beachfront restaurants to the south of town.

Cut inland here towards Plaza De Ayuntamiento and you will see **Estadio La Libertad (Old Stadium)** [151 A2] on your left-hand side. Situated right in the centre of the city, the old stadium was surpassed when the Estadio de Bata was built out by the ring road in 2007. The new stadium seats an incredible 35,000 spectators, and was expanded and renovated in 2011. Lit up at night, it's an incredible sight. However, with Estadio La Libertad's bigger brother hosting the 2012 and 2015 Africa Cup of Nations games, the old stadium has fallen into disrepair, although lower league fixtures are still played here. Continuing northeast, you will reach **Plaza Del Reloj** [151 C3], known officially as Plaza de la Libertad, which is in the very centre of the city. Apart from being home to the big clock tower that gives it its name, it also features a monument to the soldiers who died during the 3 August 1979 coup (page 29). Just over the road is an **obelisk** monument to Pope John Paul II, commemorating his visit to the country in February 1982, the first ever visit by a Pope and a huge event in this predominantly Roman Catholic country.

In the northeast of town you may also see the second **presidential complex** [map, page 154] (just in case the waterfront one by the airport was not enough). If you are heading out of town on the road to Niefang you cannot fail to notice the sprawling complex spanning both sides of the road, featuring a series of mansions, green spaces and official-looking buildings. The area is surrounded by huge walls topped with razor wire and closely guarded. Depending on which taxi driver you ask, this is either the home of the President or his eldest son Teodorín.

AROUND BATA

Those looking to escape the city often head to the resorts of Utonde north of the airport, or south to the various restaurants and lounge bars of Playa Bome. There is a working **cocoa plantation** just outside the city on the road east which makes a good day trip, and is signposted from the road. For those heading further afield, every part of Litoral Province is easily reached as part of a long day trip, including the four scientific reserves: Reserva Natural de Río Campo to the north, and Reserva Natural de Punta Ilende, Reserva Científica de Playa Nendyi and Reserva Natural del Estuario del Río Muni, in order of increasing distance, to the south. You could also visit the border towns of Río Campo and Cogo, or the coastal settlement of Mbini.

RESERVA NATURAL DE RÍO CAMPO The Río Campo Natural Reserve is a 335km^2 protected area in the northwest of Río Muni on the border with Cameroon. The area is classified as a Wetland of International Importance by the Ramsar Convention. One of the area's most famous residents is the Goliath frog, which can grow up to 32cm long and weigh over 3kg. The reserve is also frequented by a number of marine turtle species, including the green turtle, leatherback, olive ridley and hawksbill. There is also a population of hippopotamuses that live in the estuary.

Getting there If you want to explore the Río Campo Natural Reserve you are advised to organise this through a local tour agency in Malabo or Bata (pages 65 and 152), or at least get a local driver, perhaps by heading to the **shared taxi** rank in the Fabrica de Ladrilla in the Colombo district and negotiating (page 158). While your Tourism Permit will cover you in this area, there is little infrastructure in place and a driver should help with navigating through the six checkpoints you will encounter on the route north. This will also prove an excellent opportunity to put the tips found on pages 82–3 into practice.

Driving north from Bata towards the Cameroonian border, around 30km into the journey you will pass an unusual waypoint: a **light airplane** by the side of the road (located at 1°58'15.8"N 9°55'16.7"E). Every driver that plies this route has a different story about how it came to be here, perfectly intact and slowly being reclaimed by the jungle. Most stories tend to agree that it ran out of fuel on a flight from Angola back in early 2013, while being flown by a Colombian pilot who had an American onboard. He was forced to make a very successful emergency landing on the straight stretch of road and both men walked away unscathed. Beyond that, it is truly a mystery!

What to see and do The 5km stretch of beach between Punta Tika and Punta Cuche in the northwest of the reserve is a conservation site run by the **TOMAGE Project** (Tortugas Marinas de Guinea Ecuatorial; e *ayetebemme@yahoo.es, falla7@ gmail.com*) and managed by the government's Protected Areas Institute, INDEFOR. It is here between December and February every year that various species of marine turtle come to lay their eggs, while juveniles feed in the shallow rocky waters. TOMAGE also works to educate local communities on the importance of conserving the turtles rather than hunting them, and also collect eggs that are laid in areas at higher risk of poaching and predation, for safe incubation in a beach hatchery. TOMAGE runs a small eco-museum in Punta Tika where visitors can learn about sea turtle conservation, and also provides lodging in two modest beach cabins for those who want to spend the night and go on a guided turtle-watching tour to watch for nesting females. Bookings need to be made through the INDEFOR office in Bata (page 152). More information is available on their Facebook page.

At the southern coastal tip of the Río Campo reserve is **Punta Mbonda lighthouse**. Dating to 1958, this 35m-high octagonal tower sits just off a beautiful quiet beach, where you can fish in the natural rock pools and collect coconuts from the shore. Note that this area is quite close to a restricted military camp, so you should not go hiking inland here. If in doubt, seek local advice.

RÍO CAMPO Río Campo is a very small town on the infrequently crossed northern border with Cameroon. There is talk of building a bridge here over the river Ntem to link Equatorial Guinea to the town of Campo, but for now cross-border traffic is mainly by pirogue. Note that the border is frequently closed to foreigners.

RÍO CAMPO — CAMEROON

New comisario (under construction)

Comisario & border crossing point

Central market

PDGE HQ

① Ayuntamiento ②

N

Bata

Military base

0 ——— 200m
0 ——— 200yds

For listings, see pages 163–4

🍽 **Where to stay and eat**
1 Complejo Turistico Enriqueta Mokumbue
2 Pescaderia Bar

If you are not crossing into Cameroon, the other reason to come here is to fish at the mouth of the river, as this area is home to over 250 species of fish; however, you will need to bring all of your own gear. There are no tourist attractions in town but it is a good place to stock up on fresh market produce before heading over to nearby Punta Cuche or Punta Tika (see above) for a turtle-watching and camping trip. The town juts out on a peninsula into the river estuary and the crossing itself, which forms the border between Cameroon and Equatorial Guinea, is only 200m at its narrowest point. It is hard to get lost here as Río Campo is so flat and is enclosed on two sides by water. Upon arrival it is best to go and register with the *comisario* at the northern end of town. He is perfectly friendly, and the police chief even speaks English, having learned it in Swaziland.

Getting there and away It is possible to get a **shared taxi** to Río Campo from Bata by heading to the Fabrica de Ladrilla in the Colombo district (page 158). The cost is 2,000CFA per seat and cars tend to depart very early in the morning. Río Campo is a far less popular destination than places such as Niefang or Mbini, so you may have to wait around for a departure. Some taxi drivers will let you buy-out the whole car for around 10,000CFA and leave whenever you choose.

🏠 **Where to stay and eat** *See map, above.*
There is a **central market** in Río Campo where you can sometimes buy decent fish, but otherwise dining is limited to snack foods at the **Pescaderia Bar** at the southern

end of town, or the eerily silent **Complejo Turistico Enriqueta Mokumbue ($–$$$)**. It is not clear why somebody chose to build this large tourist complex in such a tourist-free area, but if you manage to find a member of staff they have a great selection of beers, serve food and can even offer the only accommodation in town. The restaurant ($$) has a courtyard with riverfront views across the border. Rooms in the hotel section have private bathrooms, double beds, air conditioning, flatscreen TVs with French satellite programmes (from neighbouring Cameroon). Rooms are between 10,000CFA and 50,000CFA depending on the size. There is also a disco here at weekends which gets rowdy.

MBINI The town of Mbini is located approximately 45km south of Bata, at the mouth of the Benito River. This whole coastal area is a Ndowe heartland. The river landscape here is dominated by the Chinese-built suspension bridge which stretches 800m over the Benito river mouth, linking the southern portion of the coastline to the capital city. The bridge is a sight to behold, especially at night when it is often lit up, but be careful taking photographs as bridges are designated 'strategic sites'.

Mbini is very similar to Río Campo in that it is a small ocean peninsula jutting into the mouth of a river. The whole town is about 600m across and you can easily get around on foot. The centre is definitely the main square's roundabout and the surrounding bars, although you will likely want to spend most of your time on the northwest coastline. As in any provincial town, your first stop should be to the nearest senior official's office to register your presence. In Mbini this is the *delgado*, a friendly but generally disinterested older woman who is based in an office opposite the Pastelaria Alice Burger. Dropping off a copy of your Tourism Permit with her secretary should suffice, and after this you will have no problems walking around town and taking photographs.

Getting there and away Mbini can be reached in an hour by **shared taxi** from Bata (factoring in the time taken passing through checkpoints). The cost is 1,500CFA per seat and cars tend to depart early in the morning. Mbini is a popular destination so you should not have to wait around too long for a departure. The taxi rank is at the southern end of Mbini and from here you can pick up taxis heading back to Bata, or continue on to Acalayong or Cogo for around 1,500CFA.

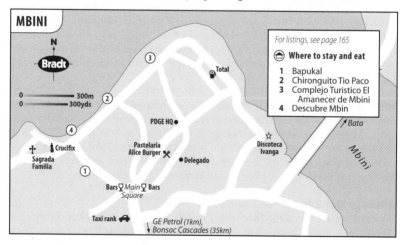

MBINI

For listings, see page 165

Where to stay and eat
1 Bapukal
2 Chironguito Tio Paco
3 Complejo Turistico El Amanecer de Mbini
4 Descubre Mbin

Where to stay and eat   *See map, page 164.*

A new hotel on the north side of the bridge was under constructionat the time of writing, which looks as if it will be the main business hotel in town upon completion. For now, the **Complejo Turistico El Amanecer de Mbini** (m *222 077 072/3/4;* e *mbini@hotmail.com;* **$$$–$$$$$**) on the northwest coastline is a good option for those looking to stay in Mbini. The restaurant and bar (**$$–$$$**) serve food from 08.00 to 22.00 daily, and there is an attractive thatch patio with sea views and a private stretch of white beach. There is also a murky-looking saltwater pool, but you are better off swimming in the sea. All rooms have air conditioning, TV and include breakfast. Prices range from 55,000CFA for a twin room in one of their mobile homes to 110,000CFA for one of their private bungalows which have two double rooms and a living room. If you come down as a group of two or more, this represents good value for money. The complex also has jet skis and kayaks which they rent out.

The Complejo Turistico El Amanecer de Mbini is also your best bet for food. A variety of meat and fish dishes are served, along with Western staples such as burgers. If you are on a budget, try **Bapukal** (**$–$$**) in town on the main roundabout, which serves delicious Senegalese cuisine in simple surroundings. Once the new hotel is finished, they should also have a restaurant.

Both **Descubre Mbini** and **Chironguito Tio Paco** are good places to relax with beers and watch the sun go down. They also serve bar snacks. You might also try braving the **Discoteca Ivanga** over by the bridge. It is a big spot in a prime location, the beer is cheap, the music is loud and most people will assume you are Chinese.

What to see
Mbini is a place of special religious significance to many in Equatorial Guinea, as it was the hometown of the former archbishop of Malabo, Rafael María Nze Abuy. A good place to start your tour therefore is the **Sagrada Familia church** in the northeast corner. Dating back to 1955, this church sadly burnt down in 2013, but has since been restored. There is a large **crucifix monument** outside by the coastline. Attached to the church is a missionary school, and the children are usually very excited to see a foreigner wandering around their town, so you may attract quite a crowd.

Around Mbini
Most of Litoral Province's population is concentrated along the coastline, and hence so is the transport infrastructure. This makes heading inland anywhere apart from towards Niefang difficult. However, 35km due east of Mbini are the Bonsoc Cascades. Situated on the very edge of Monte Alen National Park on the Río Benito (✦ 1°32'30.73"N 9°56'41.32"E), these waterfalls are 40m tall and hundreds of metres wide. The nearest village is Sinden, located 10km to the southwest. Getting there will require a local guide and appropriate equipment.

RESERVA NATURAL DE PUNTA ILENDE AND RESERVA CIENTIFICA DE PLAYA NENDYI
If you head south from Mbini, through the village of Bitika, the coastline from here is part of the **Punta Llende Natural Reserve**. This is another protected sea turtle nesting site which is administered by the TOMAGE organisation (page 162). The area is also an important foraging habitat for the endangered green and critically endangered hawksbill turtles. TOMAGE have managed to GPS tag three green turtles (named Marino, Juan Nsogo Cariño and Isidoro) in this area, and you can view their movements at www.seaturtle.org/tracking/?project_id=1001.

As with the other natural reserves, there is no tourist infrastructure here, so you will need to bring everything you need, including drinking water.

The **Reserva Científica de Playa Nendyi** is a 2.75km² area of beach that is another protected turtle nesting and foraging site, located between the villages of Cabo De San Juan and Calatrava. It is also administered by the TOMAGE organisation. Camping here is possible if organised in advance through INDEFOR in Bata (page 152), but otherwise there is no tourist infrastructure.

CABO DE SAN JUAN Cabo De San Juan is the westernmost point of mainland Equatorial Guinea. It is a great weekend destination from Bata for those with access to a 4x4 and who are looking for a deserted tropical beach to relax on, or who are perhaps interested in exploring the old colonial ruins. Try to avoid the port construction work currently being undertaken by SOMAGEC, as this ruins the ambience slightly!

In 1698, Cabo De San Juan was the site of a daring attack by French pirate Montauban, who captured an English ship carrying 350 slaves and much ivory.

During the 18th and 19th centuries this area, along with Corisco and the Elobey islands, served as commercial centres for trade between the local people and various German, American and British trading houses. The Westerners traded manufactured goods such as weaponry, textiles, alcohol and tobacco in exchange for palm oil, ivory, rubber, and woods such as mahogany, ebony and okoumé. In 1875, during the expeditions of Spanish explorer Manuel Iradier, the area became popular with European biologists due to the variety of arachnids and insects found there.

Today, you can still see the remnants of European colonisation in the form of the ruined palm oil factory, which was established by León Ururquiza Arana for the Sociedad Colonial de Guinea (SOCOGUI) in 1921. The area was also an important wood processing centre so you will find an old warehouse, timber yard, a school and a few kilometres of railroad which connected the plantation to the harbour.

The beach itself is a beautiful, deserted stretch of white sand, lined with palm trees, and it makes a great picnic or camping spot. During the week you are unlikely to see anyone else here unless some local fishermen happen upon you. At weekends you may see the occasional day tripper from Bata, but generally it remains a well-kept secret amongst the local community. Be sure to bring all your own supplies with you (especially water), as purchasing items locally is very difficult.

RESERVA NATURAL DEL ESTUARIO DEL RÍO MUNI The Río Muni Estuary Natural Reserve is a 700km² protected area created in 2000. It is home to an abundance of wildlife, including some species found nowhere else in the country. You will need a boat to explore the area, which can be hired from either Acalayong (page 168) or Cogo (page 167). The fishermen in Acalayong are happy to rent out their boats for a few hours, and will know where to go to find certain species of wildlife. Alternatively, you can set out on hikes from the main road that runs from Cogo to Ichime if you find a local guide.

The waterways in the reserve are home to a sizeable manatee population, making this the only place you can see them in the country. There are also two types of crocodile: the critically endangered African slender-snouted crocodile and the dwarf crocodile.

Río Muni Estuary Natural Reserve is believed by Birdlife International to be a potential Important Bird Area (IBA) due to the seasonal waterbirds that are attracted to its extensive areas of tidal mud- and sandflats and mangrove.

The forests in the area feature a number of primates, including the Calabar angwantibo (*Arctocebus calabarensis*) and Potto (*Perodicticus potto*). You might also see the southern needle-clawed bushbaby (*Euoticus elegantulus*), Bioko Allen's bushbaby (*Sciurocheirus alleni*), and collared mangabey (*Cercocebus torquatus*) primates.

The Río Muni estuary is also home to the red river hog (*Potamochoerus porcus*), bushbuck (*Tragelaphus scriptus*), African palm civet (*Nandinia binotata*), rusty-spotted genet (*Genetta maculata*), and African forest turtle (*Pelusios gabonensis*).

COGO Cogo sits 115km south of Bata at the mouth of the Muni River, surrounded by the Reserva Natural del Estuario del Río Muni. It is Benga territory, and before the arrival of Europeans it was administered by the king of the Benga, who also ruled Corisco and the Elobey islands. In 1843, King Bonkoro I signed an agreement with the Spanish authorities allowing commercial collaboration and indirect rule. This was replaced in 1875 by direct rule through a Spanish crown representative. Renamed Puerto Iradier under Spanish rule (after the 19th-century Spanish explorer), this town was an important trading centre with links to the interior.

Cogo is the birthplace of Dr Wenceslao Mansogo Aló, a prominent medical practitioner and activist in the political opposition party Convergencia para la Democracia Social (CPDS). The government hopes to make Cogo a commercial and tourism hub in the area, and it is expanding rapidly. A new port facility, football stadium, social housing and a bridge to nearby Akoga are under construction, and direct sea links to the island territories of Corisco and Annobón are being put in place. The redevelopment of the waterfront is breathtaking, and it is clear that the walkway by the market is intended to be a smaller version of the Paseo Marítimo in Bata, or the planned one in Malabo. On a clear day you can see all the way across the river to Gabon. There are few traces of the town's colonial past these days and the monument to the former namesake Manuel Iradier has been removed. But, in a contrast of old and new, the church overlooks the redevelopment.

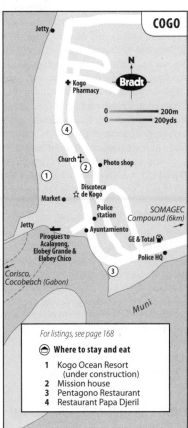

Getting there and away You can get a **pirogue** from Acalayong to Cogo for 2,000CFA, and the journey takes around 15 minutes. **Driving** to Cogo from Bata takes 2 hours on an excellent road. Equatoguineans also cross the international border to and from Gabon at Cocobeach via boat, however this route is often closed to non-nationals. In fact, a number of Western tourists have recently been refused entry or only allowed entry after paying heavy 'fines' when arriving across this border. Be sure to check local conditions before trying the crossing.

Cogo is also the arrival and departure point for the **boats** to Corisco Island. These boats, the variously numbered *Elobeyes*, are former Greek car passenger ferries and are run by the SOMEGEC construction company. The crossing takes 4 hours and is free, but you technically need a permit from the police station. In reality, the Moroccan SOMAGEC workers operating the boat do not seem to care who comes onboard and nobody checks your permit. The ship can only dock in Corisco at high tide, so it leaves Cogo 3 or 4 hours before high tide. Check locally for times.

Getting around The town of Cogo is essentially one main street running parallel to the west-facing shoreline. It is 1km long and easily navigable on foot, although the road heading out of town to the southeast is on a steep gradient. There is a large jetty which is the main point of ingress for construction materials and domestic travellers from Corisco and Acalayong, as well as international arrivals from nearby Cocobeach in Gabon.

⌂ Where to stay and eat *See map, page 167.*

At the moment there is no hotel in town, so travellers wishing to stay the night will have to try their luck by asking at the **church** and attached mission house overlooking the port (*5 rooms*; **$**), which sometimes has simple beds available. Once completed in 2016, however, the **Kogo Ocean Resort** (*54 rooms*; **$$$$$**) will be the highest-quality hotel in the region. This five-star luxury hotel has a gym, a river-facing swimming pool and bar, as well as conference rooms and a large restaurant. The 7,500m² site adjoins the new market and the red cube that is the Kogo Discoteca. If you hang around the centre for long enough you are bound to bump into one of the SOMEGEC workers who live in a compound 5km to the east of town. They may be able to suggest alternative accommodation options. If you're looking for somewhere to eat, **Pentagono Restaurant** ($) at the southern end of town is a tasty local open-air eatery that is popular with local officials. Ignore the menu, as there is only ever one thing available: whatever the lady who runs the joint has cooked up that day. This is a cheap place to relax while waiting for boat departures.

If you want a little more variety, at the northern end of town is **Restaurant Papa Djeril** ($), which serves a variety of local and Senegalese dishes. The view is not as good as Pentagono but it is cheap and cheerful.

ACALAYONG Despite being separated by only 3km of water, Acalayong and neighbouring Cogo are worlds apart. Acalayong is a town at the end of the road, quite literally. Located 110km from Bata, the asphalt stops abruptly at this waterfront settlement. Further travel by vehicle is impossible and you need to take a pirogue to reach Cogo, or else track all the way back via Mbini. Maps imply that Acalayong is of an equal size to Cogo, but in reality it is tiny. The only large structure here is the colonial C V A building, dating back to 1949. There's not much more to Acalayong, and most people visit just to pick up a boat to nearby Cogo, or to explore the estuary area from the river.

You can get a pirogue from Acalayong to Cogo for 2,000CFA, taking around 15 minutes. Acalayong is not an official international arrival or departure point, so do not take boats from here to Gabon. For this you will need to head to nearby Cogo to be stamped out of the country.

ELOBEY GRANDE AND ELOBEY CHICO The larger of the Elobey islands sits 10km off the Equatoguinean coast at the entrance to the Río Muni estuary. With an area

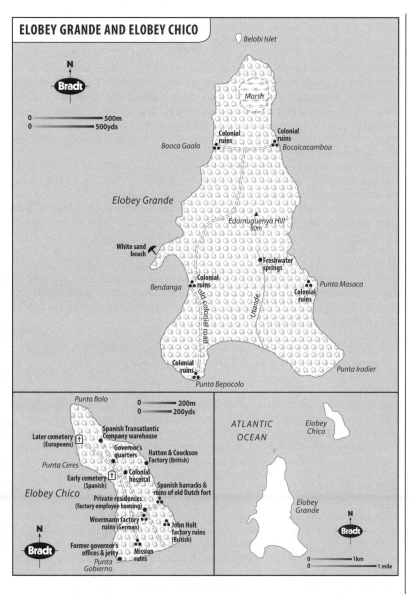

of just over 2km², it has no permanent inhabitants and is covered in dense jungle. Sitting 1km to its northeast is the smaller of the island pair, Elobey Chico. At 190m² it is truly tiny, and also has no inhabitants beyond the odd visiting fisherman. Although neither island is of any importance today, 400 years ago Elobey Chico was the central hub of an intercontinental commercial network, the archaeological traces of which are superbly preserved in its overgrown jungles.

History Archaeological evidence suggests that the Elobey islands have been visited by humans for thousands of years. More recently, they were part of the king of the Benga's territory, along with Corisco and some mainland coastal settlements such as Cogo. The islands were likely first spotted by the Portuguese explorer Lopes Gonçalves in 1475 as he was sailing along the African coast from Ghana down to Cape Lopez (modern day Port-Gentil in Gabon). Upon discovery, the whole estuary area became a scene of intense economic activity and competition between the various Western powers, particularly the Spanish, Dutch, Portuguese and British, desperate for access to African raw materials and slaves. In 1641, the Dutch set up a permanent trading post on the Río Muni mainland, and in 1648 the Portuguese built the Fort of Ponta Joko on nearby Corisco. In collaboration with the nearby Benga population, they used this island to manage slaving operations on the mainland until the early 19th century.

From their coastal bases the Ndowe peoples acted as middle men in the trade between Europeans and groups from the interior such as the Fang. In 1843, King Bonkoro I signed an agreement with the Spanish authorities formalising this commercial collaboration and indirect rule. The Elobey islands were the base for numerous trading companies, such as the Woermann Company, founded in Hamburg in 1837. European business interests preferred to locate their staff on the islands rather than the mainland due to the healthier climate and lack of tropical diseases.

In 1875, the Spanish arrangement with the Benga lapsed and was replaced by direct rule through a Spanish crown representative. When Spanish explorer Manuel Iradier visited the Elobey islands that year in preparation for exploring the region, he described the settlement on Elobey Chico as:

A real town with magnificent and comfortable buildings, numerous outbuildings, gardens and paths, forges and workshops always in use and a good dry dock.

From 1885 to 1926, Elobey Chico served as the administrative capital of the region, while the larger island hosted only a few man made structures. The Elobey islands were lumped together with Corisco and Annobón for governance purposes, and featured their own series of postage stamps which are coveted by collectors today. However, when the seat of government was moved to nearby Cogo, the islands were slowly abandoned, and remain so to this day.

Getting there and away It is possible to hire a **boat** to reach Elobey Grande or Elobey Chico from Acalayong or Cogo. The journey from Cogo to Elobey Grande is around 25km and can take 2 hours depending on your engine size. From Corisco a journey by boat is around 20km. If you are heading to Elobey Grande, fishermen will want to drop you on the southern or western shores, as the eastern side features a number of dangerous sand banks. Being dropped at Punta Bepocolo is probably more convenient if you want to walk the length of the island. For Elobey Chico, ask to be dropped at Punta Gobierno or the Spanish barracks.

In both cases prices are not fixed and you will need to negotiate for this unusual experience. Local fishermen often make the journey in pirogue but this is not recommended as the sea can get rough at the river mouth. Also be sure to make proper arrangements for getting picked up again as you may not be able to get a mobile phone signal out here!

What to see The islands are an archaeological treasure chest, especially Elobey Chico. They are also both tiny, with Elobey Grande less than 2.5km long and Elobey Chico less than 1km long, making them easy to explore once you arrive, assuming you can navigate the thick jungle cover.

On Elobey Grande you can hack your way through the jungle following the old colonial road from the southernmost point of **Punta Bepocolo** all the way up to the northern colonial outposts of **Booca Gaalo** and **Bocaicacamboa**. There was another small colonial structure over in the east at **Punta Masaca** but this is more difficult to reach. The entire island is heavily forested and there is little trace left of the limited human settlement it experienced during colonial times, but if you walk up **Edumuguenya Hill**, the highest point on the island, it should offer scenic views over the bay. There is also a great beach on the western point above **Bendanga**. Note that the ruins on Elobey Grande are much smaller and less well preserved than those on Elobey Chico, as there were never many permanent inhabitants on the larger of the two islands.

For colonial enthusiasts, Elobey Chico is the real reason to visit this area. Here you will find rusted cannons over by the **Spanish barracks** and overgrown multi-storey structures once used as warehouses, sawmills or offices for German, British and Spanish companies such as **Hatton and Coockson**, **Woermann**, **John Holt** and the **Spanish Transatlantic Company**. There are also **private residences**, a small **colonial hospital**, as well as religious buildings built for **missionaries**. There is even an isolation ward that was used for colonists suffering from sleeping sickness. The level of preservation of certain items is impressive: you can read the labelling on 100-year-old bottles of gin, or make out the name on Frederick Ely's grave, dated to 1911 over in the **later cemetery** which features the graves of numerous Europeans who worked on the islands.

CORISCO (MANDJI)

Corisco, known to the local inhabitants as Mandji, is a 14km^2 island located at the entrance of the Río Muni estuary, 44km offshore from Cogo, near the maritime border with Gabon. The population of the island numbers around 3,000 and is of the Benga ethnic group. As with the nearby Elobey islands, Corisco played an important role in the colonial history of the region. Over the past decade the government has poured investment into the island in the form of infrastructure projects such as an international airport, luxury hotels and a new port facility, in order to make it a special ecotourism zone. The stated eventual aim is to implement a special visa-free regime for the island, allowing visitors to come and enjoy the idyllic surroundings without the red tape associated with obtaining a visa. Until the planned hordes of tourists arrive, you will find Corisco to be a very quiet island, with the majority of inhabitants living over in the southwestern section, around the settlement of Combo. The airport runway runs exactly north–south over by the eastern shoreline and serves as a good reference point for navigation.

History Archaeological evidence suggests that the island was inhabited from around AD50 to 1200. The earliest known society, called the Oveng in this region, left material remains in the form of worked iron and pottery. For unknown reasons the island was gradually abandoned until the arrival of the Portuguese in the 1470s. Although the Benga are the current inhabitants, they were not on the island originally and were likely only attracted to move there due to the commercial opportunities afforded by the European presence.

By the mid 17th century, the whole estuary area (including Corisco and the Elobey islands) began to fill with Spanish, Dutch, Portuguese and British traders, all keen to seek their fortune from trading African raw materials and slaves. In 1648, the Portuguese built a fort on nearby Corisco to protect their territory from aggressive Dutch expansion in the region. From 1723 onwards, through the newly created Corisco Company, the Portuguese co-operated with local Ndowe groups in

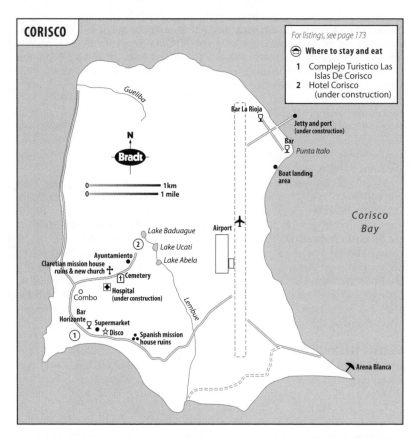

For listings, see page 173

CORISCO

Where to stay and eat
1 Complejo Turistico Las
   Islas De Corisco
2 Hotel Corisco
   (under construction)

Bar La Rioja

Jetty and port
(under construction)

Bar
Punta Italo

Boat landing
area

N

Bradt

0 ━━━━━━ 1km
0 ━━━━━━ 1 mile

Lake Baduague
Lake Ucati
Lake Abela

Airport

Corisco
Bay

Ayuntamiento
Claretian mission house
ruins & new church
Cemetery
Hospital
(under construction)
Combo
Bar
Horizonte
Supermarket
Disco
Spanish mission
house ruins

Guellba

Lembue

Arena Blanca

the trafficking of mainland African slaves across the Atlantic. In 1724, 550 slaves were processed through Corisco, shipped across the Atlantic and sold in Brazil.

The Spanish continued this commercial collaboration first with slaves and later with other products once they took over Fernando Pó in the late 18th century. They even signed an 1843 agreement with the Benga king, Bonkoro I, formalising his indirect rule on their behalf. It was not until 1875 that the Spanish began to rule directly through a crown representative, and in 1947 the last king of Corisco, Santiago Uganda, was stripped of his authority after presenting visiting Spanish ministers with a list of grievances against Spanish rule. You can visit his grave in the cemetery at the southwest of the island.

During the early years of independence the islanders were severely neglected by President Macías, who refused to send aid during a cholera epidemic on the island which killed over 10% of the population. While things are certainly better today, the local people have still had to become highly self-sufficient, or rely on Gabon for support in certain fields such as education. You will find some islanders have studied at university in Libreville (which is only 55km away) or have relatives over the Gabonese border.

Getting there and away Although Corisco International Airport was inaugurated in late 2011 at an announced cost of US$270 million, it still does not have an air traffic control tower and no commercial flight has ever landed there.

Some locals have talked of an Air France plane coming in from Libreville to test the suitability of the runway, but it is unclear exactly when foreign visitors will be able to take advantage of this large airport, or the promised visa-free regime for the island.

Currently the only reliable way to reach Corisco is on a SOMAGEC **ferry** from Cogo (page 167). There is a small shack right by the boat landing area which serves as both a departures lounge and a bar. Given that it is often raining at departure time, this is welcome shelter.

It costs 10,000CFA for a one-way speedboat to Libreville, Gabon, but it is unclear how you would stamp out of Equatorial Guinea when doing this as there does not appear to be a customs office. This is not recommended although a number of expatriates working on the island have done it.

Getting around   Assuming you arrive on a SOMAGEC boat, you will be dropped at the jetty in the northeast section of the island. Entry procedures are very relaxed (ie: non-existent) and you will not be required to register your presence or trek to the Ayuntamiento (Town Hall) to announce your arrival.

The only vehicles on the island belong to SOMAGEC, so hitchhiking or walking are your only options. This is not a problem, as the island is very small and there is always construction traffic running along the only road, so stick out your thumb and eventually one of the Moroccan workers will pick you up.

From Punta Italo, the northeastern point of the island, where a lot of the construction workers live, there is a construction track leading inland straight to the runway. The runway is your best waypoint if you ever get lost. It is impossible to miss as at over 3.5km, it is almost as long as the island itself and required a lot of forest clearance. It forms the main north–south link on the east side of the island and is perfectly safe to walk (or drive) along given the complete lack of air traffic. There is a road leading east from the southern portion of the runway to the beach of Arena Blanca, and west to the main settlements on the opposite coastline and the new luxury developments. The main waterway on the island is the small Lembue River in the south. It has three small lakes on it.

Where to stay and eat   *See map, page 172.*
There is only one functional hotel on the island at present, **Complejo Turistico Las Islas De Corisco** (*12 rooms; Pueblo Esperanza;* m *222 272 737, 222 274 932;* **$$**). Rooms have a toilet, shower, air conditioning, a fridge and a double bed. The hotel is in a great spot overlooking the southwest coastline, and has a restaurant (**$$**) and an outdoor bar area. Food is simple but tasty with lots of fish on the menu.

The **Hotel Corisco** (*60 rooms;* **$$$$$**) e jg@jgcontract.com; is currently under construction and will be the best place to stay on the island when it is completed in late 2016. Situated in a clearing near the centre of the island, it features a number of stand-alone single-storey structures with slanted roofs, in a very modern style. There is also a proposed new five-star hotel planned at **Arena Blanca**, although construction had not begun at the time of writing.

Entertainment and nightlife   The only electricity on the island is from generators, so make sure you get where you need to go before it gets dark. **Bar Horizonte** over in the village of **Combo** is a popular local spot for a beer, and is right next to the SOMAGEC housing complex, so there is usually a crowd in the evenings. Just down the road is a cramped, sweaty **disco** that blasts music until the early hours. **Complejo Turistico Las Islas De Corisco** also has a bar and a better view than Bar Horizonte.

On the other side of the island at **Punta Italo** is the beachfront **Bar La Rioja** run by Rafael (m *551 919 768*). Clientele is a mixture of the Chinese construction workers who live on that side of the island and local men. It's a very simple setup with a few bits of driftwood and some benches, but there is a good atmosphere.

Other practicalities There is almost **no phone signal** on the island, unless you stand on the eastern beaches, in which case you will be able to roam on the Gabonese network.

There is a **supermarket** (⊕ *hrs are erratic*) at the west of the island which sells a selection of canned and dried goods but you are better off asking in the villages if you want fresh produce. The hospital is currently under construction, so in the event of a medical emergency your best bet is to head to the SOMAGEC housing complex opposite Bar Horizonte and ask for help.

What to see and do **Arena Blanca** is the highlight of the island. A 1km-long sand bar stretching out into the Atlantic, the sand is pure white and the sea is crystal clear on both sides. Aerial photos of this beach are on display in many of Equatorial Guinea's airports. This is a favourite spot for SOMAGEC workers to picnic at the weekends, but outside this time you are likely to have it all to yourself. If you stand on the southern shoreline, you can see the contested island of Mbañe (page 3) around 10km away, along with the islets of Conga and Cocoteros.

There are a number of colonial ruins on the island, including those of a **Spanish mission house** and the overgrown **Claretian mission house**, which sadly burned down in the 1940s. These all date back to the time between 1885 and 1926 when nearby Elobey Chico served as the administrative capital of the region and there were more than 1,000 European traders, soldiers, colonial authorities and missionaries living across the islands.

Corisco International Airport is also interesting to explore. It feels very strange to walk around on a runway big enough to accommodate an Airbus A380. The terminal building is also unlocked, so you can wander around, or even look at the Moroccan-themed presidential terminal next door (although trying to enter this is not recommended).

There is a dirt **football** pitch over in Combo, where the majority of people live. The **fishing** in the area is also excellent, both from the beaches such as Arena Blanca and also using a pirogue. The island is great for **hiking** and it is very difficult to get lost, but beware of snakes. There are a number of venomous species on the island and there are many sections of long grass and jungle for them to hide in.

GUIDEBOOK UPDATES

You can read the latest updates and make suggestions of your own by following @BradtEGguide on Twitter or by posting a comment on the Bradt website at www.bradtupdates/eguinea.

6

Annobón (Pagalu) Province

Without an understanding of the colonial history of this region, it makes little sense that Annobón is a territory of Equatorial Guinea. It is 480km southwest of Corisco, separated from the rest of the nation by a vast stretch of the Atlantic Ocean, as well as the island of São Tomé. Annobón is an extinct volcanic island that measures just 17.5km^2, meaning you can walk across it in only a few hours. It is home to an isolated population of a few thousand residents, who speak Fá d'Ambô, a Portuguese Creole that hints at their unusual ancestry. Historically marginalised, today Annobón is changing at a rapid pace thanks to a construction boom on the island spurred on by the completion of the new airport in 2010. Head to Annobón for trekking across the volcanic scenery, whale watching and to enjoy some pristine golden beaches. Landing at the tiny capital of San Antonio de Palé on the northern tip of the island, nearly everything you need is within walking distance and if not you can always jump in a boat to explore the even smaller southern settlements. Circumnavigating the island in a decent boat takes less than 2 hours! It has never been easier to explore the least visited part of Equatorial Guinea.

HISTORY

Annobón is the southernmost island of a volcanic chain that extends into Cameroon, and is now extinct. It was uninhabited before the 16th century and can be found 160km from São Tomé and 355km off the coast of Gabon.

Sources conflict over when and by whom it was discovered. Sightings appear in the records of Spanish and Portuguese explorers as early as 1470 (eg: by Spanish explorer Diego Ramirez de la Diaz, or Portuguese explorers Pêro Escobar and João de Santarém). However, Ruy de Sequiera was likely the first person to set foot on the island in 1473/74, in the name of the king of Portugal. The name of the island derives from 'Ano Bom' (meaning 'good year' in Portuguese), and was reportedly used as it was discovered on New Year's Day.

For 150 years the island appeared on European maps, but lay uninhabited. From the 16th century onwards, the island was occupied by a deputy governor from São Tomé and slaves from Angola brought by Portuguese traders. Annobón became an important waypoint in the transatlantic slave trade, between export points such as Angola and destinations such as Central and South America. Passing ships could also stop to reprovision with water and fresh oranges (useful for preventing scurvy), which were abundant on the island. While the brutal slave trade continued, various attempts were made by missionaries to spread Catholicism on the island – starting in 1645 – but they were unsuccessful due to the hostility of the population. In 1774, the French slave ship *Duc de Gretagne* suffered a slave revolt while off Annobón, which resulted in the deaths of four crewmen.

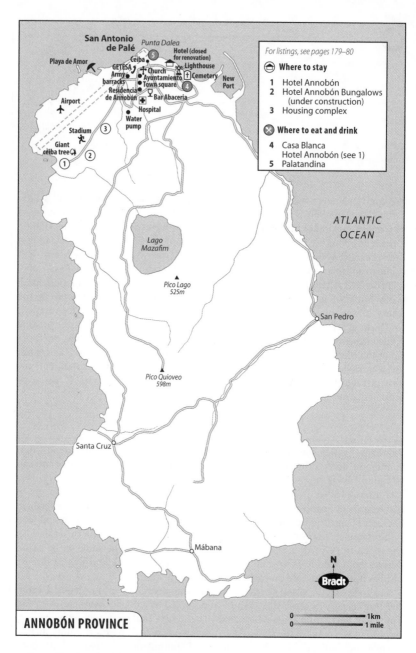

San Antonio
de Palé

Punta Dalea

Playa de Amor

Ceiba

Hotel (closed
for renovation)

Lighthouse

GETESA
Army
barracks

Church

Ayuntamiento

Cemetery

New
Port

Residencia
de Annobón

Town square

Bar Abaceria

Airport

Hospital

Water
pump

Stadium

Giant
ceiba tree

3

1

2

Lago
Mazafim

ATLANTIC
OCEAN

Pico Lago
525m

San Pedro

Pico Quioveo
598m

Santa Cruz

Mábana

N

Bradt

ANNOBÓN PROVINCE

0   1km
0   1 mile

For listings, see pages 179–80

Where to stay

1   Hotel Annobón
2   Hotel Annobón Bungalows
     (under construction)
3   Housing complex

Where to eat and drink

4   Casa Blanca
     Hotel Annobón (see 1)
5   Palatandina

In 1778, after the Treaty of El Pardo was signed, the island was lumped together with Corisco and mainland Equatorial Guinea and handed over to the Spanish. The new imperial power got off to a shaky start, as Felipe de Santos Toro, leader of the first official Spanish delegation to the island in 1778, is believed to have been killed by a group of Annobónese resistant to their new colonial masters. Spanish sources at the time, attempting to cover up this embarrassing development, stated that he died from fever. Little economic activity developed under the Spanish beyond slaving transit, with sugarcane introduction failing and most islanders engaged in subsistence agriculture and fishing. Some islanders produced a canvas material from the ceiba tree which they exported to São Tomé.

Given the lack of profits emanating from the small island, between 1827 and 1840 the Spanish government made various attempts to sell Annobón (generously packaged with Fernando Pó) to the British, for around 4.7 million reales. They almost reached a deal, but then had to back down due to the hostility of Spanish public opinion. By this time Annobón had developed a distinct society very different from that of the mainland or Fernando Pó. The original Angolan slaves (named *escravos de resgate* by their Portuguese masters) had mixed with the small transient European population. The offspring of these unions, dubbed *forros* ('slaves about to be released'), occupied a higher socioeconomic position than their fully African cousins, much like the *Emancipados* of the mainland. The *forros* developed their own Creole language, known as Fá d'Ambô, which is similar to the Portuguese Creole spoken on São Tomé. By 1836, a *forro* by the name of Pedro Pomba was even governor of the island, and most residents still thought of themselves as Portuguese rather than Spanish subjects.

In the later 19th century Annobón remained as quiet as ever, only showing up in the historical record due to the odd visit from a naturalist or explorer. After the Berlin Conference in 1885 the Spanish put a little more effort into occupying their colony, allowing a series of Claretin missionaries to set themselves up there. For the next 25 years the only Europeans permanently on the island were these missionaries (always numbering less than ten) and a small detachment of the Guardia Civil.

It was around the turn of the 20th century when French, British and Norwegian whalers began taking an interest in the autumn rainy season humpback whale migration around Annobón. The whales were known to circle the island for weeks, and had been traditionally hunted in pirogues with harpoons. By 1926, larger commercial operations had decimated whale stocks in the area and were forced to abandon their efforts.

Spanish Civil War tensions spilled over briefly on to the island when visiting governor general, Gustavo Sostoa y Sthamer, was assassinated by Sergeant Castilla, who at the time was the most senior Spanish colonial representative living on the island. It is said that the killing was linked to Castilla's impending dismissal due to his Republican leanings. Beyond this though there was no conflict on the island during this period of upheaval in Spanish society.

In the run up to independence, the Annobónese took part in the same arguments as other Equatoguineans as to whether to split the constituent parts of the country into independent nations, or construct a federal system at independence. On 30 October 1967, the Constitutional Conference on Equatorial Guinea was convened in Madrid to discuss these issues. Santiago Mun and V Castellon Ntayo represented the Annobónese at the negotiations. By the time of the elections on 22 September 1968 – which would choose the first national parliament for the newly independent nation – it was agreed that Annobón would get two elected deputies, from the total of 35. The Movement for the National Unity of Equatorial Guinea or MUNGE won both seats on the island.

The island residents suffered greatly under the reign of President Macías. In 1973, he arbitrarily changed the name of their home to Pagalu, which means cockerel in Portuguese Creole, after one of the election symbols Macías had used in the past. That same year there was a cholera outbreak on the island, which killed 192 of the 400 inhabitants. Macías refused to allow foreign aid workers on to the island to help, and when the residents appealed to Gabon for assistance, he is said to have punished them by sending in the army to execute some survivors. In 1976, all able-bodied males were deported and taken to Bioko to work in the cocoa plantations as forced labour, to make up for the departure of Nigerian workers. The underpopulated island then became a Soviet naval base for the next three years, until the end of Macías's rule.

The initial years under President Obiang were characterised by neglect. Resupply ships from the mainland often came only once a year and even then, there were no proper port facilities for medium or large ships to dock. A dirt strip runway was tagged on to the side of the small island, but at only 600m, with the end of the runway dropping into the ocean, it was an extremely hairy landing that only the most risk-hardened Soviet aviators would attempt.

In March 1988, President Obiang's government signed an agreement with a French company to allow the dumping of toxic waste on Annobón. In May, another agreement was signed with British company Emvatrex of Buckinghamshire. They rented 200ha of land on the island, on which they hoped to dig a big hole and dump two million drums of mixed chemical wastes from Europe. Greenpeace alleged that this hole was dug by convict labour. After international outcry and a diplomatic mission from neighbouring Nigeria, the agreement was eventually suspended, although it is unclear if any waste was actually dumped. However, in 1994 there were reports in the Swiss press that the government had made around US$200 million from a deal which allowed the dumping of both radioactive and toxic waste on the island by Western waste-disposal companies. Rare eyewitness accounts from people on the island attested to the storage of radioactive elements on the coast, although access for foreign visitors was very difficult due to a military blockade. As under Macías, offers of foreign aid were refused, the islanders were kept isolated and there was evidence of an increase in leukaemia, ulcers and abscesses among the population, as noted by a visiting German agronomist, German news magazine *Der Spiegel* and the Basel Action Network.

In recent years, however, things have improved for the inhabitants of the island and there have been no further reports of hazardous waste dumping. The government has invested over 200 billion CFA francs to develop the island in line with its Horizon2020 plan. On 11 October 2010, a brand new airport and port facility were opened as part of the Independence Day celebrations. The extended runway (which now juts into the northern coast) was a welcome addition, as in 2008 a plane ended up in the sea due to overshooting the short runway when coming in to land. It is now possible to reach the island regularly by plane or ferry, and there are a number of accommodation options open to tourists. Those fond of jungle hiking will also be pleased to hear that Annobón is the only territory in Equatorial Guinea with no venomous snakes (although it does have scorpions).

GETTING THERE AND AWAY

BY AIR   **Ceiba Intercontinental Airlines** fly to Annobón from Bata on Fridays and Mondays. Tickets cost 125,000CFA and can be booked only from the Bata airport ticket office (page 150), not the offices in central Bata or Malabo. It is also only possible to book on the day of departure, so get to the airport early or ask a travel agent. The flight leaves around 08.40 and is usually empty (perhaps due to the price). The journey takes 90 minutes and often experiences turbulence.

When you leave Annobón, be sure to reserve a seat on the plane the morning of departure by going to the Ceiba Intercontinental Airlines office. You will then check-in normally at the airport later that day.

BY BOAT There is a highly irregular **ferry** service to Annobón from both Cogo and Corisco, which is operated by the SOMAGEC construction company. It is free, but takes three days and there are no beds on the old Greek passenger ferries they use, so be sure to bring something to sleep on. Ask at the SOMAGEC offices in Cogo (which are on the jetty; see page 168) for more information on schedules. SOMAGEC also sometimes send a plane or boat to nearby São Tomé, which visitors might be able to hitch a lift on.

Sometimes an official government ferry calls at Annobón (either the *Djiblooh* or the *San Valentin*). Departures are from Malabo and Bata. The whole arrangement is shrouded in mystery and seemingly impossible to book.

GETTING AROUND

The only vehicles on the island are owned by the SOMAGEC construction company (who also happen to be the only importers of petrol). Your main means of transport will therefore either be hitchhiking, walking or taking a pirogue around the island. The place is tiny and there are few proper roads anyway so this is not a problem.

ARRANGING TOURS

Friendly local airport official **Arevayo** (m *222 062 663*) is able to arrange custom tours of the island, as well as accommodation and boat hire. He speaks Spanish and will always be at the airport to collect you as he works there! If you are unable to reach him, his brother **Oscar** (m *551 320 110*) is based in Malabo, speaks good English and can also make arrangements on your behalf.

WHERE TO STAY   *See map, page 176.*

There is only one hotel on the island, the **Hotel Annobón** (*55 rooms;* e *info@ hotelAnnobón.com; http://hotelAnnobón.com;* **$$$**). It is a slightly dilapidated pink building on the northwestern cliffs, but it has a lot of charm. You will be the only tourist, but there are a few long-term residents working on the SOMAGEC construction projects to keep you company. Rooms cost 50,000CFA and include breakfast, air conditioning, TV, a balcony with sea views, a fridge, a shower and bath, and a laundry service. Suites are 65,000CFA and include a small kitchen. There is a restaurant, bar, conference room and tennis court on site.

If you want to save money, there is a **housing complex** on the road to the Hotel Annobón, which has a number of holiday homes owned by wealthier Annobónese. They spend most of the year on the mainland and only visit in December. Outside these times, you can rent one of the houses for 20,000CFA per night with the help of Arrevayo (see above). The houses have a living room, a kitchen with a fridge freezer and two bedrooms that come equipped with large double beds and air conditioning. This is great value for money (**$**), but note that there is often no running water, and the electricity only comes on for a few hours at set times of the day (usually in the evenings). Local inhabitants will be able to tell you the current power schedule, and if there is no running water you can always walk to the nearby water pump to stock up.

There is a new luxury hotel under construction called the **Hotel Annobón Bungalows**. When complete in late 2016, this 9,000m² facility will be the most modern on the island. There is also a hotel on the northern beach which is currently closed for renovation.

Annobón (Pagalu) Province WHERE TO STAY

6

✗ WHERE TO EAT AND DRINK *See map, page 176.*

Finding food on the island is an issue, especially if you do not have a kitchen in which to prepare meals. The area around the town square and Residencia de Annobón has a few **street stalls** selling some fresh produce, but it is difficult to make a meal out of a pancake, doughnut, banana and tomatoes. In the evenings the fishermen will sometimes grill their catch on the beach by **Punta Dalea**, so ask around and you might get some barbecued food.

✗ **Hotel Annobón** ⏰ 07.00–09.00, noon–14.00 & 19.00–20.30 daily. This hotel restaurant (page 179) offers a 1-course set menu for 5,000CFA or a 3-course meal for 15,000CFA. The logistical issues associated with stocking the kitchen mean you can expect a lot of fish. The bar offers snacks & drinks but tends to run low on everything towards the end of the month, just before the resupply ship comes in. During my stay the 2 options were strawberry Fanta or Heineken. **$$$**

✗ **Casa Blanca Restaurant** On a ledge overlooking San Antonio de Palé; ⏰ hrs are erratic & highly dependent on when they have fresh produce. One of the best places on the island to eat dinner, where you can enjoy a delicious fish meal with a refreshing beer. **$$**

✗ **Palatandina Restaurant** Down by the beach in San Antonio de Palé. Has a limited selection of local dishes, but is often closed due to a lack of produce. **$**

ENTERTAINMENT AND NIGHTLIFE

Owing to the lack of electricity, things get pretty quiet on the island after dark, but there are a few spots with generators or batteries that keep going into the evening. In addition to the Abaceria, the bar in the **Hotel Annobón** usually has a few people in it and the bar staff are very friendly.

♀ **Bar Abaceria** ⏰ 17.00–01.00 daily. This is a popular nightspot, with a TV which usually shows sports, & the beers are cold and plentiful. Just over the road there is a games room run by a

couple of local lads & for 500CFA you can head in & play on the pool table, table football table or the PlayStation 2, which runs off a car battery.

OTHER PRACTICALITIES

Upon arrival, be sure to **register** with both the police chief (in the airport terminal building) and at the Ayuntamiento (Town Hall), which is opposite the church. The process is generally friendly and hassle-free. Give them both a copy of your Tourism Permit.

There are no ATMs anywhere on the island, and it is a **cash only** economy. There is also no internet anywhere on the island and no 3G phone signal, but it is possible to make phone calls and send text messages. You can buy phone credit over at the **GETESA** office.

WHAT TO SEE AND DO

The main attraction here is the unspoilt coastline, where you can enjoy **swimming**, **fishing** and **snorkelling**. You can hire a boat from the northern shore as long as you head over early enough, or make arrangements through Arevayo (page 179). There are also great **hiking** opportunities. It is easy to hike up the extinct volcano from San Antonio de Palé to Lago Mazafim. This scenic stretch of water has religious significance to the local community as the home of various spirits and as such you are not allowed to bathe in it, although walking around the perimeter and taking photos is fine. It may also be possible to climb to the summit of Pico Quioveo, although this would require ropes and climbing gear. This whole central portion of the island is a natural reserve, and the good news is that there are no venomous snakes, so hiking is perfectly safe. The settlements of **San Pedro**, **Santa Cruz** and **Mábana** can be reached on foot, although it might be easier to take a boat. Here people live in simple wooden shacks on the mountainside and practise subsistence agriculture and fishing.

There are few signs of colonialism (whether Spanish or Portuguese) on the island. Even the **Iglesia Parroquial Corazón de Maria** church looks new, having been completely renovated and inaugurated in 2010. However, you will find the ruins of the **old jetty** on the north coast, as well as a colonial **lighthouse** and a **cemetery** containing some 19th-century European graves.

There is an impressive **giant ceiba tree** on the road to the Hotel Annobón. This has been spared from the destruction of the building site around it as, like the lake in the centre of the island, it is believed to be sacred. There is another large tree by Punta Dalea, where you can sit and watch the fishermen at work on the northeastern shore. The entire beach is covered with pirogues which head out twice a day. There used to be some excellent surf breaking on to Punta Dalea, but now the new port is blocking it. You might still be able to find a few sets to the east of this obstruction with the right swell though.

For those hoping to relax whilst on the island, **Playa de Amor**, just to the west of the runway, is a quiet secluded beach with clear waters and bright-white sand. Here you can see children playing in small dugout canoes and the occasional fisherman land his catch of sea snails. There are rocks nearby that make it great for snorkelling and it is not too deep, so ideal for swimming too.

There is an army barracks filled with very bored soldiers located by the tunnel going under the end of the runway. They are always playing football on the patch of grass in front of their quarters, and might welcome an additional player. The stadium football pitch is probably the best place for organised sports, although it is technically in the middle of a construction site (that of the new hospital).

WHALE WATCHING Humpback whales (*Megaptera novaeangliae*) migrate northwards from their summer feeding grounds in the higher latitudes to their winter breeding grounds in the warmer, shallower waters of the tropics. They pass Annobón in the autumn each year, usually between July and October, and are known to circle the island for weeks at a time. You can see them from the shore, especially if you climb to a higher vantage point on the slope behind San Antonio de Palé or hire a boat and get closer. If you do head out to sea to see them in a vessel, do not approach closer than 100m to any whale or 50m to any dolphin. There is also an annual whale hunt, for which the islanders are famous, in which one whale is killed. Killing such a large creature using traditional methods is a complex endeavour which requires a huge amount of manpower. The islander striking the final blow is said to have to wear a mask, to prevent the animal's spirit knowing who it was that killed them.

EQUATORIAL GUINEA ONLINE

For additional online content, articles, photos and more on Equatorial Guinea, why not visit www.bradtguides.com/eguinea.

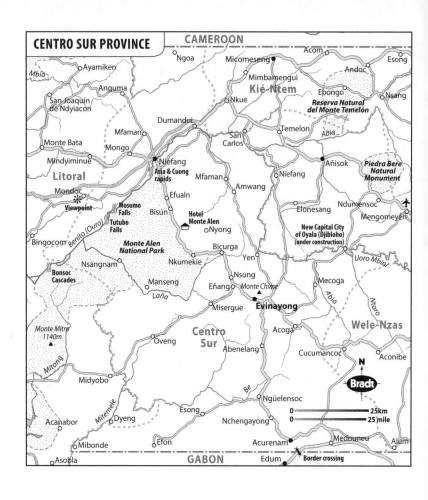

CENTRO SUR PROVINCE

CAMEROON

Ngoa
Acom
Esong
Ayamiken
Micomeseng
Andoc
Mbia
Mimbamengui
Anguma
Kié-Ntem
Ebongo
Nsang
San Joaquín
de Ndyiacon
Nkue
Reserva Natural
del Monte Temelón
Dumandui
Temelon
Abia
Mfaman
San
Carlos
Monte Bata
Mongo
Niefang
Añisok
Mindyiminue
Niefang
Asía & Cuong
rapids
Piedra Bere
Natural
Monument
Litoral
Mfaman
Mondoc
Efualn
Amwang
Mosumo
Falls
Bisún
Efonesang
Ndumensoc
Viewpoint
Hotel
Monte Alen
Mengomeyén
Tutubo
Falls
Nyong
New Capital City
of Oyala (Djibloho)
(under construction)
Bingocom
Monte Alen
National Park
Bicurga
Yen
Nsangnam
Nkumekie
Uoro Mbia
Bonsoc
Cascades
Manseng
Nsung
Mecoga
Laña
Eñang
Monte Chime
Abia
Ntoro
Misergue
Evinayong
Monte Mitra
1140m
Oveng
Centro
Sur
Acoga
Wele-Nzas
Abenelang
Cucumancoc
Aconibe
Mitong
Midyobo
Be
N
Bradt
Esong
Ngüelensoc
0   25km
0   25 mile
Acanabor
Mitemele
Dyeng
Nchengayong
Mibonde
Efon
Acurenam
Medouneu
Alum
Asobla
GABON
Edum
Border crossing

7

Centro Sur Province

Centro Sur Province is found in mainland Río Muni. A high plateau looking down over the coast, this is a lush green region of hills and mountains and is home to the most famous national park in the country, Monte Alen.

The province is sandwiched between Litoral Province to the west, Wele-Nzas Province in the southeast and Kié-Ntem Province in the northeast. Its northern extent forms the border with Cameroon, and crossing here brings you into Cameroon's South Province. To the south you find Gabon's Estuaire and Woleu-Ntem provinces. Official government estimates put the population of the province at 125,856, with the most populous town being Niefang, followed closely by the provincial capital of Evinayong. The border town of Akúrenam is the next largest settlement.

The Benito River flows through this area, and forms much of the province's northeastern border. This area is dominated by the Fang ethnic group, with Ntumu Fang in the north and Okak Fang in the south. In this region, up by the border with Cameroon, is it also possible to find Bakola-Bagyeli Pygmy tribes.

HISTORY

Archaeological excavations carried out by UNED (the Spanish National University of Distance Education) and George Washington University in the late 1990s revealed a wealth of Middle Stone Age sites along the Uoro River, which runs near the road leading from Niefang to Bata. This is evidence that Centro Sur has been inhabited by humans for millennia.

The whole of Centro Sur Province was historically occupied by Pygmy groups, such as the few remaining Bakola-Bagyeli. However, over time they were displaced by recurrent waves of Bantu migration from other parts of Africa. The Ndowe arrived between the 12th and 14th centuries from the Congo area, choosing to base themselves in the coastal Litoral Province. The Fang were later arrivals, possibly making the long migration from Nigeria down into Cameroon and Equatorial Guinea during the 17th and 18th centuries. There is a long history of conflict between the coastal groups of Litoral Province and the inland Fang, which limited Fang settlement of coastal areas for many years. The traditional demarcation line of Fang territory became the village of Niefang (meaning 'limit of the Fang'), which is around 55km directly inland from Bata, and now acts as the road hub for accessing other inland provinces as well as the provincial capital of Evinayong.

There is little evidence of Europeans venturing inland from Litoral Province before the 19th century. The few traders that were present in this region tended to stick to the southwest coast and the islands (Corisco, Elobeyes, etc), letting the indigenous Ndowe act as intermediaries for trade with the inland tribes.

Things began to change when Spanish explorer Julio Pellón toured the Río Muni coast in 1860, producing detailed maps, but it was not until Manuel Iradier's journeys that Europeans began to venture into inland Río Muni. In 1875, Iradier began a journey of over two years, using Elobey Grande as his base. He explored Corisco, travelled up the river Muni and the river Bañe and hiked into the Crystal Mountains which straddle the border between Equatorial Guinea and Gabon. During subsequent journeys he produced maps and made notes on the ethnography and languages of the areas he visited. He also travelled the left bank of the river Muni as well as the river Utamboni, and followed the Utongo River to its navigable limit. His was the most detailed exploration thus far of inland Río Muni, and a statue of him could still be seen in Cogo until independence, when it was removed as an unwanted symbol of Spanish colonialism. Numerous other scientists and adventurers followed in his footsteps, such as Amado Osorio (1884), Luis Sorela (1887) and José Valero Belenguer (1890), hoping to map out one of Africa's last 'blank spaces' or find exotic new species.

Before the beginning of the 20th century, European settlers had hardly penetrated into mainland Río Muni, and the Spanish showed no signs of wishing to occupy the space. However, in part to compensate for its losses in South America and the Philippines, and partly due to the encroachment of French, British and German interests, Spain soon started taking more of an interest in the area. In 1907, Río Muni was divided up into six administrative zones, and a Guardia Colonial (Civil Guard – a military force performing police duties) was created to protect them. In the 1920s, after the Liberian forced labour scandal (page 19), the governor of Fernando Pó, General Miguel Nuñez del Prado, militarily occupied the whole of Río Muni and press-ganged upwards of 4,000 Fang men at a time into unpaid public works projects, mainly building bridges and roads into the interior. He also shipped over 4,500 men over to Fernando Pó to work on the cocoa plantations. The most prominent of the colonial works in Centro Sur Province was the colonial road, which extended inland from Bata, but has since been replaced by the more modern Bata to Mongomo Highway.

In 1916, during World War I, Centro Sur Province acted as a transit point for the defeated German army as it retreated from Cameroon, which had been occupied by British and French forces. The soldiers, numbering over 6,000, eventually made their way to Mbini to surrender to Spanish care. Later, during the Spanish Civil War, Centro Sur saw none of the admittedly limited fighting that Bioko or Litoral Province did.

The 1938 statute of the Patronato de Indígenas (page 20), which set out a vision for the future of the colonised peoples, led to much construction on the mainland. The run up to independence, however, saw an even greater flurry of development in inland Río Muni, as the Spanish rushed to build roads, schools and hospitals in a bid to buy off the nationalists. Today, Niefang, Evinayong and Akúrenam all have surviving remnants of this colonial building spree.

Under Macías the province suffered in much the same way as the other provinces did. However, the inhabitants were fortunate to have escape routes available to them in the north (to Cameroon) and the south (to Gabon), with upwards of 90,000 citizens choosing to flee by 1976. Under President Obiang the human rights situation improved, but the influx of oil wealth has not been felt in this province as it has in the coastal regions and on Bioko island. Industrial expansion has tended to focus around Malabo and Bata, although people living in Centro Sur Province have benefited from an improved road network. The main focus for foreigners coming to this area is the Monte Alen National Park, which stretches over the boundary of Litoral Province.

The main domestic access to Centro Sur is via **road** from Bata on the coast, generally in a shared taxi. The main highway leads into Niefang, from where it is possible to head southeast to the provincial capital, or keep heading east into Kié-Ntem and Wele-Nzas provinces. There is currently no airport in this province, but it is only a 1-hour drive from Niefang to the international airport at Bata. Alternatively, the airport at Mengomeyén is only 115km along the motorway to the east.

There is no official border crossing with Cameroon in the north of Centro Sur. In the south, there is a border crossing point with Gabon at Akúrenam, but this was not open to foreign nationals at the time of writing.

Any tours of the province are best organised before arrival, through tour operators in Malabo or Bata (pages 65 and 152).

NIEFANG

Niefang, meaning 'limit of the Fang' is the second most important settlement in Centro Sur Province after Evinayong, and is the birthplace of celebrated writers Donato Ndongo and Joaquin Mbomio Bacheng (pages 55–6). The town was also the setting for Bacheng's famous 1996 novel *El párroco de Niefang*, which tells the story of a priest, recently liberated from prison under President Macías's regime.

Niefang lies on the Benito River and sits at a crossroads, acting as the traditional demarcation line between Fang territory to the east and Ndowe territory to the west. The town is sandwiched between two ranges of hills to the north and the south, which make for some picturesque scenery while driving around the area. Although it is often overcast, visitors to Niefang will also find that it is a lot drier than Bata.

Very much a transit town, there is a lot of coming and going between Bata and the interior but very few people actually stay. In fact, there are likely less than

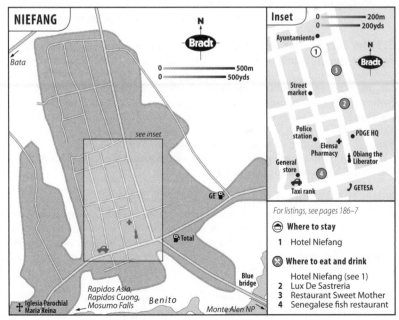

NIEFANG

Bata

0 — 500m
0 — 500yds

see inset

GE ⛽

⛽ Total

Blue bridge

Rapidos Asia,
Rapidos Cuong,
Mosumo Falls   *Benito*

✝ Iglesia Parochial
Maria Reina

Monte Alen NP

Inset

0 — 200m
0 — 200yds

Ayuntamiento ●

①

③

Street market ●

②

Police station ●   ● PDGE HQ

Elensa ✚
Pharmacy   ♟ Obiang the
General   Liberator
store
④

Taxi rank   ♪ GETESA

For listings, see pages 186–7

⊖ **Where to stay**
1   Hotel Niefang

⊗ **Where to eat and drink**
     Hotel Niefang (see 1)
2   Lux De Sastreria
3   Restaurant Sweet Mother
4   Senegalese fish restaurant

Centro Sur Province   NIEFANG

7

10,000 people living here. However, if you take the time to pause for a few hours, you will find Niefang to be a tranquil spot that gives a good indication of what life is like for the majority of Equatoguineans outside the big settlements of Malabo and Bata. The main highlights are the Iglesia Parochial Maria Reina, which has a school attached, and the daily street market in the centre of town. There are no local tour operators based in Niefang. For tourist information, try asking at the Hotel Niefang (see below).

HISTORY Niefang is a Fang territory and was historically an important trading artery linking the Central African interior to the coastal regions via overland and river routes. It was through this region that goods such as slaves, ivory and precious woods were moved by the Fang to the Ndowe traders on the coast, and their European clients. Beyond the odd missionary, trader or explorer, Europeans had little direct experience of this area until the Spanish colonial authorities expanded into the interior under Governor General Miguel Nuñez del Prado (page 20) in the late 1920s. Even then, there was little attempt at settlement, with the only colonial structure being a leper colony. It was not until the last 20 years of Spanish colonial rule that greater investment was made in the area.

Known by the Spanish settlers as Sevilla de Niefang, this rural community had their own Triana Bridge, to emulate the one found in Seville proper. In 1959, the town got a new barracks to house the Guardia Civil, and in 1973, with support from the church in Yaoundé (Cameroon), a Claretian mission was set up in Niefang. The Claretian school became the first institution of higher learning in mainland Equatorial Guinea, and had teaching staff from Granada and Madrid. President Macías closed the mission down in 1975 during his campaign against the Catholic Church, but it is back up and running today and is a prominent feature on the road into town from the coast.

The flurry of oil-backed development of the late 1990s and early 2000s seemed to pass Niefang by, although there is no doubt that the increased wealth of coastal Bata and the interior cities such as Mongomo has benefited the traders working here.

GETTING THERE, AWAY AND AROUND Niefang is a 45-minute drive east of Bata. You can jump in a **shared taxi** from Fabrica de Ladrilla in the Colombo district of Bata (page 158). The cost is 2,000CFA per seat or 10,000CFA for the whole car. There are good-quality roads linking Niefang to Monte Alen National Park, Evinayong and Añisoc over in neighbouring Wele-Nzas Province. There will be no problem finding a taxi for onwards travel at the rank in front of the general store, although you may have to wait quite a while for it to fill up if you intend to share. Most taxis are heading to Bata, but there are a few venturing inland.

The town centre is orientated on a north–south axis and is only 600m long, so you should be fine walking everywhere.

 WHERE TO STAY AND EAT   *Map, page 185.*
All of the restaurants in town also double as bars in the evening, serving up ice-cold San Miguel and truly disgusting whisky, which claims to be Scottish but is more likely Chinese. People tend to gather in front of the general store, and along the road where the market is. Restaurants in town tend to open at noon and serve food until around 21.00.

Hotel Niefang (30 rooms) At the northern end of town by the Town Hall; m 222 532 932. Hotel

Niefang is a solid budget option, which is lucky as it is also your only option. Rooms are en suite &

include AC & a TV. Advertised as having a restaurant, but this was closed at the time of writing. **$$**

✗ **Senegalese fish restaurant** Located by the taxi rank. This place is always very busy which has to be a good sign. Try to make sure the fish they give you is fresh out of the river rather than dried out of the sea. **$–$$**

✗ **Lux De Sastreria** Located in the northeastern end of town, this is another very simple affair serving grilled meats & fish. **$**

✗ **Restaurant Sweet Mother** In the northeast of town. A quiet local eatery worth visiting for the name alone. They usually have a dish of the day & a few local favourites. **$**

SHOPPING If you want to buy any non-food items you will likely find them in the **general store** by the taxi rank on the main road. The owner has deliveries coming in daily from Bata, so he might even be able to order something in from the capital if you need it desperately.

The **street market** gets going from about 07.30 and finishes around 16.00. Here you will find a selection of fresh produce but it is mainly imported Chinese goods, music and clothing. There is a relaxed atmosphere, and while you might not be keen on purchasing anything, it is a good chance to have a chat with some of the locals and find out what is going on in town that day, as well as finding out about access to the nearby rapids (see below).

OTHER PRACTICALITIES When arriving in town, be sure to **register** your presence at the police station. This is a quick process, which involves dropping off a copy of your Tourism Permit.

The owner of the **general store** (see above) has two daughters at a Spanish boarding school, so he is more than happy to exchange your euros for Central African francs.

Phone credit can be purchased in the **GETESA phone shop**.

There is one pharmacy in town called **Elensa Pharmacy** but it is poorly stocked. Try to bring everything that you need with you from Bata.

WHAT TO SEE AND DO The **Iglesia Parochial Maria Reina** is the main church and school, run by missionaries. It is seriously big considering the size of the town it is attached to, and always flooded with small children. The bell tower in particular features highly distinctive jagged architecture. The Italian-built arched **blue bridge** over the river Wele is a more recent architectural addition to the town. In the centre, you will pass a **bust of Obiang the Liberator**, but be careful taking photos as there appears to be a military base on the other side of the road. Niefang is small enough to explore in an hour, but makes for a good base from which to explore the nearby countryside, which features several impressive waterfalls.

If you follow the river 9km south of town you will find a series of rapids, including **Rapidos Asia** and **Rapidos Cuong**. Even further to the south, on the boundary of Monte Alen National Park (⊕ 1°41'13"N 10°07'30"E; see below) are the larger Mosumo Falls (Cataratas de Mosumo). To reach these you need to drive 20km out of town on the road back to Bata, then hike the remaining 5.5km southwards. Ruta47 organise tours to these raging water features and consider them a highlight of the area (page 65).

MONTE ALEN NATIONAL PARK

Monte Alen National Park is home to much of the wildlife that makes Central Africa such a popular ecotourism destination: forest elephants, gorillas, chimpanzees, crocodiles and leopards have all been recorded in this area of jungle. Finding them, however, will not be easy – partly due to poaching but mainly due to the complete lack of infrastructure within the parks. During the 1990s, Monte Alen National Park was run in collaboration with the European Commission as part of the ECOFAC Project (for the rational management and use of Central African forest ecosystems). One specific aim is to conserve Central Africa's wet tropical forests. Money was invested in infrastructure, including a series of trails and camps within the park boundaries. Rangers and guides were trained, and the local community was involved in conservation efforts. Today though, the project has been discontinued due to lack of funding, and the park has been neglected. Poachers are able to go about their work unchallenged and the jungle camps are being slowly reclaimed by nature.

Despite these issues though, Monte Alen National Park is the most accessible national park in mainland Equatorial Guinea. This 14,000km² space straddles the

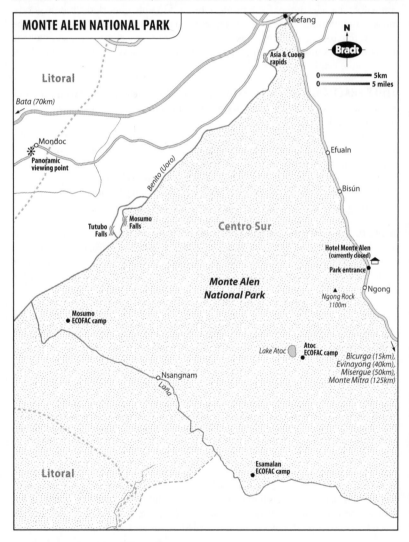

border between Litoral and Centro Sur provinces, and can be accessed from Bata in an hour, making it ideal for both day trips and longer expeditions. As long as you bring all your own gear and are prepared to do some serious hiking, you can enjoy one of Africa's least visited parks and all the animals therein. Note, however, that within the park there is little to no tourist infrastructure. Mosumo, Esamalan and Atoc ECOFAC camps are in a state of disrepair, and the trails leading to them are not regularly maintained. You are strongly advised to engage a guide to avoid getting lost (see below).

GETTING THERE AND AWAY Most visitors arrive from Bata, and there is no regular direct transport between the surrounding towns and the park entrances. From Bata, either take a **shared taxi** to Evinayong and ask to be dropped at the Hotel Monte Alen (which is just north of Ngong), or bring your own **private vehicle**. The hotel is signposted on both sides of the road, and is visible as you drive past. The entrance here is the best one to use, as you should be able to pick up a guide and porter(s) around here, although you can technically enter the park anywhere as there are no controls. Some visitors choose to get dropped off to the south of the park, at Misergue, and then hike northwards, finishing their trip at the Hotel Monte Alen. There is not much traffic on the road outside the hotel, so you may need to organise a vehicle in advance, or be prepared to hitchhike to Niefang and then hire a vehicle.

ARRANGING TOURS Trips to the park can be arranged through tour operators based in Bata (page 152). Although the Hotel Monte Alen was closed for refurbishment at the time of writing, you can still enquire here for help picking up guides and porters, as they live in the surrounding villages. Alternatively, contact **Santiago Mba**, one of the area administrators (m *222 615 708*) in advance to organise your visit. He can arrange a guide for 15,000CFA per day and porters for 5,000CFA per day, which is the official rate. He can also arrange camping equipment hire. The man supervising the renovations of the hotel is called Victorio and he should also be able to help you find a guide. At the time of writing there was no indication of when the Hotel Monte Alen would reopen.

WHERE TO STAY The Hotel Monte Alen has been closed for years, which is sad as it would be an incredible place to stay. It offers panoramic views from its perch up on the hillside at the eastern entrance to the park. **Camping** is the order of the day while in the park itself. Your guide should be able to choose suitable locations. Most visitors stick to the southeastern portion of the park, between Esamalan ECOFAC camp, Lake Atoc and Ngong Rock.

WHAT TO SEE AND DO The hike through the jungle to Lake Atoc is strenuous but offers the opportunity to see lots of wildlife, and the clearing around the lake itself makes an excellent picnic spot. It is possible to take a pirogue and explore sections of the rivers Uoro and Laña while in the park, but be aware of the **Asia** and **Cuong rapids**, as well as **Mosumo Falls**! Even more impressive are the raging **Tutubo Falls**. What they lack in height, they make up for in sheer volume of water and violent flow, especially during the rainy seasons (February to July and September to December). Generally speaking, the further from the park boundaries and a main road you get, the more likely you are to see the wildlife, due to lower poaching levels. For those serious about seeing gorillas and other large mammals, you will need to find an experienced guide and be prepared to spend days hiking around looking for them.

Evinayong sits in the rolling hills of Centro Sur at the foot of Mount Chime, which is the highest mountain in the region at 1,200m. At 630m elevation, on a clear day you can see for miles in every direction from the town and there is much less rainfall here than on the coast. It has a smaller urban population than Niefang, but a much larger rural one, with families cultivating the lush hillsides all around the settlement. There is a strong governmental presence here, with a large military base, a prison and varying telecommunications infrastructure. With a great climate, fertile soil and excellent transport links to the surrounding area, it is easy to see why this is the provincial capital.

The town is spread thinly across an east–west axis of over 4km. It is also very hilly. Driving in from the west (likely from either Niefang or Cogo), the settlement begins at the crossroads with the Total petrol station. At the eastern edge of town, three roads converge: those from the border town of Akúrenam in the south, Aconibe in the east and Añisoc to the north (where there is also a connection to the new Bata to Mongomo Highway). Here there is a large roundabout with the as yet unfinished Hotel Don Patricio. In addition to Mount Chime, there are other large peaks to the south of town, part of the Crystal Mountains range that stretches into Gabon.

In the southeast of town is the Catedral De Mision San Jose de Evinayong, an old colonial church with a yellow and white interior, marble flooring and stained-glass windows. It was fully refurbished in 2010.

HISTORY Evinayong shares the same rich history as other towns in this region, one of shifting populations and often violent interactions. The area has been inhabited for thousands of years. Groups of Bakola-Bagyeli gave way in the 17th or 18th century to migrating Fang who now dominate the entire Centro Sur area. As the Spanish moved inland at the turn of the 20th century, they considered making Evinayong their capital, given its central location and strategic communications links. In the end, the port of Bata, with an already established (albeit small) group of European colonisers, was chosen instead. The land around Evinayong is particularly

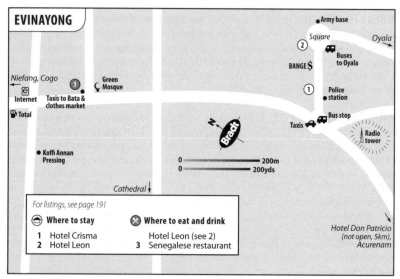

EVINAYONG

Army base

Square   Oyala

②   🚌

BANGE $ Buses to Oyala

Niefang, Cogo   Green Mosque   ①   Police station

Internet   Taxis to Bata & clothes market

Total   Bus stop

Taxis   Radio tower

Koffi Annan Pressing

0 —— 200m
0 —— 200yds

Cathedral ↓

For listings, see page 191

🛏 **Where to stay**   ✕ **Where to eat and drink**

1   Hotel Crisma   Hotel Leon (see 2)
2   Hotel Leon   3   Senegalese restaurant

Hotel Don Patricio (not open, 5km), Acurenam

lush, and the area was used by Spanish colonisers for numerous experiments in agronomy. In the 1940s, famed Spanish botanist Emilio Guinea López (1907–85) undertook many plant collecting surveys in the area, recording over 3,000 species. The town has also served as the site for a high-security prison since colonial times.

Evinayong played a significant role in the birth of modern Equatorial Guinea as it was the hometown of independence leader Bonifacio Ondó Edú, who founded both the UPLGE and the MUNGE political parties. He became the first leader of a newly autonomous Spanish Guinea on 1 January 1964 but sadly died in the early years of President Macías's rule.

GETTING THERE, AWAY AND AROUND Evinayong is well connected to the rest of the country. **Shared taxis** arrive regularly from Niefang, Aconibe and Añisoc, all costing 2,000CFA per seat. Vehicles from Akúrenam are much less regular. A driver might be willing to take you from Cogo, but this would be an unusual route and you would likely need to buy out the whole vehicle. There is a **bus service** connecting Evinayong to the planned new capital of Oyala, which departs from the square in front of the **army base**. There are also buses departing to various destinations from the **roundabout** in the southeast of town, where there is a taxi rank, too. It is possible to get a bus all the way to Bata from here. If you want to take a taxi to Bata, you need to head to the road in front of the green mosque by the clothes market and find the taxi rank there.

While the town is very spaced out, the portion of the centre you need to navigate is quite compact, so you should be able to walk everywhere (although it is hilly). Failing this, hitchhiking is not unusual.

ARRANGING TOURS There are no local tour operators in Evinayong. When it opens, the high-end Hotel Don Patricio (see below) should be able to make arrangements for visitors, but in the meantime you will need to ask around or make arrangements through an agent in Bata (page 152) or Malabo (pages 65–6).

WHERE TO STAY *Map, page 190.*

The Hotel Don Patricio is not yet open, but already looks as though it will be a much more comfortable option than the other two hotels in town. It is quite far out of the centre though, so you will need your own vehicle or be willing to jump in passing vehicles to get into town.

Hotel Leon (12 rooms) At the top of the hill on the main square; m 222 273 460. This hotel's location makes it a little quieter than the Hotel Crisma. The cheapest rooms are essentially just a double bed in a room with a fan & a shared bathroom. A little extra gets you a room with a TV, AC, shower & toilet. **$–$$**

Hotel Crisma (10 rooms) m 222 228 491, 222 633 466. Hidden down a side street on the road leading up to the army base, this hotel has a breezy but dark veranda with Chinese lanterns & comfortable sofas. All the rooms are situated around an open-air courtyard. They have very basic rooms with a fan, toilet & shower, although the water is intermittent. Good value, if a little grimy. **$**

WHERE TO EAT AND DRINK *Map, page 190.*

There are not many formal dining options in Evinayong, which is surprising considering it is the provincial capital. Over by the clothes market there is a **Senegalese restaurant** that serves tasty street food in an informal wooden shack setting (10.00–21.00 Mon–Sat; **$**). The **Hotel Leon** (see above) serves cooked local dishes at plastic tables on their porch, and assuming you can find the manager, she offers breakfast, lunch and dinner (🕐 *07.30–22.00*; **$$**). The **Total petrol station** sells snacks and refrigerated items, including some fresh baked goods (🕐 *08.00–18.00 daily*; **$$**).

There are a number of informal **bars** near the clothes market where you can pull up a stool and enjoy a beer, and this area gets quite crowded at night. The road with the police station has a number of trading establishments that turn into informal bars at night, too. The **Hotel Crisma** (page 191) veranda is a good place to enjoy a quiet drink.

SHOPPING The **clothes market** has a varied selection of goods and is open every day except Sundays, starting at around 07.30. The area just before the roundabout with the taxi rank and the bus stop also has a number of shops selling random imported goods, many of them Chinese-made. Overall there is not much on offer, and the lack of tourists in this area means that there are no art or crafts shops on the main street.

OTHER PRACTICALITIES Upon arrival be sure to walk up the hill and **register** your presence at the police station. The chief of police is friendly and has a larger-than-life-size poster of President Obiang on his wall.

There is a **BANGE Bank** by the army base with an ATM, although it lacks a Visa symbol.

The **cyber café** near the Total garage charges 500CFA for 30 minutes of internet access. The connection is slow but generally reliable.

If you need your clothes cleaned, why not visit the amazingly named **Koffi Annan Pressing**? They will be surprised to see you but will do a good job.

AKÚRENAM

Akúrenam (also known as Acurenam) is the sleepy, southern border town of Centro Sur Province and it has only recently been connected to Evinayong by a good-quality road. It should not be confused with the other town of the same name just to the west of Evinayong. The entire district has an estimated population of 20,000 but most people live in rural areas. If you are keen on a drive through the hills, then Akúrenam is 50km to the south of Evinayong.

In 1890, José Valero Belenguer visited this area on behalf of the Spanish Geographic Society and collected a number of Fang spearheads, daggers and arrows which are now on display in the Spanish National Anthropology Museum in Madrid. A subsequent expedition in 1919, led by Fernando Martínez de la Escalera, also collected a series of ethnographic material showing a history of established Fang occupation in the area.

In the town you will see the old **Tribunal de Raza** colonial building, which was used by the Franco regime following the 1938 Statute of the Patronato de Indígenas (page 20) to administer a separate brand of justice to African colonial subjects: this painted pink stone structure is hard to miss. There is also a newly refurbished **church**, Iglesia Parroquial de Akúrenam, a number of new primary schools to serve the large rural catchment area, and a significant military base.

Just down the road at the village of **Edum** there is an official border crossing point, over the river Komo (or Ncomo) to the town of Medoneu in Gabon, which has an airfield. At the time of writing this border was not open to foreign nationals, and the nearest open crossing point was all the way northeast at the Mongomo–Oyem border.

8

Wele-Nzas Province

Wele-Nzas Province is in the far east of mainland Río Muni. Much of the province is densely forested, and it was highly inaccessible until only a few years ago when the roads were improved. Conservation groups categorise this area as being part of the Monte Alen–Monts de Cristal landscape, which stretches down into much of Gabon. This is a highly biodiverse part of the world, where you should be able to find the whole spectrum of Equatorial Guinea's wildlife including tourist favourites such as gorillas, chimpanzees, forest elephants and even leopards. The province shares a southern and eastern border with Gabon, and a northern border with Kié-Ntem Province. To the west is Centro Sur Province. Crossing the southern or eastern border will bring you into Woleu-Ntem Province in Gabon.

The capital city of Wele-Nzas is Mongomo, which is the ancestral homeland of both the former president, Macías, and the current president, Obiang. It is in the Fang heartland. Mongomo serves as an important frontier town on a trade route into Gabon. However, once construction work has been completed in Oyala, Wele-Nzas will be the location of the new capital city for the entire country.

Official government estimates put the population of the province at around 157,980, with Mongomo being the largest settlement, followed by Añisoc, then Aconibe and Nsork. The Altos de Nsork and Monte Temelón national parks are located in this province. The government of Equatorial Guinea hopes that there are diamond deposits in Nsork, as it is geologically similar to Mitzic in Gabon, which is just over the border and has proven reserves.

HISTORY

The inland province of Wele-Nzas has been inhabited for thousands of years, but remained unexplored by Europeans until the 20th century. The area around Altos de Nsork used to be home to groups of Byele Pygmies, who represented the only human population for almost 15,000 years. However, the arrival of Bantu groups from the northwest changed the demographic makeup of this inland Equatoguinean region and there are now no Byele Pygmies to be found in the forests of Wele-Nzas, as they relocated northwards towards the border with Cameroon about two decades ago.

While explorers such as Paul Belloni du Chaillu did penetrate the interior of Equatorial Guinea back in the mid 19th century, there are few historical records specifically relating to this province. German traders looking for wood, rubber and ivory may have ventured this far east, but given the Fang reputation for cannibalism at the time, it is more likely they let the Ndowe groups of the coast do the negotiating with the interior tribes (page 17). The borders with Gabon were fixed in 1900 after the Treaty of Paris, much to the dismay of the Spanish negotiators, who believed the eastern limit of their territory should have been set near the Ubangi River.

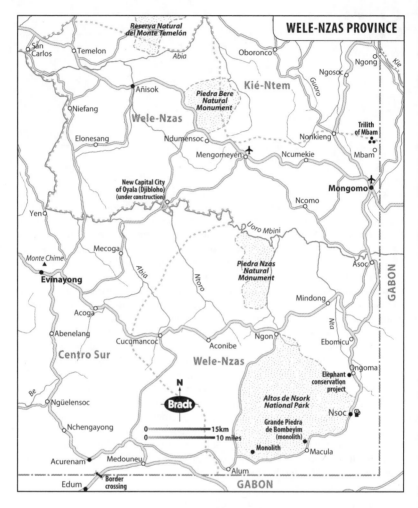

The foundation of the administrative region of Spanish Guinea in 1926 was probably the first time Spanish government representatives travelled to this area in any significant numbers, and they came mainly in search of Fang forced labourers rather than aiming to settle.

The province took on added significance after independence, as it was the ancestral homeland of both President Macías and President Obiang. In fact, in 1975 a severely paranoid President Macías relocated from Malabo to his hometown of Nsangayong, south of the regional capital of Mongomo. From this isolated spot, right on the border with Gabon, he orchestrated his reign of terror for a further four years, before he was deposed.

President Obiang has invested heavily in his home province, some would argue above and beyond the requirements for such a small and economically insignificant area. Mongomo now sports a new airport, the National School of Hotel Management, a large basilica, and a luxury hotel and conference centre. In 2013, the city even played host to the final of the beauty contest, Miss Tourism World. In June 2014, the Equatoguinean navy's latest frigate was named after the province.

Wele-Nzas promises to have a bright future. The plan is to relocate the seat of government from Malabo to Oyala once it is complete, around 2020. It is also hoped that commercial mining, for gold and other rare minerals, may be possible in the province, as artisanal miners have been known to have success in the rivers around Mongomo, Coro and Aconibe. The results of a 2012 mega-survey by Brilliant Resources Inc (a Canadian company) and Fugro Airborne Services (a Dutch company) have yet to be released due to a commercial dispute with the government (page 49).

GETTING THERE AND AWAY

Most visitors arrive by **road**. Coming from the west, the main access points are Niefang in the north and Evinayong further south. There is an official border crossing with Gabon at Mongomo, and from there you can continue driving east to the city of Oyem. Accessing Wele-Nzas from its neighbouring northern province of Kié-Ntem is difficult, as the main paved road running south from Ebebiyín crosses into Gabon before cutting back in at Mongomo.

There is a domestic airport in Mongomo, although only charter flights were arriving and departing at the time of writing. There is an airport at Mengomeyén which provides connections to the coast (Bata) with Ceiba Intercontinental.

MONGOMO

A city in the jungle, few would have heard of this place were it not for its connections to the ruling Obiang clan. Straddling the border with Gabon, this once quiet rural town has transformed into a modern city over the past decade thanks to heavy investment from the presidents, and things are not yet finished. Everywhere you walk there is a crane at work or a foreign construction team sizing up the latest planned development. The massive new Bata to Mongomo Highway connects the eastern border of Equatorial Guinea to the port city of Bata, 200km to the west. This highway, eight lanes wide in places, is not yet officially open although it is possible to drive on sections of it as you head inland. Part of the strategic Horizon2020 plan, the aim is to link Equatorial Guinea's ports to the markets of the African interior, using Mongomo as a central hub for distributing goods in this frontier region. Assuming the country is able to attract foreign importers as it predicts, the future looks very positive for Mongomo.

HISTORY Former president Macías was born in 1924 in a village called Nsangayong, a few kilometres south of Mongomo (alternative spellings are Nzangayong and Nsegayong) and he spent much of his early adulthood in the city. On 5 June 1942, current president Obiang was also born in a village on the southern outskirts of Mongomo, called Acoacam. Such is the ruling family's close connection to this city that they are often referred to as the 'Mongomo clan'.

Mongomo was an important seat of local government under Spanish colonialism, and benefited greatly from the zealous wave of Spanish investment shortly before independence. In 1960, future president Macías was able to take advantage of more relaxed rules regarding civil service positions and became mayor. Two years later, the city made the Spanish newsreels with the grand opening of their new church, the Parroquia Nuestra Senora De Guadelupe.

In 1975, when President Macías's terror was at its height, he relocated from Malabo to his ancestral village of Nsangayong, from where he ruled through

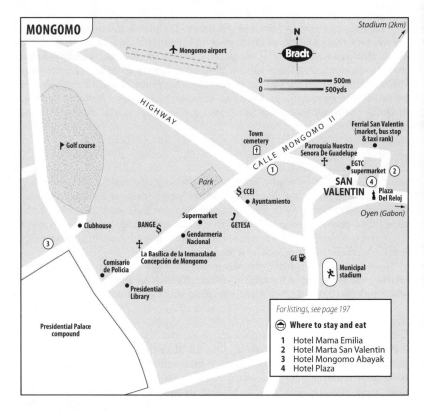

MONGOMO

Stadium (2km)

N

Bradt

Mongomo airport

HIGHWAY

0 ———— 500m
0 ———— 500yds

Golf course

Town cemetery

CALLE MONGOMO II

Ferrial San Valentin (market, bus stop & taxi rank)

Parroquia Nuestra Senora De Guadelupe ①

EGTC supermarket ②

Park

SAN VALENTIN ④ Plaza Del Reloj

CCEI

Ayuntamiento

Oyen (Gabon)

Supermarket

Clubhouse

BANGE$

GETESA

Gendarmeria Nacional

③

La Basílica de la Inmaculada Concepción de Mongomo

GE

Municipal stadium

Comisario de Policia

Presidential Library

For listings, see page 197

Where to stay and eat

1 Hotel Mama Emilia
2 Hotel Marta San Valentin
3 Hotel Mongomo Abayak
4 Hotel Plaza

Presidential Palace compound

increasingly erratic decrees. In August 1979, a bunker near Mongomo was the scene of Macías's last stand against the advancing forces of his nephew. Many people died, and the entire foreign currency reserves of the country were burned before he was captured in the jungles south of Mongomo.

President Obiang's rule has meant widespread changes for the people of Mongomo. Oil wealth has been directed towards turning the city into a model of the PDGE development plans, with an emphasis on Chinese-run infrastructure projects such as the new stadium, highway, basilica and airport. Things have not always run smoothly, however, and on 31 March 2008 there were violent confrontations between striking Chinese workers and Equatoguinean security officials, which led to tensions with China (pages 37–40). This incident has since been smoothed over and walking around the city today, you would not think it had slowed development in any significant way.

GETTING THERE AND AWAY Those arriving from the west will be greeted by a well-landscaped roundabout announcing 'Bienvenido a Mongomo' in white Hollywood lettering. The airport forms the northern boundary of the settlement, with the centre of town somewhere around the park. In the southwest of the town is the diplomatic area, where the most expensive buildings are located, along with the presidential compound, basilica, golf course and luxury Hotel Mongomo. The neighbourhood to the east around the Plaza Del Reloj (known as San Valentin) is less developed but bustling.

The easiest way to arrive is to **drive** or take a **shared taxi** from Bata along sections of the new highway. There are shared taxis to Ebebiyín, Nsoc, Aconibe, Evinayong and other destinations, and they leave from the taxi rank at Ferrial San Valentin in the east of town. Most nearby destinations cost between 1,000CFA and 1,500CFA per seat. Opposite the taxi rank you will also find the **Sin Sin Bus Line** stop, which sells tickets to Bata for 3,500CFA. They even have a waiting room with TV and a toilet.

Ceiba Intercontinental Airlines sometimes operates **flights** from Bata, but these are highly irregular and possibly for official use only. Clarify with a local tour operator such as Ruta47 before booking (page 65).

It is possible to walk **across the border** to Gabon's Oyem from Mongomo, and it is quite a busy crossing point, or to take a shared taxi from Ferrial San Valentin, which will drive you into Gabon. As with other land border crossings, be sure to check in advance if the border is open as it is subject to closure at short notice

GETTING AROUND The city is filled with **shared taxis**. They are quite carefully regulated, and official ones should display a licence sticker on the windscreen. Short hops around town cost 500CFA, and longer journeys 1,000CFA. There is a GE Petrol in the east of town by the municipal stadium. Queues here can get quite long at busy times, which tend to be early in the morning (06.00–08.00) and then again around 16.00, as people fuel up to leave town.

WHERE TO STAY *Map, page 196.*

🏠 **Hotel Mongomo Abayak** (56 rooms, 10 suites & 6 villas) Calle Koete, Mongomo; 📞 333 070 205; 📱 222 096 769; e hotelmongomo@ hotmail.com. This green giant is situated in a quiet western district, adjoining the presidential palace compound. They have everything you would expect from a 5-star hotel, including very attractive grounds & a swimming pool, but at eye watering prices. There are usually a few foreign contractors resident, but other than that this place tends to be empty apart from people using the restaurant, bar & pool. Rooms include a combined bath & shower, AC, flatscreen TV, fridge & a balcony with views of the pool (or the presidential palace if you would prefer). The rooms are quite small & crowded considering the price, but quality is good & the balcony is a welcome addition. The grounds also include a casino, nightclub, spa, gym & tennis courts. The restaurant is the best in town & serves foods imported from around the world (including lobster), & there is a delicious poolside barbecue with buffet at w/ends. The bar by the pool is also a great place to relax with a cocktail.

There are no local tour operators in Mongomo, but the hotel can arrange drivers & local excursions for residents. **$$$$$**

🏠 **Hotel Marta San Valentin** (16 rooms) In San Valentin by the clock tower overlooking Plaza Del Reloj. This hotel is in a quiet location & has large, clean AC rooms, with combined bath & shower & a TV. They are building an internet café at the back of the property. **$$$**

🏠 **Hotel Mama Emilia** (8 rooms) On a main road opposite the cemetery. There are 4 rooms with AC here & 4 without. All have a toilet, shower, bath & TV. Try to get a room as high up in the building as possible to escape the noise from the bar downstairs. **$$**

🏠 **Hotel Plaza** (10 rooms) In San Valentin by the clock tower, overlooking Plaza Del Reloj; 📱 551 694 717. This is a budget option & the only positive thing to say is that the rooms are big. You get your own toilet, access to a communal shower but no fan or AC & security is not great. If you want to save money you are better off at the Hotel Mama Emilia. **$$**

WHERE TO EAT AND DRINK *Map, page 196.*

The nightclub, casino or poolside bar at the **Hotel Mongomo Abayak** is the best place to go if you are looking to meet other expatriates. Smart dress is expected.

For those on a budget, there are a number of **street bars** in the San Valentin neighbourhood, including a large outdoor venue just opposite the **Hotel Marta San Valentin**. The **Hotel Mama Emilia** also has a bar on their terrace, which is often busy.

✕ Hotel Mongomo Abayak Calle Koete, Mongomo; ☏ 333 070 205; ⏰ 07.00–10.00, 12.30–15.00 & 18.30–22.00 daily. This high-end restaurant caters for the limited international clientele of engineers & architects who are working in the city. The menu is mainly Mediterranean with some good local fish options. Starters are the price of whole meals in some other restaurants, & the cost of lobster would actually get you a hotel room in another part of town. Perhaps only recommended if you are eating on the corporate expense account. **$$$$**

✕ Hotel Mama Emilia Restaurant On a main road opposite the cemetery (page 199); ⏰ noon–22.00 Mon–Sat, noon–21.00 Sun. The kitchen in this hotel serves a mixture of Spanish & Chinese food (not in the same dish). They often rent out the dining room for private functions, so check before making plans. **$–$$**

✕ Restaurante Plaza Situated on the ground floor of the hotel of the same name (page 197), overlooking Plaza Del Reloj; ⓜ 551 694 717; ⏰ noon–15.30 & 19.00–21.30 Mon–Sat. This is a very popular restaurant serving chicken, fish & meat dishes. The fish in particular is cheap, tasty & cooked to order. There is always a line of people picking up take-away, which has to be a hallmark of quality. **$**

SHOPPING

▥ EGTC Supermarket San Valentin, Mongomo; ⏰ 08.00–13.00 & 16.00–19.00 Mon–Fri, 08.00–13.00 Sat. A small shop, but it has both a chilled & frozen goods section.

▥ Supermarket Carretera del Museo Biblioteca Presidencial de Mongomo; ⏰ 08.00–13.00 & 16.00–19.00 Mon–Fri, 08.00–13.00 Sat. Not one for marketing itself, this vaguely named shop is large & well stocked with non-perishable items.

OTHER PRACTICALITIES Upon arrival, be sure to **register** with the *comisario*, located at the main entrance to the presidential palace. The process is generally friendly and hassle-free. Give him a copy of your Tourism Permit and be sure to compliment his camouflage patterned couch!

There is a **BANGE Bank** on Calle Mongomo II, which has an ATM but displays no Visa symbol. The **CCEI Bank** on Calle Mongomo II has no ATM.

For phone credit and SIM cards, there is a **GETESA** on Calle Mongomo II.

WHAT TO SEE AND DO The main attractions in Mongomo are the grandiose building projects. The scale of **La Basílica de la Inmaculada Concepción de Mongomo** is simply unbelievable. It was built by an Italian company over the course of five years at a cost of €13.5 million, and you can tell they used St Peter's Basilica in Vatican City as inspiration. Walking around the well-kept but empty grounds, you feel as though you might be in the Vatican itself, were it not for the jungle surroundings, and the interior is magnificent. There is a canal system opposite the basilica that local men use for **fishing**, but it is unclear how clean the water is.

Adjoining this is the **golf course**, which once again, you will find completely empty, save for a few locals using it as a picnic ground or women washing their clothes in one of the many water hazards. On this road you will also find the **presidential library**, another grand monument of glass and steel, which is sadly not open to the public. At the end of the road you reach the entrance to the **presidential palace**. In reality this is more a collection of palaces in a walled enclosure that is 2km long and over 3.5km wide. Here you will see beautifully landscaped gardens, swimming pools and water features, but do not linger in front of the entrance and definitely do not get your camera out as this will cause problems with the police. If you wish to gawp at the opulent living quarters of the Equatoguinean elite, you can do so more comfortably from the grounds of the neighbouring Hotel Mongomo Abayak.

This **Plaza Del Reloj** is built around a clock tower that has stood in San Valentin since colonial times. At the base of the tower are three rather awkwardly associated busts that neatly summarise Equatorial Guinea's turbulent transition to independence. On one side is a rather youthful-looking President Obiang, which comes as no surprise given his links to the city. However, just around the corner we find his uncle, President Macías, whose execution he presided over in 1979. The final bust is that of Bonifacio Ondó Edú, first president of the autonomous Spanish Guinea in 1964, considered by many to have been murdered by Macías (page 27).

The **park** in the centre of town, complete with playground, exercise equipment and water features, is a relaxing spot for a walk. Nearby, the **town cemetery** is also open to the public and has extensive green space.

The 15,000-seat **Stadium of Mongomo** is in the northeast part of town. It was recently upgraded to host games during the 2015 Africa Cup of Nations and is home to local Liga Semiprofesional team, Deportivo Mongomo. There is also a **municpial stadium** which sometimes hosts matches.

MENGOMEYÉN

Why Mengomeyén (also known as Mongomeyen) ended up with one of Equatorial Guinea's five international airports is a mystery. Located 145km east of Bata, there was not much going on in this town of only a few thousand people until 2006 when a swarm of international construction firms suddenly descended. Seventy-two months and €285 million later, the town was home to President Obiang Nguema International Airport; not only the largest and most modern airport facility in the country, but likely also the surrounding region. Mengomeyén seems to have been chosen due to a lucky quirk of its relative position: a short drive from both Mongomo (the president's hometown) and Oyala (the president's new capital city). Although the airport is set up to handle international flights, at the moment there is only a flight to Bata, which runs intermittently.

There is not much to do other than gawp at the airport as you cruise through on the Mongomo–Añisoc road, although the town might serve as a useful entry point to the Piedra Bere Natural Monument.

AÑISOC

Añisoc is a small town in the north of Wele-Nzas Province. There is not much to see here but it does have two things going for it. Firstly, it is located on a key transport route that links Bata to Mongomo and Oyala. Secondly, it has one of the best hotels in the province, the Hotel Joncham (page 200), which makes it an ideal base from which to explore the region.

There is a large domed church at the eastern end of town, by the square. Other than that, most of the attractions are around the town rather than in it.

GETTING THERE AND AROUND Añisoc is on the main road between Niefang and Mongomo. You can get a **shared taxi** from either of these locations to Añisoc for 2,000CFA. Añisoc is also just north of the Bata to Mongomo Highway, which you can join from the slip roads to the east and west of town. Although a little confusing, it is also possible to drive to Oyala from here, but make sure your taxi driver knows where he is going, as many local inhabitants have never visited the new city and will get very lost. It is also possible to get a **flight** from Bata to Mengomeyén airport (see above) with Ceiba Intercontinental Airlines, then take a taxi to Añisoc. Añisoc is a small town and easily explored on foot.

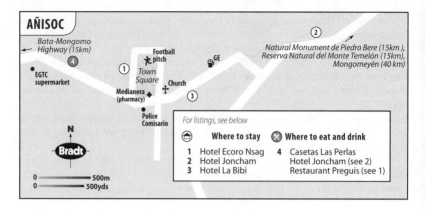

AÑISOC

Bata-Mongomo
Highway (15km)

Football
pitch

Town
Square

Church

EGTC
supermarket

Medianera
(pharmacy)

Police
Comisario

Natural Monument de Piedra Bere (15km),
Reserva Natural del Monte Temelón (15km),
Mongomeyén (40 km)

N

Bradt

0   500m
0   500yds

For listings, see below

⊖ **Where to stay**
1 Hotel Ecoro Nsag
2 Hotel Joncham
3 Hotel La Bibi

⊗ **Where to eat and drink**
4 Casetas Las Perlas
   Hotel Joncham (see 2)
   Restaurant Preguis (see 1)

🏠 WHERE TO STAY *Map, above.*

🏠 **Hotel Ecoro Nsag** (34 rooms, 4 suites) In the centre of town backing on to the town square/football pitch; ㎡ 222 141 385, 551 925 635. Rooms are quite big but dark & musty, & include AC, TV, bed & shower, but the shower is small & a wet room, which might not appeal. Some rooms have a balcony with good views of the town. There are also suites which have a living room & a couch area for triple the price of singles. Staying here I would be concerned about the large nightclub on the ground floor! $$$–$$$$$

🏠 **Hotel Joncham** (16 rooms, 2 suites) On the road heading east out of town; ㎡ 222 059 591, 555 033 393. A newly opened Spanish-run resort.

The spotless rooms are great quality & have AC, large flatscreen TVs, combined bath & shower, & a fridge. A suite costs double & includes a large living room area as well as 2 bedrooms, which is much better value for money if there are more than 2 of you staying. There is also a very good restaurant (see below) & a disco on site that is open from Thu to Sun. The hotel has an active Facebook page through which you can make reservations. $$$

🏠 **Hotel La Bibi** (6 rooms) Officially the cheapest decent rooms in the country! 5,000CFA gets you a small clean room with a fan & a double bed. Shared bathroom & shower area. Great news for those hoping to explore central Río Muni. $

🍴 WHERE TO EAT AND DRINK *Map, above.*

🍴 **Hotel Joncham Restaurant** On the road heading east out of town; ㎡ 222 059 591, 555 033 393; ⏰ noon–15.30 & 19.00–22.00 daily. This is by far the best place to eat in Añisoc. The restaurant serves traditional delicious Spanish cuisine with some Fang dishes thrown into the mix. Mains are reasonably priced & there is an extensive specials board, with wine & cheese on offer, too. An unusual place to find traditional Spanish cuisine but hopefully it will be a success. $$–$$$

🍴 **Restaurant Preguis** On the ground floor of the Hotel Ecoro Nsag (see above); ㎡ 222 141 385, 551 925 635; ⏰ 12.30–16.00 & 18.30–21.30 daily. The food looks good, a mixture of Mediterranean meat & fish dishes, but there is not much natural light in here. $$–$$$

🍴 **Casetas Las Perlas** ⏰ 15.00–late daily. This green wooden outdoor bar serves snacks during the day, including some street food. It gets very busy at night when the PA system fires up. $

OTHER PRACTICALITIES

EGTC Supermarket ⏰ 08.00–13.00 & 16.00–19.00 Mon–Fri, 09.00–13.00 Sat. The best range of produce in Añisoc, this shop has both a frozen & a chilled goods section. Run by the only English speakers in town.

✚ **Medianera Pharmacy** ⏰ 08.00–16.00 Mon–Fri. Not well stocked but your only option in town.

RESERVA NATURAL DEL MONTE TEMELÓN You can ask around in town for a local guide to take you to the Reserva Natural del Monte Temelón, where there is a variety of flora, as well as a large population of giant pangolin and apparently the critically endangered African slender-snouted crocodile. Owing to forest degradation in the surrounding region, many animals have sought refuge in this reserve, so there is a good chance you will see some wildlife, although sadly poaching is taking a toll. Some sources mention both chimpanzees and gorillas hiding in this forest, but this has not been confirmed.

NSOC

Also confusingly labelled as 'Nsork' or 'Nsok' on some maps (despite there already being towns of these names in the country), this place in the southeast corner of Río Muni is one of the most remote settlements in the country. It is not surprising that it is one of the last refuges of Equatorial Guinea's forest elephants. Here you will find none of the hustle and bustle of Ebebiyín, as there are no official links to Gabon. Nor is this a through-road to anywhere, as those wishing to visit Aconibe from Mongomo are able to swing inland well before they reach here. The drive down is an enjoyable one, cutting through the hills and passing an area of cattle and horse ranches.

Upon arrival, be sure to register with the friendly *comisario* by the town square, who may be able to recommend a guide for the area. After this, it takes less than an hour to explore the town which has a church, a covered market, a Total petrol station and only one hotel and one restaurant.

The town's hotel is the **Mbabundomo** (*11 rooms;* m *222 074 547, 222 674 535;* $). Things are pretty basic and you get a double bed, fan, a toilet and a shower out of a bucket. The building is owned by a PDGE senator, whose image seems to adorn every wall. The hotel manager is a friendly lady who can also recommend guides for the area.

The only sit-down restaurant in town is **Restaurante Senegalese** (⊕ *10.00–21.00 Mon–Sat;* $) and they serve delicious Senegalese chicken and fish dishes and also have a fridge full of cold drinks.

ALTOS DE NSORK NATIONAL PARK The entire forested area to the west of Nsoc makes up the national park, although there is no visible demarcation or signage. The main reason to head down here is to try and find the **forest elephants**. This park is home to much of the same wildlife that makes nearby Gabon's forests famous, such as common chimpanzees, gorillas, black colobus, mandrill, forest buffalo and red river hogs. Nearly every local inhabitant has a tale about the pesky elephants (usually a complaint involving eating their crops). If you ask around, you can engage a local guide to help you find them. Alternatively, you can have a go at tracking them yourself. Seeing where they have been is not difficult, as they leave a trail of dung and destruction wherever they go, and any local with a patch of land can tell you where they have been recently. Sneaking close enough to see them is another matter, as they have excellent hearing and sense of smell and use this to avoid human contact. Your guide could also walk you to the imposing rock monolith **Grande Piedra de Bombeyim**, which is located within the park. Be aware that there is no tourist infrastructure in the park, so bring everything you need with you, including drinking water.

Note that the area by the border with Gabon is quite sensitive due to suspected diamond deposits (diamonds have been found 50km over the border in Mitzic). You should not trek too far east or southeast of Nsoc.

OYALA (DJIBLOHO)

No Equatoguinean government project has attracted more international attention than the construction of the new capital city at Oyala. Situated 125km east of Bata, straddling the boundary between Centro Sur and Wele-Nzas provinces, this new city in the jungle is set for completion by 2020, when it will dethrone Malabo as the nation's seat of government.

It is hard to overstate how isolated this location is: there was literally nothing here only a few years ago, and huge swathes of jungle had to be cleared before work could even start. As you drive here on the brand new highway, there is an eerie feeling of isolation, as there is no phone signal, no traffic and no settlements by the road. President Obiang has cited security concerns as one of the reasons for needing to move the capital city inland. In this respect Oyala should deliver because access routes are extremely limited and should be easy to control.

The city is currently a hive of activity, with architects, engineers and construction companies from around the world working day and night to get the place finished on schedule. The city is laid out in a grid pattern, designed to accommodate up to 200,000 inhabitants, spread across an area of 81.5km². At the moment only the Grand Hotel Djibloho Kempinski, the golf course and the American University of Central Africa (AUCA) campus are complete, but they will soon be joined by other developments such as a zoo, hospital, presidential palace, government centre

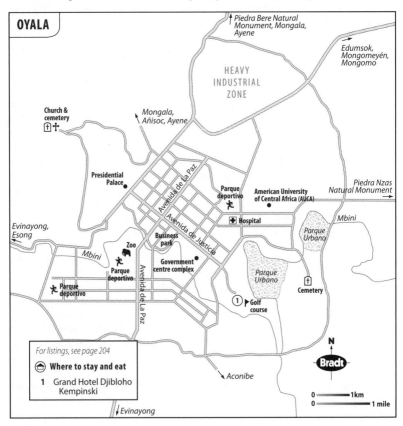

complex and business park. When completed, the Parque Urbano sections in the east of the city will be the focus of the Oyala shopping experience. This bizarre Dubai in the jungle should be part of any tour of the mainland.

HISTORY Oyala used to be a small village of a few hundred people who lived off the nearby forest. There was jungle in every direction and they were isolated. Now, they find themselves sandwiched between an eight-lane highway and what is soon to be the biggest city in the country. This rapid onset of modernity has been a mixed blessing for the people of Oyala. While they may soon benefit from improved trade links with the rest of the country, and possibly access to better healthcare, at the moment they are suffering due to a profusion of alcohol and foreign construction workers seeking prostitutes.

It is unclear exactly where the idea for building this new city came from. Was it always part of the Horizon2020 Development Plan, announced in 2007, or has it retrospectively been made to fit with its goals? There is certainly no mention of Oyala in the text itself.

What is known is that President Obiang has always been wary of threats to his hold on power. The Wonga Coup in 2004 (pages 38–9) came very close to deposing him. Then, on 17 February 2009, the presidential palace in Malabo was attacked (page 37). In a rare December 2012 interview with the BBC, President Obiang referred directly to this attack and highlighted the need for a more secure capital city. A few years down the line and the jungle has been cleared, a highway has been carved out and the cranes are working overtime to make the president's vision a reality.

Whatever the motivations, Oyala now stands as one of the biggest construction projects in Central Africa, and is expanding by the day.

GETTING THERE AND AWAY Oyala is linked to the towns of Añisoc and Mengomeyén by a road, which feeds on to the main Bata to Mongomo Highway. It is also possible to **drive** south towards Aconibe, and then head to Evinayong. The nearest airport is in Mengomeyén, a mere 25km away, where you can catch internal **flights** to Bata and on to Malabo. As very few people currently live in Oyala, you will struggle to find a **shared taxi** to the city, and may need to pay to hire a whole taxi to get you there. Be sure to explain to the taxi driver that you want to visit the new city, not the old village, and confirm that he understands where to go, as not many drivers in the area have been there.

GETTING AROUND The main road bisecting the city, the Avenida de Justicia, is 3.8km long. Running perpendicular to this is Avenida de La Paz, which is even longer. In short, you will need a vehicle to get around. It is unclear whether access to the whole site is open to the public, but there are so many foreign contractors wandering around anyway that nobody pays you much attention, and there is hardly any police presence so no need to worry about registering upon arrival. Just to be safe though, carry a copy of your Tourism Permit and make sure it specifically states Oyala/Djibloho. Also, try not to openly point a camera at anyone official-looking.

WHERE TO STAY AND EAT *Map, page 202.*
If you cannot afford a five-star hotel, consider staying in Mongomo or Añisoc and getting a taxi to Oyala for the day. Currently the only nightlife is provided by the Grand Hotel Djibloho Kempinski's restaurants, bars and nightclub. Some of the foreign construction workers head into the village of Oyala in the evenings for cheaper nightlife, but this is a sad blend of drunkenness and prostitution.

🏠 Grand Hotel Djibloho Kempinski
(450 rooms & suites, 50 private villas) m 551 694
361; e PS.Djibloho@kempinski.com, reservations.
corporate@kempinski.com. This luxury hotel
features a 1,200-guest banquet room, 2 bars, a
café, 6 restaurants serving Italian, French, Spanish
& African cuisine ($$$–$$$$), a deli, a gym,
an 18-hole golf course with club house, a retail
gallery, a nightclub, a spa & a private health clinic.
Each of the 50 private villas on the grounds has 4
bedrooms & comes with a dedicated waiting staff.
The rooms are modern, spacious & with all the
features you would expect from a 5-star luxury
hotel. You need to contact the hotel directly for
bookings, as they are not yet integrated into the
Kempinski website online booking system (at the
time of writing they had not even had their official
opening yet), although this is due to happen in
late 2015.

SPORTS AND ACTIVITIES The two **parque deportivo** sections of the city will be the
place to go for access to outdoor sports areas such as football, tennis and swimming
facilities. The Chinese are also busy building the campus of the Instituto Nacional
de Deportes, which includes two stadiums and a number of indoor sporting arenas.
For now though, there is a gym and swimming pool at the **Grand Hotel Djibloho
Kempinski** (see above).

OTHER PRACTICALITIES There is a medical clinic in the Grand Hotel Djibloho
Kempinski but any serious problems will require evacuation to the La Paz hospitals
in Bata or Malabo.

WHAT TO SEE All of the grand construction projects of Oyala are easily reached
on the road network and are free to look around. Numerous architects wandering
around taking photos means that this is one of the few places you will not be hassled
for using a camera, although caution is still advised.

The campus of the the the **American University of Central Africa (AUCA)**, with its
spaceship-like central building, is planned to attract up to 8,000 students, becoming
a centre of learning not just in Equatorial Guinea, but across the entire region.
Classes are due to start in September 2015, and those lucky enough to be studying
here will have access to seven faculties spread across nine buildings, including
faculties of Medicine, Architecture & Engineering and Agriculture & Veterinary
Studies. There will also be a library, stadium, sports centre, student residences and
a wildlife centre. e http://auca.gq/eng.

At the centre of the development is the **government centre complex**. Built
in a series of concentric circles with a large fountain in the middle, this is where
President Obiang and his relocated ministers intend to govern the country from
in the coming decades. At the moment these are the architectural highlights most
likely to be visible to visitors in early 2016. Other areas marked on the map of
Oyala, such as the zoo or the numerous parks on the east of the city, will not be
completed for a number of years.

Both the **Avenida de Justicia** and **Avenida de La Paz** are wide, long, open
boulevards which offer views of the monumental architecture as well as the
surrounding Djing jungle. As in Sipopo, their manicured lawns are maintained by a small
army of men with strimmers, fighting a constant battle to hold back the advancing
jungle.

AROUND OYALA
Piedra Bere Natural Monument This protected area spreads across the border
of Kié-Ntem and Wele-Nzas, although it is most easily accessed from Wele-Nzas
Province, specifically the road between Mengomeyén and Añisoc. Here you will

find tall granite inselbergs rising out of the forest, similar to those found at Piedra Nzas. Although I am sure geologists could give a logical explanation as to what these massive chunks of rock are doing out here in the jungle on their own, it is not surprising that the local population has constructed myths about their origins. There is also a variety of wildlife to be seen in the area, including bats in the extensive caves.

Piedra Nzas Natural Monument On the drive between Mongomo and Evinayong, or Nsoc and Oyala, you will pass the Piedra Nzas Natural Monument, a footprint-shaped area of protected parkland. In the western portion of this forest you can hike to a series of spectacular 700m-high granite inselbergs, which seem to rise out of nowhere above the treeline (✦ 1° 27' N 11° 02' E). These inselbergs have been of particular interest to biologists as they host a wide variety of distinctive plant species, such as orchids, not found in the surrounding forest. The rock formations also have a network of caves which are home to many bats.

SEND US YOUR SNAPS!

We'd love to follow your adventures using our *Equatorial Guinea* guide – why not send us your photos and stories via Twitter (@BradtGuides) and Instagram (@bradtguides) using the hashtag #EquatorialGuinea. Alternatively, you can upload your photos directly to the gallery on the Equatorial Guinea destination page via our website (*www.bradtguides.com/eguinea*).

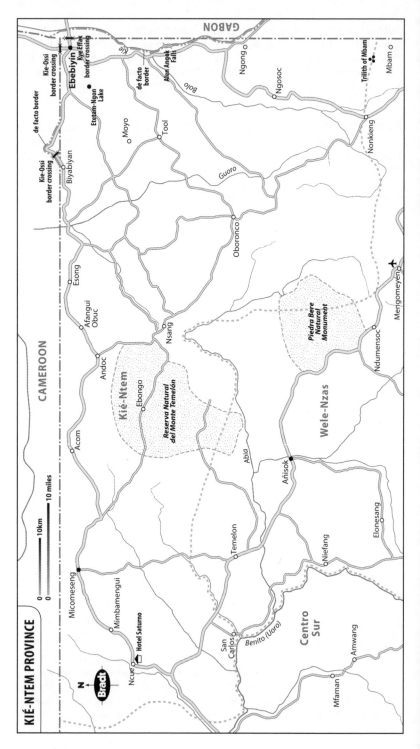

9

Kié-Ntem
Province

Kié-Ntem Province is in the far northeast of mainland Río Muni. This is a land of wide open spaces, unexplored forest and cross-border trade. Far less hot and wet than the coastal region, Kié-Ntem is a great place to camp, look for rare wildlife or perhaps even practise your French.

It shares a northern border with Cameroon, and an eastern border with Gabon (South Province and Woleu-Ntem Province respectively). Domestically, travelling south from this province you enter Wele-Nzas, and heading west you reach Centro Sur Province.

The capital city is Ebebiyín, located in the very northeast of the province, sitting on the border of Equatorial Guinea, Gabon and Cameroon. Other important settlements in the province include Micomeseng and Ncue.

Official government estimates put the population at around a quarter of a million, with Ebebiyín being the largest settlement, although accurate population figures for the town are impossible to find. The Reserva Natural del Monte Temelón (page 201) and the Piedra Bere Natural Monument (pages 204–5) both straddle the border between this province and Wele-Nzas.

Note that there are no tour operators based in Kié-Ntem Province. You are advised to make arrangements for visiting the area through companies based in Malabo (page 65) or Bata (page 152) before your arrival.

HISTORY

As with Wele-Nzas, Kié-Ntem has been inhabited for thousands of years but came very late to the 'Scramble for Africa'. Similar to its southern neighbour, it is likely that Pygmy groups had the space to themselves for almost 15 millennia until the arrival of Bantu groups from the northwest. The Bissio ethnic group, now resident in the coastal regions of Río Muni, may have transited through Kié-Ntem in search of a new home, having been displaced from their homeland in Ebolowa, southern Cameroon, by other more powerful ethnic groups.

More recently, Kié-Ntem has been the source of some tension between Equatorial Guinea and its neighbours Cameroon and Gabon. In January 2014 a deal negotiated by the Central African Economic and Monetary Community (CEMAC) was supposed to come into effect that allowed the free movement of people and goods across all members' borders. Both Equatorial Guinea and Gabon, who have far stronger economies than their other African neighbours, have blocked the deal for fear of being flooded with immigrants. This has led to huge border queues at Kie-Ossi in Cameroon. If seeking to cross at this point, be sure to seek local advice first, or check the status on http://africabordermonitor.com.

GETTING THERE AND AWAY

Domestic access to Kié-Ntem Province is usually achieved by **driving** in from the west, using the main road heading out of Niefang. Driving from Bata to Ebebiyín takes around 6 hours and the road is good. It is also possible to head north into the province from Mongomo. From Cameroon, you can drive south from Ambam and enter Equatorial Guinea at Ebebiyín, however, this crossing is subject to short-notice closures and border officials have a mixed record for allowing foreigners to cross here, even if your visa is in order. There is no domestic airport in the province.

EBEBIYÍN AND AROUND

In the far northeastern corner of Río Muni, facing Gabon to the east and Cameroon to the north, lies Ebebiyín. Compared with other locations in the country, this city feels big: big avenues, big markets, big population. It stretches 2km along an east–west axis, and with a large number of urban developments filling this space it is not thin and dispersed like Evinayong. Reliable population figures are not available, but it would not be surprising if this was the third largest city in the country after Bata and Malabo. Buoyed by recent hosting duties during the Africa Cup of Nations in 2015, and with the opportunities for cross-border trade improved by the new arterial motorway to the coast, Ebebiyín is sure to grow more in the coming years.

HISTORY Ebebiyín is very much at the centre of the Fang lands, which stretch further south than Libreville in modern day Gabon and further north than Yaoundé in Cameroon. This has been the case for hundreds of years. It is an excellent case study of the artificial nature of the boundaries that Europeans imposed on Africa during colonialism. The whole area speaks the Ntumu Fang dialect, helping to

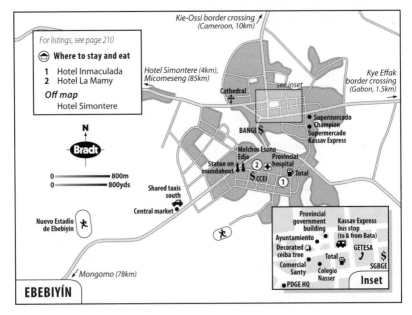

explain the modern success of cross-border trade between Gabon, Equatorial Guinea and Cameroon.

That this town came to be on the border of Spanish Guinea was a great disappointment to the Spanish colonial authorities. Spain did poorly from negotiations at the Berlin Conference (1884–85), as more powerful European nations carved out their spheres of influence on the African continent. Spain was in the unfortunate position of being sandwiched between German (Cameroon) and French (Gabon) claims. Río Muni ended up only 26,000km^2 in size, whereas Spain was aiming for 180,000km^2. This situation was finalised by the Treaty of Paris in 1900, which set the border where it remains today. Despite this agreement, the boundaries in this area are a little confusing. The eastern border between Equatorial Guinea and Gabon is officially a straight line running south from Ebebiyín (as shown on most maps and agreed at the Treaty of Paris in 1900). However, in reality, the de facto border seems to be treated as the river Kié, which gives Equatorial Guinea an extra 3km lump of territory in its northeastern corner.

During the era of President Macías, Ebebiyín became a transit point for citizens fleeing to other countries (page 28). While a terrible tragedy at the time, this diaspora created strong links between the three nations, and has served to fuel cross-border trade.

GETTING THERE, AWAY AND AROUND   Ebebiyín is well connected domestically. Both **shared taxis** and Kassav Express buses (m *222 721 516*) ply the route from Bata via Niefang, which takes around 4 hours and costs 3,500CFA. There are also shared taxis linking Ebebiyín and Mongomo for 2,000CFA per seat. It is very difficult to find a vehicle to Ebebiyín from Micomeseng, as by this point in the journey they are all full.

There are the usual shared taxis plying the main routes across town, for 500CFA per trip. Upon arrival if you get dropped off at the **Ayuntamiento** (Town Hall; by the decorated ceiba tree) in the centre of town, you should be able to walk to most locations.

Border crossings   Ebebiyín is situated on a tri-border area with Cameroon and Gabon. There is a bridge over the river Kié (or Kye) which acts as the de facto border between Equatorial Guinea and Gabon. Crossing this bridge takes you to the small settlement of Kye Effak or the larger town of Bitam in Gabon.

There is also a bridge to the north of Ebebiyín which takes you to Kie-Ossi in Cameroon.

The border between Cameroon and Gabon in this area is delineated by the river Ntem. There is a bridge at Meyo-Kye Effak.

These borders are known to close at short notice and Equatoguinean immigration officials have been recorded as refusing entry to foreign nationals at these points (even US citizens who do not require visas). If refused entry from Cameroon, your next available option on the west coast is crossing from Campo (Cameroon) to Río Campo (Equatorial Guinea). If refused entry from Gabon, try crossing from Oyem to Mongomo further south, which is a much busier crossing. Border officials are a bit more lenient about letting you out of the country (as opposed to in) at these points, although this is still not guaranteed.

WHERE TO STAY AND EAT   *Map, page 208.*
The Hotel Inmaculada bar is well stocked and they play music at weekends. For a cheap drink and some street food, head to the junction around Supermercado

Champion. There are plenty of shacks here selling cheap beer and blasting out music all night.

🏠 **Hotel Inmaculada** (23 rooms, 16 suites & 4 presidential suites) Calle San Pedro; m 222 051 148. The best hotel in town, situated in the southwest of the city. Single rooms here are good value & include all new fittings such as AC, twin beds, a big bath & shower & a fridge. There is a reasonably good buffet breakfast, & also a full menu for lunch & dinner (🕐 *07.00–23.00 daily*; $$). Pleasant bar area & pool. The suites include a large living room area & king-size beds. Staff speak Spanish, French & even some English. **$$$**

🏠 **Hotel Simontere** (20 rooms) On the western outskirts of town as you enter from Niefang & Micomeseng. This large compound has a restaurant & disco which is popular at w/ends. Rooms have AC & a double bed, but overall are not as nice as the more central Hotel Inmaculada. **$$–$$$**

🏠 **Hotel La Mamy** (24 rooms) m 222 609 481; e pperladinoss@yahoo.fr. A simple hotel with bare rooms that have a bed, mosquito net & fan. Friendly hosts & great value if you can do without AC. **$**

SHOPPING If you are looking for Fang crafts, there are a variety for sale in the village of **Afangui Obuc** (page 211).

🏪 **Central market** South of town; 🕐 07.00–17.00 daily. This huge covered market sells everything.

🏪 **Comercial Santy** 🕐 09.00–13.00 & 16.00–19.00 Mon–Fri, 09.00–13.00 Sat. The largest supermarket in town, located very centrally. A good range of fresh produce.

🏪 **Supermercado Champion** At the crossroads between the southern road to Mongomo & the eastern road to Gabon; 🕐 09.00–13.00 & 16.00–19.00 Mon–Fri. This supermarket has a decent selection of goods, including a refrigerated section.

🏪 **Supermercado Kassav Express** m 222 509 393; 🕐 08.00–18.00 Mon–Sat. Sells only non-perishable items & refrigerated drinks.

OTHER PRACTICALITIES Upon arrival, be sure to **register** at the Ayuntamiento (Town Hall), which is in the centre of town with the decorated ceiba tree outside. The bemused officials are generally friendly, if a bit slow. Give them a copy of your Tourism Permit.

There are two **Total petrol stations** in town, one central and one to the south. If you need phone credit or a SIM card, head for **GETESA**.

Banks

$ **BANGE Bank** 🕐 07.00–14.30 Mon–Fri, 09.00–13.30 Sat; e info@egbange.com. Has no ATM.

$ **CCEI Bank** Av General Obiang Nguema, Apdo 33; 🟢 333 072 196, 333 072 198; 🕐 08.00–14.30 Mon–Fri, 10.00–13.00 Sat. This massive golden structure is hard to miss. Has an ATM but no Visa symbol.

$ **SGBGE Bank** Av Principal; 🟢 333 262 020; 🕐 08.00–14.00 Mon–Fri. Has an ATM which accepts Visa.

Healthcare

➕ **Provincial Hospital** Calle San Pedro; 🟢 333 084 755; 🕐 24hrs. Near the Hotel Inmaculada. Not an international-standard facility though, so in emergencies you will need to head to Bata or Malabo.

WHAT TO SEE AND DO The town square is very picturesque, with a **ceiba tree decorated** in the colours of the ruling PDGE party and the colonial **Ayuntamiento** building. The **central market** is worth visiting, but you will need to get a shared taxi here from the centre. It is bustling and sells all manner of random goods, from Chinese imports to live animals.

At the end of Avenida Cosme Nsue Ondo in the southern part of town you will find a large **statue on the roundabout** of a lady in traditional attire picking bananas. Opposite here there is a tall column with a **statue of Melchor Esono Edjo** at the base, holding an encyclopedia. He was born and grew up locally, and is a respected economist and a former minister of finance and budgets. Ebebiyín also has a very large and new Spanish-built **cathedral**.

The newly refurbished stadium, **Nuevo Estadio de Ebebiyín**, played host to some of the group stage matches in the Africa Cup of Nations football tournament in 2015, and also the Equatorial Guinean Football Federation Women's league final in 2014. It has a capacity of 8,000 spectators.

AROUND EBEBIYÍN There are a number of potential tourist sites tucked away sites only a few kilometres from Ebebiyín, which make for good day hikes or short drives. The countryside in this part of the nation rarely sees visitors, but you should find a curious but warm welcome wherever you choose to wander. Given the lush scenery around Ebebiyín, the majority of sites listed below are outdoor attractions.

Twenty kilometres west of Ebebiyín is the small village of **Biyabiyan**, right up on the northern border with Cameroon. There is a small museum of Fang art here run by local artists. Ask around and one of the residents will open it up and show you around.

Almost equidistant between Micomeseng and Ebebiyín is the small village of **Afangui Obuc**. They have a crafts house with traditional Fang goods for sale. This area is famous from colonial times as a base for Basque big-game hunting legend Basilio Olaechea Orruño, who sadly spent much of the 1950s shooting all the gorillas in the area and the odd elephant. This hunter was legendary as a crack shot with a rifle, able to hit a stone thrown in the air from more than 50m.

The **Alen Angok Falls** on the Kié River mark the de facto border between Gabon and Equatorial Guinea in this area. The settlement here is marked on some maps as 'Adyap (Angoc)' although this is technically a village a few kilometres to the north. Alen Angok is also home to a colonial school from 1936, a dispensary and medical centre from 1937, and a military base built by the Spanish during World War II.

To the southwest of Ebebiyín is the picturesque **Etetam-Ngon Lake**. To get here, trek to the village of Bifet (Efac), and you will find it on the route to nearby Moyo village.

Right on the border of Kié-Ntem and Wele-Nzas provinces, around 17km north of Mongomo on the border road, is the mysterious stone structure **Trilith of Mbam (Esaguong)**, featuring two upright columns of stone with a third balanced horizontally between them. The location is sometimes also referred to as El Trilito de Mibang locally. These are not the only triliths in the area and some locals talked about another set near the village of Mosom Esandon, around 5km from Ebebiyín. Until this area is more thoroughly surveyed by archaeologists (which is unlikely to occur very soon) these structures will remain an intriguing mystery.

MICOMESENG

Halfway between Bata and Ebebiyín is Micomeseng, a small transit town with one main road, a market, a military radar dish and an inexplicable amount of building work happening on its periphery. Little more than a travellers' rest stop to most people, Micomeseng is located in the heart of coffee and cocoa country. It is still home to a colonial-era leprosy treatment centre, which is maintained with the help of Catholic Mission volunteers and Cuban medical experts, which hint at

Equatorial Guinea's post-colonial foreign relations (page 41). There is also a large colonial church adjoining the hospital, the Iglesia Nuestra Senhora.

 ## WHERE TO STAY AND EAT

Hotel Fidel (12 rooms) On a grass bank at the western entrance to town; m 551 445 202. This building does a good job of hiding from potential clients, & there is only a small LCD sign indicating that it is a hotel. Inside you can see the Chinese contractors have been at work as there are gold chandeliers & plastic fittings aplenty. Single rooms are clean, new & spacious. They include TV, AC, a double bed & combined bath & shower. This is good value for money in these parts. There are also suites that are much more expensive & have a larger bedroom & a living room with seating for 5. The hotel has a fairly upmarket restaurant (**$$**) but the menu is limited & the kitchen is not always open. **$–$$**

✕ Restaurante Tatiana ⊕ noon–21.30 Mon–Sat, 14.00–20.00 Sun. Situated on the side road leading to the hospital, the Tatiana offers cheap local cuisine. The chicken is good (when they have it). **$**

♀ Bar Abaceria Marisa ⊕ 10.00–23.30 Mon–Sat. In the centre of town near the taxi stop. This bar has cold beers, warm spirits & not much else.

OTHER PRACTICALITIES

✚ Clinica Wuhan On the junction of the main road & the hospital road; ⊕ 08.00–18.00 Mon–Sat. A Chinese-run pharmacy. Useful as they do not take a break for lunch.

GETESA Over the road from the police station in the centre of town. Sell SIM cards & phone credit.

✚ Micomeseng Hospital Northeast of town near the church; ⊕ 24hrs. The hospital is run down & quite crowded, as this town is a hub for the treatment of leprosy.

Police station On the main road; m 666 500 076. This is seemingly the only police station in the country with a dedicated phone number on display. Be sure to register here upon arrival by dropping off a copy of your Tourism Permit.

WHAT TO SEE Thirty kilometres west of Micomeseng is the town of **Ncue**. Here you will find a large colonial church, a GE petrol station and the Hotel Saturno (*15 rooms*; **$$**).

From Micomeseng there is a road running southeast to the town of Nsang, which passes through the **Reserva Natural del Monte Temelón** (pages 200–1).

GUIDEBOOK UPDATES

You can read the latest updates and make suggestions of your own by following @BradtEGguide on Twitter or by posting a comment on the Bradt website at www.bradtupdates/eguinea.

Appendix 1

LANGUAGE

SPANISH OF EQUATORIAL GUINEA Compared to its regional neighbours, Equatorial Guinea has a high proportion of proficient colonial European-language speakers (in this case Spanish). This is thanks to the work of various missionary groups, as well as the efforts of the Spanish government during the last period of colonial rule. Rough estimates put the number of reasonably fluent Spanish-speakers at 90% for Bioko island and the urban areas of Río Muni, with a reduction to 60% or 70% in more isolated rural communities of the mainland.

There are a lot of people from Spain and Central and South America working in Equatorial Guinea. This means that you are likely to hear a whole range of different types of Spanish being spoken. The Spanish spoken by Equatoguineans should be intelligible to anyone with experience in the language, although it does have some distinct characteristics.

In terms of pronunciation, there are a few noticeable differences. The most obvious is the lack of distinction between Spanish single /r/ and trill /rr/; usually the single sound is switched for the trill (for example, saying *trrabajo* instead of *trabajo* for work). Another audible difference is the more sing-song cadence of syllable-based tonal alternation, which might make it difficult to tell if someone is making a statement or asking a question. This change is due to the way many of the local languages are pronounced. Finally, nearly all Equatoguineans pronounce a 'd' between vowels like 'r', thus making *todo* 'all' sound more like *toro* 'bull'.

There are also some noticeable grammatical differences between Equatoguinean Spanish and Metropolitan Spanish. Prepositions such as *en*, *de* and *a* can be used interchangeably by many speakers or sometimes left out, which would be considered incorrect in mainland Spain. Often the polite, more formal form of you (*usted*) will be combined with verb endings relating to the less formal form of you (*tú*). You may also find problems with subject and verb agreement, with the third person singular used as a default, even when talking about I, you, we, etc. There are also occasional lapses of noun and adjective agreement, with little concern for the gender or the number of the object(s) being described. Most of these features are predominantly found among less fluent Spanish-speakers.

Pronunciation
Consonants

c   as in 'cat', before 'a', 'o', or 'u'; like 's' before 'e' or 'i'
d   as 'd' in 'dog', except between vowels, then like 'th' in 'that'
g   before 'e' or 'i', like the 'ch' in Scottish 'loch'; elsewhere like 'g' in 'get'
h   always silent
j   like the 'ch' in 'loch'
ll   like the 'y' in 'yellow'

ñ	like the 'ni' in 'onion'
r	pronounced as strong 'r' (note comments on difference from Metropolitan Spanish)
rr	trilled 'rr' (note comments on difference from Metropolitan Spanish)
v	similar to the 'b' in 'boy' (not as English 'v')
y	similar to English, but with a slight 'j' sound. When y stands alone it is pronounced like the 'e' in 'me'.
z	like 's' in 'same'

b, f, k, l, m, n, p, q, s, t, w, x as in English

Vowels

a	as in 'father' but shorter
e	as in 'hen'
i	as in 'machine'
o	as in 'phone'
u	usually as in 'rule'; when it follows a 'q' the 'u' is silent; when it follows an 'h' or 'g' it's pronounced like 'w', except when it comes between 'g' and 'e' or 'i', when it's also silent

Vocabulary
Essentials

Good morning	*Buenos días* (often shortened to *buenos*)
Good afternoon	*Buenas tardes* (often shortened to *buenas*)
Good evening	*Buenas noches* (often shortened to *buenas*)
Hello	*Hola*
Goodbye	*Adios*
My name is…	*Me llamo…*
What is your name?	*¿Cómo te llamas?* (informal)
	¿Cómo se llama usted? (formal)
I am from England/America	*Soy de Inglaterra/los Estados Unidos*
How are you?	*¿Cómo estás?*
Pleased to meet you	*Mucho gusto*
Thank you	*Gracias*
Don't mention it	*De nada*
Cheers!	*¡Salud!*
yes	*sí*
no	*no*
I don't understand	*No entiendo*
I don't speak Spanish	*No hablo español*
Please can you speak more slowly	*¿Podría hablar más despacio por favor?*
Do you understand?	*¿Entiende?*

Questions

how?	*¿cómo?*	what is it?	*¿qué es?*	why?	*¿por qué?*
what?	*¿qué?*	which?	*¿cuál?*	who?	*¿quién?*
where?	*¿dónde?*	when?	*¿cuándo?*	how much?	*¿cuánto?*

Numbers

1	*uno*	5	*cinco*	9	*nueve*
2	*dos*	6	*seis*	10	*diez*
3	*tres*	7	*siete*	11	*once*
4	*cuatro*	8	*ocho*	12	*doce*

13	trece	20	veinte	70	setenta
14	catorce	21	veintiuno	80	ochenta
15	quince	30	treinta	90	noventa
16	dieciseis	31	treinta y uno	100	cien
17	diecisiete	40	cuarenta	1,000	mil
18	dieciocho	50	cincuenta		
19	diecinueve	60	sesenta		

Time

What time is it?	¿Qué hora es?
Its… am/pm	Son las… am/pm
today	hoy
tonight	esta noche
tomorrow	mañana
yesterday	ayer
morning	mañana
afternoon/evening	tarde

Days

Monday	lunes	Thursday	jueves	Sunday	domingo
Tuesday	martes	Friday	viernes		
Wednesday	miércoles	Saturday	sábado		

Months

January	enero	May	mayo	September	setiembre
February	febrero	June	junio	October	octubre
March	marzo	July	julio	November	noviembre
April	abril	August	agosto	December	diciembre

Transport
Public transport

I'd like…	Me gustaría…
… a one-way ticket	… pasaje de ida
… a return ticket	… pasaje de ida y vuelta
I want to go to…	Quiero ir a…
How much is it?	¿Cuánto cuesta?
What time does it leave?	¿A qué hora sale?
What time is it now?	¿Qué hora es ahora?
The bus has been…	El autobús está…
… delayed	… atrasado
… cancelled	… suspendido

timetable	horario	car	coche
from	de	4x4	cuatro por cuatro
to	a	taxi	taxi
bus station	terminal	minibus	minibus
airport	aeropuerto	motorbike/moped	moto
port	puerto	bicycle	bicicleta
bus	autobús	arrival/departure	llegada/salida
train	tren	here	aquí
plane	avión	there	allí
boat	barco	bon voyage!	¡buen viaje!

Private transport

Is this the road to…?	*¿Es éste el camino a…?*
Where is the service station?	*¿Dónde está la estación de servicios?*
Please fill it up	*Tanque lleno, por favor*
I'd like… litres	*Quiero… litros*
diesel	*gasoil/diesel*
petrol (unleaded)	*gasolina (sin plomo)*
I have broken down	*Se me ha averiado el coche*

Road signs

give way	*ceda el paso*	one-way street	*calle de dirreción única*
danger	*peligro*	toll	*peaje*
entry	*entrada*	no entry	*prohibido el paso*
detour	*desvío*	exit	*salida*

Directions

Where is it?	*¿Dónde está?*
Go straight ahead	*Siga derecho/adelante*
turn left	*gire a la izquierda*
turn right	*gire a la derecha*
… at the traffic lights	*… al semáforo*
… at the roundabout	*… a la rotonda*
north	*norte*
south	*sur*
east	*este*
west	*oeste*
behind	*detrás de…*
in front of	*delante de…*
near	*cerca de…*
opposite	*en frente de…*

Street signs

entrance	*entrada*	closed	*cerrado*
exit	*salida*	toilets	*baños/servicios*
open	*abierto*	information	*información*

Accommodation

Where is a cheap/ good hotel?	*¿Dónde se encuentra un hotel barato/bueno?*
Could you please write the address?	*¿Podría escribirme la dirección por favor?*
Do you have any rooms available?	*¿Tiene habitaciones disponibles?*
I'd like…	*Me gustaría…*
… a single room	*… una habitación simple*
… a double room	*… una habitación doble*
… a room with two beds	*… una habitación con dos camas*
… a room with a bathroom	*… una habitación con baño privado*
How much it is per person/night?	*¿Cuánto cuesta por persona/por noche?*

Where is the toilet/ bathroom?	¿Dónde está el baño?
Is there hot water?	¿Tiene agua caliente?
Is there electricity?	¿Hay luz?
Is breakfast included	¿Está incluido el desayuno?
I am leaving today	Salgo hoy

Food and drink

Do you have a table for... people?	¿Tiene mesa para... personas?
... a children's menu?	... menu de niños?
I am a vegetarian	Soy vegetariano/a
Do you have any vegetarian dishes?	¿Tiene algún plato vegetariano?
Please bring me...	Por favor, tráigame...
... a fork/knife/spoon	... tenedor/cuchillo/cuchara
Please may I have the bill?	La cuenta, por favor

Basics

bread	pan		oil	aceite
butter	mantequilla (not burro, as in Italian)		pepper	pimienta/pepe
			salt	sal
cheese	queso		sugar	azúcar

Fruit and vegetables

apples	manzanas		onion	cebolla
bananas	bananas		oranges	naranjas
carrot	zanahoria		passion fruit	maracuyá
garlic	ajo		pepper	pimiento
mango	mango			

Fish

| tuna | atún | | squid | calamar |
| fish | pescado | | octopus | pulpo |

Meat

beef	carne (de vaca)		monkey	mono
chicken	pollo		pangolin	pangolín
pork	cerdo		porcupine	chucku-chucku
goat	cabra		sausage	chorizo

Drinks

beer	cerveza		tea	té
coffee	café		water	agua
fruit juice	zumo de frutas		wine	vino
milk	leche		palm wine	vino de palma/tope

Shopping

I'd like to buy...	Me gustaría comprar...
How much is it?	¿Cuánto cuesta?
I don't like it	No me gusta

I'm just looking	*Sólo estoy mirando*
It's too expensive	*Es demasiado caro*
I'll take it	*Lo voy a llevar*
Please may I have…	*¿Podría darme…?*
Do you accept credit card?	*¿Se acepta tarjeta de crédito?*
more	*más*
less	*menos*
smaller	*más pequeño*
bigger	*más grande*

Communications

I am looking for…	*estoy buscando…*
… the bank	*… el banco*
… the post office	*… el correo/la oficina de correos*
… the church	*… la iglesia*
… the embassy	*… la embajada*
… the exchange office	*… el cambio/la oficina de cambio*

Health

malaria	*paludismo*	condoms	*preservativos/condónes*
diarrhoea	*diarrea*	contraceptive	*anticonceptivos*
nausea	*náusea*	sun block	*crema protectora (solar)*
doctor	*doctor*	I am…	*Soy…*
prescription	*receta*	… asthmatic	*… asmático/a*
pharmacy	*farmacia*	… epileptic	*… epiléptico/a*
paracetamol	*paracetamol*	… diabetic	*… diabético/a*
aspirin	*aspirina*	I'm allergic to…	*Soy alergico/a a…*
antibiotics	*antibióticos*	… penicillin	*… penicilina*
antiseptic	*antiséptico*	… nuts	*… nueces*
tampons	*tampones*	… bees	*… abejas*

Travel with children

Is there a…?	*¿Hay…?*
Do you have…?	*¿Tiene usted…?*
… infant milk formula?	*… leche en polvo para bebé?*
nappies	*pañales*
babysitter	*niñera*
Are children allowed?	*¿Se permiten niños?*

Miscellaneous

my/mine	*mi/mis*	that (close)	*ese/esa/eso*
your (singular)	*tu/tus*	that (far)	*aquel/aquella/aquellos/*
his/her	*su/sus*		*aquellas*
our	*nuestro/a/os/as*	expensive/cheap	*caro/barato*
your (plural)	*su/sus*	beautiful/ugly	*lindo/feo*
their	*su/sus*	old/new	*viejo/nuevo*
and	*y*	good/bad	*malo/bueno*
but	*pero*	early/late	*temprano/tarde*
some	*algún/alguna/algunos/*	hot/cold	*caliente/frío*
	algunas	difficult/easy	*dificil/facil*
this	*este/esta/esto*	boring/interesting	*aburrido/interesante*

Emergency

Help!	*¡Socorro!/¡Ayuda!*	police	*policía*
Call a doctor	*llame al doctor*	fire	*incendio*
There's been an accident	*Ha ocurrido un accidente*	ambulance	*ambulancia*
		thief	*ladrón*
I'm lost	*Estoy perdido/a*	hospital	*hospital*
Go away!	*¡Fuera!*	I am ill	*estoy enfermo/a*

AFRICAN LANGUAGES OF EQUATORIAL GUINEA Equatorial Guinea hosts an extraordinary diversity of languages. If you travel around enough you may well hear Fang, Bube, Fernando Pó Creole, Fá d'Ambô or Benga being spoken. There are also some other rarer languages such as Kombe, Basek Seki, Balengue, Bissio (local Kwasio), Yasa or Bakola-Bagyeli.

Fang The most widespread African language spoken in Equatorial Guinea is **Fang**. This is the language of the majority ethnic group within the country, both on the mainland and on Bioko island. There are many dialects of Fang in Equatorial Guinea and over the borders in Cameroon and Gabon. The most common in Equatorial Guinea are Ntumu Fang and Okak Fang which are mutually intelligible.

Bube The **Bube** language is spoken by the Bubi ethnic group, who are the original inhabitants of Bioko.

Fernando Pó Creole (Pichinglis) Fernando Pó Creole (Pichinglis) is an English-lexicon Creole language spoken by those of Krio descent on Bioko. It is related to the Krio language, spoken by almost all of Sierra Leone's inhabitants.

Note: the acute accent (á) signals a high tone on the syllable, the grave accent (à) signals a low tone.

Fá d'Ambô Fá d'Ambô is the Portuguese Creole language of Annobón, which has many similarities to Forro Creole, the language spoken on nearby São Tomé and Príncipe.

Some notes on the pronunciation:

- tx = sh (as in 'shoe')
- ge and/or gi = same as Spanish pronunciation
- kh = like a Spanish 'j' or the 'ch' in 'loch'
- lh = like a Spanish 'll' or the 'li' in 'million'
- nh = like the 'ny' in 'canyon'
- Y/y = Officially known as a Voiced alveolar affricate, we do not use this much in English, but it sounds a bit like the 'ds' in 'pounds'.
- Ô is a closed vowel, like the 'aw' in 'yawn'
- ê is a closed vowel, like the 'ay' in 'play'

Kombe Kombe is a West Bantu family language spoken by a small community of the Kombe people in Río Muni (one of the Ndowe groups of the coast). It is closely related to Yasa.

Bissio Bissio is the Equatoguinean dialect of Kwasio, a widespread language of southern Cameroon that extends over the northern Río Muni border by the coast. Very little research has been done on this language in Equatorial Guinea.

English	Fang	Bube	Fernando Pó Creole
Hello	Ambolana	Ko bóyállo	Háw fá?
Goodbye	Makeyang	O sá úwe	Àdiòs/Sìdón fáyn ('stay well')
please	egugoho	tyuíi	à bég/por favor
Thank you	Akiba	Potóo/Pottó	Ténkì
yes	owe	ëë	yés
no	kaha	é'ë	nó
Do you speak English/Spanish?	Ye wa yema kobo ingles/español?	Ö la töőlënkëlési/ ëpanná?	Yù dè tók inglés/ panya?
My name is...	Me ne ewalanaha...	Nè në lé...	Mì ném nà...
Who?	Saha?	Ká bè?	Údàt?
What?	Chia?	Ké è?	Ústìn/wétìn?
When?	Oden?	Ká é he ébélő?	Ústèn?
Where?	Ove?	Ké tyë?	Úsày?
How much?	Tahayañi?	Labe'ê?	Háw móch?
toilet	ewaban	koppí	bàfrúm
police	policia	pörösía	pòlís
hospital	hospital	tyóbbo i kaaí	hòspitál
Help!	Avara!	Pulánnóo!	Hép mi!
How do I get to...?	Ye okuñi nveng...?	Ka lò m pa'a lò	Háw à gò rích...? pèlla ë...?
sleep	akeyo	lokka	slíp
eat	adji	ráa	chóp
drink	añu	ráa	dríng
good	nven	lèlè	fáyn
bad	abehe	labé	bád

OTHER LANGUAGES OF EQUATORIAL GUINEA The languages listed above should help you to communicate successfully with the vast majority of Equatorial Guinea's population. If you encounter someone who does not speak Spanish, they are highly likely to speak Fang, Pichinglis or Bube, especially on Bioko island. However, in the more rural parts of Río Muni, as well as on some of Equatorial Guinea's islands, you may encounter some of the rarer languages, such as Basek Seki, Benga, Balengue and possibly the rarest language in the whole region: Bakola-Bagyeli.

Basek Seki is a relatively unstudied language from coastal Río Muni, which is related to the Gabonese Seki language. **Benga** is spoken on Corisco island, as well as by some isolated communities on the northern Gabonese coast. Luckily, if you come unstuck with Spanish, many residents also speak French due to their close proximity to Gabon. The **Balengue** language is a Bantu language from southern Río Muni, with only a thousand native speakers spread along the coastal strip from south of Bata to the Gabonese border. The speakers of this language are considered one of the Ndowe groups of the coast. This language is also poorly understood by scholars. **Yasa** is another minority Bantu language spoken by some of the Ndowe communities of Río Muni and also northwards into Cameroon.

Lastly, the **Bakola-Bagyeli** Pygmy groups, numbering only a few hundred, are one of the smallest minorities in the country, and have their own language. Living mainly in southern Cameroon, between the Nyong and the Ntem rivers, some

English	Fá d'Ambô	Kombe	Bissio
Hello	Mantẽa	Ambolo	Bull Asigo Gi na gi
Goodbye	Mi è khabai	Cabo yoba ibocue	Me kema
please	pulusença	soso	susu
Thank you	Dezu pagà	Aquebaa	Awa
yes	txĩè	e´	aaaa yang
no	no	a´	totsa
Do you speak English/Spanish?	¿Bo khafà fá'ngééyi/ fá'lavana?	Nave capa ingles/ pañoli	Wolap ingles/español
My name is…	A khasam(à)-mu…	Dinadiame die…	Bowome…
Who?	¿Kẽ'ngẽ?	Isa?	Nze?
What?	¿Kẽ' kuzu?	Ende?	Gui?
When?	¿Kẽ' ola/ora? (or ¿K'ola?)	Isaenye?	Pil nye
Where?	¿Kẽ' khamíã?/K'khamía?	Guee?	Oyee?
How much?	¿Kẽ' khantu?/¿K'khántu?	Tangoye?	Tanguina?
toilet	khái (yi) labà/	bacaosi khá'î labà/bánho	ndosia
police	pôlôxía/khotxísima	sodie	gobina
hospital	ospital/hospital	pitale	pital
Help!	¡Socorro!/¡Zuda!	Cochene!	Cuelame!
How do I get to…?	Àma fê ku txigá…/	Napaba indi e iboco…? Kómo fê ku lhega a…	Ona me pan…?
sleep	yiunì	enanga	dasi
eat	kumì/kumù	edia	di
drink	bêbẽ'	eñia	ull nyuli
good	bweno/gaávu/bō	muasa	mba
bad	má/fẽ'ïu/mal	embeva	bio

groups are known to cross the border into northern Equatorial Guinea, ranging from Río Campo on the coast as far east as the Monte Temelón Natural Reserve.

Appendix 2

FURTHER INFORMATION

BIBLIOGRAPHY *For a general reading list, see pages 56–7.*
Archaeology
Mercader, Julio and Marti, Raquel 'Middle Stone Age Site in the Tropical Forests of Equatorial Guinea', *Nyame Akuma*, 51 (Jun 1999), 14–2 4. Print.

Vizcaya, Benita S 'Routes to Ruin', *LL Journal* 7.2 (2012). *PhD Program in Hispanic and Luso-Brazilian Literatures and Languages*. The City University of New York (2012). Print. Web.

Architecture
Furuto, Alison 'Djibloho – Equatorial Guinea's Future Capital City/IDF – Ideias do Futuro', ArchDaily website (27 Nov 2011). Web.

Ikuga, Laida Memba 'Bioko: Arquitectura y Memoria – Calendario 2013' Centro Cultural de Espana en Bata & Malabo website (Jun 2012). Web.

Culture
Cusack, Igor 'African cuisines: recipes for nation building?' *Journal of African Cultural Studies*, 2 (Dec 2000), 207–25. Web.

Cusack, Igor 'Equatorial Guinea's National Cuisine Is Simple and Tasty: Cuisine and the Making of National Culture', *Arizona Journal of Hispanic Cultural Studies*, 8 (2004), 131–48. Print.

Lifshey, Adam 'And so the Worm Turns: The Impossibility of Imperial Imitation in Una Lanza Por el Boabí by Daniel Jones Mathama', *Chasqui: revista de literatura latinoamericana*, 36/1 (May 2007), 108–20. Print.

Loboch, Francisco Zamora 'La increíble aventura de la literatura de Guinea Ecuatorial', *IberoAfrica*, 2 (2012), 51–3. Web.

Mba, Gisèle Avome 'Colonialismo y Resistencia en Cuando Los Combes Luchaban, de Leoncio Evita Enoy', *Journal of AfroEuropean Studies*, 2 (2008). Web.

Sundiata, Ibrahim 'Review: Los Bubis, Ritos y Creencias by Amador Martín del Molino', *The International Journal of African Historical Studies*, 24/1 (1991), 182–3. Print.

Economy
'African Economic Outlook: Equatorial Guinea', Organisation for Economic Co-operation and Development (2008). Web.

'African Economic Outlook: Equatorial Guinea', Organisation for Economic Co-operation and Development (2012). Web.

'IMF Country Report No.13/83: Equatorial Guinea', International Monetary Fund (Mar 2013), US Department of the Interior. Web.

'Undue Diligence: How Banks Do Business with Corrupt regimes', Global Witness (2009). Web.

'World Oil and Gas review 2013', Eni SpA (Sep 2013). Rome, Italy. Web.

Agrawal, Devendra 'Challenges Ahead at Equatorial Guinea: Execution of a grassroots LNG project on Malabo Island, EG, Central Africa', Marathon Oil Company, GasTech Presentation (13 Mar 2005). Web.

Frynas, Jędrzej George 'The Oil Boom in Equatorial Guinea', *African Affairs*, 103/413 (Oct 2004), 527–46. Web.

Mobbs, Philip M 'The Mineral Industry of Equatorial Guinea', US Geological Survey (Sep 2013). Print.

Song, Jae, Oh, Hyunseok, Lee, Chu and Chun, Hong Min 'National Economic Development of Equatorial Guinea in Horizon 2020/Desarrollo Económico Nacional de Guinea Ecuatorial para Horizonte 2020', Korean Institute for Development Strategy (2012). Web.

Education

'Financing Education in sub-Saharan Africa: Meeting the Challenges of Expansion, Equity and Quality', UNESCO Institute of Statistics (2011)

'Visualizing Rights – Fact Sheet No.9: Equatorial Guinea', Centre for Economic and Social Rights (2009). Web.

Geography

Dzurek, Daniel J 'Gulf of Guinea Boundary Disputes', IBRU Boundary and Security Bulletin (spring 1999). Web.

Government

'Equatorial Guinea at the crossroads – Report of a Mission to Equatorial Guinea', International Bar Association Human Rights Institute (Oct 2003). London, UK. Print.

Smoltczyk, Alexander von 'Volltanken in Malabo', *Der Spiegel*, 35/3 (2006), 82–101. Print. German.

Health

Ebona, Santiago Elé 'Buruli ulcer and Leprosy in Equatorial Guinea', Ministerio de Sanidad y Bienestar Social (2006), Equatorial Guinea. Web.

History

'Dispute with Spain; Arrest of Politicians after Failure of Attempted Coup; Evacuation of Spanish Armed Forces and Civilians', *Keesing's Record of World Events*, 15 (Apr 1969). Keesing's Worldwide, LLC, USA. Web.

'The 1930 Enquiry Commission to Liberia', *Journal of the Royal African Society*, 30/120 (Jul 1931), 277–290. Oxford University Press, UK. Web.

'World Illiteracy at Mid Century – A statistical study', UNESCO Education and Documentation Centre (1957). Buckdruckerei Winterthur AG, Switzerland. Web.

Aixela, Yolandà 'Of Colonists, Migrants and National Identity. The Historic Difficulties of the Socio-Political Construction of Equatorial Guinea', *Nordic Journal of African Studies 22 (1&2)* (2013) 49–71. CEA, ISCTE-IUL, Portugal. Print.

Artucio, Alejandro 'The Trial of Macías in Equatorial Guinea: The Story of a Dictatorship', International Commission of Jurists (30 Sep 1979). Geneva, Switzerland. Web.

Baynham, Simon 'Equatorial Guinea: The Terror and the Coup', *The World Today*, 36/2 (Feb 1980), 65–71. Royal Institute of International Affairs, London. Web.

Berman, Sanford 'Spanish Guinea: Enclave Empire', *Phylon (1940-1956)*, 17/4 (4th Quarter, 1956), 349–64. Clark Atlanta University, USA. Web.

Burke, Edward 'Spain's relations with Equatorial Guinea: a triumph of energy realism?', *Fundación para las Relaciones Internacionales y el Diálogo Exterior* (Jul 2008). Madrid, Spain. Web.

Burton, Richard Francis *Wanderings in West Africa, Volume 1: From Liverpool to Fernando Po* Tinsley Brothers, London, 1863. Print.

Campos, Alicia 'The decolonisation of Equatorial Guinea: The Relevance of the International Factor', *The Journal of African History*, 44/1 (2003), 95–116. Cambridge University Press, UK. Web.

Chamberlin, Christopher 'The migration of the Fang into Central Gabon during the Nineteenth Century: A New Interpretation', *The International Journal of African Historical Studies*, 11/3 (1978), 429–56. Boston University, USA. Web.

Clarence-Smith, Gervase 'The impact of the Spanish Civil War and the Second World War on Portuguese and Spanish Africa', *The Journal of African History*, 26/4 (1985), 309–26. Web.

Decalo, Samuel 'African Personal Dictatorships', *The Journal of Modern African Studies*, 23/2 (Jun 1985), 209–37. Cambridge University Press, UK. Web.

Du Chaillu, Paul *A Journey to Ashango-Land and further penetration into Equatorial Africa* John Murray, London, 1876. Print.

Eiso, Juan Manuel Davies 'Another Equatorial Guinea: Remembering, but Not for Vengeance', *Afro-Hispanic Review*, 28/2 (autumn 2009), 393–4. Print.

Erdos, Chris 'Heart of Darkness', *The Foreign Service Journal* (Apr 2008), 43–8. American Foreign Service Association, USA. Web.

Fegley, Randall 'The U. N. Human Rights Commission: The Equatorial Guinea Case', *Human Rights Quarterly*, 3/1 (Feb 1981), 34–47. The Johns Hopkins University Press, USA. Web.

Gozalbes, Cravioto E 'Las primeras exploraciones científicas de Guinea Ecuatorial', Proceedings of the International Conference: Science in the Tropics – Glimpsing the past projecting the future (2013). Lisbon. Web.

Hoffacker, Lewis 'Interview with Alan Hardy, Ambassador to Equatorial Guinea 1981–1984', Association for Diplomatic Studies and Training, Country Reader: Equatorial Guinea (2001). George P Shultz National Foreign Affairs Training Center, USA. Web.

i Güell, Miquel Vilaró and Schneider, Jürg 'Fourteen Views of Fernando Po to Save the Colony', *The PhotoResearcher*, 21 (23 Apr 2014), 38–52. European Society for the History of Photography, Austria. Web.

Ibongo, Saturnino and LeMelle, Tilden J 'The Liberation of Spanish Guinea', *Africa Today*, 14/4 (Aug 1967), 18–20. Indiana University Press, USA. Web.

Kennedy, Charles Stewart 'Interview with Lewis Hoffacker, Ambassador to Equatorial Guinea 1969–72', Association for Diplomatic Studies and Training, Country Reader: Equatorial Guinea (17 Jul 1998). George P Shultz National Foreign Affairs Training Center, USA. Web.

Kingsley, Mary H *Travels in West Africa*, J M Dent, London, 1897. Print.

Lynn, Martin 'Commerce, Christianity and the Origins of the "Creoles" of Fernando Po', *The Journal of African History*, 25/3 (1984), 257–78. Cambridge University Press, UK. Web.

Liniger-Goumaz, Max *Guinée Équatoriale – 30 ans d'État déliquant nguemiste* Editions L'Harmattan, Paris, 1998. Print.

Liniger-Goumaz, Max *La Guinee Équatoriale – un pays méconnu* Editions L'Harmattan, Paris, 1979. Print.

Mann, Simon *Cry Havoc* John Blake Publishing, London, 2012. Print.

Martin-Márquez, Susan *Disorientations: Spanish colonialism in Africa and the Performance of Identity* Yale University Press, USA, 2008. Print.

Martino, Enrique 'Clandestine Recruitment Networks in the Bight of Biafra: Fernando Po's Answer to the Labour Question, 1926–1945', International Review of Social History, 57 (2012), 39–72. Institute of Asian and African Studies, Humboldt University, Berlin. Web.

Mateu, E, Comas, D, Calafell, F, Pérez-Lezaun, A, Abade, E and Bertranpetit, J 'A tale of two islands: population history and mitochondrial DNA sequence variation of Bioko and São Tomé, Gulf of Guinea', Annals of Human Genetics, 61 (1997), 507–18. London. Print.

Mawoung, Godefroy Ngima 'The relationship between the Bakola and the Bantu peoples of the coastal regions of Cameroon and their perception of commercial forest exploitation', African Study Monographs, Suppl 26 (Mar 2001), 209–35. Kyoto University, Japan. Web.

Miller, Barry E 'Spanish Guinea: Evolution or Revolution?', Africa Today, 12/3 (Mar 1965), 8–11. Indiana University Press, USA. Web.

Moreno, Nuria Fernández 'Bubi Government at the End of the 19th Century: Resistance to the Colonial Policy of Evangelization on the Island of Bioko, Equatorial Guinea', Nordic Journal of African Studies 22/1&2 (2013), 23–43. CEA, ISCTE-IUL, Portugal. Print.

Nerín, Gustau 'Corisco y el estuario del Muni (1470–1931): Del aislamiento a la globalización y de la globalización a la marginación', (28 Jan 2015) L'Harmattan, France. Web.

Nunes, Alejandra Mahiques 'The hidden history of Equatorial Guinea: reasons behind the silence of the Spanish press around Macías Nguema's regime (1968–79)', Masters Thesis, African Studies (Jul 2013). Leiden University, Holland. Web.

Pélissier, René Don Quichotte en Afrique: Voyages à la fin de l'empire espagnol Editions Pélissier, 1992, 78630 Orgeval, France. Print (in French).

Roberts, Adam 'Equatorial Guinea: Staying Power', The World Today, 65/3 (Mar 2009), 27–8. Royal Institute of International Affairs, London. Web.

Roberts, Adam The Wonga Coup Profile Books Ltd, London, 2006. Print.

Sá, Ana Lúcia 'African Intellectuals and Cultural Diversity: Discussions of the Ethnic Question in Equatorial Guinea', Nordic Journal of African Studies 22/1&2 (2013) 105–28. CEA, ISCTE-IUL, Portugal. Print.

Shurtleff, Len 'A Foreign Service Murder', The Foreign Service Journal (Oct 2007), 51–5. American Foreign Service Association, USA. Web.

Sundiata, Ibrahim 'From Slaving to Neoslavery: The Bight of Biafra and Fernando Po in the Era of Abolition, 1827–1930' (1996). University of Wisconsin Press, USA. Print.

Sundiata, Ibrahim 'Prelude to scandal: Liberia and Fernando Po, 1880–1930', The Journal of African History, 15/1 (1974), 97–112. Cambridge University Press, UK. Web.

Van der Veen, Lolke 'The origins of the Fang: language, culture and genes: Myth and reality', Linguistics Colloquium, Centre for Language and Cognition (30 Nov 2007), University of Goningen, Holland. Web.

Language

'Fang', National African Language Resource Centre (2014). University of Wisconsin. Web.

Chumbow, S, Beban, Atindogbe, Gratien G, Domche, Engelbert and Luther Bot, Dieudonne Martin 'Classification of the languages of Cameroon and Equatorial Guinea on the basis of lexicostatistics and mutual intelligibility', African Study Monographs, 28/4 (Dec 2007), 181–204. Kyoto University, Japan. Web.

Ella, Edgard Maillard 'A theoretical model for a Fang-French-English specialised multi-volume school dictionary', Dissertation, Degree of Doctor of Literature - Lexicography (Mar 2007). University of Stellenbosch, South Africa. Web.

Lipski, John 'The Spanish Language of Equatorial Guinea', Arizona Journal of Hispanic Cultural Studies, 8 (2004), 115–30. University of Arizona, USA. Web.

Yakpo, Kofi 'A Grammar of Pichi' (2009). Berlin/Accra: Isimu Media. Web.
Yakpo, Kofi 'Gramática del Pichi' (2010). Barcelona: Ceiba Ediciones. Web.

Music

García-Alvite, Dosinda 'Strategic Positions of Las Hijas del Sol: Equatorial Guinea in World Music', *Arizona Journal of Hispanic Cultural Studies*, 8 (2004), 149–61. University of Arizona, USA. Web.

Natural history

'Advances and progress on the Flora of Equatorial Guinea', Association for the Taxonomic Study on the Flora of Tropical Africa, 19th Congress (2010). Antananarivo, Madagascar. Web.

'Meeting the Fast Start Committment – U.S. Climate Finance in Fiscal Year 2012: Equatorial Guinea', US State Department (2012). Web.

Beudels-Jamar, Roseline, Lafontaine, René-Marie, Devillers, Pierre, Redmond, Ian, Devos, Céline and Beudels, Marie-Odile 'Gorilla. Report on the conservation status of Gorillas', CMS Gorilla Concerted Action Technical Series, 17 (2008). UNEP/CMS Secretariat, Bonn, Germany. Web.

Cabezas, F, Aedo, C, Barberá, P, Estrella, M, Fero, M, Velayos, M, de Wasseige, C and Devers, D (eds) 'Forests of the Congo Basin – State of the forest 2010', Publications Office of the European Union (2011). Luxembourg. Web.

Del Val, Jaime Pérez Evans, M I and Fishpool, L D C 'Important Bird Areas in Africa and associated islands: Priority sites for conservation', pp265–272, Pisces Publications, Cambridge, 2001. Print.

Honarvar, Shaya 'Bioko island – Where the wild things are… for now', Bioko Biodiversity Protection Program (10 Mar 2012). Drexel University, USA. Web.

Hughes, R H and J S '4.4 Equatorial Guinea', *A Directory of African Wetlands* (1992), 499–505. Cambridge University Press, UK. Print.

Larison, Brenda, et al 'Biotic surveys of Bioko and Rio Muni, Equatorial Guinea', Biodiversity Support Program (25 Jun 1999). USA. Web.

Sunderland, Terry C H 'A biodiversity assessment of the Monte Mitra forest, Monte Alen National Park, Equatorial Guinea', Smithsonian Institution (Nov 2005). Washington, DC, USA. Web.

Thorhaug, Anitra 'Botany in Equatorial Guinea & in the Island Nation of São Tomé and Príncipe', *The Plant Science Bulletin*, 55/3 (2009). Botanical Society of America, USA. Web.

Tollens, Eric 'Potential Impacts of Agriculture Development on the Forest Cover in the Congo Basin', World Bank Report (30 Jun 2010). Catholic University of Leuven, Belgium. Web.

Politics

'Briefing Paper: Excerpts from the U.S. Case against Teodorin Nguema Obiang of Equatorial Guinea', Open Society Justice Initiative (2013). Web.

Coleman, Norm and Levin, Carl 'Money laundering and foreign corruption: enforcement and effectiveness of the Patriot Act – Case study involving Riggs Bank', Permanent Subcommittee on Investigations, United States Senate (15 Jul 2004). USA. Web.

Norris, Carolyn 'Equatorial Guinea: The position of refugees and exiles in 2001', UNHCR Emergency and Security Service (Dec 2001). Web.

Silverstein, Ken 'The secret life of a shopaholic: how an African dictator's playboy son went on a multi-million dollar shopping spree in the U.S.', Global Witness Report (17 Nov 2009). London, UK. Web.

Vines, Alex 'Well oiled – oil and human rights in Equatorial Guinea', Human Rights Watch (Jul 2009). Washington, DC, USA. Web.

WEBSITES
General
www.exteriores.gob.es/portal/es/serviciosalciudadano/siviajasalextranjero/paginas/recomendacionesdeviaje.aspx Spanish foreign Ministry travel advice

www.gov.uk/foreign-travel-advice UK Foreign and Commonwealth Office travel advice

Investment and commerce
www.beac.int Bank of Central African States

www.cbc-bank.com/index.php CBCGE Bank

www.cceibankge.com CCEI Bank

www.embassyofequatorialguinea.co.uk/introducing-business-in-equatorial-guinea Equatorial Guinea embassy in London local business advice

www.equatorialoil.com/Index.html Republic of Equatorial Guinea Ministry of Mines, Industry and Energy

www.guineaecuatorialpetrol.com/e_index.html GE Petrol, national oil company of Equatorial Guinea

https://guinee-equatoriale.bgfi.com BGFI Bank Group

www.losanuncios.net Fortnightly news ads magazine distributed free across the country

http://malabo.usembassy.gov/doing-business-local.html US embassy in Malabo local business advice

History
http://patrimonioguinea.com Historic architecture of the country

www.trasmeships.es A history of shipping and Equatorial Guinea (Spanish only)

Natural history
http://africanbirdclub.org/countries/Equatorial-Guinea/introduction A thorough overview of what to expect when birding in Equatorial Guinea

http://bioko.org/wildlife/ Bioko Biodiversity Protection Program

www.birdlife.org Great resource from a global partnership of independent bird-related organisations

News
www.africa.com/news/news,equatorialguinea.html Daily news feed of stories from Equatorial Guinea

www.diariorombe.es Opposition news site, often provides much more interesting and up-to-date news than the official portals

http://elpais.com Spanish newspaper with coverage of Equatorial Guinea

http://equatorialguineainfo.blogspot.co.uk Another official news portal of the government of Equatorial Guinea

http://fr.africatime.com/guinee_equatoriale/guinee_equatoriale Daily news feed of stories from Equatorial Guinea (French only)

www.gacetadeguinea.com Monthly news magazine published in Equatorial Guinea

www.guineaecuatorialpress.com One of the official news portals of the government of Equatorial Guinea

www.guineequatoriale-info.net Trilingual news site on Equatorial Guinea and the region

NGOs and humanitarian sector
www.asso-sherpa.org Anti-corruption NGO which brought a legal case against Teodorín Obiang in France (French only)

www.egjustice.org Equatoguinean-run human rights website based in USA

http://en.rsf.org/equatorial-guinea.html Reporters Without Borders has reports on freedom of expression, freedom of information and censorship within Equatorial Guinea

www.hrw.org/africa/equatorial-guinea Human Rights Watch has numerous detailed reports on Equatorial Guinea and its leadership

www.transparency.org/country#GNQ_Chapter Anti-corruption NGO which brought a legal case against Teodorín Obiang in France

Political

www.africa-confidential.com/browse-by-country Detailed country-specific political analysis covering the whole continent (some areas require subscription)

www.cia.gov/library/publications/the-world-factbook/geos/ek.html *CIA World Factbook*

www.state.gov/r/pa/ei/bgn/7221.htm US State Department factsheet on US relations with Equatorial Guinea

Telecommunications

www.getesa.gq National Telecom Company

www.hitstelecom.net/hitsafrica.asp Kuwati-based company running the HITS mobile phone network

www.orange-guinee.com Orange mobile phone network in Equatorial Guinea

TWITTER ACCOUNTS

@BradtEGguide Official updates account for this guidebook

@OscarScafidi Author's account

@Bioko_BBPP Bioko Biodiversity Protection Program

@CaptSFM Ex-SAS 'mercenary' and key organiser of the Wonga Coup

@carlosmdiaz Manager of Grand Hotel Djibloho Kempinski

@ccemalabo Spanish Cultural Centre in Malabo

@ChathamHouse Independent analysis and debate on international affairs

@CronosAirlines Regional airline based in Malabo

@DiarioRombe Opposition news site

@DrewCronin Primatologist and conservationist working for BBPP

@EGEmbassy News about Equatorial Guinea from the embassy of Equatorial Guinea in Washington, DC

@EGembassyUK Official feed of the Equatoguinean embassy in London

@EGJustice Human rights NGO

@empleoguinea Employment portal for Equatorial Guinea jobs

@EnjoyEqGuinea Official government tourism feed

@FracturesPhoto Spain-based photography group with work from Equatorial Guinea

@guinealia Official tourism portal for Equatorial Guinea

@LouiseRedvers Freelance journalist with a focus on Africa and the Middle East

@radiomacutoinfo Opposition radio station

@Ruta47 Tour agency based in Malabo

@SofitelMalabo Official hotel feed

@tortugasmarinas TOMAGE turtle conservation group

@TutuAlicante Executive Director of EGJustice NGO

@UD_Adventures UK-based tour company offering organised trips to Equatorial Guinea

@UNED (Universidad Nacional de Educación a Distancia) Spanish university that runs distance-learning courses in Equatorial Guinea

Index

Entries in **bold** indicate main entries; those in *italics* indicate maps